MAKING US CRAZY

Making Us
CRAZY

DSM: The Psychiatric Bible and the
Creation of Mental Disorders

HERB KUTCHINS and **STUART A. KIRK**

Constable · London

First published in the United States of America by
The Free Press, a division of Simon & Schuster Inc., 1997
First published in Great Britain 1999
by Constable and Company Limited
3 The Lanchesters, 162 Fulham Palace Road
London W6 9ER
Copyright © Herb Kutchins and Stuart A. Kirk 1997
ISBN 0 094 79710 2
The right of Herb Kutchins and Stuart A. Kirk to be identified as authors
of this work has been asserted by them in accordance with
the Copyright, Designs and Patents Act 1988
Printed in Great Britain by
St Edmundsbury Press Ltd, Bury St Edmunds, Suffolk

A CIP catalogue record for this book
is available from the British Library

TO

GINA SICILIANO-KUTCHINS

PO KUTCHINS

CAROL ANN KOZ

C O N T E N T S

INTRODUCTION

Dorothy Rowe

The Diagnostic and Statistical Manual is an American invention for use by American psychiatrists. Why should it concern us here in Britain?

It should concern us greatly because, like MacDonalds and Microsoft, it's here and affecting our way of life, and not always to our benefit. Indeed, we have much cause for concern because it is being used increasingly by mental health professionals in their daily work and in relation to the law and to health insurance. The use of the *DSM*, as Herb Kutchins and Stuart Kirk have said, reflects "a growing tendency in our society to medicalize problems that are not medical, to find pathology where there is only pathos, and to pretend to understand phenomena by merely giving them a label and a code number."

In Britain this tendency is not a new growth. It was well established when Henry Maudsley, after whom the famous London psychiatric hospital is named, wrote in 1885,

> It is not our business, as it is not in our power, to explain psychologically the origins and nature of any of these depraved instincts; it is sufficient to establish their existence as facts of observation, and to set forth the pathological conditions under which they are produced; they are facts of pathology, which should be observed and classified like other phenomena of disease.[1]

Does a model of the mind in terms of disease accurately reflect how we think, feel and act? There is a huge body of evidence which suggests that it does not, but this is the assumption on which the profession of psychiatry is built. When in the late eighteenth century doctors realised that they too could make money out of providing asylums for lunatics but that, to do so, they would have to compete with a variety of landlords already providing such accommodation, they needed a rationale which would show them to be the only people with the necessary expertise. So they invented mental illnesses with the same flair, imagination and awareness of current opinions which the authors of the *DSM* demonstrate today. Andrew Scull in his book *Museums and Madness* wrote, "From about 1815 onwards a veritable spate of books and articles purporting to be medical treatises on the treatment of insanity began to appear."[2]

By the Parliamentary Acts of 1828 and 1845 the medical profession acquired the virtually exclusive right to direct the treatment of those deemed to be insane. Around the same time Parliament directed local counties and boroughs to provide asylums for the lunatic poor. Consequently, outside each town and city, huge, handsome edifices were erected and surrounded by farms to provide work and sustenance for the inmates. These asylums were vile and horrible places, the exact opposite of what people in distress need, but they served the purposes of the State well because they removed from society those who couldn't or wouldn't work, or were a trouble to other people.[3]

The development of asylums and psychiatry followed a similar pattern in the USA. One major difference between American and British psychiatrists was that, in the first half of the twentieth century, many American psychiatrists were influenced by Freud while British psychiatrists eschewed what they thought was an unhealthy interest in the workings of the mind. When I came to England from Australia in 1968 and worked in asylums and university departments of psychiatry, I found that the psychiatrists spoke of Freud only when they wanted to show that they were men of learning. In their work they stuck to diagnosis, medication and electroconvulsive therapy. British psychiatrists ignored the early editions of the *DSM* and instead worked on their own classificatory system which was later incorporated into the World Health Organisation's *International Classification of Diseases* (ICD). However, as revisions of the *DSM* got larger and more stuffed with medical terminology British psychiatrists began to see its usefulness.

To maintain their assertion that psychiatry is a science, psychiatrists have to do research and get their research published. Using the *DSM* as a measuring instrument might enhance the chances for a psychiatrist outside the USA of getting his papers published there. The seventies saw the growth of international teams of researchers who looked at phenomena such as schizophrenia which was deemed to be an illness found in all societies. The *DSM* became the measuring instrument in such research.

This research had to be reported, and so large international conferences began to be organised. The members of the American Psychiatric Association and the Royal College of Psychiatrists and similar institutions in other countries greatly enjoy international conferences because they enhance psychiatrists' prestige and give them somewhere pleasant to go. The international pharmaceutical companies, strong supporters of the APA and the Royal College, like international conferences because they allow the companies to distribute their largesse among those who can best enhance the sale of their products. (The Royal College explains the failure of anti-depressants to cure depression as underprescribing by doctors. If the pills don't work give your patient more of the same.) In world-wide trade the pharmaceutical industry ranks second only to the international arms trade, and the sale of mind-altering drugs is a major part of the pharmaceutical industry's business.[4] It is immensely convenient for the pharmaceutical industry if psychiatrists all around the world use the *DSM*. It simplifies research and sales.

In the USA the use of the *DSM* and the requirements of health insurance companies create enormous issues which are examined in this book. In the UK health insurance is much more limited, but psychiatrists, psychologists and therapists working privately use either the *DSM* or the *ICD* so that their patients can make effective health insurance claims. Lawyers like everything neat and cut and dried, so a psychologist's report based on the *DSM* is greatly appreciated. In the competition between psychiatrists and psychologists for business some psychologists in the UK use the *DSM* in the hope of appearing more professional. Most, if not all, National Health Service departments of clinical psychology contain a copy of the *DSM IV* because the psychologists, even though they might deplore it, see the *DSM* as the future. Psychologists can easily be seduced by jargon, and, indeed, a psychologist cannot be deemed to be fully qualified until he or she can use jargon fluently.[5] The *DSM* supplies plenty of jargon.

However, in ordinary practice psychiatrists don't go rushing for the *DSM* every time they have to make a diagnosis. They rely, as they have always done, on their clinical intuition.

A psychiatrist's clinical intuition is a wonder to behold. I have been studying psychiatrists since the early sixties. Over those decades I have compared notes with my colleagues and we have agreed that such clinical intuition operates as a thing in itself, untrammelled by the psychiatrist's past experience, his age, gender, nationality, religion, and by the opinions and prejudices he might bring to other matters. It has the force and clarity of Absolute Truth, for indeed it is Absolute Truth. Or so he would have us believe.

Such clinical intuition is at the centre of the *DSM*. As Herb Kutchins and Stuart Kirk record, to create a diagnostic category all the *DSM* committee had to do was "pick a label, provide a general description based on clinical wisdom, develop a menu of diagnostic criteria, check the proposed criteria with advocates for the new category, decide how many must be met to use the diagnosis, counter opposition (if any), and presto – you have a new mental disorder."

Clinical wisdom is the product of clinical intuition. This book chronicles the operation of such clinical wisdom in some important areas of human experience and shows how the *DSM* makes it possible for victims to be blamed, ordinary behaviour to be turned into pathology, homosexuality to be changed from being a disorder to not being a disorder, the effects of trauma to be ignored and then turned into a pathology, modest, compliant women to be diagnosed as mentally ill for being what society expects them to be, aggressive, sexist men to be protected from the stigma of mental illness, difficult patients to be punished, and racial prejudice to masquerade as science.

Such clinical wisdom produced the *DSM*, but not easily. A vast amount of work was carried out by people devoted to the task. Why is the *DSM* so important to psychiatry? My colleague Lucy Johnstone, author of a brilliant critique of British psychiatry, *Users and Abusers of Psychiatry*[6] answered this question. She wrote, "If there is no agreement on basic classification, then the field of psychiatry can never be developed into a science. To admit the central role of value judgements and cultural norms is to give the whole game away. The *DSM has* to be seen as reliable and valid, or the whole enterprise of medical psychiatry collapses."[7]

Validity is certainly the key issue for the *DSM*, but its authors prefer to concentrate on reliability, on getting psychiatrists to agree to use certain language in a certain way. Herb Kutchins and Stuart Kirk wrote,

> *DSM* is a book of tentatively assembled agreements. Agreements don't always make sense, nor do they always reflect reality. You can have agreements among experts without validity. Even if you found four people who agreed that the earth is flat, that the moon is made of cheese, that smoking cigarettes poses no health risks, or that politicians are never corrupt, such agreements do not establish truth.

Certain psychiatrists might be prepared to admit that some of the disorders listed in the *DSM* mightn't be particularly valid, but all would insist that there are two mental illnesses whose validity has been proved beyond all reasonable doubt, schizophrenia and depression.

Not quite. The body of literature questioning the validity of the concept of schizophrenia is huge. One such critic, the psychologist Mary Boyle, wrote,

> The crucial difference between medicine and psychiatry can perhaps be best summarised by saying that whereas medical scientists study bodily functioning and describe patterns of it, psychiatrists behave as *if* they were studying bodily functioning and as *if* they had described patterns there, when in fact they are studying behaviour and have assumed—but not proved—that certain types of pattern *will be* found there . . . Given the central role attributed to schizophrenia, the vast literature surrounding it and the research effort to validate claims made about it, it seems reasonable to suggest that it functions as the prototypical psychiatric disease.[8]

R. Bentall and colleagues reviewed the research into schizophrenia and concluded, "Given that schizophrenia is an entity which seems to have no particular symptoms, which follows no particular course and which responds to no (or perhaps every) particular treatment, it is perhaps not surprising that aetiological research has so far failed to establish that it has any particular cause."[9] The psychiatrist A. M. Mortimer, beginning a review of the concept of schizophrenia, said, "In some quarters schizophrenia has gained the reputation of a graveyard of research. Few findings stand the test of time, most of the pieces of this particular jigsaw seem to be missing, and it is not easy to make sense of those that are available. Even 'hard' scientific findings fail to be replicated."[10] Two years later a survey of the views of psychiatrists in the south-west region of England on the diagnosis, aetiology, management and prognosis of schizophrenia "indicated a diversity of thinking and clinical practice about diagnosis, aetiology and prognosis: management of schizophrenia being the only aspect with a relative consensus. This study supports the notion that the understanding of schizophrenia is largely individualistic and remains an ill-defined condition despite recent attempts to standardise and delineate it as a diagnosable entity with defined characteristics, treatment and outcome."[11]

My particular interest has been depression about which I have researched and written a great deal. As well as my academic papers, I write for the general public and since 1978, when my first book was published, a large number of people have written or spoken to me and said that the way I describe depression, as arising out of the way we see ourselves and interpret the world, has proved valid for them and provided a means whereby they could leave the prison of depression.[12] They found that the psychiatrist's explanation that depression is caused by a gene or a "chemical imbalance" of the brain did not accord with their experience. When people tell me about being told that they had a "chemical imbalance" they always speak in a doubtful, puzzled way. They might welcome an explanation which absolves them of any responsibility for their distress, but they find nothing in the explanation which accords with their experience. Those people who have been told that their "chemical imbalance" is a result of their "depression gene" speak of their worry that they have passed, or will pass, this gene on to their children.

If I had a pound for every time I've encountered a psychiatrist announcing that the gene for depression is about to be discovered I might be as rich as Bill Gates, but such announcements have not produced the gene because, as geneticists like Professor Steven Jones [13] are always explaining, genes cannot explain complex behaviour. As for this nonsense about chemical imbalance, no one knows what a balanced brain might be. Research on patients who are already depressed might show alterations in brain chemistry, but, as psychiatrists should know, a correlation cannot be considered to be a cause. A particular alteration in brain chemistry would have to be demonstrated invariably to precede depression, and this has not been done. Meanwhile, there is an increasing body of evidence that cognitive therapy enables people diagnosed with schizophrenia or depression to lead ordinary lives. No amount of cognitive therapy will cure the undoubtedly genetic disorder of cystic fibrosis, so how can it be so effective with depression and schizophrenia?

The search for evidence of the schizophrenia gene and the depression gene has followed some wayward paths. Grave doubts have arisen about the truthfulness of early twin study researchers,[14] while more recent studies of identical twins separated early in life do not attempt to assess the nature of the environments where the twins grew up. When separated twins show similar behaviour, the question needs to be asked about the probability of that behaviour occurring in that environment. For instance, if one male twin grows up in a Catholic family in Liverpool and the other in a Catholic family in Dublin what is the probability that each twin will marry a woman called Mary and have a keen interest in football? The idea that, if a grandmother, mother and daughter each develop depression, they must each have the depression gene is as silly as the idea that if a grandmother, mother and daughter all vote Labour they must have the Labour gene. (Could New Labour be merely a mutation of the Labour gene?)

Why do psychiatrists cling so tenaciously to the belief that there are such things as mental illnesses which have a physical cause? It is not simply that this is the assumption which makes possible the existence of their profession. After all, the profession of astrology, which once had power, disappeared from all but the popular media when its basic assumptions were shown to be false. The profession of psychiatry is maintained because it has two roles, and the second role is necessary to the body politic, the State. Psychiatrists have a duty to their individual patients but they also have a duty to the State, to help maintain public order. In this second role psychiatrists do not simply incarcerate the unruly and keep them quiet. They also provide an explanation of behaviour which stops protests against the State.

The USA covers a huge land mass and contains many divergent groups of people. It is a savage country with murder both a means of self-expression and of State reprisal. Yet it does not constantly threaten to fragment in the way that smaller countries, like the UK and Spain, do. The USA remains a unit because most of its populace hold, or say they hold, two ideas—a belief in God and a belief in America. Not to believe in the American Dream, that every American can, by hard work and trust in America, succeed in reaching their goals, is un-American.

These two beliefs, if true, should ensure that the American people, as their politicians like to call them, are always happy. But patently many Americans are not happy. This unhappiness must not be allowed to threaten the stability of the State. Unhappy people must be explained away. The unhappiness of the poor can be explained away by saying that the poor are lazy. But what explanation can there be for the unhappiness of people who are not poor, who are educated and live in comfortable circumstances? It cannot possibly be that society is at fault, that institutions like marriage, or methods of child-rearing, or racist or sexist practices, all concerns of the State, are at fault. It cannot be that God does not always protect the good and punish the wicked or that the American Dream is an illusion. The fault must lie in the individual, in his genes.

In the UK the current crop of politicians like to profess a belief in God, but they can't assume that all the population does likewise. There's no British Dream, no sin of being un-British. But the State does have a great interest in keeping the populace quiet. The poor are told they're lazy and greedy, and the comfortably-off unhappy are told that the cause of their distress is in their genes. Anyone who protests against the State is merely demonstrating his mental disorder. (Benjamin Rush, the father of American psychiatry, coined the mental illness of "anarchia" for people who were unhappy with the American political structure. He found that the people most prone to this disease were negroes and poor whites.[15] This illness seems to be quite similar to one that used to be found in the USSR—"paranoid delusions of reforming the State".)

The validity of that mental disorder is not called into account. The *DSM* avoids the problem of validity by ignoring the putative cause of mental disorder. The *DSM* discusses neither cause nor cure. The whole of the *DSM* reflects the desire to pin down and to categorise the flux of human experience rather than to enter into it in the hope of understanding how another person perceives himself and his world. In psychiatry 'twas ever thus. In that other bible of the profession *Clinical Psychiatry* the authors Eliot Slater and Martin Roth, great names in the pantheon of British Psychiatry, advised their fellow psychiatrists that, "It is the objective world in which we live and to which the subjective world must pay deference. It is more important to know what the facts are than what the patient makes of them."[16] This is actually a claim to possess a superhuman power to know the Absolute Truth, to perceive reality directly, unimpeded by the interpretations which mere human beings have to make of a reality which is forever beyond their grasp.

Yet psychiatrists are doctors and should know from their study of physiology that human beings are not physically capable of apprehending reality directly. All our brain ever lets us know are the interpretations our brain/mind makes of reality. What is currently known of how the brain operates has been summarised as, "The human brain forms and maintains a model of the world and itself within that world. This model can be used to explain the past events and predict the future."[17] The authors of the *DSM* are steadfastly uninterested in the models of the world which their patients have created. Yet it is these models which have determined the patients' behaviour. As it is for all of us, what determines our behaviour is not events but how we have interpreted events.

The *DSM* cites many different behaviours as evidence of a mental disorder. Its authors do not inquire about the interpretations which led to these behaviours. These behaviours are described in terms which make them appear to be unusual, strange, even bizarre. Yet, if the interpretations which led to the behaviour are examined they can be seen to be ordinary interpretations, well within the range of most people's experience. Here I could choose any of the behavioural symptoms listed in the *DSM* to illustrate my point, but I shall select Criteria 7 for Major Depression Episode. "feelings of worthlessness or excessive or inappropriate guilt." The *DSM* states,

The sense of worthlessness or guilt associated with a Major Depressive Episode may include unrealistic negative evaluations of one's worth or guilty preoccupations or ruminations over minor past failings. Such individuals often misinterpret neutral or trivial day-to-day events as evidence of personal defects and have an exaggerated sense of responsibility for untoward events. For example, a realtor may become preoccupied with self-blame for failing to make sales even when the market has collapsed generally and other realtors are equally unable to make sales. The sense of worthlessness or guilt may be of delusional proportions (e.g., an individual who is convinced that he or she is personally responsibly for world poverty).[18]

This way of behaving is not, as the *DSM* would have us believe, an epiphenomenon, mere foam on the tide of a mental disorder. It is a way of seeing oneself and one's world which follows naturally and logically from a set of ideas which most people from all cultures and societies hold. It could be argued that this set of ideas in their more extreme form are more prevalent in societies with a Christian tradition, but the existence of depression in most, if not all societies, suggests that this set of ideas is universal. Indeed, one part of this set of ideas is essential if people are going to live together in groups.

This part is concerned with how we bring up children. Babies come into the world concerned solely with their own interests but they have to learn to fit in with the demands of their family and of society. Consequently the message each baby is given is, "As you are, you are not acceptable. You have to learn to be good." Societies differ in the precise definition of "good", but good is what children must become. Most of us learn to be experts in being good. By being good I mean thinking of yourself as never being good enough but always having to strive to be better. This idea is implicit in the American Dream and is quite explicit in the Christian belief that we are born in sin and must meet certain standards in order to be saved. If we fail to live up to the standards set by our society and by ourselves we sink in our own estimation. We doubt our worth.

While this way of thinking makes us good members of society the burden of always feeling not good enough and having to strive to be better can be very onerous. Childhood isn't easy, even for children in the most loving of families. But most of us find hope in some ideas presented to us as a way of understanding the world. When we are small children we soon discover a set of ideas which operates in our family. It is, "If you're good you get rewarded. If you're bad you get punished."

In most families children are encouraged to generalise these ideas to the whole world and come to believe that we live in a Just World where goodness is rewarded and badness is punished. This is what all religions teach, though they differ on what they call good and bad, reward and punishment. The belief in God professed by most Americans implies a belief in the Just World. In the UK there are many people who would say that they are not at all religious but they believe that somehow, in the end, justice does prevail. The belief in the Just World enables many children to grow up believing that their life story is one where they will eventually be rewarded for their goodness and where, if they're good, nothing bad will happen to them and their loved ones.

However, as John Lennon said, life is what happens while we're making other plans. Sooner or later we discover that there is a discrepancy between what we think our life is and what it actually is. If we are lucky, this discrepancy proves not to be so large that we cannot make suitable adjustments without too much pain. But for those people who later become depressed the disaster that befalls them creates too big a discrepancy to be overcome by a small adjustment to one's ideas. Sometimes this disaster is obvious to outside observers, sometimes it is a disaster known only to the person, a private loss and disappointment, but, whichever, the disaster comes as a threat to the integrity of the individual's sense of being a person. If you have held unquestioningly the idea that if you are good nothing bad can happen to you, and if you have always striven to be good, then a disaster like the death of your child or the unfaithfulness of your husband creates in you the feeling that your very self is fragmenting, crumbling, even disappearing. This feeling of the imminent annihilation of you as a person creates an immense fear. Many depressed people can describe this fear while others try not to remember this most horrible experience and instead talk only of the depression suddenly coming over them for no apparent reason. Every adult knows the threat and the fear which follows the discovery that you have made a major error of judgement, yet it features in psychiatric textbooks only as the symptom called Panic.

Whenever we encounter a disaster we ask, "Why in the whole scheme of things did this happen?" This question was repeated over and over in the cards and condolences left in mourning for Princess

Diana. There are only three possible answers to this question. Either it was my fault, it was someone else's fault, or it happened by chance. However, a belief in a Just World rules out chance. The choice is between blaming yourself or blaming other people. Blaming other people is extremely popular. Conspiracy theories about the princess's death were on the Internet within minutes of the announcement of her death. But good people, really good people, believe that it is wrong to blame others. They must always take responsibility and blame themselves. Thus a good person can always deal with the threat to the integrity of their self by blaming themselves for the disaster. This explanation puts all the pieces back together again. They can always say, "If I'd been a really good parent my child would not have died," or "If I'd been a really good wife my husband would not have left me for someone else." In blaming themselves for the disaster they see that they were even more wicked than they had thought. It follows that if they had been derelict in that responsibility they must have been derelict in other responsibilities. After all, does not each of us play a part in maintaining world poverty and despoiling the planet?

Thus Criteria 7 of the Major Depressive Disorder, intense feelings of guilt and worthlessness, is not a symptom but a logical outcome of a person's way of seeing himself and his world. All depressed people struggle with universal moral issues. When such a person speaks of his guilt and worthlessness, to say in reply, "That's just your illness talking" is both stupid and cruel. To explain a person's behaviour in terms of "you have a mental disorder" is stupid. It explains nothing, but creates a fictitious entity whose existence can be demonstrated only in a circular argument. When I first became an undergraduate in 1948 an era was coming to an end in how behaviour was explained. This was in terms of instincts, and I learned to recognise a circular argument. It went,

"Why does this person behave like this?"
"Because he has this instinct."
"How do you know he has this instinct?"
"Because he behaves like this."

Substitute "mental disorder" for "instinct" and you have the basic line of reasoning used by the authors of the *DSM*. This is not science.

When my colleague Lucy Johnstone teaches her student nurses and undergraduate psychology students about the *DSM* and *ICD* she asks them to consider the following questions:

Are these social or medical judgements?

Why should doctors have any special role in passing judgements about unusual forms of behaviour or experience?

On what kind of basis are these judgements made?

What values and norms is the psychiatrist likely to bring to the process, and who might be expected to be over-represented in mental health statistics as a result?

Is this a legitimate medical activity, or a disguised form of social control?

What implications are there for the practice of psychiatry and the role of psychiatrists within it?[19]

I suggest that those who read this book should ask themselves these same questions. Lucy reports that her students are "invariably alarmed and horrified". The readers of this book will be equally alarmed and horrified, but at the same time they will be most usefully informed and most greatly heartened by the clarity of thought and the wisdom of Herb Kutchins and Stuart Kirk in their study of the *DSM*.

---

1. *Responsibility in Mental Disease*, Kegan Paul, London, 1884.

2. Penguin, Harmondsworth, 1972.

3. Dorothy Rowe, *Beyond Fear*, HarperCollins, London, 1987.

4. Dorothy Rowe, *The Real Meaning of Money*, HarperCollins, London, 1997.

5. Lucy Johnstone, "'I hear what you're saying': How to Avoid Jargon in Therapy", *Changes*, Vol 16, Number 3, 1998.

6. Routledge, London, 1989.

7. Personal communication, 6 November 1998.

8. *Schizophrenia: a scientific delusion?* Routledge, London, 1990.

9. Bentall, R., Jackson H.F., Pilgrim, D. "Abandoning the concept of 'schizophrenia'", *British Journal of Clinical Psychology*, 1988, 27, 303–324.

10. Mortimer, A. M. "Phenomenology: its place in schizophrenia research", *British Journal of Psychiatry,* 1992, 161, 293–297.

11. Gavin Cape, Daniel Antebe, Penny Standen and Christine Glazebrook "Schizophrenia: The views of a sample of psychiatrists", *Journal of Mental Health*, 1994, 3, 105–113.

12. *Depression: the Way Out of Your Prison*, second edition, Routledge, London, 1997; *Breaking the Bonds*, HarperCollins, London, 1991; *Choosing Not Losing*, HarperCollins, London, 1991; *Beyond Fear, op cit*.

13. *Language of the Genes*, Flamingo, HarperCollins, London, 1994.

14. Richard Marshall, "The genetics of Schizophrenia:axiom or hypothesis?" in R. Bentall ed., *Reconstructing Scizophrenia*, Routledge, London, 1990.

15. Thomas Szasz, *The Manufacture of Madness,* Delta, New York, 1970.

16. Baillière, Tindall and Cassell, London, 1970.

17. Terence Picton and Donald Stuss, "Neurobiology of Conscious Experience", *Current Opinion in Neurobiology,* 4, 1994, pp. 256–65.

18. *Diagnostic and Statistical Manual of Mental Disorders,* fourth edition, American Psychiatric Association, Washington DC, 1994.

19. Personal communication, *op cit.*

PREFACE

In the last few days, we found the following stories in our morning news-papers:

- John G. Bennet, Jr., who had become the toast of Philadelphia as founder of the Foundation for New Era Philanthropy (a Ponzi scheme that bilked millions from such institutions as the American Red Cross, the Salvation Army, and Harvard University), pleaded no contest when his legal defense strategy was disallowed by a federal judge; he now faces years in prison for fraud, money laundering, and tax violations.

- Under the new federal welfare law, passed last year, legal immigrants who are elderly or disabled will lose welfare benefits if they are not citizens. Under new citizenship rules, they may not take the oath of allegiance and become citizens unless they can understand what they are saying.

- A Jordanian soldier opened fire on a group of Israeli schoolgirls, killing seven of them. Speculation about the precipitants of the violence and the soldier's motivation ensued.

- Geoffrey Rush won an Academy Award for best actor in the movie *Shine* for his portrayal of David Helfgott, amid controversy about Helfgott's real musical ability and the film's depiction of his life and troubles.

- A leading medical reference book, the authoritative *Physicians' Desk Reference,* or PDR, which physicians use when prescribing drugs, was

found to contain outdated, incorrect advice that may harm patients
who have taken overdoses of some medications.

- There is wide speculation about a cult leader and his followers, most of
whom committed suicide.

- Jon Westling, the president of Boston University, is involved in a highly
visible lawsuit about his authority to set academic standards.[1]

To most readers these snippets of news would appear to have little in
common. In fact, they all involve, in one way or another, issues of mental
disorder and medical authority: the con man tried to use a psychiatric defense, legal immigrants may now have to pass tests of their mental states,
political violence brings commentary from psychiatrists, the authenticity
of the Oscar winner's portrayal of Helfgott is questioned by a psychiatrist,
a widely used medical manual is found to contain errors, the nation tries
to fathom why bright people join cults, and a university questions the experts' use of the diagnosis of learning disabilities. It is precisely because
issues of psychiatric diagnosis, commentary by psychiatrists on all manner of social issues, and the use of medical authority are so ubiquitous in
our lives and because we are so vulnerable to the misuse of psychiatric diagnosis and authority that we wrote this book. There is a growing tendency in our society to medicalize problems that are not medical, to find
psychopathology where there is only pathos, and to pretend to understand phenomena by merely giving them a label and a code number.
There may, indeed, be comforts to be gained by these maneuvers—and
money to be made—but in this book we question the legitimacy of this
tendency and describe its risks.

To pursue this goal, we take the reader into the world of the psychiatric
bible, the *Diagnostic and Statistical Manual of Mental Disorders* (DSM). Although this world may be unfamiliar to many readers, it is a world that affects all of us. As the authoritative manual of the American Psychiatric
Association, DSM defines, classifies, and describes what the association
says are mental illnesses. It is much more than an obscure psychiatric reference book. It is the repository of a strange mix of social values, political
compromise, scientific evidence, and material for insurance claim forms. In
this book we tell how this influential manual has evolved, how diagnoses
get invented and abolished, and how the manual gets used and misused.

It is relatively easy to make DSM appear absurd, as was done recently in
an article in *Harper's* magazine titled "The Encyclopedia of Insanity: A Psychiatric Handbook Lists a Madness for Everyone," where DSM is de-

scribed as "a book of dogma" in which "human life is a form of mental ill-ness."[2] We admit that we, too, have at times given in to the temptation to poke fun at DSM. But in this book we want to do more; we try to explain what it is about the structure of DSM and the processes used in develop-ing it that makes the enterprise of creating mental disorders so vulnerable to distortion and misuse. We are critical, to be sure, but we also try to be constructive. Our book is not meant to be a treatise addressed to the de-velopers of DSM and offering advice on how to revise the manual, nor are we salesmen peddling some newfangled classification system. Rather, this book is addressed to the general reader who is often mystified by what gets labeled as mental illness and who seeks to comprehend how it is that psy-chiatrists go about the business of inventing categories of mental disorder.

One such inventor, the highly respected research psychiatrist Robert L. Spitzer, unavoidably receives more than a fair share of our attention, per-haps misleading the reader into thinking we harbor some animosity toward him. Quite the contrary. We respect and like him and his work. Spitzer is one of the most thoughtful, dedicated, productive, and intellectually formi-dable people to work on the development of DSM. Our attention to his ideas, his writings, and his style of management is in exact proportion to his broad influential role over two decades and his masterful political skills in creating the modern-day DSM. Although we realize this is small comfort to him, it is probably fair to say that without Spitzer's ability and career-long commitment to creating diagnostic categories, we would never have found very much in DSM worthy of our energies for the last 15 years.

Had we known at the time we began to notice the phenomenal suc-cess of DSM that it would be demanding our attention for all these years, we might well have chosen some other vocation. Our persistent fussing over DSM, which has led to two books and a score of articles on the manual as we tried to decipher its many puzzles, has been engrossing but not without costs: our reading habits have been distorted; our files are overflowing with all manner of psychiatric minutiae; we have become persona non grata among our more conventionally oriented mental health colleagues; and, we fear, our friends and family have been search-ing quietly for the right DSM category for us.

For our efforts we have received needed and timely support. For that support we wish to thank the following: the institutions that have paid our salaries while we pursued our concerns—California State University, Sacramento, and the University of California, Los Angeles; the Rockefeller

Foundation's Study and Conference Center in Bellagio, Italy, where we spent a month in residence as visiting scholars at the incomparable Villa Serbelloni while completing the first draft of this book; the graduate students and colleagues who responded to our presentations of this material at seminars and conferences; and our friends Tony Platt, Howie Becker, Mary Beth Montgomery, Jerry Wakefield, and Karen Staller, who have been exposed to our DSM ramblings for many years. We have attempted to incorporate the keen, often unacknowledged, insights from the latter throughout the book, although we accept responsibility for our presentation of those insights (and for not heeding their advice more often!). When the project wandered, Susan Arellano, our editor at The Free Press, corralled our efforts, offered encouragement, and helped us maintain a focus. In the final weeks of work, Toby Troffkin earned our deep gratitude for her mastery of detail and her skill in fixing our prose.

Finally, there are those private debts that we incurred, ones that can never be adequately described or repaid. The first author wishes to thank Stuart, Carrie, Mari, and Albert Kutchins for the wit, insight, and support that made the writing of this book possible. Kayakers, hikers, and bikers from Sayulita to Pokhara have humanized the effort, particularly Doc, Reyna, Kal, and Rishi. Gina's management skill was only one of many ways that she cared for me and kept the project moving in the darkest times, and Po's implacability was an inspiration. The long march that Stuart Kirk and I have shared across the entire continent has lasted longer than either of us will admit and has often left us bruised and battered, but none of it would have been possible without him.

The second author is grateful, first, to Herb Kutchins, because it was he, not I, who began raising questions about DSM and because he invited me to join him in the struggle to answer them. Throughout our collaboration, he has insisted that we ask significant questions and not settle for the easy, conventional answers. This book is one result of his intellectual prodding. I am also grateful to Ryan and Jim and the entire early morning gang at the R.S. for their camaraderie every weekend in the blurred canyons of the Santa Monica Mountains. Most importantly, I am grateful to Allison and Brandon for making me proud and for making me laugh, and to C.A. for love that never wavers and companionship that sustains a full life.

All these sources of aid and comfort truly kept this project from making us both crazy, we hope.

Making Us
CRAZY

1 DOUBTING THOMAS

Psychiatric Diagnosis and the Anita Hill Controversy

When Anita Hill accused Clarence Thomas of sexual harassment before a Senate committee, the televised proceedings captured the attention of the American public as few events have since Watergate. The impact of Hill's accusations are still reverberating, and it is not surprising that American psychiatry played an important, if shadowy, part in her ordeal. The *New York Times* reported that "while the Clarence Thomas hearings unfolded on the television screens, Republican defenders of the Supreme Court nominee and their Democratic opponents engaged in a behind the scenes struggle to use psychiatry for strategy and, in some cases, as ammunition for their arguments."[1]

Republicans attacked Hill, first by calling her a liar and then by claiming that she was suffering from delusions. After Hill passed a lie detector test, her critics relied more heavily on the theory that her complaints were the result of romantic fantasies. One senator said that he had been contacted by psychiatrists who suggested that she may have been suffering from delusions. "Schizophrenic," "out of touch with reality," "delusion," and "fantasy" were terms repeated in the testimony against Professor Hill without medical substantiation—but not without psychiatric consultation.

Republicans enlisted the assistance of a psychiatrist, Parke Dietz, the

1

subject of a *New Yorker* profile appropriately titled "Witness for the Prosecution." Usually, Dietz tries to demonstrate that notorious criminal defendants are not insane. For instance, as a government witness Dietz tried, unsuccessfully, to establish the sanity of John Hinkley, who attempted to assassinate Ronald Reagan. In the Thomas hearings, Dietz was asked to support an allegation that Anita Hill was mentally ill.

During the hearings, while many Americans were riveted to their television sets, Dietz was in the office of Senator Danforth, Thomas's sponsor. The psychiatrist offered opinions about a mental disorder that may have been afflicting Hill. "Dr. Dietz said he provided a description of the disorder known as 'erotomania,' in which the delusion is that another person, usually of a higher status, has romantic interest in the subject." Although Danforth insisted that the psychiatrist had no role in the questioning, the *New York Times* reported that the "Republicans used the testimony of John Doggett 3d, who said that Professor Hill had shown a romantic interest in him, to introduce the idea that she may have been suffering from erotomania."

The White House also made a foray into psychopolitics by flying in a psychiatrist, Jeffrey Satinover. His involvement was the result of a casual dinner conversation with Jamie Bush, a nephew of the former president. During the meal Satinover said that "he had treated a couple of patients who suffered from erotic delusions. . . . [He] had been struck by the impression that neither Hill nor Thomas appeared to be lying; this disorder could be the explanation. He also had heard about the affidavit John Doggett had made stating that Hill had fantasized about him."[2]

When he eventually saw Doggett testify, Satinover changed his mind. Doggett made extravagant claims that Hill had erotic fantasies about him, but the flimsy evidence he offered was unconvincing, if not ridiculous. Although Satinover repudiated his initial diagnosis of erotomania, his first assessment was used by politicians to impugn Hill's credibility. In the end, Dietz also refused to sign an affidavit attesting to Hill's mental illness but the damage was done and senators pressed on with their accusations.

In order to counter the theories of Dietz and Satinover, the Democrats brought in their own experts. According to the *New York Times,* "To explain why Professor Hill had not publicly accused Judge Thomas until 10 years after the harassment she said occurred, they interviewed psychiatrists who were prepared to testify that this was typical behavior." Although the Democrats eventually decided not to call on him to testify, their star witness was to be Robert Spitzer, a Columbia University psychiatrist. He provided a statement that Hill's "behavior was inconsistent with her having a mental disorder, at least a disorder that would have caused her to make these charges." Spitzer told the *New York Times* that "her behavior was entirely consistent with that of victims of sexual harassment" and that she did not have any delusions. Spitzer, Dietz, and Satinover were not the only psychiatrists who volunteered their opinions. The *New York Times* reported that senators of both parties "were inundated with letters and fax messages from psychiatrists with off-the-cuff opinions about Professor Hill, an apparent violation of the American Psychiatric Association's code of ethics." Whatever the ethical issues may be, complaints of sexual harassment routinely prompt psychological evaluations of the women who make the charges and psychiatrists are often enthusiastic participants in the proceedings.[3]

Psychiatrists who participate in events such as the Clarence Thomas hearings go far beyond their professional roles and responsibilities. Every psychiatrist is a physician, a professional whose principal mission is to heal and comfort the sick and to prevent the spread of illness. The activities of Dietz, Satinover, Spitzer, and their colleagues had nothing to do with the treatment or prevention of disease, but the American public is accustomed to psychiatrists becoming deeply involved in political and legal struggles, which are far removed from medical treatment.

The *New York Times* questioned the ethics of psychiatrists' making a diagnosis of someone they have never met, because the American Psychiatric Association (APA) prohibits this conduct. The ethical standard at issue is the "Goldwater rule," adopted after the 1964 presidential election. During that campaign, many psychiatrists responded to a one-page questionnaire devised by a magazine. The results were summarized in a full front-page headline— 1,189 PSYCHIATRISTS SAY GOLDWATER IS PSYCHOLOGICALLY UNFIT TO BE PRESIDENT!—and the accompanying story reprinted psychiatrists' responses to the poll.[4] After Lyndon Johnson used the findings in his campaign, the APA had second thoughts about this type of political psychiatry and prohibited members from offering specific professional opinions about people whom they had not personally interviewed. This prohibition seemed to apply to the activities of Drs. Dietz, Satinover, and Spitzer in the Anita Hill case.

Dietz circumvented the APA proscription because he did not actually make a diagnosis of Hill but only provided information about a diagnostic category, erotomania. He asserted that his intention was simply to educate senators, at least the Republicans, who referred to him as "our psychiatrist."[5] Although Dietz did not directly accuse Hill of entertaining fantasies, he observed that "it would be tragic if that possibility were left unexplored."[6] Furthermore, he reported that there are "many thousands of people who incorrectly believe that famous people have done something to them."[7]

Newsmen asked Paul Applebaum, a member of the APA's ethics committee, to comment on the activities of Dietz. Since there was a real possibility that a complaint would be filed, it was surprising that a member of the ethics committee would offer an opinion without a thorough investigation. He concluded that "Dr. Dietz's account of his involvement suggested that he did not violate this ethical code and appeared to be trying to educate the Senators on complex medical issues." Applebaum said that if Dietz "wasn't offering comments directly on the psychopathology or lack of psychopathology of people he hadn't examined, it is hard to call that an ethical violation." Applebaum observed that Dietz's "involvement may have backfired, but you can't blame him for that." Applebaum was less charitable toward Dietz's clients, the Senate Republicans: "I have many more problems with the behavior of those who then took that information and did what Dr. Dietz himself refused to do."[8]

When the *New York Times* questioned Spitzer about ethical issues, he said that he was aware of the guidelines for professional ethics and that he did not believe he had violated them, because he did not offer a formal diagnosis. However, he did provide a statement rejecting the claim that Hill suffered from delusions, and he proposed the alternative explanation that she had acted like a victim of sexual harassment. The *New York Times* reported, "None of their colleagues said Dr. Dietz or Dr. Spitzer, neither of whom was paid, violated the profession's code."[9]

Although the news reports provided a very revealing account of psychiatry at work, there are some facets of the story that warrant further examination. Some of the unreported aspects of the story are to be found in the private world where psychiatrists invent diagnostic categories that are used to label people. Dietz and, to an even greater extent, Spitzer are important participants in the creation and propagation of psychiatric diagnoses.

THE DIAGNOSIS MAKERS

Robert L. Spitzer is more than a professor of psychiatry, he is the godfather of modern psychiatric diagnosis. He is the principal author of the *Diagnostic and Statistical Manual of Mental Disorders, Third Edition* (DSM-III), often referred to as "the psychiatric bible."[10] When it was published in 1980, DSM-III revolutionized American psychiatry. Under Spitzer's direction, detailed instructions for making evaluations were officially adopted by the American Psychiatric Association for the first time, and claims were made that the new manual was scientifically sound. We will show that the claims made for the accuracy and scientific value of DSM-III and subsequent editions of the manual are questionable, but there is no doubt about the widespread acceptance of DSM-III and its enormous impact. For more than a quarter of a century, Spitzer led the fight to establish the credibility of DSM, and its success is in no small measure the result of his tireless efforts. Spitzer is very adept at making diagnoses. Not only has he identified the mental disorders of individual clients, but he has also created new diagnostic categories for mental disorders. In fact, he has undoubtedly designed or refashioned more new diagnoses than any other living person in the field of mental health. He has been very involved in inventing a number of diagnoses concerning sex and gender, as we will discuss in chapters 3 and 5.

Victimizing Hill

In 1989, Spitzer proposed another new diagnostic category, Victimization Disorder: "The diagnosis of Victimization Disorder is made when, following the experiencing or witnessing of one or more episodes of physical or psychological abuse, coercion into sexual activity, or being the victim of a violent crime, the individual develops a distorted view of the self, the victimization experience, the perpetrator, and the environment." The proposal elaborated on "the distorted view" the victim develops by offering thirteen descriptive criteria, some of which may be pertinent to understanding what Spitzer meant when he said that Hill's behavior was entirely consistent with that of a victim of sexual harassment:

- Stigmatization, i.e., the feeling that one has been permanently damaged by the victimization experience
- Feeling isolated or unable to trust or to be intimate with others
- Overinhibition of anger or excessive expression of anger
- Exaggeration of the powers of the perpetrator
- Lack of believing that authority figures will come to one's help even when help is clearly available

- Fearfulness of being revictimized even in the absence of apparent danger
- Hypervigilant, i.e., increased scanning of environment for potential danger[11]

By the time the Hill–Thomas confrontation occurred two years later, in 1991, Spitzer had circulated the proposal for the diagnosis Victimization Disorder. By applying these criteria to Anita Hill, an adept diagnostician could answer many of the questions raised by the senators who interrogated her. Why did she keep silent for so long? (Obviously, she felt that she had been stigmatized, permanently damaged by Thomas's harassment.) Why didn't she share the information, except for some very secret conversations and furtive telephone calls to friends? (She felt isolated and unable to trust others.) Why did she seem so calm—almost detached—when she testified before the committee? (Clearly it was an overinhibition of her anger.) Why had she, on the other hand, felt driven to testify about what many consider to be casual sexual overtures made a decade earlier? (What better way to describe her reaction than as an excessive expression of anger?) Why hadn't she complained at the time of the offense? (Another obvious answer: she exaggerated the powers of the perpetrator, Thomas. Furthermore, she probably did not believe that authority figures would come to her help.) As to fearfulness of revictimization, didn't Hill leave the employ of Thomas soon after he approached her for the second time? Even though he had stopped making advances, she was obviously hypervigilant and had therefore aborted a promising career in the federal government because of the possible danger in her environment.

Spitzer's observation that Hill was not suffering from a mental disorder contained a provocative reservation; he said that no mental disorder from which she was suffering would have caused her to make accusations against Judge Thomas. Was he suggesting that she had some other mental disorder? He concluded that she seemed to be a typical victim of sexual harassment. What better diagnosis was there for such a person than his newly constructed Victimization Disorder?

Unfortunately, with this (as with many other diagnoses) there are serious problems. Hill's behavior did *not* reflect a distorted view of reality but an accurate assessment of what she could expect if she reported her complaints.

- She was stigmatized; that is, she was permanently damaged by her experience.
- She was isolated and unable to trust her associates. This was amply il-

lustrated by the testimony in support of Thomas by the other women who worked for him at the Equal Economic Opportunity Commission (EEOC), who disparaged Hill.

- If she showed her anger, she would jeopardize her promising career. Any doubt about the risk to her career should be allayed by the testimony of the dean of Oral Roberts Law School, where Hill went after she resigned from the EEOC. Without hesitation, the dean said that he would have fired her if she had made her charges against Thomas when she worked at Oral Roberts.

- She had every reason to fear the power of Thomas and to fear that he would harass her again. Hypervigilance was not only reasonable but necessary for her to maintain in order to survive in her perilous surroundings.

- The hearings painfully demonstrated that authority figures would not help her even though they were clearly available. After all, even when she made her charges before the marginally more sympathetic Democratic Senate, rather than to the Republican Reagan administration, her claims were rejected.

Although Hill exhibited behavior that appeared to meet the criteria for Victimization Disorder, her view of reality was not distorted. Her actions were a prudent, realistic reaction to a dangerous situation. The response to her complaints during the Senate hearings demonstrated how realistic her fears were.

There was another stumbling block in concluding that Professor Hill's problems were symptoms of Victimization Disorder. Many people, particularly psychotherapists who worked closely with sexually abused women, questioned the validity of Spitzer's proposed disorder. The comments of a feminist therapist, Laura Brown, who worked with survivors of sexual abuse, are illustrative.[12] According to Brown, the reactions of many patients who have been abused or harassed are analogous to bereavement and are somewhat normal, although painful, responses to an abnormal life event. The experiences of survivors of victimization and exploitation "are clearly painful to them, and they wish to relieve their distress." Brown concluded that she "would not classify those responses as being clearly a disorder, or, if a disorder, as being necessarily distinct in character from post traumatic stress disorder." She objected to the characterization of sexually abused patients' reactions as being a distorted view of reality, which is the hallmark of the diagnosis of victimization disorder. On the contrary, Brown believed that it is important to recognize that survivors' fears are accurate, and she argued that it is important to the patient's healing process to validate the realities of these patients.

After Brown and her colleagues made strenuous objections to the adoption of Victimization Disorder, the American Psychiatric Association's task force decided not to include it in the newest version of the diagnostic manual, DSM-IV.[13] They did not acknowledge that they were responding to the objections of feminists, but they frequently declared that they intended to avoid the kind of embarrassing confrontations they had experienced in the past.

Erotomania

Although the APA showed restraint about adopting a new diagnosis for victims of abuse and harassment, there were plenty of officially recognized diagnoses in the DSM that were used to interpret Anita Hill's behavior. As we have seen, the one that captured the imagination of her Republican detractors was erotomania. Delusional Disorder, Erotomanic Type, is a newcomer to DSM. It was first included in a 1987 revision,[14] which was supervised by Robert Spitzer, and Parke Dietz played an important role in drafting the text that describes it. Erotomania has been mentioned in the literature for more than a century, although all commentators have described it as an extremely rare disorder and many doubt its existence. The diagnosis of erotomania is based partly on the work of the French psychiatrist de Clerambault. He proposed a category of delusional disorders called *les psychoses passionelles* and included among them one called *erotique*.

The primary characteristic that erotomania shares with other types of delusional disorders is a single well-organized set of delusions held by a person who may function very well in other aspects of life. Erotomania and the other delusional disorders are roughly differentiated from schizophrenia because of the focused, self-contained nature of the sufferer's delusions. The usually well-organized life of those who suffer from delusional disorder is in marked contrast to the chaotic disintegration that is often characteristic of schizophrenia.

The official DSM-IV description of Delusional Disorder, Erotomanic Type states that "the predominant theme of the delusion(s) is that a person, usually of higher status, is in love with the subject." Hill never testified that she thought Thomas was in love with her, only that he made sexual advances. Furthermore, when John Doggett testified that Hill had delusions about his feelings for her, this was not evidence of erotomania, either. What he seemed to be suggesting was that Hill had something like an emotional equivalent of nymphomania, an ability to quickly develop a high school crush on him (and, by implication, on Thomas). This behavior is not erotomania, which is a focused, obsessive, delusional love for a particular person.

Some commentators take issue with the DSM diagnosis of erotomania. They believe that erotomania is not a delusion that women develop but a fantasy that men have invented. As a follow-up on the Anita Hill story, the *New York Times* published an article about this issue.[15] The article quotes Phyllis Grosskurth, a feminist historian of psychoanalysis, as saying, "This is just another form of misogyny. . . . It's like nymphomania. Men so wish that there were women like that out there." To illustrate the point that Hill's erotomania was a man's fantasy, the *New York Times* referred to an assessment of Anita Hill published by an economist, Jude Wanninski. "I never met either of them," Wanninski confessed, "but it strikes me that she may have felt a genuine attraction to the real Clarence Thomas." The *New York Times* characterized Wanninski's observations as fantasies about Hill's fantasies, "using the same kind of breathless italicized prose usually found in Harold Robbins novels." Wanninski described Thomas as "handsome, polished, brilliant, a man of the world" and Anita Hill as "25, bright and comely. She works for him. She is available." Wanninski believed that Thomas would "surely have been tempted by Hill" but that "he would have known there could be no return, one step is a slippery slope." The *New York Times* concluded, "Mr. Wanninski could not bring himself to accept that a woman could reject someone as handsome and successful as Mr. Thomas." Wanninski's clinching argument was, "Why would she say no?"

Doubting Thomas

In all of the talk about psychiatric disorders, one thing stands out above everything else: the public controversy was about Anita Hill's psychiatric condition, whereas few people expressed doubts about Judge Thomas's mental health. It is no more appropriate for clinicians to diagnose

Thomas on the basis of his public statements or from charges made by others than it is for them to diagnose Hill. But those who speculated about a diagnosis for the woman who complained did not reciprocate by offering an assessment of the man she accused.

In addition to possibly having psychological problems related to the sexual feelings and fantasies that were implicit in the charges against him, Thomas manifested behaviors that can be found listed as symptoms of mental disorder in DSM. These include manipulativeness and willingness to distort the truth in order to gain personal goals; volatility and explosive displays of intense anger; callousness and lack of empathy or remorse; irritability; and a pattern of shifting beliefs coupled with overzealousness. That Thomas displayed these behaviors is not disputed; they were present in words and actions that were seen and heard by millions of television viewers. Besides the basic complaint about Thomas's inappropriate sexual advances, there were also persistent allegations of other behaviors, including an inordinate interest in pornography, which was acknowledged by both his enemies and some of his friends. These are the kind of behaviors with which psychotherapists often have a field day. Although they frequently construct elaborate interpretations of personality and behavior from far less information, their speculations about Thomas were muted.[16]

The indifference to the diagnosis of pathology in the man as compared with the inordinate attention to real or imagined symptoms displayed by the female victim is not peculiar to the Thomas–Hill situation. Feminists, as well as many others, have complained about the persistent focus on the psychology of the victim and the blind eye that is often turned on the person who is accused of victimizing her. The imbalance is apparent not just in the way clinicians respond to individual cases or in the one-sided interpretations that are applied only to women. This tendency to manipulate and distort definitions of pathology exists in the structure of psychiatric diagnosis, that is, in the psychiatric bible itself and the way it is created. And it should be no surprise that the targets of these distortions often include the relatively powerless, including women, minorities, and gay people.

THE IMPORTANCE OF THE PSYCHIATRIC BIBLE

On the shelf of every mental health professional is a copy of the *Diagnostic and Statistical Manual of Mental Disorders*. The American Psychiatric Association's 900-page reference book attempts to describe and classify each one of over 300 mental disorders. Even though it is poorly organized, offers no suggestions for treatment, presents its material in wooden prose, and costs $55, each edition of the manual is destined to sell more than a million copies. Few other professional reference works are so regularly stocked in trade and college bookstores, and few are read by so many laypeople. And none have so broad an impact on so many sectors of life.

Part of the power of DSM derives from its attempt to distinguish mental disorder from other human troubles. Although to some laypeople the importance of the distinction may not be immediately clear, it is an enormously consequential one. DSM is a claim for professional jurisdiction by the American Psychiatric Association. The broadness of this claim provides justification for the scope of psychiatric expertise and a basis for requests for governmental and private support. But it does more: it proposes how we as a society should think about our troubles. By creating categories for certain behaviors, DSM determines which behaviors should be considered a result of illness or disorder and should therefore fall under the purview of psychiatrists and other mental health professionals. Mental disorder is, by definition, a matter of internal dysfunction, an indication that something harmful has gone wrong with a person's mental apparatus. Thus, to label specific behaviors as mental disorders, as was done with Anita Hill, is to instruct us to see the behavior as a direct result of a malfunction of the individual.

DSM is a guidebook that tells us how we should think about manifestations of sadness and anxiety, sexual activities, alcohol and substance abuse, and many other behaviors. Consequently, the categories created for DSM reorient our thinking about important social matters and affect our social institutions. The diagnostic manual, for example, is used frequently in the judicial system when questions are raised about a defendant's mental capacity, intentional state, or cognitive abilities. In legal cases involving guardianship, child custody, criminal liability, fitness to stand trial, and determination of the extent to which defendants have the capacity to appreciate the consequences of their acts, testimony about diagnostic categories is frequently invited, and the guidelines provided by DSM are therefore introduced.

Courts are only one of the social institutions that use DSM. In schools throughout the nation, children who are having problems with their academic work, their peers, their teachers, or their families are being labeled by the users of DSM as suffering from disorders that carry labels like Oppositional Defiant Disorder, Conduct Disorder, or Attention-Deficit/Hyperactivity Disorder. These children may be placed in special classes, dismissed from school, or given medication. From prisons to child welfare agencies, DSM is shaping how we think about problems and determining who gets labeled as having a mental disorder.

But the effect of DSM is broader than its use in courts, schools, and social agencies. Inevitably, psychiatric concepts and the behaviors they "medicalize" seep deeply into our fiction, theater, movies, language, humor, and view of ourselves and our neighbors. At times, it is even difficult to distinguish between our psychiatric science and our humor. For example, a recent article in the prestigious *American Journal of Psychiatry* proposed adding to DSM a mental disorder characterized by "uncontrolled buying" or "frequent buying of more than can be afforded."[17] In a January 1997 *New Yorker* article, "Just Click No," one psychiatrist proposed in jest a DSM category of Internet Addiction Disorder only to discover that many people considered themselves addicted to the Internet and quickly joined self-help therapy groups.[18] One psychologist, Dr. Kimberly Young, has apparently already asked the APA to give official recognition to the disorder, an action that will pave the way for insurance companies to reimburse addicts for therapy.

In fact, one of the most powerful effects of DSM is due to its connection to insurance coverage: DSM is the psychotherapist's password for insurance reimbursement. Whether you are depressed or just blue, manic-depressive or just moody, anxious or just high-strung is not simply a matter of semantics; it is the key to millions of dollars in insurance coverage for psychotherapy, hospitalization, and medications. This vital connection exists because all mental health professionals must list a psychiatric diagnostic label, accompanied by appropriate code number, on their claims for insurance reimbursement. DSM provides the key to the dollars not only from private health insurance carriers but also from massive government programs such as Medicaid, Social Security Disability Income, benefit programs for veterans, and Medicare. Because of the financial incentives structured into the development and use of DSM, decisions about which human problems get included as mental disorders in DSM and who qualifies for the reimbursable diagnostic label are vulnerable to pressure from advocacy groups, professional associations, and corporations.

The pharmaceutical companies, for one, have a big stake in psychiatric diagnosis. It is well known that drug companies provide substantial funding for the American Psychiatric Association's conventions and major scientific journals and reap enormous profits from the expanding market for psychiatric medications. They also fund a substantial number of psychiatric researchers. It is less well known that some pharmaceutical companies have contributed directly to the development of DSM. The companies have a direct financial interest in expanding the number of people who can be defined as having a mental disorder and who then might be treated with their chemical products. For this reason, drug companies are disturbed by the findings of many surveys that have found that a majority of people whom DSM would label neither define their own problems as mental illness nor seek psychiatric help for them.[19] For drug companies, these unlabeled masses are a vast untapped market, the virgin Alaskan oil fields of mental disorder.

DSM helps the drug companies in tapping this territory by identifying those new customers. The New York Times described a new diagnostic instrument, derived from DSM, that helps them do just that.[20] It is a 26-item checklist that was designed to be self-administered by general medical patients so that primary care physicians can quickly spot anxiety, depression, substance abuse or alcoholism, and somatoform disorders (i.e., physical symptoms with no medical explanation) among people who have come to the clinic for relief from, for example, the flu or a sore back. The physician, using a companion DSM-based instrument, can make a psychiatric diagnosis in an average of only eight minutes and can then, presumably, prescribe medication or make a referral to a psychiatrist. The Times article quotes one of the developers of this checklist as saying, "To diagnose and treat those four categories, you don't need psychiatric training." Thus, this new checklist, called Prime-MD, is the Alaskan pipeline for the pharmaceuticals, a method of gaining direct access to an immense new market.

The architects of DSM, including Robert Spitzer, are the main developers of Prime-MD (Spitzer, Williams, Kroenke, et al., 1994). Pfizer, one of the country's largest drug companies, paid for the development of Prime-MD and holds the copyright to it. Pfizer has already paid for the training, at symposiums, of more than 6,000 primary care doctors in the use of Prime-MD. As part of the training, in case the physicians miss the obvious point, they hear a lecture on psychopharmacology. The New York Times, in its understated way, concludes, "Pfizer presumably stands to benefit if the doctors prescribe its psychiatric medications."[21] Furthermore, the developers of Prime-MD, concerned that busy primary care physicians may not take the few minutes needed to use it, explain to them in their promotional article exactly how they should request third-party reimbursement for their time administering Prime-MD and reassure them that payment is likely.[22] The pump, indeed, has been primed.

DSM is also having an enormous impact in the halls of science. Its categories of disorder, its definitions of those disorders, and its general approach to describing and understanding human problems have had a tremendous effect on the research and higher education community. Psychiatric researchers who seek funding from the National Institute of Mental Health (NIMH), the major sponsor of psychiatric research, must do so using the DSM categories and definitions. Thus, DSM provides a template for new knowledge, shaping what scientific questions get asked— and which ones get ignored.

The effects of DSM on the knowledge development enterprise will last for a generation. The effects of DSM-driven research on public policy are more immediate. Congress and state legislatures use statistics on the number of people in the United States who suffer from mental illness as one basis for allocating public funds to various health programs. They look to public health epidemiologists for those statistics, and epidemiologists use DSM-based categories and definitions to count the mentally ill. To the extent that DSM is flawed, these national counts of the mentally ill are misleading to public policymakers.

The private citizen should also be concerned about the basis for DSM diagnoses. It is, in the end, private citizens who are labeled with these official psychiatric diagnoses, diagnoses that can be stigmatizing and consequential in ways that are almost impossible for the individual to control. For example, a young lawyer, Molly, consulted a psychotherapist because of the distress she was suffering in an abusive personal relationship. The therapist, in order to receive reimbursement from Molly's health insurance company, exaggerated the severity of the distress and distorted the extent to which it was due to Molly's own mental problems rather than to her partner's violent behavior. A DSM diagnosis of mental disorder was offered to the managed care company with a plan for individual treatment. The use of a psychiatric medication was encouraged by the managed care company, and one was prescribed. Molly left the abusive personal relationship; ended treatment after six weeks, when she was feeling better; and never took the medication. Two years later, she is shocked to learn that she now has a psychiatric history of mental disorder and that her medical records are available to her current (and any future) employer, other insurance companies, the state, and just about anyone else who may want to know. Not only did the use of DSM in this case distort the nature of the problem (and perhaps compromise the treatment received), but the label itself (and perhaps some of the therapist's reports) stuck to the individual in computerized information systems accessible to many organizations. This lack of privacy and confidentiality, of course, is not the fault of DSM, but it is a major reason why the public should be concerned about DSM's validity and the accuracy of its use.

THE CONVENTIONAL AND CRITICAL VIEWS

The conventional view in psychiatry is that diagnoses are names for pathological conditions that are "discovered" by scientific methods. DSM, in this view, is a scientific classification system that carves nature at its joints. Both the making of a diagnosis of an individual and the identification of a category of illness, such as schizophrenia, are the results of careful, systematic scientific inquiry. The American Psychiatric Association has gone to great lengths to promote the conventional view of how diagnoses are created. By naming an illness and placing it within a classification system of diseases, psychiatry makes claims about what is normal and what it views as its legitimate domain—the terrain of madness.

There are certainly many people who are troubled and plenty of individuals and families made miserable by mental illness. DSM is intended to describe these illnesses and identify those who have them. But DSM oversteps its bounds by defining how we should think about ourselves; how we should respond to stress; how much anxiety or sadness we should feel; and when and how we should sleep, eat, and express ourselves sexually. Although people inevitably base these judgments on personal and social values, the APA tries through DSM to extend its professional jurisdiction over daily life by arguing that its descriptions of illnesses are based on science. The APA has revised its classification system three times during the last 17 years, each time claiming that the resulting document and its expanded list of disorders are based on research.

In this book we examine critically how the APA creates categories of mental disorders. After 17 years of studying the constant revising of DSM, we have difficulty reconciling what the APA claims about the manual with what actually happens in its creation. The story told here is not the conventional one of science triumphing over the mysteries of nature. Rather, we trace how the psychiatric profession struggles with various political constituencies to create categories of mental disorder and to garner support for their official acceptance.

In pursuing this story, we identify several themes. The first is the increasing "pathologizing" of everyday behavior. In its approach to defining mental illness and in its actual use by clinicians, DSM is sweeping increasing numbers of human problems into the realm of psychiatric disorder and medical jurisdiction. In this growing arena, the interests of the psychiatric establishment to expand reimbursable problems are pitted against the cost-containment interests of the insurance companies and the weakness of the scientific evidence. The second theme is the fragility of science in the face of political advocacy. Although the conventional view claims that science and hard evidence underlie decisions about DSM, we find that political negotiation and advocacy—as well as personal interest—are just as, and often more, important in determining whether a mental disorder is created. A third theme is how DSM can be an instrument that pathologizes those in our society who are undesirable and powerless; this occurs not because of any malicious intent but because of unspoken cultural biases about what should be considered normal and what should be considered disease.

A PREVIEW OF THE BOOK

These themes are illustrated throughout this book by case studies that analyze how scientific claims are manufactured and promoted, how disorders are invented, and how science is often subordinated to social and political influences in the development and use of the diagnostic categories contained in DSM. On the surface, the negotiation appears to be a process of sifting through scientific evidence, but barely concealed beneath the surface is an intricate process that involves old-fashioned political horse-trading, complex economic considerations, elaborate systems for consensus building, and other mechanisms for mobilizing power and negotiating social conflicts. These processes involve carefully brokered negotiations among the developers of DSM, other mental health professionals, and the advocates for people to whom the labels may be applied, while attempts are made to keep an eye on how a wider public audience may react to the creation or deletion of a particular category of mental illness. Mental disorders are no longer easily created by any one small group. It takes a village, so to speak, a coalition of groups both within and outside the American Psychiatric Association. If nobody has the power to call the shots unilaterally, how do we decide who is crazy? We get the best view of this process when there are public disputes regarding particular diagnostic categories. Consequently, our book uses information that is generated by such disputes to illustrate its general themes.

In an earlier book, *The Selling of DSM: The Rhetoric of Science in Psychiatry*,[23] we examined the making and marketing of the third edition of DSM by focusing on the most salient scientific problem of the 1970s, diagnostic reliability, and on how the developers of DSM created, managed, and used that scientific problem in the service of reforming the official diagnostic manual. In this book, we move well beyond that territory to examine in detail the politics and scientific basis of specific diagnostic categories that have created controversy. In telling these stories, we attempt to reveal how professional biases can sweep seemingly normal behavior into categories of mental illness, how definitions of mental illness often mask gender and racial bias, and how the interpretation of scientific data is often distorted to serve the purposes of powerful professional groups.

In the opening of this chapter we used the Clarence Thomas–Anita Hill confrontation as an illuminating example of the role of psychiatric diagnosticians in a dramatic political struggle. From it you learned of the potential destructive power of psychiatric diagnosis and saw how it was marshaled at the highest levels of our political system to defend Clarence Thomas by skewering his accuser. You saw the enormously arbitrary discretion that DSM permits in placing people in mental illness categories and how newly minted proposals for DSM categories can rapidly be pressed into political service. We presented the use of leading psychiatrists as hired guns, ready to quickly draw DSM from their holsters to defend or attack Anita Hill's character and veracity, and showed how the psychiatric establishment obsessed over the proper diagnosis for a courageous woman while it completely ignored the equally significant question about the mental health of her tormentor.

In chapter 2 we provide a general background about the *Diagnostic and Statistical Manual of Mental Disorders*. We briefly review its origins and the role of classification in science. We describe DSM's recent history and the way it achieved such phenomenal status within the mental health field. This chapter informs readers of the significance of the debates that have taken place about DSM and explains the organizational structure that is used by the APA to manage revisions of the manual. We pay particular attention to the issue of scientific validity and its neglected role in the invention of diagnoses. We argue that the process of developing diagnostic categories has been similar to other types of professional decision making, where status, reputation, and turf are dominant considerations.

In chapter 3 we discuss one of the most publicized diagnostic controversies: the shifting status of homosexuality in the diagnostic manual. Well-publicized protests by gay activists led to the elimination of homosexuality from DSM-II[24] in 1974. This struggle was a watershed event because the ad hoc procedures the APA used to resolve the controversy became the model for the "revolutionary" development of DSM-III and for subsequent revisions. In this episode we see vividly the salience of political factions and the effects of their campaigning and maneuvering in constructing and deconstructing diagnoses that potentially affect millions of functioning and presumably normal citizens. Definitions of mental disorder are revealed to be particularly susceptible to external pressures and contemporary culture, in a way not easily matched by physical disorders like influenza, TB, or cancer.

In chapter 4 we describe the reinvention of a psychiatric diagnosis under political pressure from an outside advocacy group. The diagnosis War Neurosis had disappeared from DSM until the Vietnam veterans pressured the American Psychiatric Association. We examine the creation of Posttraumatic Stress Disorder (PTSD),* a diagnosis that was reluctantly included in DSM for the first time in 1980 in spite of the opposition of many leading psychiatric experts. Once accepted into the manual, PTSD became one of the most popular diagnoses, used increasingly to cover a growing assortment of problems. The unexpected success of PTSD is a fascinating story. It was championed initially by Vietnam veterans, who had to wage a guerrilla war to have the diagnosis included in the manual.

---

*In DSM-III and DSM-III-R, this diagnosis is written Post-Traumatic Stress Disorder; in DSM-IV it is written Posttraumatic Stress Disorder.

Ironically, in the march of PTSD to success as a diagnosis, its purposes were reversed. It was originally designed to label the psychological damage to soldiers who were perpetrators or witnesses of violence. Now it is used increasingly for women and children who are victims of domestic abuse and rape.

Chapter 5 tells a very different story, a saga about the gender politics of DSM. With little warning, the developers of DSM invented a new diagnosis, Masochistic Personality Disorder, based on psychoanalytic theories of masochism. With the political advantages enjoyed by insiders and on the thinnest scientific evidence, they rapidly advanced the new category from proposal to official candidate for inclusion in the manual. Unexpectedly, their proposal created a firestorm of criticism from feminist psychotherapists and others for being blatantly gender biased. Because of the much-publicized controversy that ensued, there is a rich record of how DSM developers actually go about making "scientific" decisions about what to include in the manual. This chapter traces the controversy; reviews the scientific evidence offered for the new diagnosis; and describes the political maneuvers that resulted in the inclusion in DSM of the revised diagnosis, relabeled as Self-Defeating Personality Disorder (SDPD), as a special category in 1987. SDPD's final downfall came several years later when feminists succeeded in banning it from DSM-IV. After the battle was lost, the weakness of the scientific support for the diagnosis was finally revealed by its own proponents.

In the process of defeating SDPD, its opponents provided an illuminating counterpoint by proposing their own new diagnostic category: Delusional Dominating Personality Disorder. The proposed new diagnosis was designed to capture the dominating, harmful behaviors often promoted by male socialization in our culture. The proposal for DDPD was both satirical and serious. Although DDPD appeared to be conceptually parallel to SDPD, it was handled very differently by the committees planning DSM-IV. The politics of gender played a pivotal role in the consideration of this diagnostic category.

Chapter 6 examines how psychiatric diagnoses, once created, can be used to protect and rationalize psychiatric malpractice. It makes this point with a review of the writings of psychiatrists who have argued that patients seduce their therapists and entice them into other kinds of professional misconduct. The psychiatrists advance the novel argument that these patients falsely accuse their therapists of transgressions because *the patients* suffer from an identifiable illness, namely, Borderline Personality Disorder. This chapter describes the evolution of Borderline Personality Disorder, a peculiar but frequently used diagnostic category that has been used to label difficult patients and those who accuse their therapists of having sexual relations with them, and explores the diagnostic illogic that psychiatrists have used to explain their own misbehavior.

Chapter 7 traces the misuse of psychiatric diagnosis applied to African Americans from the days of slavery to the present. On the title page of DSM is the seal of the APA, which includes a bust of Benjamin Rush, "the father of American psychiatry," a man who concluded that the blackness of Africans was due to a form of leprosy. The perception that African Americans suffer from inherent pathological conditions was given credence in 1840 by the first United States census report on the incidence of insanity. The data were presented as demonstrating that freedom led to insanity among African Americans and slavery promoted mental stability for slaves. Census figures were used by Southern politicians to reinforce the need for slavery as a protection for African Americans. The newly formed APA (1844) continued to report the data even after they had been discredited. In the antebellum period, psychiatrists continued to promote the theory that manumission caused insanity. Later, after World War II, the APA's official journal reported that increases in admissions of blacks to mental hospitals after *Brown v. Board of Education* (the landmark desegregation case) was due to propaganda promoted by Communists and labor organizers. The tradition of conflict between psychiatry and African Americans continues today, and it is often expressed, unsurprisingly, in the uses of diagnosis.

The last chapter distills what can be learned from the diverse diagnostic stories in the earlier chapters. What is it about DSM that makes it so vulnerable to misappropriation and misuse? Why have its scientific ambitions been so often thwarted? Why are psychotherapists unwittingly pushed into the strange new world of deliberate misdiagnosis? Can anything be done? We will conclude with some modest suggestions.

2 PATHOLOGIZING
EVERYDAY BEHAVIOR

As you reflect on conversations you have had during recent weeks, you recall that your cousin, a rising young stockbroker, complained of not sleeping well; a writer friend who is finishing a novel admitted to being unable to quit smoking cigarettes; a former high school classmate and rival confessed to still bearing grudges against you; a colleague at work, who is single, appears to always choose to be alone after work and on weekends; a close friend confided that she has almost no sexual desire for her husband; your supervisor's 10-year-old is in trouble at school; your neighbor's teenager has been caught shoplifting; your old college roommate telephoned and admitted she was hungover from another weekend beach party; your partner has been feeling blue; and your sister can't stop obsessing about a former boyfriend. In addition, you are really worrying about an upcoming speech you must make at a national convention.

Individually, none of these problems strikes you as extraordinary. Although they may be unpleasant and distressing experiences, they are ordinary ones, ones we all feel from time to time, and they usually subside. During those conversations you had with your friends and associates, you were able to put aside your own worries and respond appropriately with support and advice. You recognize that these routine problems provide the bumpy texture of human life.

But, according to DSM-IV (the latest version, published in 1994), they also provide the texture of mental illness. In fact, each of the behaviors above is listed as a criterion for one or more mental disorders:

- Not sleeping: Major Depressive Disorder
- Smoking: Nicotine Dependence
- Bearing grudges: Paranoid Personality Disorder
- Being alone: Schizoid Personality Disorder
- Lack of sexual interest: Hypoactive Sexual Desire Disorder
- Trouble at school: Oppositional Defiant Disorder
- Shoplifting: Conduct Disorder
- Hungover: Alcohol Abuse
- Feeling blue: Dysthymic Disorder
- Obsessive thoughts: Obsessive-Compulsive Personality Disorder
- Worrying: Generalized Anxiety Disorder

Where you thought your friends were just having normal troubles, the developers of the American Psychiatric Association's diagnostic bible raise the possibility that you are surrounded by the mentally ill. Equally disconcerting to you, you may be among them.[1] This easy inclusion of so many common quirks and experiences is what we refer to as the pathologizing of everyday behavior. Other behaviors defined by DSM as possible symptoms of mental disorder include, among others, frustration, anger, difficulty concentrating, restlessness, increased appetite, weight gain, often losing one's temper, being easily fatigued, muscle tension, avoidance of almost all genital contact with a sexual partner, recurrent inability to maintain an adequate erection, recurrent delay in orgasm (for a woman) following normal sexual excitement, having extremely frightening dreams, being inappropriately sexually seductive, theatricality, showing arrogance, lacking empathy, being preoccupied with being criticized, and difficulty making everyday decisions. Under what circumstances and with what logic can such everyday behaviors be transformed into symptoms of mental disease?

The story of that transformation is the story of the *Diagnostic and Statistical Manual of Mental Disorder,* a story of the struggles of the American Psychiatric Association to gain respectability within medicine and maintain dominance among the many mental health professions. It is a story of science and of politics, of facts and fantasies. At the heart of the story (and often lost in the parade of committees and the minutiae of scientific reports) are two seemingly intractable scientific problems that DSM has attempted to solve: diagnostic validity and reliability. We will need to briefly visit these two topics in this chapter to explain why DSM now includes so many specific everyday behaviors as symptoms of mental illness and why doing so has not helped the APA improve either the validity or the reliability of DSM.

Let's begin this story by tracing how DSM might categorize that hypothetical symptom of mental disorder that we assigned to you—your anxiety about an upcoming speech.

WHAT, ME WORRY?

Alfred E. Newman's signature remark in *Mad* magazine could now be written "What, Me Crazy?" because worry and anxiety have become big business in the United States. DSM-IV says 5 percent of the population (about 12 million Americans), two-thirds of them women, will have Generalized Anxiety Disorder (officially coded as 300.02) in their lifetime. The pharmaceutical companies—the makers of Prozac, Xanax, and beta blockers for stage fright—love those numbers because they represent a vast and growing market. Your anxiety about your upcoming speech makes you part of that vast market. The drug companies have products that they would like you and your physician to use. Sure, giving a speech can be worrisome, but how do normal discomforts become possible signs of mental illness?

First, you must appreciate that the notion of mental disorder is what social scientists call a construct. Constructs are abstract concepts of something that is not real in the physical sense that a spoon or motorcycle or cat can be seen and touched. Constructs are shared ideas, supported by general agreement. Democracy, alienation, conservatism are constructs, abstract ideas that have some degree of shared meaning within some groups. Mental illness is a construct, a shared abstract idea. Later in this chapter we will address some problems that have occurred in trying to gain agreement about the meaning of mental disorder. But for now, be aware that constructs such as Generalized Anxiety Disorder are held together by agreements and that agreements change over time. The category itself is an invention, a creation. It may be a good and useful invention, or it may be a confusing one. DSM is a compendium of constructs. And like a large and popular mutual fund, DSM's holdings are constantly changing as the managers' estimates and beliefs about the value of those holdings change.

For example, the meaning of an anxiety-based mental disorder has been officially changed in DSM three times just since 1979. As a method of illustrating the evolving creations, let's review how various versions of DSM may have been used to categorize your discomfort about your public presentation. In DSM-I, used from 1952 to 1968, we would look under the category Psychoneurotic Disorders, disorders whose chief characteristic is anxiety, which may be felt "directly" or may be "unconsciously and automatically controlled" by "defense mechanisms."[2] Anxiety, DSM-I explains, is "a danger signal felt . . . by the conscious portion of the personality" (p. 31). Unlike psychoses, psychoneurotic disorders may not involve gross distortions of external reality; instead, there are periodic "maladjustments." According to DSM-I, your particular discomfort could be from either of two psychoneurotic disorders: Anxiety Reaction or Phobic Reaction. Anxiety Reaction is "diffuse" and "characterized by anxious expectation." Phobic Reaction, we're told, is anxiety that is "detached from a specific idea, object, or situation in the daily life and is displaced to some symbolic idea or situation in the form of a specific neurotic fear" (p. 33). These creations are deeply embedded in the theoretical beliefs of psychoanalysts, the dominant group in psychiatry at the time DSM-I was created.

In DSM-II, used from 1968 to 1979, we find in the class Neuroses, two labels similar to those in DSM-I. One disorder is labeled Anxiety Neurosis (Code 300.0) and is described as "anxious over-concern extending to panic and frequently associated with somatic symptoms"; we are told that it "must be distinguished from normal apprehension or fear, which occurs in realistically dangerous situations."[3] Neuroses, in general, the manual explains, "manifest neither gross distortion or misinterpretation of external reality, nor gross personality disorganization." Little more is said. Thus, according to DSM-II, unless you are Salman Rushdie scheduled to deliver a public address in Tehran, your anxiety about your speech could be considered "over-concern" and therefore the symptom of a mental disorder.

Another possible label for your problem in DSM-II is Phobic Neurosis, described as the "intense fear of an object or situation which the patient consciously recognizes as no real danger to him. The person's apprehension may be experienced as faintness, palpitations, perspiration, tremor or panic, that may represent displaced fears of some other unconscious object." We would certainly need to know more about the extent of your apprehension and how you experience it to use these old DSM-II categories.

In 1980, DSM-III (used from 1980 to 1986) eliminated the entire construct of neurosis, rejecting a prior agreement (which, one might say, became not so agreeable) but not discarding the construct of anxiety itself. Instead, DSM-III created a broad new class of mental disorders, called Anxiety Disorders, and split and relabeled many neuroses as specific types of this disorder. For example, Anxiety Neurosis was dropped as a label, but the general problems it described were split into Panic Disorder and Generalized Anxiety Disorder. Phobic Neurosis was dropped and replaced by five types of Phobic Disorder: Agoraphobia, or fear of the outdoors (with and without panic attacks); Social Phobia; Simple Phobia; and Separation Anxiety Disorder (for children). By 1980, you may have fallen into one of these seven categories of disorder, depending on the specific nature, context, duration, and symptoms of your worrying about your upcoming speech. If these categories were not sufficient, other anxiety-ridden diagnoses were available, such as Adjustment Disorder with Anxious Mood.

In the revised DSM of 1987 (referred to as DSM-III-R), further changes were made in the subtypes of Anxiety Disorders and other minor changes were made in the criteria. In 1994 still more changes were made for DSM-IV, the current manual. Some of these latest changes are rather difficult to decipher, as the constructs keep changing and multiplying like guppies. The constant revising provides the illusion that knowledge is changing rapidly (it is not) and that more specific categories are likely to be more valid and used more reliably (which is also not necessarily the case, as will be shown). The section of DSM-IV about Anxiety Disorders begins by indicating that Panic Attack and Agoraphobia (formerly stand-alone disorders) are not defined as disorders themselves but as features of other Anxiety Disorders. Thus, your worrying about your upcoming speech would currently need to be reviewed against the descriptions of at least the following categories:

Panic Disorder with Agoraphobia
Panic Disorder without Agoraphobia

Agoraphobia without History of Panic Disorder
Specific Phobia (replacing the former Simple Phobia)
    Animal Type (e.g., fear or avoidance of dogs, spiders)
    Natural Environment Type (e.g., fear of storms, water, heights)
    Blood-Injection-Injury Type (e.g., fear of seeing blood, getting an
        injection)
    Situational Type (e.g., fear of tunnels, bridges, flying, elevators, etc.)
    Other Type
Social Phobia (fear of a social or performance situation)
Obsessive-Compulsive Disorder
Generalized Anxiety Disorder
Anxiety Disorder Due to a Medical Condition
    with Generalized Anxiety
    with Panic Attacks
    with Obsessive-Compulsive Symptoms
Substance-Induced Anxiety Disorder
    with Generalized Anxiety
    with Panic Attacks
    with Obsessive-Compulsive Symptoms
    with Phobic Symptoms
Anxiety Disorder Not Otherwise Specified

Simply reviewing the detailed descriptions of all these possibilities would probably increase your worrying! Included in the defining criteria of these Anxiety Disorders are such normal experiences as sweating, chills, fear of losing control, fear of being in a crowd, various fears of objects or situations, excessive worry, restlessness, irritability, muscle tension, sleep disturbance, and so on. To be sure, having one simple, transitory symptom is unlikely to qualify you for a DSM diagnosis, but the criteria lists contain many common behaviors that most people have experienced and that are not rare. Furthermore, this dizzying array of mental disorders contains just a few of the more likely disorders that might be used to diagnose your difficulties.

The difficulties experienced by your circle of friends and acquaintances could be subjected to the same genealogical search through the many versions of DSM. In each search, what one is tracing is the evolution of American psychiatry's attempt to define the boundaries of its jurisdiction, the profession's own manifest destiny. Rather than gaining any substantive understanding of your difficulties, you gain a far more interesting glimpse of psychiatry's struggle to define its domain and expand its range.

At this point in your DSM inquiry, your speech-giving troubles have already alerted you to the two major scientific problems of DSM. The first alert is the apparent complexity of determining what category, if any, fits you best. DSM now has so many different possibilities that it would be reasonable to assume that clinicians have more, rather than less, trouble using the recent editions. Whereas earlier there were two possible labels, now there are over twenty. Ironically, the developers of DSM have promoted this great elaboration of categories and the endless list of specific symptoms as an attempt to make diagnosis easier for clinicians and to increase the likelihood that different clinicians will agree on how to label a particular person's problem. This is the scientific problem of diagnostic reliability. We will review this later in this chapter, and in the last chapter we will discuss some of the reasons why DSM fails to solve this problem.

You are also not at all convinced that what you and your friends are experiencing belong in categories of mental illness at all. However unpleasant or painful your experiences and regardless of whether therapy or medication may help, you intuitively reject the idea that these common hassles are truly signs of mental disorder. Your concern gets to the heart of the second scientific problem, the problem of diagnostic validity.

Defining a mental disorder involves specifying the features of human experiences that demarcate where normality shades into abnormality. Defining mental disorders creates these boundaries. That is why DSM, which is a compilation of these definitions, is so important. Determining when relatively common experiences such as anxiety or sadness or memory lapses should be considered evidence of some disorder requires the setting of boundaries that are largely arbitrary, not scientific, unlike setting the boundaries for what constitutes cancer or pneumonia. Because these boundaries are arbitrary, agreements must be hammered out among a few psychiatrists serving on special committees. Where the boundaries are set determines how prevalent a disorder is "discovered" to be in the population.[4] If the threshold for the disorder is set too low, making many common experiences evidence of mental disorder and therefore characterizing many people as mentally disturbed, the diagnosis may be ridiculed publicly, as happened with the inclusion of a caffeine-related disorder. Making the criteria stringent may make it easier for the public to accept a new disorder (it is so extreme and rare that it intuitively seems to be abnormal), but such stringency may render the disorder so uncommon that clinicians or researchers may have no practical interest in it. Thus, creating diagnoses involves both scientific and political considerations.

DEFINING A MENTAL DISORDER: THE PROBLEM OF VALIDITY

If mental disorder is a construct, an abstract idea held together by agreements, the construct's *validity* refers to the extent to which those agreements make sense. DSM is a book of tentatively assembled agreements. Agreements don't always make sense, nor do they always reflect reality. You can have agreements among experts without validity. Even if you found people who agreed that the earth is flat, that the moon is made of cheese, that smoking cigarettes poses no health risks, or that politicians are never corrupt, such agreements would not establish truth. You can find agreement even about untruths. Validity is less about agreements and more about truth. In practice, scientists are concerned about both reliability and validity, because they seek truth.

The notion of validity is an important one in the social and behavioral sciences, particularly among psychologists concerned with measurement and diagnosis.[5] Classification is, in the crudest way, a form of measurement, a method of determining whether phenomena have the particular characteristics for membership in a class. Questions about the meaningfulness of the concept of mental illness, just like questions about the substantive meaning of relatively abstract concepts such as intelligence or anxiety, involve the issue of validity of scientific constructs. Having an operational procedure for determining whether a phenomenon belongs in a class, such as the checklist of symptoms in DSM, does not substantiate what that construct or class is.

Recent editions of DSM have attempted to address this problem, because critics of psychiatry have been asking whether mental illness is a valid concept conceptually distinct from other kinds of human difficulties. The French philosopher and historian Foucault viewed mental illness as a justification for medical power.[6] The American psychoanalyst Szasz has spent a lifetime arguing that mental illness is an inappropriate metaphor to disguise the bitter pill of moral conflicts.[7] Scheff, a sociologist, viewed mental illness as a "residual category," a label used by lay people and experts alike when a person's behavior defies other explanations.[8] All these authors suggested that mental disorder is merely a judgment that devalues some behaviors. Mental disorder, they said, is not a scientific or medical concept but a lay concept and a value judgment.

Earlier editions of DSM completely ignored this problem. DSM-II, for instance, made no attempt to provide a conceptual definition of mental disorder. Instead, it offered general, vague descriptions of specific disorders that had evolved over the years through professional consensus. For example, one disorder, Inadequate Personality, was defined as "ineffectual responses to emotional, social, intellectual and physical demands . . . inadaptability, ineptness, poor judgment, social instability, and lack of physical and emotional stamina." Although such a description found agreement among those developing DSM-II, it hardly silenced critics who raised questions about construct validity. Regardless of agreements that had been made to promote Inadequate Personality as a mental disorder in DSM-II, the diagnosis disappeared from the manual by 1980. The concept of inadequate personality, like neurosis, was an agreement gone bad.

Defining Disorder

It may come as a surprise to those unfamiliar with American psychiatry that until 1980—almost 140 years after the founding of the American Psychiatric Association and 28 years after DSM was first published—DSM provided no formal definition of what constitutes a mental disorder. Why should American psychiatry need a definition of mental disorder at all? Why not simply claim that any phenomenon that psychiatrists treat is a mental disorder? To some extent that had been the de facto definition of mental illness. Whatever psychiatrists wanted to treat was generally accepted by the public and other professions. But not anymore. Now we have many professional and self-help groups that claim expertise in helping with life's problems; social workers, clinical and community psychologists, psychiatric nurses, marriage and family counselors, and self-help groups provide services to alcoholics, drug abusers, battered women, and many others. By 1980, psychiatry as a medical specialty needed to demarcate its boundaries but to do so in some conceptually coherent way, not merely by asserting its presumed authority.

For many years, the American Psychiatric Association successfully pushed the issue aside, but gay activists in the early 1970s demanded an explanation for why homosexuality was considered a mental disorder (see chapter 3 for a discussion of these events). It was a question about validity, and the crisis it created for the APA forced the association to wrestle with the problem.

As with so much that is in the DSM, the APA had to wrestle over more than the definitions. The psychiatrists had to fight with the psychologists' association over professional turf. The dispute arose when Robert Spitzer, who had earlier managed the battle over the exclusion of homosexuality and who had recently been appointed to create DSM-III, attempted to develop a general definition of mental disorder that could guide the work of his task force. When he presented his ideas the following year, he made the assertion that "mental disorders are a subset of medical disorders."[9] (p. 4). This statement, which was unnecessary for the definition, attempted to establish that mental disorders are fully within the province of medicine, a notion that caused a storm of protest from the American Psychological Association.[10] The psychologists' demands that the offending phrase be abandoned led to a brief standoff with the APA. In the short run, no compromises were reached and no agreement about professional turf was achieved. But when DSM-III was released in 1980, the disputed phrase had been dropped. What was learned, however, was that defining mental disorders is not only conceptually difficult but also politically controversial.

Nevertheless, in DSM-III, for the first time, a definition of mental disorder was offered. Few people paid any attention to the definition itself, since most of the interest was in the 300 disorders described in the manual's 500 pages. There was no rigorous debate about whether the brand-new definition of mental disorder itself was conceptually adequate or even whether it was used systematically to decide what is pathological and belongs in DSM and what should be excluded. In fact, the definition was never meant to guide those decisions. It appeared to be there to fill an embarrassing void in earlier editions of DSM. An official compendium of mental disorders should, after all, make some effort to define what a disorder is.

In the last three editions of DSM, the same general definition is provided:

> In DSM-IV, each of the mental disorders is conceptualized as a clinically significant behavioral or psychological syndrome or pattern that occurs in an individual and that is associated with present distress (a painful symptom)

or disability (impairment in one or more important areas of functioning) or with a significantly increased risk of suffering death, pain, disability, or an important loss of freedom. In addition, this syndrome or pattern must not be merely an expectable *and culturally sanctioned* response to a particular event, for example, the death of a loved one. Whatever its original cause, it must currently be considered a manifestation of a behavioral, psychological, or biological dysfunction in the individual. Neither deviant behavior (e.g., political, religious, or sexual) nor conflicts that are primarily between the individual and society are mental disorders unless the deviance or conflict is a symptom of a dysfunction in the individual, as described above.[11]

These few sentences and the lengthy discussions in the psychiatric literature that had preceded them largely failed to provide the conceptual coherence needed to guide the development of the manual.

The Promise of a Valid Definition

In the few sentences of its definition of mental disorder, DSM attempts to address many complex but contested issues.[12] The definition is a distillation of decades of rumination.[13] First, it locates mental disorder as a phenomenon that occurs "in the individual," thereby countering critics who contend that mental disorder is either transactional or mere social deviance. Moreover, by defining mental illness as an internal dysfunction, DSM's definition parallels our cultural understanding of physical disorders. With psychiatry's recent turn toward the biological, this parallelism in conceptualization and treatment approach positions psychiatry more effectively as a full partner with other medical specialties.

Second, the definition implies that something within the individual has gone wrong, that there is a dysfunction. By defining disorder as a dysfunction, it tries to include some notion of internal pathology that causes the symptomatic behaviors. The problem with defining disorder in terms of dysfunction, however, is that dysfunction itself requires a definition and DSM does not provide one.

Third, the definition requires that disorder must have harmful effects to the individual, that is, distress, disability, or pain. Dysfunction alone is not enough; dysfunction must have negative effects. These harmful effects, since they often occur to the individual in some social context, introduce considerations external to the individual.

Fourth, the definition avoids any requirement that the etiology or cause of the disorder be identified or that the disorder be understood through the lens of some theoretical system of explanation. Eschewing etiology allows the DSM's developers to claim that the manual is descriptive and atheoretical and avoids the many controversies in mental health that swirl around the murky topic of causation.

The Failures of DSM's Definition

The test of the validity of DSM's definition of mental disorder is whether it allows us to separate disorders from nondisorders. In this regard, DSM's definition is inadequate. Here are some of the more obvious problems:

EXPECTABILITY

The definition's requirement that disorders not be "expectable" responses to events implies that disorders are unexpected and rare, that they are statistically unusual. But DSM provides no logical reason why disorders need to be unexpected or rare to be disorders. During some periods, the flu and allergies are both expected and common. Does that mean that they are not illnesses?

What about mental conditions that *are* rare (i.e., statistically unexpected) and undoubtedly cause distress or disability, such as the condition of people who exhibit extreme degrees of selfishness, cowardice, slovenliness, foolhardiness, gullibility, insensitivity, laziness, or lack of talent?[14] These mental conditions appear to meet DSM's definition of mental disorder, yet they are not in the manual and are generally not considered as disorders. On this count, the DSM definition is too broad to be valid.

In other respects, the unexpectable response clause appears to be too narrow to be valid. For example, the definition excludes from the list of disorders any expectable response to environmental events. But what is unexpectable is often a direct function of our knowledge and ability to accurately predict events, not merely an attribute of a syndrome. The unexpectable clause, if taken seriously, would exclude as disorders some of the conditions that are already included in the manual as disorders. For example, a now expectable response to extreme trauma is Posttraumatic Stress Disorder (PTSD), one of the popular new disorders added to DSM (see chapter 4). Depression is an expectable response to major loss. Antisocial behavior can be an expectable response to socialization into a criminal subculture. In physical medicine, lung cancer is an expectable effect of heavy smoking and AIDS is an expectable effect of engaging in unprotected sex with an HIV positive partner, but clearly lung cancer and AIDS are disorders. To the extent that science provides an understanding of the cause of a disorder, thereby rendering it expectable under specified conditions, DSM's definition would eliminate that condition as a disorder. Clearly, the expectable response clause is invalid.

But even if clearly invalid, the expectable response clause gives DSM great leeway in designating behaviors as symptoms of mental disorders. It allows the unusual and seemingly inexplicable—as when the child of educated, well-to-do parents does poorly in school—to be defined as craziness.

IMPAIRMENT

The definition requires that a mental condition cause impairment or disability in an important area of functioning.[15] This criterion can lead to overinclusiveness. The problem is that the definition fails to distinguish impairments that are relevant to the meaning of disorder from what we might call normal inabilities. For example, illiteracy involves the inability to read, and in our society being unable to read surely impairs functioning. Nevertheless, illiteracy is not viewed as a mental disorder. The disability clause would suggest that a short man's inability to play professional basketball, a clumsy person's inability to work as a waiter, an intellectually below-average person's inability to become a scientist, or a very selfish person's inability to form intimate relationships could all be classified as physical or mental disorders, that is, as internal conditions that impair functioning. Intuitively, we recognize that the simple lack of physical or mental ability, regardless of its consequences, should not be considered a disorder. Therefore, impairment is insufficient as a criterion of disorder.

IN THE INDIVIDUAL

Finally, the "in the individual" requirement is ambiguous. The definition attempts to distinguish disorders from mere social deviance by locating the disorder as internal to the person and not merely as a reaction to a stressful or noxious environment. But in medicine, diseases produced by exposure to environmental toxins (e.g., radiation) are still diseases; injuries caused by externally produced traumas (e.g., car accidents) are still physical injuries. Similarly, a child who is extremely fearful because he is abused by a parent may have an anxiety disorder, a widow who is left penniless may be depressed, and a battered wife may have a sleep disorder. DSM's formal definition of mental disorder (which, in fact, is not used consistently throughout the manual) appears to exclude these conditions simply because they may be reactions to the immediate environment. This is clearly faulty. Whether a mental condition is or is not a reaction to an immediate external event should not determine whether there is a mental dysfunction. Mental conditions frequently mediate between environmental stresses and resulting impairments. Thus, the issue is not simply whether the disorder is "in the individual" or how it was caused but whether it represents a *mental dysfunction*.

DSM's definition, which can be both too broad and too narrow, remained confused enough to allow the developers of DSM to have enormous discretion in what to include in the manual and how to describe those conditions. In that sense, the definition's weaknesses were useful. But in terms of offering a conceptually valid framework, the definition fails because it neglects to provide a systematic analysis of the concept of dysfunction, a concept on which most discussions of disorder are grounded.

DYSFUNCTION

Dysfunction, as a 1992 article by Wakefield in *Psychological Review* argues, implies that some mechanism that should have worked has failed. A function can be construed as any mechanism of the organism that is designed to operate in a certain way. When that mechanism does not work as it was designed to, it has failed in its natural function. This failure is called a dysfunction. When the heart stops pumping blood, when the eye cannot see, when the brain cannot process and interpret routine information, we refer to the failure as a dysfunction, because the heart is designed to pump blood, the eye to see, and the brain to process information. This apparent simplicity, however, encompasses some important conceptual issues. The major one involves determining the purpose of a mechanism, that is, what the mechanism was designed to do.

In everyday life we have little difficulty thinking about the function of devices that people have created: toasters function to warm bread, eye glasses help us see, telephones facilitate long-distance communication. It is easy to determine that cars were designed for transportation or that watches were made to record the time of day. The function of each of these artifacts is the original purpose for which it was designed. Its function is to produce a specific effect. We conclude that we have identified a dysfunction in the device if the toaster does not toast the bread, if the spectacles are cracked and we cannot see, or if the telephone doesn't allow our voice to be heard.

This analysis can be extended to mental mechanisms as well.[16] When our mental mechanisms dysfunction, we speak of mental disorders. But this approach to identifying mental disorders *requires that the natural functions of mental mechanisms be known before claims of dysfunction can be made.* Because we have limited knowledge of the purpose for which many mental mechanisms were designed, the arguments for what constitutes a mental dysfunction are frequently confused, tautological, and controversial. For example, consider Lily, a 35-year-old accountant who for two weeks has been feeling sad, has displayed a diminished interest in most activities, has not been sleeping well, has had no energy, and has had trouble concentrating. A clinician using DSM would classify Lily as having a mental disorder (i.e., Major Depressive Episode), reasoning that these "symptoms" are being caused by an internal mental dysfunction. But they may be caused by temporary feelings and are not necessarily signs that her mental mechanisms are dysfunctioning. In fact, if Lily has just ended an important intimate relationship; has been passed over for a long-sought-after promotion at work; has lost her possessions in a house fire; or has been transferred by an employer to a new location away from friends, family, and the familiar, feeling blue and distracted is not a sign of dysfunction; on the contrary, her response is a sign of normality, an indicator that she can love and feel loss, has career aspirations, and has a capacity to become attached to personal belongings and to family, friends, and community. Thus, the everyday behaviors that DSM uses as criteria of mental disorders do not necessarily indicate any mental dysfunction at all! The creators of DSM did not take on the task of developing a comprehensive statement of the purposes of our cognitive, emotional, and behavior patterns, a task that would have revealed the huge gaps in our knowledge; instead, they substituted the much easier task of identifying suspicious everyday behaviors.

Elucidating the concept of mental disorder allows us to understand some of the confusion about particular mental disorders. Additionally, it also provides us with a perspective to use in examining some of the debates about mental disorders that continually gain publicity. For example, recent news articles about the "discovery" of "shadow syndromes" display the logical outcome of many of DSM's confusions. In a *New York Times* article titled "Quirks, Oddities May Be Illnesses," we find a bid by some psychiatrists to consider people who do not meet the full criteria for a specific mental disorder as having a milder form of that disorder, a shadow of the real thing.[17] Given DSM's approach to identifying disorders by providing a Chinese menu of specific behaviors and requiring that some arbitrary number of these behavioral criteria be met before the diagnosis is used, these mental illness entrepreneurs are proposing that people may have the disorder even if they only exhibit a few of the required symptoms. As every psychotherapist realizes, this proposal, if taken seriously, might qualify more people for insurance coverage, but, as Frederick Goodwin, the former head of NIMH, complained, managed care companies may discount their therapists' claims.

Perhaps we should not be surprised to read on the front page of the *Los Angeles Times* an article ("Mild Depression Common and Harmful, Study Finds") in which respected psychiatrists report that one in nine adults has some symptoms of the shadow syndrome of depression.[18] In DSM, five of nine criteria must be met for depression, criteria such as deep sadness, apathy, fatigue, agitation, sleep disturbances, and appetite change. Is it any wonder that when the threshold is lowered from five to only two that more people are discovered to be suffering from "subsyndromal depression" or "shadow depression"? The article reports that some psychiatrists are concerned about such attempts to "make an illness out of what looks to be life's normal ups and downs," about how the psychiatric establishment is expanding "into everyday life and [defining] it in terms of medical conditions." There is even a warning about the feeding frenzy that the drug companies may have; "It's clearly of concern if this enlarges the market share of the pharmaceutical industry," one psychiatrist mentioned.

These proposals to lower the threshold even further for behaviors that constitute a mental disorder are understandable, given the fact that DSM contains no workable definition of mental disorder. The definition in the manual does not govern what conditions get included as disorders, and the content and number of criteria that must be met to qualify for each disorder are largely arbitrary. The manual has no consistent requirement that the everyday behaviors used as diagnostic criteria actually be the result of mental disorder and not the result of other life experiences. In the shadows is a stockpile of proposals to add new mental disorders to the next edition of DSM.

Because of the many conceptual confusions about what constitutes a mental disorder, the ease with which DSM's clumsy definition allows conditions to be moved into the manual, and the severe limits of scientific knowledge regarding the purpose of mental mechanisms, the construction of DSM involved much more than the assembling of scientific conclusions and the making of technical decisions. It involved negotiations among contending interest groups of theoreticians, researchers, clinicians, hospitals, clinics, and drug companies—and, at times, potential patients. Changing the psychiatric nosology involves struggles among constituencies and requires a balancing of conflicting interests. Over time, the process of changing the DSM has become much more elaborate. This growing complexity is illustrated in the last four revisions of the nomenclature of the APA.

CONSTRUCTING THE PSYCHIATRIC BIBLE

The pace of changing the psychiatric bible has increased. There have been four different diagnostic systems since 1979. With each change, mental disorders are created, eliminated, or radically redefined. The revisions can seldom be explained by advances in science but can often be explained by the shifting fortunes of various powerful factions within the American Psychiatric Association.

The process of revising DSM has become elaborate. With each revision, the approval of changes in the manual moves through multiplying layers of advisers, work groups, task forces, governance committees, and boards. In this increasingly elaborate process, more and more participants are invited to play some role in the revision. Their names and titles are prominently displayed in the published manual, lending superficial legitimacy to the product. But, just as important, the involvement of a larger number of groups has made the task of revising the nosology much more politically complex. In the most recent edition, more than 1,000 names are listed. Since available scientific data seldom provide definitive answers to questions, most issues must be handled through complicated behind-the-scenes negotiation.

Nonetheless, in each new revision the claim is made that the manual has achieved greater validity and more precision. Every change, even ones that are abandoned within a few months, is presented as a science-guided decision in which mistakes have been corrected, ambiguities have been clarified, and new knowledge has been incorporated. And since the final product, incorporating hundreds of minor and major changes, is never directly tied through citations to research articles, the claims of science-at-work are difficult to verify or dispute.

All of the recent efforts to revise DSM began by discrediting the scientific status of the then current edition. Typically, the developers assert that the process being used for their version is scientifically superior to the preceding one. When revision is complete, the developers proclaim that the brand-new version represents a vast improvement over the old, and they encourage everyone to purchase the new publication and its paraphernalia (casebooks, tapes, videos, instructional manuals, worksheets, computer programs, etc.). All too soon, a new task force questions the scientific status of the latest version of the manual. This cycle of denigration, enthusiasm, and denigration makes an old system appear antiquated and a new system necessary, a marketing strategy pioneered by the automobile industry.

Certainly some form of classification is needed. A profession whose mission is to understand and treat mental illness must show convincingly that it can describe and recognize illness when it occurs. If there are different varieties of psychiatric illness, psychiatrists need to identify what those types are and how they are distinguished. By reducing and organizing information into categorical systems, we learn to make sense of our experiences and the world around us. Modern science depends on classifications. Medical classifications of diseases have led to the advancement of knowledge and to effective treatment.

Although descriptions of madness and its subtypes have been around since the ancient Greeks,[19] a handful of unofficial, broad categories appeared to be sufficient until the last half of the 20th century. By 1994, however, the count had grown to over three hundred categories, and the number appears to be rising. Moreover, categories of disorders are now carefully encrusted in a professionally approved classification system.[20]

The earliest classification systems of mental disorders in the United States were developed by the federal government for the U.S. Census, which played a predominant role in psychiatric nosology for almost a century.[21] By the 1880 census, there were seven official categories of mental disease: mania, melancholia, monomania, paresis, dementia, dipsomania, and epilepsy. In 1904 and 1910, two special surveys were conducted to enumerate the institutionalized insane. The one in 1904 was particularly concerned with race and ethnicity and the growing fear that large-scale immigration of presumably inferior groups could be somehow indicated by statistical studies of patients in asylums.[22]

In subsequent years census officials became more interested in the need for a standard nosology and asked the American Medico-Psychological Association, the forerunner to the APA, to appoint a committee on nomenclature to facilitate the collection of data. Psychiatrists who were beginning to involve themselves in a broader array of community problems beyond the administration of mental hospitals and who were adopting a broader vision of their social mission began to see how accurate social statistics could be used to guide mental health planning. In 1913, the association created a Committee on Statistics.[23] By 1918 the association produced, with the cooperation of the National Committee for Mental Hygiene, the first standardized psychiatric nosology: the *Statistical Manual for the Use of Institutions for the Insane.* The manual offered 22 principal categories. It emphasized biology and the physical body, a perspective that was congruent with the fact that most psychiatrists practiced in mental hospitals and many patients, perhaps a majority, had severe physical as well as mental problems. Moreover, the somatic nosology reflected the nature of psychiatric care.[24] Developed in 1918, the manual was adopted by the U.S. Census and was used to survey mental institutions annually, a tradition that was continued by the National Institute of Mental Health after World War II. This manual went through ten editions between 1918 and 1942 while retaining its somatic orientation. In 1935 it was incorporated into the first edition of the American Medical Association's *Standard Classified Nomenclature of Disease,* a system that classified all medical conditions.[25]

These revisions in nosology, however, were of only marginal significance to psychiatrists and their patients. The categories were broad, and psychiatric treatment at the time was nonspecific. The struggles to develop a systematic nomenclature, from the earliest decades of the 19th century, were motivated by administrative and governmental needs, not by demands from practitioners.[26] This is a pattern that has persisted.

World War II produced the next revision. The experiences of psychiatrists during the war were responsible for the first major change in psychiatric nosology and were embodied in the *Diagnostic and Statistical Manual: Mental Diseases,* now commonly referred to as DSM-I. Published in 1952, this was the first edition of a diagnostic manual published by the American Psychiatric Association. DSM-I reflected the major political and theoretical shifts that had occurred in American psychiatry. The somatic tradition had given way to psychodynamic and psychoanalytic perspectives, which had achieved ascendancy in the profession by the middle of the 20th century in part because of the immigration of many psychoanalysts fleeing Nazi oppression. These new viewpoints (more so than the somatic theories) emphasized the role of environment and the variety of less severe forms of disturbance that could benefit from the attention of the psychiatric profession. Clinicians increasingly worked with noninstitutionalized populations and those suffering from less severe disorders, which were identified as neuroses and personality disorders rather than psychoses.

A consideration of these developments and others resulted in the more modern classification represented by DSM-I. This manual, produced in one year (1949–1950) by a working group and published in 1952, reflects the ascendancy of new leadership in the profession.[27]

Making DSM-II

DSM-II, published in 1968, was a small spiral-bound notebook of less than 150 pages that clinicians could purchase for $3.50. DSM-II opened with a list of the 10 members of the Committee on Nomenclature and Statistics who developed the manual and of the 30 other members who had served on the committee in the previous 20 years. Developing the successor to DSM-I was justified primarily as a response to the nation's treaty obligation to keep its nosology in rough alignment with the World Health Organization's *International Classification of Diseases* (ICD), a list of diseases that includes mental disorders and is revised every decade in consultation with health officials from many countries.[28] DSM-II expanded the number of disease categories and continued the psychodynamic traditions of DSM-I.

By contemporary standards, making DSM-II was a relatively private and simple process, more like changing rules and regulations within one organization than negotiating treaties among many rival factions, each with a very different objective. In 1965 the APA assigned the task of preparing a new manual to its Committee on Nomenclature and Statistics. The process of revision involved a small committee of experts (eight members and two consultants) who worked privately and quickly to make many changes in the manual. Robert Spitzer, who was to become a major spokesperson for psychiatric diagnosis for two decades, served as one of the key consultants and emerged after publication of the manual as a major defender of it.[29] By February 1967 a draft manual was circulated to 120 psychiatrists; after being revised, it was approved by the APA in December 1967, and it became effective on July 1, 1968.

There is very little information about the process of developing DSM-II. An accompanying promotional article published in the *American Journal of Psychiatry* in June 1968 avoids mention of any controversies or disputes that may have arisen in the revision and, instead, simply reports how the new manual differs from the former version.[30] Yet new categories of disorder were added, the nomenclature was organized in a different way, the recording of multiple psychiatric diagnoses and associated physical conditions was explicitly encouraged, qualifying phrases were changed, and numerous revisions were made in the definitions of disorders.

What is striking about these first reports about DSM-II is that they were presented as matter-of-fact updates and reorganizations of categories, rather than as changes that represent major rethinking or new decision-making standards. The changes are explained simply, sometimes with but often without any rationale. Almost completely absent is any attempt to justify the many changes on the basis of scientific evidence. In the words of the committee chairman, "The Committee has attempted to put down what it judges to be generally agreed upon by well-informed psychiatrists today."[31] As with earlier nosologies, DSM-II was intended primarily to reflect, not to change, the current practice of psychiatry. The publication of DSM-II drew no public attention or concern. Some clinicians appreciated its simple administrative uses; few viewed it as a treatise on psychiatric philosophy or treatment.[32] For psychiatric researchers, DSM-II was nearly useless as a scientific guidebook.

Making DSM-III

There are many reasons why the APA decided to revise DSM-II. No doubt the demands that homosexuality be eliminated from the manual caused great discomfort, particularly after gay activists staged protests at the annual APA conventions (see chapter 3). Furthermore, many researchers, including some who were highly respected within the profession, criticized both the theoretical foundations of the diagnostic system and the reliability of diagnostic practices. There were many other pressures that have been less publicized. For example, in order to obtain approval from the federal government to sell a new medication, the drug industry must conduct clinical trials with the new product and document its effectiveness for individuals with specific, defined disorders. If psychiatric diagnoses cannot be made reliably, it is difficult to determine for whom a drug may be effective.[33]

Third-party support for psychotherapy grew rapidly during the 1970s, and this led to an unprecedented expansion of outpatient treatment. Insurance companies and other third-party payers often required diagnoses, and they pushed for a closer relationship between diagnosis and treatment.[34] This focused more attention on diagnosis, and as a result the deficits in the existing diagnostic system, DSM-II, became more evident.

Public protests, disturbing research, third-party financing, and clinician dissatisfaction all played some part in the mounting pressure on the American Psychiatric Association. The pressures were not necessarily consistent or well focused, nor was it certain that more tinkering with the diagnostic manual was the solution to many of these concerns. Although the decision to revise the manual was made within five years after the publication of DSM-II, what the APA hoped to achieve is unclear. What is clear, however, is that the leaders of the APA had no idea how important DSM-III would become for the association or how different it would be from the earlier editions.

Millon, one of the original members of the DSM-III Task Force and, by his own estimate, one of those most responsible for encouraging the APA to undertake a major revision of the manual, has offered a detailed and revealing account of the early development of DSM-III.[35] It is apparent from his account that the task force was eager to capitalize on a political opportunity presented by a unique historical moment in American psychiatry. From the beginning, members of the task force wanted to make a radical change in psychiatric nosology. They had no interest in a cosmetic updating of DSM-II. They recognized the inherent difficulties of developing a classification system: American psychiatry and the field of mental health were more fragmented and diverse than they had been in 1960. According to Millon, the task force members "recognized that no ideal

classification was possible in clinical psychopathology" and that "no consensus would ever be likely found" among mental health professionals
". . . . as to how a classification might be best organized, . . . no less what
it should contain."[36] The developers knew that it was impossible to organize a classification system that would satisfy multiple constituencies
with different views about etiology, prognosis, structure, and treatment.
One advantage of the DSM-III Task Force was that it was chaired by
Robert Spitzer. Although he had been intimately involved with DSM-II
and had become its public defender when it was published, he was now,
less than five years later, spearheading its complete demise.

The DSM-III Task Force was predisposed to include many new diagnostic categories. Millon admitted that their intentions were to "embrace
as many conditions as are commonly seen by practicing clinicians."[37]
While the task force initially required that any potentially new category
be specified by diagnostic criteria and distinctness, the ultimate inclusion
test was in part political, based on such criteria as whether the diagnosis
was used with reasonable frequency, whether interested professionals and
patient representatives offered positive comments about it, and whether
the new condition maximized the manual's utility for outpatient populations.[38] For DSM-III, the mentally ill were by definition those seen by psychiatrists. DSM-III desired for every client a reimbursable diagnosis, if not
quite a chicken in every pot.

The guiding philosophy of the DSM-III Task Force during its first year,
when the ground work and structure for the new manual were being
firmly planted, was to err on the side of inclusion of new categories. One
motivation was the desire to make the new manual reflective of the array
of conditions practitioners confront, particularly in outpatient settings,
where psychiatric treatment increasingly took place. Understandably,
many practitioners wanted to see an expanded array of problems to reflect the diversity of patients they were treating, such as people with various interpersonal and family problems. The challenge was in not
committing the error of defining as mental disorder any problem treated
by a psychiatrist. A second motivation was the wish to expand psychiatric
turf to capture more fiscal coverage from third-party reimbursements,
which had become much more important to the financing of mental
health care.

Although there were many innovations in the new manual, the most
important one was the introduction of specific criteria for each diagnosis.

For example, in the previous version of the manual, the entry for schizo-phrenia fills less than three pages. The entry begins with a single short paragraph describing the disorder, and this is followed by additional one-paragraph descriptions of schizophrenia subtypes, such as paranoid schiz-ophrenia and hebephrenia. In contrast, the entry in DSM-III is 13 pages of densely printed text. The 10-page description of the disorder culminates in a chart that lists more than 23 criteria that must be considered in order to make a diagnosis. This is followed by more text describing each of the subtypes and listing additional criteria. For instance, to make a diagnosis of Schizophrenia, Catatonic Type, five additional criteria must be evaluated after the 23 basic ones for schizophrenia are considered.

Many controversies surrounded the making of DSM-III, but perhaps the most symbolic was the proposal to drop the use of one word—*neuro-sis.* Neurosis, a disorder that presumably resulted from intrapsychic con-flicts, had long been the mainstay of psychoanalysis. The DSM-III Task Force early on proposed to banish the term from the manual because it strongly implied a cause for certain disorders and the new manual was being designed to be atheoretical and descriptive. Many psychodynami-cally oriented psychiatrists were alarmed by this proposal to radically re-fashion the language of psychiatry, and strong opposition developed from the professional associations of psychoanalysts.[39] From 1976 until the final approval of DSM-III, an acrimonious conflict flared between mem-bers of the DSM-III Task Force and the psychoanalysts. The contending factions, suspicious of the intentions of their opponents, battled over the word *neurosis,* arguing about whether and how it might be included in the manual. The battle took place at conferences, committee meetings, in psychiatric newsletters, and in personal correspondence. There were pro-posals and counterproposals; agreements were hammered out, and com-promises were made and then unmade. There were hard-liners and those who threatened, and there were peacemakers and those who wanted to conclude a deal. Toward the end it looked as if the battle would escalate out of control, threatening to publicly embarrass American psychiatry and to prevent the final approval of DSM-III after five years of effort. Fi-nally, after all the posturing and silliness, DSM-III was approved, with the symbolic use of the controversial term *neurosis* used in parentheses in sev-eral places. The Board of Trustees of the APA approved DSM-III because there was too much "bureaucratic momentum" behind the new man-ual.[40] After six years of preparation, a substantial financial expenditure, and the promotion of the manual in many APA journals and in the popular press, it would have been hard to reject the new product.

In contrast to its immediate predecessor, DSM-III is an oversized volume, 500 pages long, that sold for more than ten times the price of the earlier manual. Everything about it is bigger. Swollen in length and in importance, it contains long lists of those who participated in its creation. In a section of the introduction entitled "Cautions," readers are advised that "the use of the manual for nonclinical purposes, such as determination of legal responsibility, competency or insanity, or justification for third-party payment, must be critically examined in each instance within the appropriate institutional context" (p. 12). The architects of the manual knew that these were the concerns of greatest importance to most of its users.

The text of the manual includes elaborate instructions for its use, which were particularly important since many features were new to most mental health professionals.[41] The bulk of DSM-III is devoted to descriptions of the specific disorders—there were now 265. Many, such as Post-traumatic Stress Disorder, appeared for the first time (see chapter 4), and many others had been deleted. For instance, neurasthenia (nervous exhaustion), the most popular diagnosis throughout the rest of the world, was dropped from DSM-III. The greatest expansion occurred among the children's disorders, an area relatively neglected previously, compared to adult disorders. The entry for each specific disorder is far more elaborate than the simple one-paragraph description in DSM-II. The principal change is a list of criteria that must be satisfied for each diagnosis. In order to make a diagnosis, the clinician had to identify in the patient the specific symptoms listed as the criteria. These were met only if a certain number of symptoms could be identified in the patient. In addition to listing essential and associated features, the entry for each disorder contains information about age of onset, course, impairment, complications, predisposing factors, prevalence, sex ratio, and familial pattern—with all of it sounding very scientific and very medical.

Finally, in an appendix, there is a report of the reliability data from the field trials. This 14-page report consists of a 2-page description of the field trials, three tables, and an 8 1/2-page list of the names, degrees, and institutional affiliations of the more than 600 field trial participants. We will return to this report in a moment.

Making DSM-III-R

DSM-III was published in February 1980 to great acclaim. It was immensely successful—beyond anyone's wildest expectations—both in terms of distribution and use. But, astonishingly, after so much time and effort and such an enthusiastic reception, almost immediately planning began on its revision. In May 1983, with DSM-III barely three years old and DSM-IV expected in 1990, the formal revision process began, with the appointment by the APA of the Work Group to Revise DSM-III. The work group was composed of eight psychiatrists and chaired again by Robert Spitzer.[42] Like its predecessor, it used 25 advisory committees and involved over 230 consultants. Two drafts of the revision were made available to the public, one in October 1985 and a final one in August 1986. The revised manual, the *Diagnostic and Statistical Manual of Mental Disorders* (third edition, revised), or DSM-III-R, was published in May 1987. In size, character, and structure, DSM-III-R was an unmistakable younger, if larger, sibling of DSM-III.

This move to revise DSM-III almost as soon as it was published was quite different from the path taken with DSM-II. The quick move to revise had strategic advantages. For one, DSM-III became a moving target for all those who had criticisms. By presenting the manual as provisional, not final, as one important step in an ongoing scientific process, the APA muted the force of criticism and offered opponents future opportunities for change. Developing a manual in perpetual motion was a strategic advantage in deflecting opposition, but it was also a potential disadvantage to those who wanted to maintain the structure of the new system and secure the major changes in the structure of DSM that had been made. With victory still fresh, task force members now had to open the door for modifications.

Although participation by outsiders in the revision process was encouraged, the Work Group to Revise DSM-III tried to control controversy. Members of subcommittees were handpicked, and other resource experts were restricted in their involvement.[43] Even the process of making minor changes was tightly controlled. Spitzer and his wife were members of almost every subcommittee. To interested professionals, the work group maintained the guise of pursuing minor, technical improvements, and these within rigid parameters.

In fact, many more substantial changes were in progress, but these were not broadcast. In the end, four of the five basic dimensions (i.e., axes) of the DSM-III diagnostic system were refashioned. Over half of the more than 200 diagnostic categories were changed, many in extensive ways. And, significantly, more than 30 new diagnostic categories were added. Most of these changes passed without controversy, until feminist psychotherapists confronted the APA about the proposed inclusion of three new psychiatric disorders, which they viewed as having serious negative consequences for women—Paraphilic Rapism, Premenstrual Dysphoric Disorder, and Masochistic Personality Disorder.[44]

By appearing to be just tinkering with the old system, the developers avoided any demands that their revisions undergo new field trials or tests for reliability. In fact, no new reliability studies were conducted, and the reliability appendix symbolically included in DSM-III was dropped when DSM-III-R was published. In changing DSM-III, research psychiatrists tightened their grip on psychiatric nomenclature. And they did so without admitting to outsiders that what they had just hailed as the great scientific achievements of DSM-III were so quickly cast off.

Making DSM-IV

Only four months after DSM-III-R was published, at a time when most clinicians and researchers had not had time to review or become familiar with the new version, the APA Committee on Psychiatric Diagnosis and Assessment met to explore possible timetables for the publication of DSM-IV. In May 1988, the Board of Trustees of the American Psychiatric Association appointed another task force to begin work on the fourth edition of the DSM. Allen Frances, who served on the Work Group to Revise DSM-III and had participated on the Personality Disorders Subcommittee of the DSM-III Task Force, was appointed as chair of the DSM-IV Task Force. Even as copies of DSM-III-R were making their way into the offices of clinicians, the APA nosologists were already focusing their attention on what needed to be changed. Clearly, before clinicians could develop informed judgments about the new manual and before any research could begin, a replacement entered the design phase. Planned obsolescence, long a dominant theme of the American auto industry, was adopted by the American Psychiatric Association for the business of psychiatric diagnosis. New editions of the manual made the old editions useless and sent clinicians and others scurrying to the bookstores for the latest version.

In many respects, the procedure for developing the new manual was the same as that which was used for DSM-III and repeated with DSM-III-R. A task force of experts, almost all of them psychiatrists, was appointed by the APA to oversee the work. Thirteen specialized work groups were assembled. These advisory committees comprised more than a thousand members, advisors, and consultants who were experts in specific disorders, and each work group was charged to scrutinize carefully the diagnoses in its subject matter area.[45] Their proposals were reviewed by the task force and incorporated into a draft of the manual, which was then subject to further review by an elaborate hierarchy of committees within the APA, the whole process culminating in the final approval by the association's board of trustees.

Frances wanted to produce DSM-IV without controversy or conflict. He wanted to avoid the confrontations that had plagued DSM in the past and reduce the sources of controversy that had embarrassed American psychiatry. It was evident that he did not envision any revolutionary new paradigm that would change diagnostic procedures or concepts.

Frances's announced conservative strategy had some interesting implications. The basic rule was not to accept any changes that did not have sound empirical support.[46] This meant that in the absence of compelling evidence, DSM-IV ratified the sweeping changes first incorporated into DSM-III. This conservative approach to innovations, along with the commitment to avoid controversy, had the ironic effect of institutionalizing the radical expansion embodied in DSM-III, regardless of DSM-III's shaky empirical foundation.

But the process of producing DSM-IV—or at least how it was initially presented to the APA membership—was quite different from the one used for earlier revisions of the manual. One difference was that it was initiated amid controversy about whether a new revision was even needed. For example, Zimmerman argued that the frequency of manual revisions—all championed by researchers, not practitioners—actually impeded the use of scientific findings to improve the manual;[47] since it took years to develop and implement studies to test the categories in each revised manual, the rapid changes to DSM could not be informed by the careful research that was needed. He questioned whether constant revisions really improved diagnostic reliability or validity, the ability of researchers to study these matters, or the quality of psychiatric care provided to patients and asked whether the constant revisions might have more to do with financial considerations of the APA. Kendell also suggested that one explanation for the APA's increasingly frequent revisions of DSM was to reap the "huge and unexpected profit" that DSM-III and subsequent editions generated.[48]

Against this backdrop of criticism, the DSM-IV Task Force went to great lengths to assure mental health professionals that changes incorporated into DSM-IV would not be arbitrary or whimsical. There was an explosion in the number of committees and experts involved and in the elaborate processes designed to control decision making. Two early conferences to discuss methodological issues in the construction of DSM-IV were held. Elaborate outlines were developed for the review and synthesis of available empirical data.[49] There was a steady and concerted effort by the developers of DSM-IV to get the word out about why DSM-IV was necessary and how it would be better than previous versions. The process of revision was described as both rigorous and open, a claim that some found strained.[50]

Although a fountain of information poured out of the DSM-IV Task Force, there were still no clear answers to the question, What is all of this massive effort producing other than a deluge of preliminary publications?

In May 1994, DSM-IV was released, a 900-page volume that despite the hundreds of changes from DSM-III was indisputably its offspring. Its release was reported in major national newspapers. It has the same guiding philosophy as DSM-III, as well as the same structure and many of the same problems. It has 16 chapters, each containing descriptions of a class of disorders, and 10 appendices of various kinds, including a list of 1,000 consultants. It is presented, as were its two immediate predecessors, as an evolving scientific document that represents the best from the brightest. How can we even begin to evaluate such a massive classification scheme? This brings us back to the fundamental issue of reliability, because an unreliable classification system, whether for research or for practice, is an invalid one.

IS DSM RELIABLE?

Hundreds of scientific claims are made by the developers of each revision of DSM. Some claims pertain only to single diagnostic categories, but other claims are about the manual in its entirety. The most central scientific claim about DSM as a whole was made in 1980, when DSM-III was touted as a much more reliable classification system than earlier versions of the manual (reliability being the extent to which clinicians can agree on diagnoses for patients). The developers argued that high reliability was necessary for DSM to be a useful classification system.

Why were the developers of DSM-III, who were primarily researchers, so concerned about this technical issue of reliability? Why did they, much more than clinicians, view it as such a significant problem? If mental disorders are constructs, as we explained earlier, held together primarily by agreements about their meaning, reliability serves as a practical test of those agreements. If, in examining patients, clinicians or researchers cannot agree on who has a particular anxiety disorder or mood disorder or schizophrenia—or even whether someone has any mental disorder or not—the agreements about these constructs are suspect. Even if psychiatrists agreed in principle about the general meaning of, say, Panic Disorder with Agoraphobia, they would be having a problem with reliability if they disagreed about which people qualified for that diagnosis. But a serious problem with reliability causes an even greater concern.

The primary purpose of classification systems, such as DSM, is to structure and enhance agreements, and the purpose of DSM's elaborate diagnostic criteria was specifically to improve diagnostic agreements. The developers knew, perhaps better than most, that an unreliable classification system would be of no use to researchers and would only undercut psychiatry's attempt to gain greater respectability in scientific circles in general and within medicine in particular. In fact, if reliability is not good, the practical validity of the constructs that DSM embodies, that is, the diagnoses, is called into question. If DSM is unreliable, it cannot be used to distinguish mental disorders from other human problems. In practical terms, this means that many people will be diagnosed with the wrong disorder and that clinicians will frequently disagree about which one is correct. It means that some people who do not have any mental disorder (although they may have other kinds of difficulties) will be inappropriately labeled as mentally ill and those who may have a mental disorder will not have it recognized. It means that reimbursement systems tied to diagnostic categories will be misused. It means that when the National Institute of Mental Health announces how many Americans suffer from mental disorder, the numbers may be grossly inaccurate. And it means that when medications or types of psychotherapy are specifically targeted for those with particular mental disorders, they may be used with the wrong patients. That is why the claims that DSM-III had improved reliability were so significant in the campaign to sell the new manual.[51]

As DSM-III approached its publication date, its developers, possessing data from special field trials, were not shy about promoting their product as having reliability (compared with that of DSM-II) that was "far greater," "quite good," "higher than previously achieved," "so much better than" expected, and "particularly encouraging."[52] In an article published in 1982, they went further and described DSM's reliability as "extremely good."[53]

In making their claims, the developers presented data in the form of large tables using a relatively new statistic, called kappa, which was designed as a measure of agreement.[54] These tables were not readily interpretable by most mental health professionals, nor were any direct comparisons with DSM-II presented. Most clinicians were in no position to critically evaluate the studies upon which these numbers were based. They accepted the claims of the developers of the impressive new manual that it was reliable and therefore scientific.

The claim of greatly improved reliability has been widely (if uncritically) accepted, even by some scholars. For example, a former president of the American Psychological Association stated that DSM-III, unlike its predecessors, was a much more reliable system for classifying psychiatric disorders.[55] The late Gerald Klerman, a prominent psychiatrist, praised DSM's reliability and wrote that "in principle, the reliability problem has been solved."[56] Even critics of DSM were quick to accept that it had greatly improved reliability.[57] For example, in an otherwise critical discussion of DSM, one psychologist stated that "DSM-III fixed that problem [reliability] once and (possibly) for all . . . and . . . resulted in . . . unprecedented levels of diagnostic agreement."[58] These statements attest to how firmly the belief of improved reliability had been planted.

This belief system marked a dramatic shift of opinion from the early 1970s, when the unreliability of diagnosis became the focus of sustained attention. Because the claim of greatly increased reliability was broad, clear, significant, and frequently made by the developers of DSM, it provides a pivotal test of the credibility of DSM's scientific claims. In *The Selling of DSM,* we examined all the evidence bearing on this central claim.[59] How do the data presented by the developers of DSM-III compare with what we know about the reliability of diagnosis before DSM-III? Did the development and inclusion of all the diagnostic criteria (DSM's major innovation) of everyday behaviors for each diagnosis actually improve clinicians' ability to agree on the proper diagnoses of patients? This was, after all, the central task of the revolutionary new manual.

As we have shown in great detail elsewhere, the reliability problem did not get much better with DSM-III. In fact, no study of DSM as a whole in a regular clinical setting has shown uniformly high reliability. And most studies, including the DSM field trials themselves, provide little evidence that reliability has markedly improved, much less been "solved" as a problem.

The most recent major study was quite instructive, because it was conducted by some of the principal participants in the transformation of DSM and utilized all of the techniques that had been developed to improve diagnostic reliability. The study was conducted at six sites in the United States and one in Germany.[60] Experienced mental health professionals at the seven sites were selected to be interviewers and were given extensive special training in how to make accurate DSM diagnoses. The clinicians were given all the latest aids that had been developed over two decades to improve the reliability of psychiatric diagnosis. They were trained and supervised by a research team that was perhaps the most experienced in the world at conducting diagnostic studies. Following this extensive training, pairs of clinicians interviewed nearly 600 prospective patients. The objective was to determine if the clinicians who saw the same client would agree on which diagnosis, if any, was appropriate. Could they reliably make diagnoses using DSM?

Because of the great care that was involved with this study, it should have produced the highest diagnostic reliability possible in a supervised research setting. We would expect that diagnostic agreement would be considerably lower in normal clinical settings, where the staff is not knowingly involved in an international research project. The findings of this elaborate reliability study were disappointing even to the investigators. The kappa values (the statistical measures of reliability) were not that different from those statistics achieved in the 1950s and 1960s— and in some cases were worse. What this study demonstrated was that even when experienced clinicians with special training and supervision are asked to use DSM and make a diagnosis, they frequently disagree, even though the standards for defining agreement are very generous. That is, agreement on diagnosis was defined for this study as agreeing on the *class* of diagnosis, not on the specific diagnosis. Thus, if one of the two therapists interviewing a person made a diagnosis of Schizoid Personality Disorder and the other therapist selected Avoidant Personality Disorder, the therapists were judged to be in complete agreement on the diagnosis because they both found a personality disorder—even though they disagreed completely on which one! So even with this liberal definition of agreement, reliability using DSM is not particularly good. Mental health clinicians independently interviewing the same person in the community are as likely to agree as disagree that the person has a mental disorder and are as likely to agree as disagree on which of the over 300 DSM disorders is present.

Twenty years after the reliability problem became the central scientific focus of DSM, there is still not a single major study showing that DSM (any version) is routinely used with high reliability by regular mental health clinicians. Nor is there any credible evidence that any version of the manual has greatly increased its reliability beyond the previous version. The DSM revolution in reliability has been a revolution in rhetoric, not in reality. Despite the scientific claims of great success, reliability appears to have improved very little in recent decades. Some defenders of DSM are quick to point out that medical diagnosis in general is often unreliable, too. That defense strikes us as interesting but hardly reassuring.

If the unreliability of diagnosis were widely recognized and if there were no scientific patina to DSM, the use of everyday behaviors as indicators of mental disorder would be more rigorously questioned by the public. The illusion that psychiatrists are in agreement when making diagnoses creates the appearance of a united professional consensus. In fact, there is considerable professional confusion. Serious confusion about distinguishing mental disorders from nondisordered conditions and the inability of clinicians to use the manual reliably make the development and use of DSM vulnerable to a host of nonscientific pressures. If well-trained and well-intentioned therapists often fail to agree on specific diagnoses, how can the incompetent or purposely deceptive diagnostician be identified? How can specific medications and other therapies be targeted to people with specific diagnoses, if clinicians don't agree on who has those disorders? How can managed care companies determine that the correct treatment is being used for a particular mental disorder if there is widespread uncertainty about the accuracy of DSM diagnoses? The unreliability of DSM is a chronic problem that the psychiatric establishment tried unsuccessfully to solve and would now rather ignore.

3   THE FALL AND RISE OF HOMOSEXUALITY

The best way to appreciate how mental disorders are invented is to understand how one diagnosis, homosexuality, was expunged from DSM. Elimination of the diagnosis from the manual represented a significant change in the way organized psychiatry dealt with sexual behavior. The exclusion of homosexuality had an even greater impact: it provided a blueprint for reformulating the entire diagnostic system. Ad hoc procedures devised to remove homosexuality from DSM became the APA's system for making changes in the manual, a system that resulted in DSM-III and revolutionized modern psychiatric diagnosis.

The dispute over homosexuality was more than an intramural argument among competing psychotherapists or a quarrel between psychoanalysts and their dissatisfied gay customers. The psychiatric supporters of the diagnosis and their gay challengers understood that the decision to delete homosexuality from DSM would have far-reaching consequences. It was the first step in legitimating lifestyles on the basis of recognition of sexual diversity. The assumption of heterosexuality that was taken for granted in American culture gave way to a new pluralism in ideas about gender and lifestyle. Today's debates over same-sex marriage, health benefits for domestic partners, civil rights of gay people and lesbians, and acceptance of gays in the military would not be possible if homosexuality

were considered to be pathological behavior. Although many of these issues have not been settled, they would not even be considered seriously
if homosexuality were interpreted as a medical condition. In order to understand the impact of eliminating homosexuality from DSM, it is useful
to carefully examine not only the circumstances that led to the declassification of the diagnosis but also the aftermath of that conflict. In this
chapter we review the changing status of homosexuality as an official
DSM diagnosis, assess the current understanding about the diagnosis,
and analyze some future trends.

The description of the controversy over homosexuality that follows is
quite extensive. We had several reasons for including this detailed narrative. First, unlike many of the other controversies over diagnosis, this
one has a public record; the major factions chose to make their opinions
known. This is unique. Generally, negotiations over diagnoses are conducted in private, and the record is not available. In most cases all the
public knows is the final result and the official explanation that appears
in DSM. The dispute over homosexuality provides us with a unique
glimpse into the inner workings of the American Psychiatric Association
and allows us to understand precisely how diagnoses evolve. This is not
an obscure academic debate. The decision about the diagnosis of homosexuality affected not only the millions of people who are gay but millions more—their family members, employers, insurers, and therapists.

Second, the way psychiatrists have conceptualized homosexuality at
different times is a key to understanding how they think about their work.
These concepts provide a foundation for understanding their approach to
sex and gender and are also basic to understanding their concept of mental disorder. Whether or not homosexuality is classified as a psychiatric
illness depends upon what psychiatrists consider to be normal and what
they define as a mental disorder.

Third, the homosexuality controversy illustrates one of our major
themes, namely, that science is often not central to the decision to include or exclude a diagnosis from DSM. The dispute over the inclusion
of homosexuality in DSM was not about research findings. It was a 20-
year debate about beliefs and values. Although the professionals who
formulated diagnoses couched their arguments in the language of science, the actual influence of empirical data was negligible. More often
than not, the issues were settled by political compromises that promoted personal interests.

DSM AND THE DIAGNOSIS OF HOMOSEXUALITY

When DSM was first published by the American Psychiatric Association in 1952, Freud's influence was apparent in the way in which the disorders were organized and in the diagnoses that were included.[1] There were three major divisions of the functional (nonorganic) disorders: psychoses, neuroses, and personality disorders. Among the latter was Sexual Deviation, the diagnosis used for homosexuality.

A separate diagnosis of homosexuality first appeared when the manual was revised in 1968.[2] The new edition, DSM-II, listed homosexuality as one of the sexual deviations. The full text read as follows:

302 Sexual deviations. This category is for individuals whose sexual interests are directed primarily towards objects other than people of the opposite sex, toward sexual acts not usually associated with coitus, or toward coitus performed under bizarre circumstances as in necrophilia, pedophilia, sexual sadism and fetishism. Even though many find their practices distasteful, they remain unable to substitute normal sexual behavior for them. This diagnosis is not appropriate for individuals who perform deviant sexual acts because normal sexual objects are not available to them.[3]

Homosexuality was the first of 10 sexual deviations listed after this single paragraph, quoted above, that was carried over from DSM-I. Homosexuality was given a separate code number, but there was no specific description of this new diagnosis (or of any of the others). It was just added as a new category, one of the 10 "sexual deviations" that included a variety of behaviors ranging from those as mild as Voyeurism to the much more dramatic Sadism.

No one, inside or outside the APA, liked DSM-II very much. There was growing dissatisfaction with psychiatric diagnosis among scientists, professionals, and the general public during the 1960s (as we described in chapter 2).[4] On the other hand, DSM-II was not a matter of major concern, since few people used the manual. Diagnosis had little to do with psychotherapy, and extensive use of the manual to determine eligibility for payment (the principal reason it has become so important to mental health professionals) was just beginning. The fermenting unhappiness over DSM came to a head in the fight to eliminate the homosexuality diagnosis.

There are four strands to the story about the decertification of homosexuality: (1) historical changes in the concept of homosexuality; (2) the emergence of a militant gay movement; (3) the transformation of psychiatry and its professional organization, the American Psychiatric Association; and (4) an internal struggle in the field of psychoanalysis.

THE SOCIAL CONSTRUCTION OF HOMOSEXUALITY

The record of prosecution of homosexual behavior is brutal, horrifying, and unending. Recently, revisionist historians have argued that in non-Western cultures (as well as in earlier societies) homosexuality has been tolerated and even accepted to a much greater extent than we have been led to believe, but no one can deny the excessive cruelty that has been a frequent response to homosexual behavior throughout the world.

Social institutions responsible for control of homosexuality have changed over time. As Western civilization, especially in English-speaking countries, became secularized at the end of the Middle Ages, the responsibility for controlling unacceptable sexual behavior shifted from the church to the criminal justice system. During the 19th century a new struggle began as to who would be responsible for control of deviant behavior. The medicalization of deviance, as this process has often been called, began to supplant the criminalization of many kinds of objectionable or "immoral" conduct, and the social response shifted from punishment to treatment. Actually, the conflict between the medical and the criminal justice paradigms has often been overstated, and the distinction between punishment and treatment has been less apparent than is often suggested. Nonetheless, treatment was compared to punishment as being more enlightened, scientific, and humane.[5] Although treatment was advertised as an advanced approach to deviance, it did not take long for the recipients of it to question whether it was a more humane, more desirable alternative to earlier social sanctions.

Treatment of homosexuality has been a source of difficulty and pain for homosexuals ever since the idea for therapeutic intervention first began to compete with criminal punishment as the desired societal response to homosexuality during the 19th century.[6] The following is a partial list of the medical and other therapeutic interventions to which gay men and lesbians have been subjected:

Surgical intervention
  Castration
  Vasectomy
  Pudic nerve section
  Lobotomy
  Sterilization
  Clitoridectomy
  Hysterectomy
Chemical intervention
  Sexual stimulants
  Sexual depressants
  Hormone injection
    Estrogen
    Testosterone
    Pregnant mare serum
    Desiccated thyroid
    Pranturon (a pituitary gonadotropic)
  Pharmacological shock: matrazol
  LSD
Psychological intervention
  Abstinence
  Adjustment therapy
  Psychoanalysis
  Hypnosis
  Aversion therapy
    Hypnotic
    Shock
    Emetic
    Desensitization
    Covert sensitization (the patient imagines pictures of
      homosexuals and vomits on them)
  Group psychotherapy
  Desensitization (using pornographic materials)
  Primal therapy
Other Procedures
  Anaphrodisiac (cold sitz baths)
  Electroshock[7]
  "Homo-Anonymous" (patterned after AA)

One of the more remarkable reports about the medical treatment of homosexuals is that German physicians renewed questionable experiments on these devalued patients less than two decades after the Nazi era. In the 1960s and 1970s, West German physicians "revived the 'third sex' theory of homosexuality and gave it a new twist by performing surgery on homosexual men—some thirty between 1962 and 1979—destroying part of the hypothalamus where they hypothesized the 'female center' of the brain to be located."[8]

This episode is of current interest in light of the highly publicized speculation and research reported by LeVay and others that areas of the hypothalamus are involved in the sexual orientation of homosexuals.[9]

THE EMERGENCE OF THE GAY LIBERATION MOVEMENT

In 1947, Kinsey reported that there were more homosexuals than most people thought and that many "normal" men committed homosexual acts. Although the report questioned many basic assumptions about sex and gender, homosexuality continued to be treated as a sexual deviation. Gay groups that began to organize soon after the publication of the Kinsey Report seldom challenged the depiction of homosexuality as deviance. The primary interest of these fledgling groups was in reducing criminal penalties for homosexual acts. Their general strategy was to emphasize the similarities between gays and straights, and their basic tactics were education and gradualism. The most significant organization of homosexuals in the fifties and early sixties, the Mattachine Society, advocated greater tolerance and decriminalization. Their attitude about causation was that insufficient information was available to draw conclusions and that more research was needed. The nascent homophile organizations of the forties and fifties were very conservative, and they, reflecting the general political climate, were often staunchly anti-Communist. According to Bayer, "So fearful was the leadership of the [Mattachine] Society that it even cautioned against aggressive collective lobbying."[10] It was not until the late 1960s that the newer, more radical organizations challenged the fundamental assumption that homosexuality was a sexual deviance.

Gay activists did not wake up one morning and decide to march down to the American Psychiatric Association to demand the declassification of homosexuality from DSM. Before they protested, they had to become a movement, and they had to develop militancy. The turning point was the Stonewall Riot in 1969, when police and gays battled for days in the streets of Greenwich Village. The Gay Liberation Movement was born in the aftermath of Stonewall.

Even after the emergence of the Gay Liberation Front, activists did not immediately seize upon DSM as the focus for their complaints. They were interested in other aspects of psychiatry, particularly the psychiatric treatment (both psychoanalysis and behavior modification) of homosexuality. One of the first protests was not to the American Psychiatric Association but to the American Medical Association (AMA). In 1968, even before Stonewall, protesters demonstrated at the AMA national convention and objected to a speech by the psychoanalyst Charles Socarides. They asked the AMA to schedule speakers who opposed the interpretation of homosexuality as psychopathology and to include representatives of what was then called the homophile community. They also asked that research be conducted in a "value-free manner." What they wanted was research free of the homophobic bias of Socarides and his psychoanalytic colleagues.

There were many differences between the homophile groups of the fifties and early sixties and the gay liberation groups that emerged from the Stonewall riots. The confrontational politics of the latter reflected a fundamental change in self-perception. Their members stopped being homosexuals and became gay. They transformed themselves into a community with a unique public lifestyle. Fundamental to this transformation was the decision to stop apologizing for their condition. As one gay activist put it, "By the late 1960's we began to see that discussing the cause and nature of homosexuality would not help us. We began to insist on our rights . . . to demand what was ours."[11]

They cut the Gordian knot—or perhaps it was the umbilical cord. Gays insisted that their infantile psychosexual relationships with their mothers and fathers were no longer relevant to determining their fate. The question of causation was no longer significant in their newly politicized, rights-oriented approach, and debates about the value of psychotherapy or other treatments were deemed equally irrelevant. Among the most radical of the groups, it was considered improper even to discuss these matters with psychotherapists, and those who did were accused of collaborating with war criminals.[12] Conrad and Schneider have summarized the transformation:[13]

The stigma of the old meanings surrounding "homosexual" had to be removed and a new, more positive definition substituted. Under these circumstances homosexuals gradually would become "gay" and proud and public. . . .

Underlying this transformation, however—and this is perhaps the center of the irony involved—is the assertion that indeed there are homosexuals and there is something called "homosexuality"—the entity on which most traditional moral opprobrium rested. But it has become an entity morally transformed. Leaders of movement organizations, supported by a much larger population of sympathetic others, have de-emphasized questions of etiology. They argue that, short of academic and rarefied scientific debates about sexuality in general, there is no particular importance in search[ing] for the cause of something that is good. Although the question of cause may remain important at the individual, biographic level, redefinition has turned attention to what homosexuality is. It has become a "sexual preference," an "identity" (or "role" . . .) and a life "style."

Furthermore, the transformation also involved collectivizing the problem of homosexuals. No longer was the problem an individual moral struggle to overcome temptation and avoid sin or a psychological struggle to overcome overwhelming desires. Edmund White has observed that

Americans—Emersonian rhetoric notwithstanding—believe in a kind of communitarianism rather than individualism. In the United States, where so many political factions are linked to ethnic identity, homosexuals have been astute in presenting themselves as something very much like a racial or cultural entity. Perhaps our history as a haven for persecuted religious sects makes us want to defend the rights of groups rather than of that universal and abstract being, the individual citizen.[14]

THE INNER WORLD OF PSYCHIATRY AND PSYCHOANALYSIS

During the late 1960s and early 1970s, most practicing psychiatrists had a psychoanalytic orientation. Although a psychoanalytic interpretation of homosexuality held sway in psychiatric circles, a dispute was brewing. The reigning version, which characterized homosexuality as a reaction to a cold, rejecting father and an overprotective mother, was that of Charles

Socarides, Irving Bieber, and their associates. A cure was implicit in the theory of psychosexual development: psychoanalysis could uncover the infantile conflict, and this would resolve the homosexual's longings. Although this was the orthodox view, it was not the opinion of Freud but a position that had been formulated by later psychiatrists, especially in the United States.

The generally accepted psychoanalytic interpretation of homosexuality had been under attack since shortly after World War II, when the Kinsey Report was published and a new antipsychoanalytic view of homosexuality began to emerge. Kinsey, an anthropologist, claimed that homosexuality occurs more frequently than previously believed and that the demarcation between homosexuality and heterosexuality is not a sharp line. Throughout the postwar period the interest in more sociological interpretations grew, as exemplified by the work of Evelyn Hooker, a psychologist who studied successful homosexuals and concluded that homosexuality is not a mental illness.

Even within the psychoanalytic establishment there were challenges, and the revisionist approach of Judd Marmor, who later became a president of the APA, began to crowd out the interpretations of Bieber and Socarides. Marmor was a Los Angeles–based psychoanalyst who began his practice in the 1940s. His patients included movie actors and writers who were professionally successful but wanted to change their sexual orientation. Describing his early patients, Marmor said, "The gay men I saw were caught up, for the most part, in the common myth that it was bad to be gay and that if they possibly could, they ought to try to be heterosexual. I was sympathetic to their wishes to try to become straight if they could."

Marmor assessed his therapeutic successes more modestly than many of his psychoanalytic colleagues: "We all used to think in those days that psychoanalysis could cure everything, from chilblains to homosexuality. But I wasn't too successful. Some were able to function bisexually but most of them remained gay."[15] As a result, he gradually transformed his work from trying to reform the activity of gay patients to helping them accept their orientation and deal with the problems they experienced as homosexuals. "I very quickly realized—since I wasn't judgmental about them being gay—that if I couldn't help them achieve heterosexuality, which they assumed they wanted, then my job was to help them accept their gayness and live effectively within that scheme of things." As a result of his changing therapeutic approach, Marmor gradually began to reformulate his theoretical orientation, but he continued to believe that homosexuality is a sexual deviation. "The first time I heard Dr. Evelyn Hooker state that homosexuality was not an illness," he said, "I wasn't prepared to go all the way. This was in 1956 when she presented her study of gay men. I was sympathetic to what she was saying but I wasn't totally convinced. I still had a feeling that it was a developmental deviation." But Marmor's views began to change, and in 1962 he published "Sexual Inversion: The Multiple Roots of Homosexuality" in order to challenge prevailing psychoanalytic views.

Disputes about the genesis and treatment of homosexual patients were part of a bigger struggle among psychiatrists over psychoanalysis. Until quite recently, psychoanalysis was the basic theoretical perspective in psychiatry. The period after World War II was the heyday of Freudian treatment in this country, but dissatisfaction mounted in the late sixties. Freudian theory was vulnerable because of the limited success of psychoanalytic treatment and the paucity of hard scientific data to support psychodynamic explanations for behavior. This conflict found its way into the efforts to improve DSM.

A major objective of the research-oriented psychiatrists who were revamping DSM during the 1970s was to eliminate psychoanalytic influences from the manual, and the fight about homosexuality was the opening salvo in the battle. These struggles over the psychodynamics of homosexuality, as well as over other psychoanalytic concepts, were fueled by a reorganization of psychiatric practice. There was a transformation from a private-practice-centered, psychoanalytically based profession to a research-oriented, university-dominated discipline influenced by the descriptive approach of Emil Kraepelin.

The change in the profession was mirrored by the career of the psychiatrist who was at the center of the fight to declassify homosexuality—Robert Spitzer. Originally trained as a psychoanalyst, Spitzer spent his career as a university professor working on issues of diagnosis. He acknowledged that he knew little or nothing about the treatment of homosexuals. He was not particularly sympathetic to gays; he had other interests. His concerns about homosexuality had more to do with how mental illness was defined. His thinking was deductive: first define mental illness and then evaluate whether homosexuality meets the definition. Although Spitzer has been unable to create a satisfactory definition of mental illness, despite repeated attempts, one principle that has guided his efforts has been a commitment to eliminate psychoanalytic assumptions. The search for a satisfactory definition of "mental disorder" and the creation of a classification system free of psychoanalytic concepts seem to be far removed from the concerns of gay demonstrators, but the debate over these two problems played a central role in the struggle to remove the diagnosis of homosexuality from DSM. The declassification of the diagnosis of homosexuality should be understood in the context of the broader debate within the APA about eliminating psychoanalytic assumptions from the theoretical formulation of the concept of mental illness.

EXPUNGING HOMOSEXUALITY FROM THE MANUAL

Over a four-year period, from 1970 to 1973, the principal staging ground for protests over psychiatric diagnosis was the annual convention of the American Psychiatric Association. The struggle began with angry confrontations by gay activist outsiders demanding to be heard; they denounced presenters whom they considered their enemies and threatened violent disruption of the proceedings. These scenes were replaced by presentations by gays and their supporters that were designed as an alternative to the sessions offered by psychoanalysts and other therapists on the treatment and cure of homosexuality. This format gave way the next year to a carefully moderated session in which professionals, some of whom were gay, debated with their psychiatric opponents in the same forum. As the process moved from confrontation to reasoned debate, the participants changed, the issues became more abstract, and the concerns of protesters gave way to those of professionals.

The initial confrontations were directed by outsiders, consumer groups that had no stake in maintaining the stature of organized psychiatry. Although on the surface it seems that these protesters were less effective in obtaining their objectives than professional groups of insiders who succeeded them, one must recognize that it was their militant strategy of disruption that led to major change. Later, when the action was dominated by those within the psychiatric profession, there was a partial reinstatement of homosexuality as a psychiatric diagnosis (i.e., as Ego-dystonic Homosexuality) even though pro-gay psychiatrists were more influential in the APA than were those who believed that homosexuality is a pathological condition. The impact of the outsiders on this dialectic is worth noting. A decade later, when there was a renewed protest that originated outside the profession, the vestigial diagnosis of Ego-dystonic Homosexuality was deleted. Even though gay psychiatrists were far more prominent and better organized as time went on, their efforts were ineffective when compared with the impact of outside agitation.

One of the earliest events in the struggle over the diagnosis of homosexuality was a demonstration at the 1970 convention of the American Psychiatric Association.[16] The demonstrators confronted Irving Bieber and other, lesser-known, psychiatrists and hurled profanities and accusations at them. They took over a meeting and denounced aversive treatment techniques. When the gay speakers seized the microphone and demanded to be heard, many psychiatrists were enraged (one asked that police shoot the protesters).

After the meeting, one psychiatrist, Kent Robinson, took it upon himself to contact leaders of the gay organizations, although he was unfamiliar with gay groups and did not even know a gay psychiatrist. Subsequently, he persuaded the APA to include gay speakers in the next national annual conference in Washington in order to prevent more disruptive confrontations.

Although they had obtained their original goal, a panel where they could present their position, the gay protesters were not satisfied. The best efforts of the APA to avoid disruptions were thwarted by gay demonstrators, along with Vietnam veterans and other activists, who continuously disrupted the 1971 Washington meeting. This was not spontaneous street theater but a planned assault (the demonstrators had even checked the building layout in order to plan their attack). At the conference, gays asked to meet with the APA's Committee on Nomenclature to present a demand to delete homosexuality from DSM. Although nothing came of this effort, it was the first attempt to directly address the diagnostic issue and it represented a significant refinement of the protesters' strategy.

If the disruptions caused by the demonstrators during the 1971 convention obscured a gradual change in the gay approach, the next year's conference in Dallas left no doubt that a transformation was occurring. (At this meeting there were no presentations that were antithetical to the views of gay activists.) Instead of forcing an objectionable exhibitor to close down, as they had done in Washington, the gay demonstrators maintained their own booth in the exhibition area, a practice they continued in subsequent years. Once again a session was arranged to present the gay activists' point of view. But this presentation was different from that of the previous year: three psychiatrists were part of the panel. One was Judd Marmor (soon to become the president of the APA), who had attacked recent publications by Charles Socarides. However, the most dramatic impact was made by Dr. Anonymous, a cloaked and hooded psychiatrist who declared that he was gay. He also revealed that more than two hundred other members of the APA were homosexuals and that some of them were members of the Gay Psychiatric Association, which met socially but secretly during the annual APA meetings.

Awareness that the number of gay psychiatrists was so large cannot be overestimated. In various accounts of the incidents that led to the declassification of homosexuality, it appears that recognition that there were homosexual psychiatrists was persuasive in a way that formal scientific studies were not. The attempt to erase the distance between physician and subject seems to have been an important factor. Since some prominent psychiatrists were homosexuals, it was much harder to argue that homosexuality was a disability and that being gay was dysfunctional.

The presence of gay psychiatrists, most of whom were still in the closet, became even more important at the next annual meeting, which was the culmination of this series of confrontations. During 1972, a number of events took place that set the stage for the resolution of the dispute over the diagnosis of homosexuality. A key event was an accidental encounter between Robert Spitzer, who was on the verge of revolutionizing psychiatric diagnosis, and gay activists. In October 1972, more than a hundred gay demonstrators disrupted a meeting of behavior therapists that Spitzer was attending. This was Spitzer's first contact with gays protesting against therapeutic abuse, and he stayed behind to talk with a protest leader, Ron Gold. Spitzer described the encounter as follows: "I went to this conference on behavioral modification which the gay lib group broke up. I found myself talking to a very angry young man. At that time I was convinced that homosexuality was a disorder and that it belonged in the classification, I told him so."

Gold also described the exchange: "[Spitzer] said he believed in the illness theory. I said, alright, who do you believe? And he hadn't read any of it. . . . But he happened to know Socarides and thought he was a nut. Whom do you believe? Bieber? I don't know. Have you read it? No. But they all believed it."[17] The outcome of this encounter was that Spitzer agreed to arrange a meeting between gays and the APA's Committee on

Nomenclature and to schedule a panel on homosexuality at the next APA convention in May 1973 in Honolulu.

This chance encounter has been described in several different reports,[18] but there is a disingenuous quality to the story. Spitzer, by all accounts, was not familiar with the literature on homosexuality and had little clinical experience with homosexuals, yet as a result of an accidental meeting he agreed to undertake a major role in the struggle. He knew that during the next year the decision would be made about who would head the effort to revise the manual, an assignment considered the capstone of a career, yet he was willing to risk his future in the biggest public battle then confronting the APA.[19] As it turned out, Spitzer's participation in the declassification of homosexuality as a mental disorder demonstrated that he was the person to undertake the difficult task of revolutionizing psychiatric diagnosis. During 1972–1974 he resolved an embarrassing dispute for the APA without capitulating to either the psychoanalytic faction or the gay activists; if there was any question about who should head the upcoming revision of DSM, Spitzer's performance in the controversy over homosexuality added to his stature. Furthermore, when disputes later emerged in the development of DSM-III, he was deferred to, on the basis of his performance in this debate, as a master of the professional politics involved in developing an acceptable nosology.

The Committee on Nomenclature agreed to hear the gay activists. Once again, Spitzer offered a disingenuous explanation for the decision: "We couldn't think of any good reason not to meet them."[20] Perhaps not, but there were many good reasons for the committee to proceed in a manner different from the one they adopted. The committee did not consult psychoanalysts who opposed declassifying homosexuality, yet they quickly publicized their consultation with gay leaders. On the day after their meeting (February 9, 1973), the New York Times quoted the committee chairman as saying that some change was indicated and that the committee intended to prepare a resolution in time for the APA's annual meeting. This deadline was not met, despite the apparent enthusiasm of the committee, because Spitzer refused to incorporate a recommendation to declassify homosexuality in a position paper he was asked to coauthor for the committee.

The 1973 convention was not punctuated by the dramatic confrontations that had occurred in prior years, but several events had a major impact on the conflict over the diagnosis of homosexuality. As he had promised, Spitzer organized a panel that included psychiatrists on both sides of the controversy, and a gay speaker. Unlike the previous years' panels, which were consciousness-raising sessions conducted by gay activists and supportive psychiatrists, the 1973 panel debated the merits of the controversy. The whole atmosphere had changed dramatically in the three years since the protesters had created so much pandemonium that some conventioneers demanded a refund of their airfares.[21] In contrast, the 1973 panel's audience, which numbered almost a thousand, responded positively to the argument that homosexuality is not a pathological condition. The proceedings were subsequently published in the *American Journal of Psychiatry,* and the media made optimistic predictions that soon homosexuality would be dropped from DSM.

Another event at the 1973 conference had a profound effect on the outcome of the homosexuality diagnosis controversy. Spitzer, who had never knowingly met a gay psychiatrist, was invited to attend a social meeting of the Gay Psychiatric Association. Although some participants were upset by Spitzer's surprise appearance, many were persuaded to explain how they felt about the day's events. "Spitzer heard homosexual psychiatrists declaring . . . that 'their lives had been changed by what they had heard at the panel discussion.'"[22] This exchange helped to persuade Spitzer that many homosexuals (among them, psychiatrists) function at a high level. It gave Spitzer such an "emotional jolt" that he quickly prepared a proposal for the deletion of homosexuality from DSM.[23]

Actually, Spitzer's proposal did not entirely eliminate homosexuality from the manual.[24] Spitzer concluded that homosexuality per se did not warrant a diagnosis, but he believed that those who were troubled by their sexual interests should be given a new diagnosis—Sexual Orientation Disturbance. He rejected the position of gay activists and their chief proponent in the APA, Judd Marmor, that homosexuality is a normal variant of sexual behavior. Instead, he proposed a middle ground between their position and the assertion by Socarides, Bieber, and their allies that homosexuality is pathological.

Spitzer's reasoning was tortuous. In order to answer the question of whether homosexuality is an illness, Spitzer felt it was necessary first to define mental disorder. This, he decided, is a behavior that is accompanied by subjective distress or a generalized impairment in social effectiveness or functioning. Since Spitzer had met at the APA meeting gays who did not suffer from subjective distress because of their sexual orientation and who were obviously high functioning, he felt that homosexuality could not be considered a mental illness.

On the other hand, Spitzer did not want to give homosexuality the stamp of normalcy. He decided that homosexuality could be considered a form of irregular sexual behavior. But, reasoned Spitzer, if psychiatry was to broaden its diagnostic system to include "suboptimal" behaviors as mental disorders, it would have to recognize such phenomena as celibacy, religious fanaticism, racism, vegetarianism, and male chauvinism as diagnostic categories. Spitzer's choice of examples, obviously meant to be humorous, reveals a great deal about whom he was trying to persuade, namely, white males who believed that racism and sexism differed from the disorders they diagnosed and treated. In *Homosexuality and American Psychiatry,* Bayer offers an admiring evaluation of Spitzer's proposal:

> The position paper as well as the proposed new diagnostic category [sexual orientation disorder] thus attempted to provide a common ground for those who had been locked in combat for the past three years. To homosexual activists it granted the removal of homosexuality from the Diagnostic Manual, allowing them to claim a stunning victory. To psychoanalytically oriented psychiatrists, it stated that their own view of homosexuality as suboptimal was not being challenged but rather was not central to the restricted concept of psychiatric disorder. To those seeking an end to the pattern of disruptions that had beset psychiatric meetings, the new classification provided a formula that could remove the APA from the center of controversy. Finally for psychiatrists concerned with the extent to which the psychiatric nosology had become a tool in the hands of government officials attempting to deprive homosexuals of their rights, the proposed shift promised to put an end to such unwanted collaboration. That all this could take the form of a theoretical refinement rather than a political accommodation made the proposal more attractive to those willing to yield polar positions defined in the course of conflict. (Pp. 128–129)

However, none of the participants in this controversy viewed Spitzer's handiwork in this way. The Committee on Nomenclature refused to adopt his proposal, although it did adopt a companion resolution that called for recognition of the civil rights of homosexuals. The chair of the committee suggested conducting a survey of APA members to determine whether Spitzer's proposals would elicit a strong reaction. Nevertheless, Spitzer's proposal, without committee approval, was bucked upstairs to

THE FALL AND RISE OF HOMOSEXUALITY   71

the Council on Research and Development. The head of the council rejected the suggestion of a survey as "ridiculous," saying, "You don't devise a nomenclature through a vote." Ultimately, of course, this is precisely what the APA did.

The Committee on Nomenclature was not the only group that rejected Spitzer's compromise. Ron Gold, Spitzer's gay ally, objected to the proposal, particularly because the proposed new diagnosis, Sexual Orientation Disturbance, was only for homosexuals. Gold urged the APA to simply delete the homosexuality diagnosis from the manual. Judd Marmor also objected to Spitzer's proposal because of the description of homosexuality as "irregular" rather than as "a variant form of sexual development."[25] Despite reservations by many of its members, the Council on Research and Development voted unanimously to adopt Spitzer's proposal, because they felt that they should not override the recommendation of a committee they had appointed to evaluate a scientific issue. Their logic seems shaky, since the proposal was not recommended to them by the Committee on Nomenclature; it was Spitzer's work.

Next to review the proposal was the Assembly of District Branches, a group that was more representative of the rank-and-file clinicians than any other committee in the APA hierarchy. The proposal was overwhelmingly approved, but the assembly recommended the elimination of pejorative phrasing, such as the reference to homosexuality as an "irregular" form of sexual behavior.

Finally, in December 1973, after the approval of yet another committee, the Reference Committee, the matter was considered by the APA's board of trustees. After listening briefly to objections from the opponents, the board voted unanimously to delete Homosexuality from the diagnostic manual and to replace it with the diagnosis of Sexual Orientation Disturbance, but the board amended the description of the disorder to satisfy the objections of the assembly.[26] Although Spitzer had proposed the word *irregular,* the final text described homosexuality as "one form of sexual behavior."

Newspapers across the country featured stories announcing the revision. Many of the stories missed the nuances of the compromise Spitzer had engineered. For example, a *Washington Post* headline reported DOCTORS RULE HOMOSEXUALS NOT ABNORMAL. The headline ignored a careful statement by the APA president to the effect that the association had not declared homosexuality to be normal. Spitzer also made a statement that attempted to clarify his position:

> This is not to say that homosexuality is normal or that it is as desirable as heterosexuality. . . . Many people will interpret this [decision] to mean that we are saying that it is normal. We are not saying that; we're not saying it is normal. The terms normal and abnormal are not really psychiatric terms.[27]

His statement infuriated gays, but it made little difference in the public perception of what had happened.

Spitzer was not done tinkering, but it was a while before he had an opportunity to revisit the issues. First, other participants had scores to settle. Charles Socarides collected 200 signatures on a petition for a referendum of the APA membership to overturn the decision.[28] Ironically, Socarides and Bieber complained that scientific concerns had been subjected to political pressures by gays, but now they justified the use of a political device to reverse a decision they disliked. Although many people ridiculed the idea that a scientific issue could be settled by a plebiscite, the APA scheduled the referendum for April 1974.

The outcome was significant to individuals as well as the organization. Personal careers were deeply affected. For example, not long after the decision, Judd Marmor replaced Irving Bieber as the author of a chapter on homosexuality in a leading psychiatric textbook. A new group of experts with views more sympathetic to gays and lesbians were being called on to express their opinions about homosexuality in court proceedings, in the popular media, and in professional publications.

Robert Spitzer was among those most directly affected. He had just been appointed as chair of the newly formed committee to revise DSM. He joined gay activists in drafting a letter signed by all the nominees in an upcoming election for president and vice president of the APA. The letter was paid for by funds secretly raised by gay groups and was sent to the entire APA membership. Spitzer recognized that this was a risky strategy, but he felt that the stakes were very high. As he later acknowledged, "We knew the other side would be angry with what we did. Frankly I was very worried by the referendum. We were very apprehensive and we didn't win by much. If we had lost I would probably have been asked to resign and just after becoming Chairman at that."[29] The vote, although not overwhelming, was decisive, but describing the outcome as close served Spitzer's purposes in later stages of the conflict over the diagnosis of homosexuality.[30]

Before the sequel to this debate is described, four aspects of the controversy deserve to be highlighted since they reoccurred repeatedly in the conflicts over the revisions of DSM. First, proponents on every side claimed that they were being scientific and that their opponents were not. A fallback position was that the scientific evidence presented by their opponents was invalid and should therefore be discounted—this position was easy enough to maintain by invoking the basic standards of scientific research. None of the psychiatrists involved in the controversy had done studies that could pass muster as definitive scientific research, but before a decision could be made, each side had to couch its arguments in terms of scientific standards. The presentation by gay activists to the Committee on Nomenclature was important in this respect; the activists were careful to mobilize whatever scientific reports were available to support the declassification of homosexuality. The earlier disruptions of APA meetings by gay rights groups had been crucial in bringing the issue of the classification of homosexuality to the attention of the association, but a scientific rationale was also needed before the APA and its committees could act. *Science* was a rallying cry and *politics* a term of denigration.

Second, Spitzer's strategy was to maintain that he was operating from a position of authority and that those who attacked him were operating from a position of weakness. Even when he did not have the support of the Committee on Nomenclature, his proposal was seen as its recommendation. There is an excellent illustration of this strategy in the events surrounding the referendum conducted by the APA. In addition to the circulation of a letter signed by the leaders of the organization supporting the decision of the board to delete the diagnosis of homosexuality from DSM the strategy was reflected in the way the referendum was worded. Members were asked to vote on whether they were in favor of the decision of the board of trustees or opposed to it. In this way, Spitzer's position was persuasive to both liberals, who wanted to declassify homosexuality, and to some conservatives, who wanted to maintain the status quo and to reestablish the traditional authority of the organization.

A third important phenomenon, which reappeared in later struggles over DSM, was the sense that Spitzer was taking control in a stalemated situation and resolving it and that without his intervention the APA would not act. Actually, far more leadership was provided by Judd Marmor, who had much greater popular support than Spitzer. Marmor, who had been much more forthright about his position that homosexuality is not pathological, was elected president of the APA within months after the board declassified homosexuality and the Socarides referendum was defeated.

Some of the psychoanalysts in opposition to the declassification of homosexuality have a far different explanation of how these events unfolded. Charles Socarides has offered the following account:

> When the gay panelists challenged the APA delegates [at the 1971 convention] to "break the monopoly" enjoyed by those who said that homosexuality was a disorder, a small minority inside the APA began laying plans to see how they could re-classify homosexuality—that is, take it off the APA's list of disorders. . . .
>
> But the time was not ripe. It would get riper after our next meeting in Dallas in 1972.[31]

The Socarides account goes on to describe a report that he and a group of psychiatrists in New York made that contained the finding that homosexuality is a disorder of psychosexual development. When Socarides tried to have the report adopted by the local branch of the APA, they rejected it because they concluded that it had too a great a psychoanalytic bias. Socarides claimed that the local branch was being manipulated by the national organization:

> At the national level a group of politically active psychiatrists—some of them gay—was forming. They called themselves the Committee for a Concerned Psychiatry (CFCP). Over the next few years their lobbying and their electioneering led to a seizure of the presidency and the chairs of the APA. They gave strong support to Alfred Freedman in his election as president of the APA, and it really made a difference: in an election where more than 10,000 voted, Dr. Freedman won by two votes. Then the CFCP helped to set up John Spiegel and Judd Marmor in the chairs, ready to move up into the presidency—which with the support of the CFCP, they did. Then each of them—Freedman, Spiegel and Marmor—later delivered what the CFCP wanted; they each played important roles in the move to delete homosexuality from the Diagnostic and Statistical Manual.[32]

Socarides also has a different interpretation of the process by which the Committee on Nomenclature decided to meet with gay spokesmen about homosexuality:

In mid-1973, the president of the American Psychiatric Association, John Spiegel, and the vice president, Judd Marmor, had brought the Nomenclature Committee of the APA to a meeting at Columbia University with representatives of the Gay Activist Alliance, the Mattachine Society, and the Daughters of Bilitis to discuss the deletion of homosexuality from [DSM]. I discovered that the chairman of the Nomenclature Committee, Dr. Henry Brill, had been shunted aside on this matter, and a new subgroup was formed, the Nomenclature Task Force on Homosexuality, to be headed by Dr. Robert Spitzer. . . .

I heard nothing until a reporter from *Newsweek* asked if I were invited to attend the upcoming celebration cocktail party scheduled for December 15 or 16 at APA headquarters in Washington . . . [to celebrate] "the greatest of gay victories—the purging of homosexuality from the realm of psychiatry."[33]

Although this conspiratorial interpretation of events by Socarides has not been fully corroborated, he does offer a somewhat less one-dimensional account than the generally accepted version.[34] Clearly, leaders with more socially progressive ideas took over the APA just prior to the declassification of homosexuality.[35] Very little has been written about the historic change in the profession that was marked by the election of Albert Freedman in 1971. In a recent interview, he acknowledged that his write-in candidacy was engineered by members of CFCP who had been organizing for several years to overthrow the old guard. Furthermore, other efforts by gay activists were creating pressure to eliminate the diagnosis of homosexuality. A proposal of the Massachusetts Psychiatric Association to declassify homosexuality had been favorably received, and it appeared to have a good chance of being adopted when it was withdrawn in deference to Spitzer's efforts. This proposal was originally drafted by Richard Pillard, a gay psychiatrist, at the behest of the Massachusetts group's leader, Lawrence Hartmann, who went on to become president of the APA some years later and who was recently "outed" by militant gay groups at an annual meeting of the APA.

What Spitzer had to offer was his involvement with the nomenclature committee, which had general responsibility for psychiatric diagnosis and DSM, but, as we know, he was never able to get the backing of the committee for his proposal. Although the story has generally emphasized Spitzer's ability to get things done, there is another way of looking at it, in which Spitzer is seen as part of a larger movement involving the leadership of the APA. In this version, Spitzer is not a lone gunman shooting down the entrenched defenders of orthodox psychoanalysis who had a stranglehold on organized psychiatry. This is not a matter that can be settled. The reason for raising the issue here is to indicate the bias in the generally accepted interpretation of the APA's declassification of homosexuality, an interpretation that has emphasized the importance of Spitzer's contribution but has failed to provide an adequate description of the political milieu in which he operated so successfully.

The fourth and final aspect of the controversy is how symbolic it was and how unimportant its consequences were for psychiatric treatment. The decision to declassify the diagnosis of homosexuality had important ramifications, but it had very little impact on the therapeutic enterprise. The choice of therapy for gay patients is usually based on the psychiatrist's theoretical orientation, not on the diagnosis. Psychoanalysts who adhere to Socarides' position still try to reform gays with reparative therapy, and gay psychiatrists often try to help gay patients accept their gender and sexual preferences. Although Spitzer insisted on the adoption of a new diagnosis, sexual orientation disturbance, that was to be limited to homosexuals, the impact of this revision was inconsequential. Consider the following interview of Lawrence Hartmann.

HARTMANN: If you're seeing a homosexual patient and had to fill out an insurance form, I would still . . . not use the word *homosexual*. I think it is such a damaging word.
INTERVIEWER: What is the most convenient one?
HARTMANN: *Depression* is easy, *anxiety neurosis* is easy, *adjustment reaction of adulthood or adolescence*. Usually a patient has quite a few worries. . . . I write as brief notes as I can. I use as vague and general categories as I think are compatible with the truth. Insurance companies realize that they are getting watered down diagnostic labels in order not to harm the patient.[36]

Removal of the homosexuality diagnosis from DSM was of little consequence in terms of treatment decisions, but gay activists realized the symbolic significance of the APA's decision about the diagnosis. Although they were angry with Spitzer for introducing the new diagnosis of Sexual Orientation Disorder and for his refusal to recognize homosexuality as a normal variation of sexual activity, they pushed for the APA press conference that announced the change in nomenclature.

The psychoanalytic opponents also felt that the decision was a monumental one. In an interview, Socarides made a sweeping evaluation of the impact of the decisions:

> SOCARIDES: In some ways, the gay community in this country are like a bunch of confused kids. They knew they had these mysterious sexual compulsions. They knew they weren't happy. And then the nation's psychiatrists said, in effect, "Hey, you're okay. Go out and have fun."
> INTERVIEWER: So they did?
> SOCARIDES: Yes.
> INTERVIEWER: And then what happened?
> SOCARIDES: Some gays and their families who might have looked for psychoanalytic help just never considered it an option. Now they could grow a new delusion courtesy of the American Psychiatric Association. But that was only the beginning. The APA decision led to a number of decisions by policymakers all over the country. They decriminalized sodomy in half of the country. That led to the rise of gay bathhouse culture. And that fueled the century's most horrific plague, the plague of AIDS.[37]

Socarides exaggerated the significance of the decision to declassify homosexuality, just as Hartmann minimized the importance of the diagnosis. But the decision was meaningful for its symbolic significance for psychiatry and its importance in a wider cultural context, if not for its impact on individual treatment. If homosexuality were still considered a mental illness, business and insurance companies would not be offering health coverage for domestic partners, the army would still be using psychiatry to screen suspected homosexuals for discharge, and many of the other advances in gay rights would not be part of our culture. Nevertheless, the accomplishments should not be exaggerated; there are still enormous difficulties that beset gays and lesbians. But there has also been great progress, and the first step was the action by the APA to remove the homosexuality diagnosis from DSM.

ONCE MORE INTO THE BREACH: EGO-DYSTONIC HOMOSEXUALITY AND DSM-III

After the 1974 referendum, Spitzer went back to the drawing board. He was dissatisfied with the definition of mental disorder he had used to justify replacing the psychiatric diagnosis of homosexuality with Sexual Orientation Disorder in DSM-II. He created a new definition of mental disorder for DSM-III, and he believed that this new formulation required another revision of the diagnosis of homosexuality to replace Sexual Orientation Disorder. First he proposed to name this new diagnosis Homodysphilia and then he suggested calling it Dyshomophilia; it finally appeared in the next edition of the APA's diagnostic manual (i.e., DSM-III) as Ego-dystonic Homosexuality (EDH), a diagnosis for those who are troubled about their homosexual impulses.

The adoption of EDH proves that not every change in DSM-III was the result of outside political pressure or new scientific evidence. This new diagnosis was not a response to a new problem in the way that Post-traumatic Stress Disorder was needed to account for the difficulties of Vietnam veterans. It did not result from any new scientific discovery or newly reported research (in fact, there was so little interest in it that EDH was only a diagnosis for seven years, until it was deleted in 1987). The inclusion of EDH in DSM-III was not a response to political pressure from any organized group within or outside the American Psychiatric Association. There was no significant pressure by Bieber, Socarides, or their allies who had fought so hard to retain the diagnosis of homosexuality; they appeared to have given up the fight. The major impetus for the change came from Spitzer himself.

There was some opposition to EDH, principally from within the American Psychiatric Association. There was an exchange of letters between Spitzer and gay leaders and their psychiatric supporters who opposed the new diagnosis, but eventually Spitzer prevailed. Gay activists decided against another public battle, one they feared they might lose, since the APA was beginning to shift back to a more conservative orientation. By not publicizing the inclusion of Ego-dystonic Homosexuality in the diagnostic manual, they felt that there would continue to be a public perception that the APA had abandoned homosexuality as a pathological condition. (The wisdom of the gay activists' decision was confirmed in 1987, when Ego-dystonic Homosexuality was quietly eliminated from the next revision of the manual, DSM-III-R.)

Although it had almost no impact on the diagnosis and treatment of sexual problems, the short career of Ego-dystonic Homosexuality as a mental disorder can shed light on the forces that mold modern psychiatry. This episode illustrates how important public opinion and outside interest groups are in determining psychiatric diagnosis. Although gay psychiatrists were much better organized after the 1974 campaign that eliminated the diagnosis of homosexuality from DSM-II, they proved to be ineffectual in their efforts to prevent the inclusion of Ego-dystonic Homosexuality in DSM-III. It was not until outside groups brought pressure to bear for its elimination that EDH was finally dropped from the next revision, DSM-III-R.[38]

Why did Spitzer reopen the diagnostic controversy over homosexuality? It was important to him to establish that diagnostic categories are dictated by scientific considerations, not political ones, particularly the political resolution of the fight over homosexuality in 1974, when the question was settled by a plebiscite. When the controversy over homosexuality resurfaced during the preparation of DSM-III, it was handled quietly, for the most part within the confines of the decision-making structure that Spitzer had established. In fact, Spitzer was the only one who subsequently publicized the controversy. On the surface, the process by which EDH came to be included in the diagnostic manual seemed to illustrate that DSM-III was free of political influences; it also demonstrated Spitzer's mastery over the process and his ability to keep the discourse from becoming overtly political. Spitzer controlled the process, and the debate remained scientific—within the special meaning that he and his colleagues gave to the term.[39]

There were two major aspects of the controversy. One was a name change for Sexual Orientation Disorder, the diagnostic category that had been agreed to by the APA in 1973. The second was the creation of more specific descriptions and criteria for the disorder, in keeping with the rest of the activity involved in the development of DSM-III.

The dispute about homosexuality resurfaced in 1976, after Spitzer made a proposal for certain diagnoses to be included in the section of the manual concerned with gender role disorders. Among the diagnoses was one called Homodysphilia, which was Spitzer's idea for the DSM-III version of Sexual Orientation Disorder, the category that had replaced Homosexuality in the 1974 dispute. Spitzer sent his proposed revisions to the Advisory Committee on Sexual Disorders, one of more than a dozen advisory committees that had been organized to review diagnostic proposals and to make recommendations to the DSM-III Task Force.

The response was immediate. Richard Green, a psychiatrist and lawyer, objected to both the process of revising the sexual disorders section and the proposal to change the diagnostic entry Sexual Orientation Disorder.[40] He reminded Spitzer that the advisory committee was composed initially of members who constituted "a select body of experts representing various aspects of human sexuality" and that these experts had worked "diligently" to prepare revisions for DSM-III.[41] Green told Spitzer, "Then there was an influx to the task force of representatives from your own institution and a diminution in the roles played by the expert members."[42] He also complained that although he had submitted an extensive commentary on gender role disorders, Spitzer had made no response to that work for nearly a year. As Green told Spitzer, there had been no response "until a note of a few days ago requesting, within a matter of days, views regarding extensive modifications. There was also in that note, a new diagnostic term, 'homodysphilia.' . . . There was, apparently, no polling of myself, Dr. Lief, Dr. Gebhard, or Dr. Fortney-Settlage with respect to this change. Thus you are putting on record members of a Task Force as recommending a term which some might regard as a neologism, without explanation and without regard for our views."

Green felt that it might not be clear what role he had played in the decision-making process, and he did not want it to appear that he was responsible for the final product. He threatened to make his position known to the membership of the APA. He told Spitzer, "I feel it imperative that you state to the APA the role you have played in this Nomenclature Task Force with respect to terminology, decision making, and the process and criteria by which additional members were selected, as well as the roles played by the original task force members." And with that, Green resigned.

Spitzer responded that with the exception of Homodysphilia all of the modifications had been discussed with various committee members and memos about the changes had been sent to all committee members. Although he acknowledged that he should have discussed the term Homodysphilia with the committee, he claimed that they had talked about the limitations of the old term. Spitzer asserted that "the committee was aware of the lack of specificity in the term Sexual Orientation Disorder, which could equally apply to other disorders involving sexual arousal such as fetishism and pedophilia" in addition to distress over homosexual arousal patterns. Spitzer complained that he was continually asked why a better term could not be found "for the category of homosexuals in distress about their sexual arousal" and explained that in response he had coined the term Homodysphilia, which had "met with much humor but real acceptance." Spitzer pointed out that although his term was a neologism, it was no more so than Sexual Orientation Disorder.[43]

Although Spitzer rejected their complaints, Green and his allies continued to protest against the proposed revisions.[44] Green and Richard Pillard, a leader of the Gay, Lesbian and Bisexual Caucus, wrote to a number of leading psychiatrists. Judd Marmor protested directly to Spitzer. George Winokur, a member of the Advisory Committee on Sexual Activities, was against Spitzer's proposal but did not want to get involved in a controversy. He suggested, "No new words without new data." Warned Winokur, "The creation of new words leaves us open to the epithet 'clown.'"[45]

Green did not believe that the dispute was just a quibble over words and decided to take matters into his own hands by polling advisory committee members. He did not ask respondents to vote for or against Spitzer's proposal. Instead, he asked committee members to rank the following alternatives:

1. Eliminate the category of Sexual Orientation Disorder and instruct manual users to choose one of the catchall categories—Other Gender Disorder of Adult Life or Psychosexual Disorder Not Otherwise Classified—as a diagnosis for homosexuals who are distressed about their condition
2. Eliminate Sexual Orientation Disorder entirely and identify the kind of distress the homosexual patient feels as the disorder. Thus, if the patient's primary mental state is depression, that would be the diagnosis, and the notation would be added that the selected diagnosis is "secondary to discomfort over homosexual (or same sex) sexual arousal pattern"
3. Retain Sexual Orientation Disorder or Dyshomophilia among the paraphilias, the overall category for sexual perversions
4. Retain Sexual Orientation Disorder but include two subtypes: homosexual and heterosexual

Green's wording made both Sexual Orientation Disorder and Dyshomophilia appear to be distasteful terms that deserved to be eliminated.

Spitzer, temporarily outmaneuvered, hastened to inform members of the Advisory Committee on Sexual Disorders that Green's four choices did not reflect the current thinking of the "authors of the Dyshomophilia category description."[46] He asked the committee members to indicate whether they agreed or disagreed with a proposal that represented the authors' (meaning Spitzer's) current thinking. His proposal was to include Dyshomophilia but to move it from the section listing the paraphilias (i.e., recurrent, intense, sexually arousing fantasies, sexual urges, or behaviors) to another section describing psychosexual disorders. He characterized his position as a compromise, rather than as one side of a debate: "It is true, as some have suggested, that the concept of dyshomophilia takes a middle position regarding the pathological status of homosexuality, even though the text states that homosexuality per se is not regarded in DSM-III as a mental disorder." Spitzer stated the justification for his view: "I believe that in our current state of ignorance this is a scientifically defensible position." He appealed to the committee to reject politics, and he redefined the dispute as a conflict over the removal of dyshomophilia rather than the addition of it to the manual. "I believe that if we removed dyshomophilia from DSM-III we could be justifiably accused of responding to political pressure." He reminded the committee of their professional, clinical commitment: "There is little doubt that the clinical description of dyshomophilia is a real clinical entity and that relatively specific treatment programs are designed for this condition (including gay counseling services)." He ended with a mild threat: "If the majority of members of the Psychosexual Advisory Committee do not support this view, the matter will then be brought to the Task Force on Nomenclature," where all of the disputants would be allowed to present their views. The implication was that opposition would be futile and would simply undercut the authority of the advisory committee. (In a memo to the Advisory Committee on Sexual Disorders dated July 8, 1977, Spitzer suddenly began referring to it as the Psychosexual Advisory Committee.)

It seemed like a no-lose political maneuver, but Spitzer was unable to obtain the mandate he sought. He had, however, managed to reframe the debate and to prevent Green from obtaining the support he sought. Subsequently, he informed Green, "I am pursuing each of the members [of the advisory committee] to collect their view on the Dyshomophilia issue. From the results so far, it appears that neither side is likely to have a clear majority, and therefore almost certainly the issue will go to the Task Force." Spitzer invited Green to prepare material for their review. He also told Green of "an extensive discussion" of the dyshomophilia issue with Judd Marmor and Lester Grinspoon, the chair of the Council on Research, which was the committee above the Task Force on Nomenclature and Statistics in the APA hierarchy. It is hard to know what was said at this meeting. Since there had been a bitter exchange of letters between Marmor and Spitzer during the previous summer, Spitzer's characterization of his communication with Marmor and Grinspoon may be an understatement. At any rate, Marmor and Spitzer were invited to a meeting of the Council on Research for a private airing of the conflict. The upshot of this meeting was that members of the Council on Research washed their hands of the matter. Shortly thereafter, the Assembly DSM-III Liaison Committee also decided that they did not want to become involved.

It seems that Spitzer gained the upper hand by maneuvering so that the issue would be resolved by the task force. If the Advisory Committee on Sexual Disorders did not agree with him, they would lose, since Spitzer appeared to control the task force. Before he went to the task force, Spitzer asked the advisory committee to consider a different name for the disputed disorder. Judd Marmor had suggested Distress about Homosexual Impulses, rather than Dyshomophilia. Marmor reasoned, "To create a new term which potentially lends itself to new generations of homosexual individuals being snidely referred to as "Dyshomophiliacs" is contrary to everything that we are all trying to accomplish. . . . The forthright diagnosis of a syndrome called "Distress over Homosexual Impulses" allows for no possible confusion and carries with it no possible derogatory implication.[47] Marmor's suggestion opened the door to the reintroduction of the word *homosexuality* into the title for the disputed diagnostic category. Spitzer told the advisory committee that he disagreed with Marmor's terminology but supported one committee member's suggestion to call the diagnosis Homosexual Conflict Disorder. Spitzer asked committee members to choose between the three terms.

After the advisory committee agreed with his latest recommendation for a new name, Spitzer turned his attention to obtaining approval from the task force. He informed them that the Advisory Committee on Psychosexual Disorders was unable to reach a consensus about a diagnostic category for homosexuals in conflict over their sexual arousal patterns. He explained that Green "does not accept the majority decision of the Advisory Committee and wishes to take the matter to the Task Force and if necessary even to the Assembly of the APA," and announced, warning the task force, "I believe it is very important that we pay a great deal of attention to the procedural issues involved in settling this dispute." He enclosed information provided by various participants in the conflict and ended his memo by asking task force members to choose among the following options:

1. The majority position of the Advisory Committee on Psychosexual Disorders is sustained; i.e., Homosexual Conflict Disorder appears in the classification immediately prior to Other Psychosexual Disorders. Suggestions for possible changes in the . . . text for this condition should be enclosed.
2. The minority position of the Advisory Committee . . . is sustained; that is, a reference to this condition should be one of the examples noted in Other Psychosexual Disorders.
3. The Task Force should meet with some of the participants in this controversy so that further discussion may clarify some of the issues.
4. Other.

The pattern is familiar by now. Spitzer must have been aware that the wording of his questionnaire would influence the results. Predictably, his position was identified as the majority position, and the task force endorsed it. Other options were not included for the task force to consider, such as retaining the existing title for the disorder or adopting another, less pejorative, term.[48]

The yearlong debate was now over but not before another title, Ego-dystonic Homosexuality (EDH), was adopted and some changes were made to satisfy hesitant members of the task force. Green objected: "I cannot accept the logic of ego dystonic homosexuality. To begin with, I'm not sure where the 'ego' is. Many psychiatrists, particularly behaviorists, may wonder about this as well."[49] The use of the concept of the ego, which is at the heart of Freudian psychology, was inconsistent with Spitzer's overall effort to expunge psychoanalytic influences from DSM-III. It is ironic that Spitzer accepted this term at the same time that he was in the midst of a furious debate with psychoanalysts.

Despite their threat to appeal the decision, Green and his allies did not press their campaign any further. Members of the Gay, Lesbian and Bisexual Caucus of the APA had actually expressed dissatisfaction with Spitzer's approach to the diagnosis of homosexuality as early as 1975, and they had threatened to take militant action.[50] Although they were aware of the outcome of the debate, they did not appeal the matter.

Among the gay activists' reasons for dropping the matter was their awareness of the increasingly conservative mood in the country and of an upsurge of homophobia at the same time as the 1977 DSM conflict over homosexuality. This was the year Anita Bryant headed a nationally publicized referendum campaign in Miami to repeal legislation to protect gay rights. There was a feeling that the same backlash was occurring within the APA. An article in *Time* titled "Sick Again?" reported the results of several polls that indicated that many psychiatrists were having second thoughts about the pathology of homosexuality.[51]

On the other hand, there was still a commitment in the APA to fight the classification of gays as mentally disturbed. During the same time as the DSM-III dispute, the APA took public stands that were sympathetic toward gays. In 1977 the APA president, Jack Weinberg, protested against the refusal of the United States government to naturalize homosexuals. Weinberg argued that the deletion of homosexuality from the DSM necessitated a revision in immigration laws that excluded gays.[52]

Apprehensive about erosion of their achievements within the APA, gay activists decided not to fight against the task force decision, particularly since the general public was almost completely unaware of the most recent revision. A member of the DSM-III Task Force who acted as liaison to the gay community, communicated his reservations:

> I personally feel that it would be destructive both to the gay rights movement and to psychiatry for this issue to be publicly debated and voted on at this time. I think that the general public views official psychiatry as having decided that homosexuality per se is not a mental illness, and the risks of losing what the press would describe as a debate regarding homosexuality should forestall anyone from carrying this debate beyond the Task Force to the Assembly . . . or the APA general membership.[53]

Others who had opposed Spitzer were also unwilling to proceed. Judd Marmor, the most powerful person among the opponents, signaled his reluctant acquiescence: "I think that the discussion of the draft is a reasonable one and I personally would accept it even though I would have preferred no separate category at all for homosexuality."[54]

What was gained by the debate? Homosexuality was back in the manual. (However, it was dropped quietly in 1987, when gay activists and their allies threatened to reopen the subject during a very embarrassing controversy between Spitzer and a group of feminists over new diagnostic categories that offended them. By then the gay activists had learned to use the internal politics of the APA to their advantage, but in 1977 things looked different.) Spitzer, who seemed to have an endless amount of energy to engage in battle over the diagnosis of homosexuality and to simultaneously participate in many other bruising fights as well, was the undisputed master of the process. He had his way, and he avoided a public political controversy. For Spitzer, this was a triumph of science over politics, even though there was no discussion of data, and his victory involved endless maneuvering and compromising. In a special sense, politics had been avoided, since the controversy remained within the domain of the committees that decided "scientific issues" and had not been the subject of public protests, as the hierarchy of the APA had feared.

When DSM-III was published, it contained a lengthy description of Ego-dystonic Homosexuality that began as follows:

302.00 Ego Dystonic Homosexuality. The essential features are a desire to acquire or increase heterosexual arousal, so that heterosexual relationship can be initiated or maintained, and a sustained pattern of overt homosexual arousal that the individual explicitly states has been unwanted and a persistent source of distress.

This category is reserved for those homosexuals for whom changing sexual orientations is a persistent concern.

To qualify for a diagnosis a patient had to meet the following criteria:

A. The individual complains that heterosexual arousal is persistently absent or weak and significantly interferes with initiating or maintaining wanted heterosexual relationships

B. There is a sustained pattern of homosexual arousal that the individual explicitly states has been unwanted and a persistent source of distress.[55]

NOT WITH A BANG: DSM-III-R AND THE END OF HOMOSEXUALITY

From the time Ego-dystonic Homosexuality was first included in DSM (in 1980) until it was dropped in 1987, it attracted very little attention. Even when EDH was finally dropped, there was no fanfare. The official explanation offered by the APA was an unrevealing paragraph in DSM-III-R:[56]

This category has been eliminated for several reasons. It suggested to some that homosexuality itself was considered a disorder. In the United States almost all people who are homosexual first go through a phase in which their homosexuality is ego-dystonic. Furthermore, the diagnosis of Ego-dystonic Homosexuality has rarely been used clinically and there have been only a few articles in the scientific literature that use the concept. Finally, the treatment programs that attempt to help bisexual men become heterosexual have not used this diagnosis. In DSM-III-R, an example of Sexual Disorder NOS are cases that in DSM-III would have met the criteria for Ego-dystonic Homosexuality.

Bayer offered a more complete description of the demise of EDH, but he did not adequately explain what transpired. He wrote, "Surprisingly the first challenge came not from organizational representatives of gay and lesbian psychiatrists, but from the chair of the Committee on Lesbian and Gay Concerns of the American Psychological Association, Alan K. Maylon."[57] At first blush, it may seem surprising that the initiative came from outside the psychiatric profession, but reform efforts to depathologize diagnoses, especially those that involve issues of sex or gender, almost always come from outside organized psychiatry. Few reforms of any kind come from within a profession (even though there may be many powerful and sympathetic insiders) unless they involve struggles for power.

Because of the existence of two officially sanctioned groups representing gay interests within psychiatry, this inactivity may seem surprising. "Either because of timidity or because of an inadequate appreciation of the internal functioning of the DSM-III review process," Bayer wrote, "neither the [American Psychiatric Association's] Committee on Gay, Lesbian and Bisexual Issues nor the Association of Gay and Lesbian Psychiatrists pressed to have the issue of 'ego-dystonic homosexuality' placed on the agenda."[58] Neither timidity nor inadequate understanding of the DSM review process explains the reticence of the psychiatric insiders on this issue. They knew more about the review process than the outsiders who finally initiated action, and they had not been timid about promoting their professional interests. Their initial inactivity is better accounted for by their structural position within organized psychiatry.

In the fall of 1985, Maylon, a psychologist, seized the opportunity offered by the row between Spitzer and feminists who opposed his attempt to incorporate three new diagnoses—Masochistic Personality Disorder, Paraphilic Rapism, and Premenstrual Dysphoric Disorder—into DSM-III-

R, the forthcoming revision of the manual.[59] The adverse publicity over these diagnostic proposals threatened to undermine the respectability that psychiatric diagnosis had gained with the publication of DSM-III. Once more, psychiatrists were being ridiculed for their insensitivity to women and for abandoning scientific procedures in their haste to invent new diagnoses.[60] The last thing the American Psychiatric Association wanted was to widen the controversy, especially if it included the subject of homosexuality, which had been a source of so much derision for the association in the past. Furthermore, since the general public believed that the issue of the normalcy of homosexuality had been settled, it was feared that a new highly publicized dispute over the diagnosis of homosexuality would cause confusion for all, not to mention embarrassment for the APA.

On the other hand, the public attitude toward homosexuality was not as tolerant as it had been in the early seventies. The AIDS epidemic was a new source of antipathy, one that no one could have imagined at the time of the 1974 debate over homosexuality. Given the growing antagonism toward the gay community, one might wonder why the APA, always sensitive to public opinion, responded to pressure to liberalize its position toward gays by dropping Ego-dystonic Homosexuality. It is necessary to recognize that the issue was not how the public felt about AIDS or homosexuality but about the public's faith in psychiatric diagnosis. A highly publicized fight over EDH would certainly have done damage, irrespective of the final outcome.

The same factors that led to the adoption of EDH in 1980 also led to its deletion in 1987. Before the publication of DSM-III in 1980, gay activists decided against a battle to oppose EDH, because they were afraid that they might lose and that the publicity would undermine the public perception that homosexuality was no longer a psychiatric disorder. Prior to the publication of DSM-III-R in 1987, the APA decided against a battle to retain EDH in order to avoid more adverse publicity than it was already receiving as a result of encounters with feminists.[61] Furthermore, EDH had little intrinsic value for practitioners or researchers.

Maylon's attack was embarrassing because he used Spitzer's own arguments for the adoption of Ego-dystonic Homosexuality. In 1981, Spitzer had restated his opinion that EDH was a compromise that was justified, declaring that "the concept of disorder always involves a value judgment."[62] Using this statement to his advantage, Maylon asserted that the recognition of EDH was a political decision and not a scientific finding. According to Bayer, "In making the argument, the opponents of ego-dystonic homosexuality thereby sought to seize the professional high ground by defending the norms of science in psychiatry against what they characterized as the value-laden efforts of Spitzer and his supporters."[63]

Once protesters outside of psychiatry decided to make a stand, they were joined by gay psychiatrists, and no organized constituency within the profession supported EDH. Spitzer put up a fight, and initially he seemed to be winning. The first opportunity the gay protesters were given to make their case was a hearing in December 1985 before an Ad Hoc Committee of the Board of Trustees and the Assembly of District Branches, the two principal governing bodies of the APA. The main reason for this meeting was to review the objections of feminist protesters to the three proposed diagnoses that were troubling them. Less than an hour was spent on the status of Ego-dystonic Homosexuality; most of the meeting was taken up with the other diagnoses. Committee members seemed sympathetic to the gay representatives, but they initially decided to retain EDH in the manual. Although Spitzer had his way about EDH, the committee members gave him less support in regard to the other diagnoses; they decided to include them in a special appendix. Members of the ad hoc committee may have believed they made a judicious compromise by assigning the diagnoses that feminists opposed to an appendix, but the public's response was not favorable. Derisive reports about the meeting and the APA's encounters with feminists appeared in major news publications, although EDH was not mentioned. Both feminists and gay groups continued to press their demands for the elimination of the disputed diagnoses.

After the December meeting, Spitzer wrote a condescending letter to those who wanted to drop EDH, a letter in which he attempted to justify why he had opposed their protests.[64] He explained why his committee had not thoroughly reviewed Ego-dystonic Homosexuality. He claimed that, first of all, such a review would have required time-consuming meetings with critics as well as proponents of EDH and was unnecessary. Spitzer wrote, "The issues that you [critics] have raised are well known, so it would be unlikely that the members of our Advisory Committee would change their position on this matter, even after extensive discussion. (Of the nine members of the Committee, seven are strongly opposed to dropping the category.)" Spitzer's second reason was that since a chapter on EDH was scheduled for a forthcoming volume by the APA's Task Force on the Treatment of Mental Disorders, it would be inconsistent to eliminate the diagnosis from DSM.[65] He complained that the protest was initiated too late in the review process and that it would be more satisfactory to consider the issue during the next revision of DSM. Finally, waving a red flag, Spitzer reminded the protesters that the concept of Ego-dystonic Homosexuality was a compromise between those who wanted homosexuality itself classified as a diagnosis and the protesters, who wanted it to be understood as a normal variant of sexual behavior.[66]

The justifications offered for EDH became more contradictory and less convincing as the debate continued. In the 1970s debate over homosexuality, the arguments offered by the psychoanalytic proponents of homosexuality as psychopathology were often based on flimsy scientific evidence and on Victorian moral assumptions that were embarrassing to the American Psychiatric Association. Under those circumstances, Spitzer's middle position seemed like a face-saving compromise. In 1987, Spitzer was no longer in the middle, and his assertions were denounced as value judgments that lacked scientific support. Although the decision of the ad hoc committee was discouraging to many gay protesters, the comments by Spitzer increased the level of opposition among psychiatrists who were gay. A past president of the Association of Gay and Lesbian Psychiatrists complained that Spitzer's letter was "an embarrassment to the profession."[67] Other statements made by Spitzer were seized upon by protesters to support their conclusion that EDH was unscientific.

Partly because of the mounting opposition, the APA convened an ad hoc group to reconsider EDH. The result of the meeting was that the APA decided to drop the diagnosis. According to Bayer, Spitzer realized that sentiment had shifted, and he simply capitulated. Little more has been said about this sudden reversal. An interesting postmortem appears in Bayer's *Homosexuality and American Psychiatry:*

> What is remarkable about this final curtain is the silence with which it fell. None of those who had been described as unalterably opposed to deletion seemed to care very much in the end. It was as if the struggle over words— diagnostic labels—ultimately did not matter to them, since in the "unofficial" world of clinical practice the existence of a clinical label was viewed as

of secondary importance. The virtual silence of the psychoanalytic community could well have reflected a similar conclusion.[68]

HOMOSEXUALITY IN DSM-IV AND BEYOND:
THE DIAGNOSIS THAT DARE NOT SPEAK ITS NAME

What about psychiatrists who still want a diagnosis for patients who
come to see them for treatment of homosexuality? The whole matter is
now handled in a rather obscure manner. It is difficult to identify the
oblique reference to homosexuality in the current edition of DSM, but for
someone who is complaining about a problem of unwanted homosexuality there is still a diagnosis:

> **302.9 Sexual Disorder Not Otherwise Specified. This category is in-
> cluded for coding a sexual disturbance that does not meet the criteria
> for any specific Sexual Disorder and is neither a Sexual Dysfunction nor
> a Paraphilia. Examples include . . . (3) Persistent and marked distress
> about sexual orientation.**[69]

With the deletion of EDH from DSM, psychiatrists have seemingly
agreed not to call their clients homosexuals, although they have indirect
ways of identifying homosexuality. It will come as no surprise that psychiatrists are still deeply involved in efforts to diagnose homosexuals
(although, at least for the time being, without the aid of DSM). At present there are two noteworthy trends that may lead to the relabeling of
homosexuals as mentally ill, and many of the participants in the earlier
struggles have triggered some of the most recent activity. Both psychoanalysts who fought to retain the diagnosis of homosexuality and some
of the psychiatrists who worked to eliminate it are deeply involved in efforts to identify factors that produce homosexuality. In turn, these efforts may lead inevitably to the reclassification of homosexuality as a
DSM diagnosis.

WHO IS IN THE CLOSET NOW? NARTH

The political landscape of mental health organizations has changed dramatically in regard to issues concerning gays and lesbians since the declassification of homosexuality. The secret Gay Psychiatric Association has
been replaced by groups such as the very public Association of Gay and

Lesbian Psychiatrists and the American Psychiatric Association's official Committee on Gay, Lesbian and Bisexual Issues. Other mental health organizations have also institutionalized the interests of gays, lesbians, and their allies; an example is the American Psychological Association's Committee on Lesbian and Gay Concerns. All of these groups were active in the final campaign to eliminate Ego-dystonic Homosexuality from DSM.

The influence of gay psychiatrists is growing throughout the world. In 1996, at its 10th world congress in Madrid, the World Psychiatric Association (WPA) held a symposium called Perspectives on Affirmative Gay Psychiatry, its first-ever scientific panel devoted to the unique aspects of being a gay or lesbian psychiatrist treating gay or lesbian patients. The symposium discussant was Melvin Sabshin, the chief administrator of the American Psychiatric Association, who lavished praise on the panel. Among the topics discussed were issues of gay Asians, the impact of stigma on gay psychiatrists and patients in many countries, the role of the APA in fighting homophobia, and a survey of discrimination against gays in German psychoanalytic institutes. Informal gatherings at the world congress were also significant, as was true earlier, when gay psychiatrists began organizing activities at the American Psychiatric Association annual meetings. "In some cases this was the first chance gay psychiatrists had to meet other psychiatrists from their own country, as was the case with several psychiatrists from the host country, Spain," one organizer commented.[70]

The growing influence of gay and lesbian psychiatrists and patients suggests how far-reaching the impact of eliminating homosexuality from DSM has been. Therapists are coming out of the closet with a vengeance, their gay clients are benefiting from a more affirmative approach to treatment, and it is increasingly difficult to use psychiatry as a device to stigmatize gays and lesbians.

But new developments threaten this progress. Two contending factions in the field of mental health are deadlocked in a debate about the nature and causes of homosexuality; one faction stresses biological and genetic interpretations while the other offers a psychoanalytic explanation. The psychoanalytic faction has founded an organization called the National Association for Research and Treatment of Homosexuality (NARTH). Its president is Charles Socarides (another campaigner from the 1970s, Irving Bieber, was an active participant until his death not long ago). The organization was founded in 1992, and its meetings are synchronized with the annual conference of the International Psychoanalytic Association. NARTH offered the following information about a recent annual meeting in San Francisco:[71]

> We will be advertising the NARTH Conference as being held at the Marriot Hotel Downtown, which is the location of the International Psychoanalytic Association meeting being held at the same time. *This is not the actual location of the conference.* Only pre-registered attendees will know that the actual conference location is the Hyatt. There will be no walk-in participants accepted. We have registered at the Hyatt as the "National Association of Research and Therapy." The reason for this subterfuge is this: we hope to avoid any possible disruption from pro-gay picketers. While there may be no picketing at all, we thought we best take this relatively simple precaution.

This letter tells us more than it intends. It tells us that the reborn movement for psychoanalytic and other "reparative" treatments of homosexuality is in the closet; its leaders act very much like closeted gays did two decades ago.

The presidential address given by Socarides at this conference also reflected the theme of persecution and discrimination. It was a long account of a trip he made to England to accept an award and give a speech. Gay demonstrators had disrupted one meeting and had forced him to hide in a locked room for 40 minutes until order was restored. The following day another event was canceled, and his hosts reconvened at a restaurant for a private celebration. All of this was recounted with very good humor by an old warrior who obviously relished the confrontations. His audience of 70 or 80, who laughed with him, was composed of psychiatrists, other therapists, and religious officials. The Reverend Louis Sheldon of the Traditional Values Coalition worked the crowd, shaking hands with newcomers and assuring them, "We're so glad you could join us."[72] The presentations mixed conventional scholarship with revival-type stories by redeemed former homosexuals and right-wing attacks that linked homosexuality with communism, pornography, pederasty, sadism, and a long list of other evils. Among the presenters was Jeffrey Satinover, who had educated Republican senators about erotomania during the Hill–Thomas confrontation (see chapter 1). Since then, he has been prominent among those psychotherapists who champion analytic treatment for gays in an effort to encourage heterosexuality.

NARTH has been in existence for six years, and during that time it has battled gay advocates who try to prevent therapists from engaging in "reparative therapy" to transform "obligatory" homosexuals into hetero-sexuals. NARTH has successfully opposed those resolutions condemning the therapeutic treatment of homosexuality that have been considered by the American Psychiatric Association, the American Psychoanalytic Associ-ation, the AMA, and other professional organizations. NARTH claims, as gay activists once did, that it represents the hidden sentiments of a great many therapists and patients and that it is battling against entrenched spe-cial interests. When attempts are made to condemn their work, members of the organization invoke patient rights, in particular, the right to treat-ment.[73] In the current political climate, NARTH presents itself as a lonely advocacy group battling the establishment through its Committee on Aca-demic and Professional Intimidation and other channels.

Issues of diagnosis are an important concern for NARTH members. The 1973 struggle in the APA was a pivotal historic event for them, and it is mentioned frequently in their newsletter. They are also interested in current diagnostic changes. The full front page of a recent issue of their newsletter was devoted to a story with the headline PEDOPHILIA NOT AL-WAYS A DISORDER. The article includes the following:

> According to the new DSM-IV, a person is no longer a pedophile simply be-cause he molests children or fantasizes about molesting children. He is a pe-dophile ONLY if he feels bad or anxious about what he's doing, or if his pedophilia impairs him in an important area of functioning.
>
> Now a child molester must show "clinically significant distress" (Guilt or Anxiety) or be impaired in an important area of his life such as work or so-cial relationships. If he feels no guilt or anxiety, and is otherwise functioning reasonably well, a child molester would be violating the law, but he would not be psychologically disordered.[74]

In a sidebar that accompanies the article, Dr. Reuben Fine observes that "the only conclusion to be drawn is that the APA is in a state of serious moral and intellectual decline." NARTH is often concerned with the links between homosexuality and other sexual practices, such as pe-dophilia and sadomasochism. By showing close links between homosex-uality and sexual practices that are more objectionable to the general public, NARTH emphasizes pathology. This strategy is the opposite of the initial efforts of gay activists, who put forward examples of homosex-uals who led normal, successful lives and differed primarily in their sex-ual preferences.

Although they have maintained an interest in DSM, no significant effort was made by NARTH members to reintroduce homosexuality into the manual during the DSM-IV revision process. However, the existence of an active and vital organizational structure is a precursor to serious efforts to introduce, as well as to eliminate, diagnostic categories. In this respect, NARTH can be viewed as the beginning of an organized force that can renew the fight for a diagnosis of homosexuality. This once again parallels the conditions that preceded the fight against the diagnosis of homosexuality in the sixties and early seventies, when gay advocacy groups organized. As we have shown, organized and militant gay protests were necessary precursors to the campaign against the diagnosis of homosexuality. Conversely, in the current political climate, the emergence of a strong pressure group such as NARTH may be a catalyst for the resurrection of a diagnosis of homosexuality.

HOMOSEXUAL BIOLOGY AND HOMOSEXUAL GENES

Biological and genetic findings are more likely than efforts by organizations like NARTH to result in repathologizing homosexuality. Ironically, these reports come not from researchers who have been identified as homophobes but from supporters of gay interests, and prominent among them are gay psychiatrists.[75] Their work, if it proves to be successful, may provide an essential contribution to the medical identification of homosexuality.

Another irony—the whole subject seems to be a series of unending reversals—is that some of the psychiatrists spearheading the effort to prove that homosexuality is genetically predetermined were leaders of the earlier campaign to rid DSM of homosexuality. Richard Pillard has played a key role in the current controversy, just as he did during the 1974 campaign. Pillard was one of the first psychiatrists to publicly identify himself as gay, and he drafted resolutions to remove homosexuality from DSM (which were withdrawn to permit the adoption of Spitzer's compromise proposal). When Spitzer reintroduced Ego-dystonic Homosexuality into DSM several years later, Pillard was a leader of the opposition. In recent years Pillard has been conducting studies of twins, and he has coauthored research reports that offered the first evidence in the contemporary debate about the genetics of homosexuality. His work is still one of the most important contemporary investigations into the biology of ho-

mosexuality, along with contributions by Anton LeVay, a gay neu-
roanatomist, and Dean Hamer of the National Cancer Institute.

There is an intense debate raging about the validity of the evidence
that has been presented by these researchers. There are serious methodological issues, as well as many questions about the validity of conclusions that have been drawn from the limited data that have been
published. At best, the reports of the three researchers are preliminary.
They need to be replicated by others and augmented by more information about the biology and genetics of homosexuality before any firm conclusions can be accepted. Everyone on all sides of the debate concedes
that there is no satisfactory explanation at this time of the way that genetics or other biological factors contribute to the determination of sexual
orientation or gender identity.[76]

Long before the scientific issues are settled, the political fallout from
this controversy will be felt. In fact, the political issues surfaced immediately after publication of the initial reports of genetic sources of homosexuality. Here is the political argument in its most simplified form: If
homosexuality is biologically determined, and especially if it is genetically
programmed, homosexuals cannot be considered culpable for their activities. Since their sexual orientation is not a matter of choice, they should
not be subjected to discrimination any more than any racial, sexual, or
other biologically determined group. Therefore, gays ought to be able to
assert their constitutional rights against discrimination in employment,
housing, military service, and other aspects of daily life.

An extreme form of the argument is that homosexuality is the result of
a genetic abnormality, and that gays and lesbians are therefore protected
under the provisions of the Americans for Disability Act (ADA). This interpretation invites a question: What is the disability from which homosexuals suffer? There is none currently included in the DSM. If this
position prevails, the disorder requires a diagnosis.

The hypothesis that homosexuality is the result of a genetic abnormality has not been universally accepted, even in the gay community, although it seems to be gaining popularity. There is widespread, although
not unanimous, support for the theory that homosexuality is genetically
determined. For many gay men there is a sense that their subjective experience has been validated by recognition that their sexual preferences are
predetermined. A survey of gay and bisexual men reported in the *Advo-
cate,* a leading gay magazine, found that "even though science has not

documented the mechanism for the biological origins of homosexuality, nine out of ten men believe that they were born with their sexual orientation."[77] Repeatedly, gay men report that their earliest memories are that they felt different, that they were attracted to males, and that they were never interested in females. Initially, this subjective feeling was said to differentiate gay men from lesbians, who, it was claimed, often become aware of their sexual preferences later, during adolescence or midlife. More recently, many lesbians, especially younger ones, have challenged this distinction; they claim that they also have felt same-sex affinity from their earliest years.[78]

Even more controversial is the next step in this argument, namely, the belief that antipathy toward gays will be reduced once homosexuality is recognized as a predetermined biological characteristic. Even the scientists most supportive of biological determinism are divided on this point. "LeVay believes that biological evidence that homosexuality is innate might defuse opposition to it from religious conservatives." Hamer has characterized this hope as "extremely naive."[79]

There has been little evidence that the thinking of gay opponents will be changed by biological or genetic evidence. Some of the opponents simply reject the genetic explanation as unnatural.[80] Even if the biological evidence is accepted, this will not necessarily lead to an about-face by gay critics.[81] Recognition of biological determinism is a two-edged sword. It is quite possible that religious fundamentalists will see this biological difference as a mark of the devil and as justification for the persecution of unrepentant gay people.

The use of data about the immutability of sexual orientation to establish legal rights for homosexuals is even more controversial, but this has not deterred some gay spokesmen. As soon as reports of genetic links to homosexuality were released, Richard Green, another veteran of the DSM battles,[82] told newspapers that legal protections would increase "if we can demonstrate that sexual orientation is due to an inborn brain distinction."[83] The controversies that surround the research data and the possible negative fallout from this legal approach have not deterred advocates from using the research on genetics and biology of homosexuality, most prominently in *Romer v. Evans,* a challenge to an anti-gay-rights amendment to the Colorado constitution.[84] Green testified in the case, as did Hamer, and the Colorado courts held that the amendment was unconstitutional, a decision subsequently affirmed by the United States Supreme

Court. The case was not decided on the basis of biological or genetic findings, but these issues have been recognized in other cases. In a case in 1994, a district court judge declared that homosexuality is an "involuntary state of being."[85]

It is not surprising that scientific issues have been overshadowed by political considerations, but in the field of research about the biology and genetics of human behavior, preliminary findings have been accepted as conclusive evidence and used to decide policy with breathtaking speed. We have witnessed a rush to publicize new findings about the genetics of alcoholism, schizophrenia, and manic depression, many of which were later retracted. Despite the repeated renunciations of earlier reports and findings, the belief is growing that each of these mental disorders has been found to have a genetic source. The cumulative effect of these reports has been that they substantiate each other, at least in the popular literature. Although many have been retracted, the reports about the inheritability of mental disorders are the scaffolding for the current discussion of the biogenetics of homosexuality.

There are many similarities in the way attitudes about schizophrenia, alcoholism, manic depression, and homosexuality have evolved, but there is a significant difference in the debate over the genetics of homosexuality. In each of the other cases, there is an assumption that there is a mental disorder whose genetic roots may have been uncovered, but homosexuality appears to be the mental disorder that dares not speak its name. We do not want these observations to be interpreted as our belief that homosexuality is a mental disorder or that it should be a DSM diagnosis. Far from it: We do not believe homosexuality is a mental illness. The point we are making is that, in addition to the efforts made by many traditional psychoanalysts, the position taken by some gay psychiatrists and their supporters may increase the pressure to restore the diagnosis of homosexuality to DSM.

WHAT'S NEXT FOR DSM?

The new controversy about the genetics of homosexuality reopens the question of whether or not homosexuality is a disorder. This in turn will inevitably lead to the question, If homosexuality is a disorder, should it be restored to DSM? There is very little support in the APA for restoring homosexuality to DSM, but this can change quickly.[86] Although the reclassification of homosexuality does not seem to be a possibility at this time, storm clouds are gathering. Many of the institutional reforms attempted by gays have backfired, for example, the legalization of same-sex marriage and banning the persecution of gays in the military.[87]

The attitudes of mental health professionals about diagnosis and treatment are volatile.[88] The events described in this chapter indicate that a major shift involving the reclassification of homosexuality is quite possible. Because of the lack of a coherent definition of mental disorder, it has been easy to move homosexuality in and out of the American Psychiatric Association's diagnostic manual. The process of deciding on which diagnoses to adopt for the manual has become more and more elaborate—but not necessarily more scientific. The story of the declassification of homosexuality as a mental disorder shows that recognizing and classifying mental disorders is an elaborate process in which political considerations, personal interests, and economic pressures are major factors. Throughout the entire struggle over the inclusion or exclusion of homosexuality from DSM, the minor role played by scientific research has been striking. The decision to eliminate DSM had a major impact on psychiatry, and it has meant a great deal in terms of some of the major social issues of the day. But it was a political debate, not a scientific one. A decision to return the homosexuality diagnosis to the manual may be justified on the basis of new genetic research data, but it, too, will be based on political considerations far more than on the validity of scientific findings.

4 BRINGING THE WAR BACK
TO DSM

While DSM was undergoing radical revision in the 1970s, many consumers of mental health services intensified their interest in psychiatric diagnosis. Some wanted to prevent stigma by deleting invalid diagnostic categories, such as homosexuality. Other groups sought recognition for their suffering and saw DSM as a way to achieve their goal; however, it was no easier for outsiders to include a disorder in DSM than to delete one. Despite the obvious enthusiasm the APA displayed in fashioning new categories of mental disorders and the tremendous increase in diagnoses in the new manual, many proposals were rejected.

Nevertheless, some outsiders were able to persuade the APA to adopt a new diagnosis. Among the most successful were Vietnam veterans, who introduced a new term, Post-traumatic Stress Disorder (PTSD), into the manual. The story of the suffering they experienced is well known, but less is known about their political campaign to add PTSD to DSM-III. Their work has been described in detail by a sociologist, Wilbur Scott.[1]

The campaign was driven by the need to obtain concrete benefits for Vietnam veterans, who had received inhumane treatment at their homecoming. In recent years, a great deal of blame for the veterans' suffering has been attributed to criticism of the veterans by antiwar activists. But well-documented reports from veterans indicate that many of their psychiatric difficulties emanated from the brutal events they participated in during the war, the official cover-up of these horrors, and the unwillingness of government leaders and established veterans' groups to provide services for those who were suffering. It was precisely the same officials who had argued most vociferously for the need to support the war effort who were also slashing funds for psychiatric causalities of the war. The antiwar protesters, many of whom were Vietnam veterans who were horrified by what had occurred on the battleground, fought to make public the traumatic experiences of Vietnam and to expose the official denials of these events. Part of this struggle involved a campaign to include PTSD in DSM-III.

THE MADNESS OF WAR

In order to understand the struggle for official recognition of PTSD, it is useful to know how the psychological impact of combat was interpreted in previous wars. Since the beginning of recorded history, soldiers have suffered severe disabilities that were not the result of physical injury. Herodotus described an Athenian soldier who lost his sight when the man next to him was killed in 490 B.C. at the Battle of Marathon, even though the blinded warrior "was wounded on no part of his body."[2] Blindness, deafness, paralysis, and even death without physical injury have been reported over and over again during wars. In the 18th century there was a great deal of concern about men who abruptly died on the battlefield without any wounds. One theory of the time was that the wind of the cannon balls led to undetectable internal injuries that were responsible for the mysterious deaths.

Soldiers reported other disabilities that had no somatic component. Uncontrollable fear often rendered troops unfit to fight. Physicians were often asked to treat soldiers' psychological problems, and it is not surprising that they created diagnoses for them.

> Swiss physicians in 1678 were among the first to identify and name that constellation of behaviors that make up acute combat reaction or PTSD. Nostalgia was the term they used to define a condition characterized by melancholy, incessant thinking of home, disturbed sleep or insomnia, weakness, loss of appetite, anxiety, cardiac palpitations, stupor and fever.[3]

Similar diagnoses were formulated by physicians in other countries. The

Germans called it *heimweh* or homesickness, the French described it as *maladie du pays,* and the Spanish referred to it as *estar roto* ("to be broken").

In America, psychiatrists have always had an important role in our wars (see Table 4-1). Benjamin Rush, the father of American psychiatry, whose bust appears on every letter, book, and communication from the American Psychiatric Association, was surgeon general of the Continental Army during the American Revolution. But the first organized response to psychological difficulties of combatants occurred during the Civil War. As a result of new weapons—improved repeating rifles, Gatling guns, and artillery that allowed airbursts—the strategy of war changed and the emotional impact on fighting men intensified. The problem was so widespread that military commanders and doctors pleaded for a system to screen out recruits susceptible to psychological breakdowns.

There was no Civil War policy concerning psychological casualties. At first, physicians simply mustered out recruits who broke down on the battlefield. "They were put on trains with no supervision, the name of their home town or state pinned to their tunics, others were left to wander about the countryside until they died from exposure or starvation."[4] As a result of public reaction to this tragedy, the first military hospital for

TABLE 4-1

WAR-RELATED MENTAL DISORDERS OF U.S.
MILITARY PERSONNEL

	War	Mental Disorder
1.	Civil War	Nostalgia
2.	World War I	Shell shock
3.	World War II	Battle fatigue
4.	Korean War	Brainwashing
5.	Vietnam War	Post-traumatic stress disorder
6.	Gulf War	Gulf War syndrome[a]

[a]Unlike Vietnam veterans, Gulf War campaigners do not want their suffering to be interpreted as a mental illness and have argued that Gulf War syndrome is a physiological condition, possibly the result of exposure to toxic chemicals.

Adapted from K, Hyams, F.S. Wignall, and R. Roswell, "War Syndromes and Their Evaluation: From the U.S. Civil War to the Persian Gulf War," *Annals of Internal Medicine* 125 (5) (1996):402.

the insane was opened in 1863, and the most common diagnosis of its inmates was "nostalgia." Despite the medical diagnosis, military physicians continued to attribute the condition to malingering. The hospital closed after the war, and there was no subsequent organized effort to deal with psychiatric casualties. Many wound up in the soldiers' homes that were opened around the country. The administrator of one home reported that he was puzzled by an increase in the need for his hospital's services over time; on the basis of his assumption that psychological disturbances were a result of combat pressure and were caused by a desire to avoid battle, he had expected them to disappear, not to increase, once the war was over.

In the 1905 war with the Japanese, the Russian army was the first to claim that the psychological breakdown of combat soldiers is a legitimate medical condition that requires treatment. Their approach, which was to treat psychiatric casualties close to the front in order to return them to combat, has been accepted as the basis for psychiatric intervention by most modern armies, even though their success rate was less than 20 percent. This strategy of forward treatment, based on the principle of proximity, has been forgotten and then rediscovered repeatedly by military psychiatrists since that time.

In World War I prolonged artillery bombardment of troops pinned down in the trenches was relieved only by suicidal assaults that resulted in staggering casualties. Like the soldiers of past wars, many of the disabled troops who had no observable physical injuries suffered from somatic symptoms ranging from paralysis, blindness, and deafness to twitching and cramps. Emotional reactions (including phobias), severe anxiety, and depression were common. These somatic and emotional conditions were identified as "shell shock."

German and Austro-Hungarian physicians originally believed shell shock to be the result of an organic impairment of the nervous system.[5] Since the physicians could not treat these organic injuries, shell-shocked soldiers were usually sent to the hospitals in the rear. Theories changed as troop casualties depleted the fighting forces, and the Central Power physicians began to interpret symptoms as a malady of the will or as an unconscious attempt to escape from duty into illness. This was sometimes described as a "neurosis of defense." Underlying this diagnosis was a pervasive assumption that these psychological casualties were malingerers who produced symptoms in order to receive pension payments ("greed neurosis" or "pension struggle hysteria") or to avoid combat. For a period of time during the war, Central Power physicians used electroshock treatment as a remedy, thus creating a more fearful alternative to returning to the trenches. They also used isolation and permanent baths to encourage submission. Brunner reports that "war psychiatrists not only took it upon themselves to strengthen the will of neurotic soldiers and restore them to battle fitness, but also to guard the state from the daunting financial burden of pension payments and compensation after the war.[6]

The German Psychiatric Association announced that its one mission was "to serve our army and the fatherland."[7] Members of the Viennese Psychiatric Association expressed a similar commitment, namely, that their "cardinal point of view ought not to be determined by the individual case, but by the welfare of . . . [their] so closely allied armies." Even Sigmund Freud was initially thrilled by the participation of his country in the war. When the Austro-Hungarian armies were unable to achieve any victories, he confided to a colleague, Karl Abraham, that he lived "from one German victory to the next."[8] He publicly criticized partisanship of scientists, but privately he dismissed his statements as "topical chit-chat." It was only in the later stages of the war, when defeat of his country and their allies seemed imminent, that Freud became pessimistic and declared that war was a disaster. Many of Freud's followers were less facetious and more openly partisan; they enlisted in the armed service and participated in military efforts to treat "war neurosis." Officials from Germany and Austro-Hungary attended and contributed financial support to the Fifth Psychoanalytic Congress in 1918. They were interested in how psychoanalysis could improve the treatment of emotionally disabled soldiers. Many of Freud's followers believed that "a great moment had come for psychoanalysis."[9]

American psychiatrists also committed themselves to restoring their troops to combat. They, too, abandoned the theory that shell shock was a physiological condition. Under the leadership of Thomas Salmon, who later became president of the American Psychiatric Association, psychiatrists were posted with each army division. The objective was to treat "war neuroses" as quickly as possible near the front lines. Treatment consisted of a few days of rest and relaxation, with the expectation that soldiers would resume combat. American psychiatrists claimed great success by returning 65 percent of their patients to duty.[10]

By the start of World War II, the Salmon doctrine was forgotten, a curious case of official amnesia. The initial response to psychological problems was to use psychiatrists to screen out those recruits who were considered emotionally unfit for service; more than 1 million draftees were rejected.[11] Despite these careful screening procedures, the rate of psychiatric casualties during combat remained high; psychiatrists were unable to predict who would become psychologically disabled in combat. One reason for the problem was that the program had a partially hidden agenda: to screen out homosexuals from the military.[12] This lead to the disqualification of a large number of recruits, without regard to their actual qualifications for combat. These two factors—the rejection of a large number of draftees and high rates of psychological casualties on the front lines—combined to produce a manpower crisis. Midway through the war, military commanders found they were unable to maintain troop levels, and this led to a reformulation of psychiatric ideas about treatment.

World War II was fought in a different manner than World War I. It was a fast-moving war in which trench warfare played a small role. Although there were reports that some troops suffered from shell shock, a new problem (or a new name for an old problem)—combat fatigue—began to be of greater concern to military commanders and psychiatrists. In 1944, the army reinstituted the Salmon doctrine, which states that combat exhaustion is a temporary reaction to battlefield stress. The intervention followed from the diagnosis; battle fatigue was considered a transient condition that could be cured by sleep and a hot meal. Army psychiatry was reorganized to move support services close to the front, and psychiatrists were discouraged from sending soldiers to hospitals in the rear. The theory was that the further away soldiers were sent from the front lines and the more they penetrated into the treatment system, the more they deteriorated. It seemed to make perfect sense, and it slowed the attrition of combat troops. The famous World War II novel *Catch-22* parodies the thinking behind the Salmon doctrine: those who asked to be relieved from combat were obviously sane whereas only those who did not think they were crazy were suspect. That is, the war neurosis called combat fatigue was a normal condition, and those who denied that they suffered from this condition were abnormal.

The experience of World War II was forgotten (another outbreak of amnesia) by the time the Korean War broke out several years later. At the beginning of the war, psychiatric casualties were evacuated to a large facility in Japan. When troop losses became too high, psychiatrists reinstituted the Salmon program and once again reduced the number of those relieved from combat because of emotional difficulties.[13]

The Salmon doctrine was firmly in place when the American military buildup began in Vietnam. In the early years of the war, the official rate of breakdown was 5 per 1,000, one-fifth of what it was in the Korean War even after the Salmon doctrine was adopted. The usual explanation for this transformation is that the reorganization of military psychiatry resulted from new discoveries about psychiatric diagnosis and treatment, but critics claim that diagnoses were reformulated to meet the demands of the military.[14] It may be that recognition of the minor and temporary nature of many psychiatric combat problems led to an understanding of the need to treat combat fatigue promptly and to discourage soldiers from assuming the sick role. A better explanation is that military policy makers encouraged psychiatrists in the service to downplay the severity of the problems from which soldiers suffered, especially when psychiatric casualties exceeded the conscription of replacements.

As early as World War II, prominent psychiatrists with military experience reported that often the symptoms of combat fatigue were not temporary and that they sometimes persisted for months or years.[15] The delayed reaction to combat that some soldiers experience was also observed. Despite these reports, military psychiatry was organized in a manner that emphasized the temporary nature of symptoms and disregarded the long-term psychological impact of combat.

Wherever the pressure came from, by the time of the Vietnam War the official goal of military psychiatry was to maintain the fighting force, and this was accomplished by diagnosing most psychiatric casualties as combat fatigue due to temporary, battle-related stress. The New York Times reported that "the rapid return to combat of those with battle fatigue, when it was used in the Vietnam War, made for a ratio of one psychiatric casualty for every four medical ones in that war, a rate that is considered low."[16] Psychiatrists who endorsed this approach ignored one of the basic axioms for dealing with traumatic events, an axiom widely accepted long before the Vietnam War: when the emotional impact of a traumatic event is denied or suppressed, the problems continue to fester and the disturbance reemerges sometime later, often in strange and unanticipated ways. The death of a loved one is one well-known illustration of this problem. When a survivor of this loss refuses to acknowledge the death or to allow adequate time to grieve, health problems and bizarre behavior often occur later. Survivors who immediately throw themselves back into work and daily routines are at great risk of later breakdowns. It is a tenet of mental health treatment that adequate time for grieving is necessary to prevent future difficulties.

Post–World War II military psychiatry ignored these principles of diagnosis and treatment. The result was that by the time of the Vietnam War, "depending on intensity of fighting experienced by soldiers and the morale of their unit, rates for post traumatic stress disorder among Vietnam veterans who saw combat was between 15 and 50 percent."[17] Among Vietnam veterans, the types of traumas that led to PTSD included witnessing or participating in atrocities, seeing grotesquely mutilated bodies, or going on particularly dangerous missions.[18] Those who were most likely to suffer from PTSD were those who suffered from battle fatigue, but military psychiatrists, far from identifying combat fatigue as an early warning, were involved in exactly the opposite strategy, namely, minimizing the seriousness of the complaints and pushing soldiers back into combat as quickly as possible.

VIETNAM VETS AND THE BATTLE OVER DSM

To compound the problem for Vietnam veterans, when DSM-II was published in 1968, in the middle of the Vietnam War, Gross Stress Reaction, the diagnosis for battle fatigue that had been included in the original DSM-I, had been deleted. The revised manual blanketed this category into a more general one entitled Adjustment Reaction of Adult Life. Although it was the transitory nature of combat fatigue that was implicit in the diagnosis of Gross Stress Reaction, even this pale acknowledgment of the psychological impact of war experience was diluted by the DSM-II revision. One explanation is that since the developers of DSM-II did not have wartime military experience, the profession collectively forgot the lessons of World War II—another case of professional amnesia. After the publication of DSM-II, there was no realistic way to use the manual to account for the trauma caused by wartime experiences or for the aftermath of these psychological injuries.

This pattern of denial continued after the Vietnam War. The Veterans Administration (VA) was unwilling to admit that the severe psychiatric problems beginning to flood the clinics and wards of their hospitals were principally the result of experiences in Vietnam. They argued instead that patients were suffering from long-term psychiatric disorders that induced delusional thinking about the war.[19]

The official denial of the impact of war on the emotional life of veterans was only changed as a result of organized political pressure by veterans' groups. The first steps in obtaining treatment and other benefits for psychiatric disabilities were to identify the disorder from which veterans suffered, to give it a name, and to have it included in DSM. The initial phase in this process was recognition among the veterans and the allies they formed in the mental health professions that patients who had seen combat were not delusional but were describing real events that caused their suffering. If they were having delusions, they could be diagnosed as psychotic, and their flashbacks and panic about the war could be dismissed as symptoms of preexisting disorders and not as behavior caused by the war.

One of the first professionals to recognize the problem was Sarah Haley, a social worker with the VA. On her first day on the job, just after graduation from a Boston school of social work in 1969, Haley interviewed a very disturbed veteran who reported that he had witnessed members of his unit kill large numbers of women and children at My Lai. The veteran had not participated in the slaughter, and afterward several members of his platoon threatened to kill him if he reported what happened. One soldier threatened that someday he would kill him anyway, to prevent him from talking.

The My Lai survivor came to the VA because he felt terrified and was unable to sleep. He complained that his wartime comrades were going to kill him, although he could offer no proof. Haley believed his story and prepared to discuss it at a staff meeting. Here is her report of the meeting:

> The staff assembled to discuss all the information and reach a diagnosis and treatment plan. When we met, the intake log already had a diagnosis filled in: paranoid schizophrenic. I voiced concern. The staff told me that the patient was obviously delusional, obviously in full-blown psychosis. I argued that there were no other signs of this if one took his story seriously. I was laughed out of the room. I was told that it was my first day and I just didn't understand how things worked. . . . I was aghast. These professionals denied the reality of combat. This [denial] clouded their clinical judgment. They were calling reality insanity![20]

Although the general policy of the VA was to dismiss the impact of the war on veterans' problems, Haley discovered that some other staff members also recognized the reality of war experiences:

> The three or four people in my clinic who were listing war neurosis . . . they would see as their job, their task, to talk with the person about what had happened in Vietnam. . . . Oh you lost this buddy, you lost that buddy and that happened. What do you think about it now? Oh, I see, you blame yourself. You think that if you had only [acted differently], this wouldn't have happened. I see. No wonder you feel so terrible. . . . The people who thought that these fantastic stories were . . . just indications of psychotic thought-processes would give them anti-psychotic medication . . . [or] they were seen as . . . character disorders. . . . This person must still be having symptoms because—it's not that combat is so bad—it's just that they're weak sisters.[21]

Soon after her first encounter with the My Lai survivor, Haley linked up with the local chapter of the Vietnam Veterans Against the War and began sending them information about sympathetic staffers and warning them to avoid the others.

Haley and the other subversive VA staff members were not alone in their effort to assist the Vietnam veterans. The veterans made contact with sympathetic psychiatrists and worked especially closely with two of them—Robert Jay Lifton and Chaim Shatan. Lifton was an antiwar activist who had done studies on the survivors of Hiroshima and on the Chinese brainwashing of American prisoners during the Korean War. Shatan, who was also opposed to the Vietnam War, was a psychoanalyst who had received training in combat disorders; he was concerned about the deletion of the combat-related diagnosis from DSM-II. The two were invited to join a rap group, an emerging form of self-help devised by the veterans. Lifton and Shatan did not conduct the group as professionals; they were invited to be participants, since they were familiar with emotional problems related to combat, experiences that troubled the veterans. The knowledge shared during these meetings, as well as the contacts that Lipton and Shatan made, were important in the ensuing campaign to incorporate PTSD in DSM-III.

Shatan, Lifton, and the veterans appeared on a panel that was attended by more than 800 people at the 1971 meeting of the American Orthopsychiatric Association (AOA). The meetings and journals of the AOA became vehicles for publicizing the problems of the veterans. At the 1972

AOA annual meeting, Shatan introduced the term Post-Vietnam Syndrome to describe the mental anguish that veterans were suffering. Shortly thereafter, he used the term in a *New York Times* article. The article triggered enormous interest, and requests for assistance poured in, both to him and to veterans' groups.

Lifton was also busy. He wrote *Home From the War,* which discussed the atrocities of war, detailed the story of the My Lai survivor, and criticized the relationship of American psychiatry to the military as an "unholy alliance that was a major impediment to postwar adjustment of troubled veterans."

During this period, Lifton, Shatan, and the veterans created a network of mental health professionals, ministers, university professors, and others; a conference in 1973 resulted in the formation of the National Veterans Support Network. When the organization applied for financial aid, it was rejected by many foundations. Jack Smith, the network's coordinator, described the problem: "The foundations were saying, well this is really a government problem. Why are you coming to us? And we were saying, because the government denies there is a problem."[22] In order to document the need for foundation support, the network organized an empirical study of the impact of military service and of the unmet needs of Vietnam veterans.

Other events soon overshadowed the plans of the network. Publicity over the battle about homosexuality after the APA announced its intention of revising DSM led to a tremendous influx of inquiries to the APA about other possible changes in the manual. When an attorney, preparing a defense of traumatic war neurosis, asked if the combat-related diagnosis of Gross Stress Reaction was going to be reinstated, Robert Spitzer replied that no change was planned. The information quickly filtered back to the veterans, who were surprised by the news and decided to intensify their political efforts, since consumer advocacy had proved to be decisive in the homosexuality controversy.[23]

THE MOBILIZATION

Two of the goals of the veterans' campaign were to create greater public awareness of the psychiatric problems of Vietnam veterans and to educate psychiatrists. One of their most successful events was an all-day radio marathon on a New York City radio station. They also increased the number of presentations they made to professional audiences.

Although they regularly made presentations at American Psychiatric

Association meetings, neither Shatan nor Lifton were insiders in the association. Then they formed an alliance with John Talbott, a future president of the APA and editor-in-chief of the organization's popular journal *Psychiatric Services*. Talbott had been psychiatrist in Vietnam and he had recommended the reintroduction of Gross Stress Reaction into DSM-III as early as 1969.[24] He had also become aware of the refusal of the VA to recognize cases of veterans suffering from postcombat stress reactions.[25]

Talbott arranged for Shatan, Lifton, and the veterans to give presentations at meetings of psychiatrists in New York and at the 1975 annual meeting of the American Psychiatric Association, where they were joined by Sarah Haley, who had published an article, "When the Patient Reports Atrocities," in the prestigious *Archives of General Psychiatry*. Arrangements were also made for this group to meet with Spitzer at the convention. Talbott expected that it would be difficult to convince Spitzer to include a new category that recognized postcombat stress. Talbott's assessment of the situation at the time of the meeting was as follows:

> [Spitzer] started out being a very data driven person. . . . If the data aren't there, the thing doesn't exist. The pressure groups began to rise and say, "Look, this should be in and this should be out." . . . And he would say, "There aren't any data!" . . . I think that he started out saying, we're going to throw DSM-II out the window, we're going to have zero-based budgeting, as it were. . . . And what he ended up doing was a two-part process, one, setting up task groups who were experts in the field, and two, subjecting it to a political process in the American Psychiatric [Association] that ensured that it would be adopted by them.[26]

Not only did those fighting for a postcombat stress diagnosis have to deal with Spitzer's hard-nosed attitude toward requests for changes, but they had a special problem in that Helzer and Robins, two important experts on psychiatric diagnosis who were very influential in the formulation of DSM-III, believed that no separate category was necessary to diagnose the psychiatric disturbances of military survivors of war trauma. Furthermore, they had "hard data" to support their position, unlike the veterans and their psychiatric allies, who could offer only a rapidly growing number of anecdotal accounts of the veterans' suffering. At the brief meeting with Shatan, Lifton, and their allies at the 1975 APA convention, Spitzer challenged them to disprove the Helzer and Robins findings.

Spitzer was confronted with an embarrassing divergence between the views of recognized professional authorities within the psychiatric establishment who subscribed to the same research ethos he did and the insistent demands of a special interest group, the veterans, who were rapidly gaining public sympathy. The problem was similar to the homosexuality struggle, and he used that earlier experience as a model to respond to the veterans' demands. Spitzer's task was to translate the political conflict into a scientific debate and to frame it in such a manner that the veterans could prevail. If they failed, the APA would once again appear to be foolish.

Spitzer's first step was to challenge the Vietnam veterans to participate in the scientific debate by producing convincing scientific arguments. The veterans accepted the challenge by creating a new structure called the Vietnam Veterans' Working Group (VVWG), which systematically gathered evidence to justify the inclusion of a postcombat disorder into the manual. The VVWG eventually obtained information on 700 veterans.

The VVWG held a follow-up meeting with Spitzer several months later and presented some of the evidence they had developed, particularly data on the similarities between the experiences of combat veterans and those of concentration camp survivors. As a result of their contacts with Holocaust researchers, the VVWG began to think about veterans' problems as a manifestation of the same psychological disorder as that experienced by survivors of various catastrophic traumas. By conceiving of the disorder in broader terms, VVWG members were able to strengthen their scientific argument by using the accumulated research about Holocaust survivors. Using the analytic process developed by the French sociologist Bruno Latour to explain how frequently occurring natural disturbances are defined as illnesses when a number of social groups become interested in them, one could say that the disease was gaining allies.[27]

Spitzer was not yet convinced by these new ideas, but he took the second step in transforming the political struggle into a scientific dispute. Although he made it clear that the veterans' group still had to prove their claims, he organized a DSM-III advisory committee that could introduce the new diagnosis into the manual. A favorable report from this committee was the first step in the long process of approval through the hierarchy of APA committees. The new body, the Committee on Reactive Disorders, consisted of three members of the DSM-III Task Force—Nancy Andreasen, Lyman Wynne, and Spitzer—as well as Shatan, Lifton, and Jack Smith, the only participant without a college degree among the scores of members of the DSM-III Task Force advisory committees.

No member of the Committee on Reactive Disorders opposed a special diagnostic category for combat-related mental problems. Representation of only one side of the debate in this critical decision-making body echoed the earlier exclusion of antigay psychiatric authorities from key meetings of APA groups that deliberated on the diagnosis of homosexuality. Although the decision-making process seemed to encourage a complete assessment and although Spitzer was tough on the veterans' groups, the actual process was managed in a manner that favored them.

The chair of the Reactive Disorders Committee, Andreasen (an influential insider) held the key to success.[28] Because she had done research on the psychiatric problems of burn victims, she was familiar with post-traumatic disturbances. Spitzer instructed her to work closely with the veterans' groups, and they devised a strategy to enlist her support. The veterans invited her to participate in a panel on combat disorders at a meeting of the American Orthopsychiatric Association.

In the months before the meeting, the VVWG made alliances with other specialists who dealt with victims of catastrophes. As VVWG members' concepts broadened, they were able to use the data from related areas and the support of scientists who did research in these fields; for instance, they found that survivors of industrial catastrophes often suffer from posttraumatic stress that is similar to that of war veterans. They also made alliances with researchers who studied workers' compensation claims.

At the Orthopsychiatric meeting, the VVWG participants presented case histories they had collected from their rap groups. Sarah Haley presented data she had surreptitiously gathered, data that seemed to be especially interesting to Andreasen. Haley described her participation as follows:

What I did was stay after work at the VA and, without anybody knowing it, I went through all of the records of Vietnam veterans who we had seen in a year. I looked at what their diagnoses were. What I looked at was the official, the DSM-II diagnosis—the official one that you had to put down in the record. But then in parentheses [for some] was a working diagnosis. The working diagnosis was usually "traumatic war neurosis." And so what I said was, "Look it, Nancy, we had to give these guys diagnosis [consistent with DSM-II], but if you look at what some clinicians are actually doing, they're basing their treatment on the fact that they recognize in these fellows similar traumatic war neuroses as they saw in the Second World War and Korean War Veterans." That really turned her around.[29]

It was not carefully designed scientific research that persuaded the hard-headed scientist Andreasen but evidence of actual clinic experience. Andreasen said that she had observed stress reactions among burn patients that were similar to the veterans' descriptions. By sharing their personal experiences with clinical problems, the veterans' group convinced Andreasen to become an ally.

The VVWG also refined a proposal for a new diagnostic category—Catastrophic Stress Disorder (CSD)—and presented it at the 1977 APA annual meeting. They proposed that a traumatic event be considered the only significant cause of CSD. The psychiatrists who opposed the proposal still maintained that the veterans' symptoms could be diagnosed by using existing diagnostic categories of depression, schizophrenia, and alcoholism, but the veterans now had stronger alliances within the APA, better access to the decision-making process, and a great deal of anecdotal evidence.

Nonetheless, the veterans' proposal violated basic guidelines about theory and research that had been established for DSM-III. Whereas those involved in the creation of the new manual were attempting to eliminate etiology from their description of disorders, the veterans' proposed diagnosis linked a specific cause, catastrophic trauma, to the disorder. Their proposal relied heavily on Freudian theory, especially the idea that repressed trauma results in neurotic symptoms. Neurosis was eliminated as an organizing category in DSM-III (and eventually the word itself was dropped from the manual), but the theoretical construct was embedded in CSD. Furthermore, the veterans' anecdotal evidence, although abundant, was not the kind of rigorous empirical data that Spitzer and his colleagues recognized as a prerequisite for any revision. In this respect, CSD fell short of the announced intentions of the developers of DSM-III. Nonetheless, the demands of the veterans had been sufficiently transformed into the language of science that they were accepted. The working group presented their proposal to the Committee on Reactive Disorders in 1978, and after another name change, this time to Post-traumatic Stress Disorder, and some other revisions, the proposal was accepted by Spitzer, Andreasen, and Wynne, adopted by the DSM-III Task Force, approved by the APA, and appeared in DSM-III with the diagnostic criteria listed in Table 4-2.

TABLE 4-2

DIAGNOSTIC CRITERIA FOR POST-TRAUMATIC STRESS DISORDER

A. Existence of a recognizable stressor that would evoke significant symptoms of distress in almost everyone.

B. Reexperiencing of the trauma as evidenced by at least one of the following:

    (1) recurrent and intrusive recollections of the event

    (2) recurrent dreams of the event

    (3) sudden acting or feeling as if the traumatic event were reoccurring, because of an association with an environmental or ideational stimulus

C. Numbing of responsiveness to or reduced involvement with the external world, beginning some time after the trauma, as shown by at least one of the following:

    (1) markedly diminished interest in one or more significant activities

    (2) feeling of detachment or estrangement from others

    (3) constricted affect

D. At least two of the following symptoms that were not present before the trauma:

    (1) hyperalertness or exaggerated startle response

    (2) sleep disturbance

    (3) guilt about surviving when others have not, or about behavior required for survival

    (4) memory impairment or trouble concentrating

    (5) avoidance of activities that arouse recollection of the traumatic event

    (6) intensification of symptoms by exposure to events that symbolize or resemble the traumatic event

SUBTYPES

Post-traumatic Stress Disorder, Acute

A. Onset of symptoms within six months of the trauma.

B. Duration of symptoms less than six months.

Post-traumatic Stress Disorder, Chronic or Delayed
Either of the following, or both:

    (1) duration of symptoms six months or more (chronic)

    (2) onset of symptoms at least six months after the trauma (delayed)

Reprinted with permission from the *Diagnostic and Statistical Manual of Mental Disorders, Third Edition*, Copyright 1980 American Psychiatric Association.

DIAGNOSTIC MIGRATION FROM PERPETRATORS TO VICTIMS: PTSD IN THE POST-VIETNAM ERA

The inclusion of PTSD in DSM was the result of Vietnam veterans' efforts to obtain recognition, treatment, and compensation for disabilities that were a result of their war experiences. Although some veterans, such as the celebrated My Lai survivor, witnessed gross human rights violations, others had committed them. In advocating for the adoption of PTSD, veterans did not differentiate between those who committed atrocities and those who simply witnessed them. Whether they were combatants who inflicted injury or those who were noncombatants, all were considered participants who suffered the aftereffects of a brutal war.

Originally, the VA saw things the other way. Many veterans were denied benefits by the VA because they had not participated in combat while they were in Vietnam. Vietnam returnees who had not engaged in actual fighting challenged this policy. Noncombatants claimed that they suffered from PTSD because they had observed traumatic events or had otherwise been affected by them. Thus, a major impetus for adopting the disorder was the need to recognize the mental suffering of those soldiers who had witnessed atrocities but had not pulled the trigger themselves.

Most people who have received the diagnosis of PTSD since it was included in DSM have a very different history from the Vietnam veterans. Since its first recognition as a disorder in DSM-III in 1980, PTSD has become one of the most frequently used diagnoses. It is used principally to explain the suffering not of soldiers who commit or witness atrocities or of perpetrators of violence but of victims of abuse, especially of sexual mistreatment. There are several historical trends that have led to this development. Among them is the growing recognition of the traumatic effects of rape, sexual harassment, child beating, and spousal abuse.[30] The major impetus for recognizing these problems came not from Vietnam veterans but from the women's movement, whose concerns were championed by conservative politicians interested in providing a justification for expanding law enforcement powers. The convergence of support from the left and the right fueled a drive to crack down on perpetrators, a drive that needed some way of demonstrating that victims suffer from impairments even if they do not show signs of debilitating physical trauma. PTSD fit the bill for claims of delayed, long-term, or permanent damage to victims even if they do not display physical lesions.

Some have questioned the applicability of PTSD as a diagnosis for victims of nonmilitary trauma. For instance, Ziskin, an attorney and psychologist, reviewed the research on PTSD in an authoritative handbook for trial lawyers and concluded, "Thus, it appears that the question of generalizability of the studies on combat related stress disorder to civilian populations has not been resolved at this point."[31] Robert Spitzer responded to problems in applying PTSD to victims of abuse by proposing several new diagnoses: Masochistic Personality Disorder (the subject of chapter 5) and Victimization Disorder (discussed in chapter 1). These proposals were rejected by both experts and consumers. He, in turn, rejected other proposals, including an attempt to include a disorder for children who were victims of sexual abuse. Spitzer also tried to identify the disorders of perpetrators (Sadistic Personality Disorder and Coercive Rapism), and outsiders proposed Delusional Dominating Personality Disorder (see chapter 5) and Racist Personality Disorder (see chapter 7). None of these proposed diagnoses has been made an official part of DSM.

PTSD has become a catchall category used to identify an increasingly wide pool of problems that originate in traumatic life events and are not attributable to preexisting intrapsychic malfunctions. Although it has been argued that not all people react to psychological trauma in the same way and that some people have a constitutional predisposition for PTSD, clinicians and researchers continue to look for the precipitants of PTSD in life events.[32]

ACUTE STRESS DISORDER AND MORE (OR LESS) TRAUMA

The limitations of PTSD as a diagnosis led to changes in the latest edition of DSM that enable practitioners to more readily assign a psychiatric diagnosis to those who have been exposed to trauma. One change is the adoption of a new category, Acute Stress Disorder (ASD). The diagnosis of PTSD can only be made four or more weeks after the initial trauma. The new diagnosis of ASD is made during the first four weeks following a traumatic event. This makes sense inasmuch as many people have an emotional reaction, often a severe one, as an immediate, direct consequence of their trauma. ASD is useful to clinicians who want to make a diagnosis when they see clients immediately after an event such as a rape, a plane crash, or some other disaster. The new diagnosis does broaden the range of stress-related disorders, however. The Vietnam veterans used PTSD to explain delayed reactions, often many years after the war. ASD is used to account for an immediate reaction to a severely disturbing event. If symptoms persist for more than a month, the diagnostician is instructed to make a new diagnosis (if the symptoms meet the criteria for PTSD, that diagnosis is substituted for ASD). The criteria for the new diagnosis of ASD are found in Table 4-3.

A second revision also broadens the concept of trauma and increases the number of potential candidates for a diagnosis of PTSD. The definition of what constitutes a trauma has changed significantly since 1980. Originally, the events that precipitated PTSD were supposed to be so unusual that they were, as DSM-III-R put it, "outside the range of normal human experience." This restrictive phrase was dropped in DSM-IV. Since trauma, such as the death of a loved one, is a normal, if distressing, part of the life cycle, it initially seemed to make sense to distinguish common painful life experiences from more severe catastrophes. But the restrictive definition of a traumatic event in DSM-III and DSM-III-R was criticized for two reasons: First of all, a psychologically disturbing event may not be outside the realm of common human experience. Americans have been forced to recognize that rape and other forms of sexual assault happen much more often than they had thought. The full extent of family violence is another dirty secret that only recently has received widespread public recognition. Although they are common, rape, child abuse, and family violence can all produce the symptoms of PTSD. The second problem with the concept of trauma as it was described in DSM-III and DSM-III-R is that not all the cases of PTSD result from severe assault. Some people are traumatized by a persistent low-level stressful event. Chinese water torture is based on the notion that the most mundane occurrence—water falling on the forehead drop by drop—can drive someone mad if it is repeated frequently enough. Chinese water torture is not a common occurrence, but other types of persistent everyday events can be very disturbing, such as persistent sexual or racial harassment on the job. In such cases, there is no single incident that adequately qualifies as a trigger for PTSD, but when harassment occurs day after day, the cumulative effect can be traumatic. For these reasons, the diagnosis of PTSD was revised to include many ordinary events that can precipitate stress reactions. The newly revised criteria for PTSD are found in Table 4-4.

TABLE 4-3

DIAGNOSTIC CRITERIA FOR 308.3 ACUTE STRESS DISORDER

A. The person has been exposed to a traumatic event in which both of the following were present:

(1) the person experienced, witnessed, or was confronted with an event or events that involved actual or threatened death or serious injury, or a threat to the physical integrity of self or others

(2) the person's response involved intense fear, helplessness, or horror

B. Either while experiencing or after experiencing the distressing event, the individual has three (or more) of the following dissociative symptoms:

(1) a subjective sense of numbing, detachment, or absence of emotional responsiveness

(2) a reduction in awareness of his or her surroundings (e.g., "being in a daze")

(3) derealization

(4) depersonalization

(5) dissociative amnesia (i.e., inability to recall an important aspect of the trauma)

C. The traumatic event is persistently reexperienced in at least one of the following ways: recurrent images, thoughts, dreams, illusions, flashback episodes, or a sense of reliving the experience; or distress on exposure to reminders of the traumatic event.

D. Marked avoidance of stimuli that arouse recollections of the trauma (e.g., thoughts, feelings, conversations, activities, places, people).

E. Marked symptoms of anxiety or increased arousal (e.g., difficulty sleeping, irritability, poor concentration, hypervigilance, exaggerated startle response, motor restlessness).

F. The disturbance causes clinically significant distress or impairment in social, occupational, or other important areas of functioning or impairs the individual's ability to pursue some necessary task, such as obtaining necessary assistance or mobilizing personal resources by telling family members about the traumatic experience.

G. The disturbance lasts for a minimum of 2 days and a maximum of 4 weeks and occurs within 4 weeks of the traumatic event.

H. The disturbance is not due to the direct physiological effects of a substance (e.g., a drug of abuse, a medication) or a general medical condition, is not better accounted for by Brief Psychotic Disorder, and is not merely an exacerbation of a preexisting Axis I or Axis II disorder.

Reprinted with permission from the *Diagnostic and Statistical Manual of Mental Disorders, Fourth Edition,* Copyright 1994 American Psychiatric Association.

TABLE 4-4

DIAGNOSTIC CRITERIA FOR 309.81 POSTTRAUMATIC STRESS
DISORDER

A. The person has been exposed to a traumatic event in which both of the following were present:

    (1) the person experienced, witnessed, or was confronted with an event or
events that involved actual or threatened death or serious injury or a threat
to the physical integrity of self or others.

    (2) the person's response involved intense fear, helplessness, or horror.
Note: In children, this may be expressed instead by disorganized or agitated behavior

B. The traumatic event is persistently reexperienced in one (or more) of the following ways:

    (1) recurrent and intrusive distressing recollections of the event, including
images, thoughts, or perceptions. **Note:** In young children, repetitive
play may occur in which themes or aspects of the trauma are expressed.

    (2) recurrent distressing dreams of the event. **Note:** In children, there may
be frightening dreams without recognizable content.

    (3) acting or feeling as if the traumatic event were recurring (includes a sense
of reliving the experience, illusions, hallucinations, and dissociative flashback episodes, including those that occur on awakening or when intoxi-
cated). **Note:** In young children, trauma-specific reenactment may occur.

    (4) intense psychological distress at exposure to internal or external cues
that symbolize or resemble an aspect of the traumatic event.

    (5) physiological reactivity on exposure to internal or external cues that sym-
bolize or resemble an aspect of the traumatic event.

C. Persistent avoidance of stimuli associated with the trauma and numbing of

(continued)

All of these changes in the diagnosis of PTSD seem reasonable and
compassionate until we evaluate their overall impact. Responding to
criticism about the enormous growth in the number of diagnoses in
successive editions of DSM, Allen Frances, the psychiatrist in charge of
the latest revision, asserted repeatedly that the APA was raising the
threshold for inclusion of new diagnoses in the manual. Although he
never specified where the new, higher thresholds were, he gave the impression that the APA was going to seriously restrict the number of additional people who could be given a psychiatric diagnosis. But DSM-IV
demonstrates that even without adding new categories it is possible to

general responsiveness (not present before the trauma), as indicated by three (or more) of the following:

(1) efforts to avoid thoughts, feelings, or conversations associated with the trauma

(2) efforts to avoid activities, places, or people that arouse recollections of the trauma

(3) inability to recall an important aspect of the trauma

(4) markedly diminished interest or participation in significant activities

(5) feeling of detachment or estrangement from others

(6) restricted range of affect (e.g., unable to have loving feelings)

(7) sense of a foreshortened future (e.g., does not expect to have a career, marriage, children, or a normal life span)

D. Persistent symptoms of increased arousal (not present before the trauma), as indicated by two (or more) of the following:

(1) difficulty falling or staying asleep

(2) irritability or outbursts of anger

(3) difficulty concentrating

(4) hypervigilance

(5) exaggerated startle response

E. Duration of the disturbance (symptoms in Criteria B, C, and D) is more than 1 month.

F. The disturbance causes clinically significant distress or impairment in social, occupational, or other important areas of functioning.

Specify if:
Acute: if duration is less than 3 months
Chronic: if duration of symptoms is 3 months or more

Specify if:
With Delayed Onset: if onset of symptoms is at least 6 months after the stressor

---

Reprinted with permission from the *Diagnostic and Statistical Manual of Mental Disorders, Fourth Edition,* Copyright 1994 American Psychiatric Association.

vastly increase the number of people who can receive a diagnosis. The changes in the wording of the PTSD diagnosis are an excellent illustration. The alteration of a single eight-word phrase describing the precipitating trauma has made millions more people eligible for a diagnosis.[33] Although it is important to recognize the suffering of these victims, it is a major leap to identify characteristic reactions to assaults, abuse; and harassment as symptoms of mental disorder; this practice leads to the complaint that psychiatrists and other mental health workers are blaming the victim.

The importance of these changes was appreciated immediately by a vast audience, including a legion of professionals, many of whom were not psychotherapists. Shortly after the publication of DSM-IV, the California Trial Lawyers Association broadcast the news to its members in an article titled "The New DSM-IV: Is It Easier to Prove Damages?"[34] The answer is "Yes, of course!" The list of reasons why it is easier starts with the changes in PTSD and includes the addition of Acute Stress Disorder. In effect, a self-selected group of professionals in the APA has altered public policy in major ways without public sanction. It may be a very good idea to make it easier to gain compensation for psychological injury, but the definition of such injury is being made without public debate, moreover, the APA and its minions will not even acknowledge that they are creating public policy. As they explain it, they are simply making diagnoses (and in the process making many more of us crazy).

THE NEW PROFESSIONAL ARMY AND ITS SYMPTOMS

A new war, the Persian Gulf conflict, has again produced unexplained suffering among its survivors. Veterans complain of a variety of symptoms, including depression, lack of concentration, weight loss, and insomnia, and their condition has been identified as Gulf War Syndrome (GWS). Returnees suspect that their physical and psychological complications are due to exposure to biological and chemical agents.[35] Army and Veterans Affairs (VA) doctors reject many of these claims, and often diagnose the complaints as Postraumatic Stress Disorder. The diagnosis of PTSD often hampers the recognition of the actual illnesses that afflict these veterans. By making diagnoses of PTSD, government physicians and other officials avoid accusations that troops were exposed to toxic materials.

There is speculation that some symptoms of GWS are a reaction to chemical warfare agents used either by the Iraqi or the American military. Until recently, the Iraqi and American governments have denied that they engaged in chemical or biological warfare and have refused to acknowledge the existence of Gulf War Syndrome as a disability for which American troops are entitled to compensation.

Several years ago, scientists began offering new explanations for Gulf War Syndrome.[36] *Nature Medicine* reported that U.S. and Israeli troops used a drug, pyridostigmine (Mestinon, Regonol), as prophylactic against anticipated damage from possible attacks of nerve-gas-tipped missiles from Iraq. Researchers described the case of an Israeli soldier who had a severe reaction to the drug, and they offered a hypothesis about the way the drug alters brain functioning in a manner that produces the symptoms of Gulf War Syndrome.

The pyridostigmine hypothesis has not been accepted by officials, and new revelations have increased the speculation about other causes of GWS. It may not be a reaction to prophylactic drugs but actual contact with toxins that causes GWS. For many years, the CIA and the Department of Defense hid information that U.S. military personnel were imperiled by poisonous chemicals when they detonated captured Iraqi weapons and explosives. Reluctantly, the armed services and the intelligence agency have revealed information about explosions during the destruction of Iraqi chemical warfare agents that may have contaminated American and allied troops. These incidents may be the source of many of the physical and emotional complaints of veterans.

It is still too early to determine how much contact Gulf War veterans had with toxic chemicals, but one thing is generally accepted: a relatively small percentage of Gulf War veterans are suffering from PTSD as it is conceptualized in DSM. Although the psychological problems of Gulf War veterans have been acknowledged, as a general rule they have been inextricably tied to physiological problems. It will be necessary to develop new psychiatric diagnoses to account for the difficulties of Gulf War veterans, just as the problems of veterans of past wars have led to the creation of new categories of mental illness.

PTSD TODAY

Most of the basic assumptions that led to the creation of PTSD have been called into question by both critics and supporters of DSM. It would be hard for the Vietnam veterans and their psychiatrist allies who fought for recognition of the syndrome to recognize the diagnosis as it is presently formulated. These twists and turns in the evolution of PTSD have not gone unnoticed. The handbook prepared by Ziskin for attorneys (so that they can attack forensic experts) offers this critique:[37]

> PTSD is one of the outstanding illustrations of the effects of the "Chronic Change Syndrome" (our term) from which the DSMs seem to suffer . . .

classification and description of reported disorders subsequent to traumatic events seems to be a matter of controversy and constantly changing viewpoints.

We need to be aware that the overwhelming bulk of research on PTSD has been done with Vietnam War veterans and, therefore, is of doubtful applicability to civilians. . . . It is our impression that, as of 1994, war service related PTSD has become an infrequent forensic issue. Two decades have passed since the Vietnam War, and the Gulf War seems unlikely to have produced a substantial number of PTSD cases. Therefore it seems likely that disability claims related to PTSD in veterans would for the most part have been resolved by now. The other forensic issue in which combat related PTSD has been raised is the insanity defense . . . the use of PTSD diagnoses in insanity defenses peaked in 1983. . . . Reviewing court records . . . of 8,163 cases in which there were insanity pleas, only 0.3% (28) were based on a diagnosis of PTSD. . . . Hopefully there will never be another generation of combat related PTSD. In any event, because of the changes . . . [in revisions of DSM after 1980], even with veterans the use of prior research is questionable.

Further, the newness of the formalized diagnosis appearing for the first time in 1980, with significant changes in 1987 and 1994, precludes generalizations from research in the 1980's and early 1990's, leaving very little in the way of well-validated knowledge concerning this disorder . . . research about the psychological effects of disaster continues to be hampered by the diverse conceptualizations and methodologies. . . . [D]iagnostic criteria are a "moving target" (continually changing) meaning that "by the time research is conceptualized, executed, analyzed, described and published, the results will be described in terms of earlier diagnostic criteria."

There were 11 changes made in the diagnosis of PTSD in 1987, when DSM-III-R was printed, and 15 changes when DSM-IV was published in 1994.[38] There are 175 combinations of symptoms by which PTSD can be diagnosed. Ziskin presents a series of examples in which patients who cannot be diagnosed with PTSD in one edition of DSM can be given this diagnosis in another one, even though the symptoms remain the same. He also points out that because a diagnosis can be made by choosing from a long list of symptoms, it is possible for two people who have no symptoms in common to receive a diagnosis of PTSD, even if the same edition of DSM is used to make both diagnoses.

Many of the "defining" features of PTSD are shared with dozens of other diagnoses. Furthermore, it is difficult to distinguish between maladaptive and healthy responses to stress or pressure. Ziskin, too, observes that "it can be difficult to say whether reactions to purportedly stressful events are most appropriately identified as healthy or unhealthy."[39]

Of all the many problems in regard to PTSD, none is more significant than its use as a diagnosis for victims of such violent crimes as rape, domestic violence, and sexual abuse (especially of children). Do mental health professionals need to make a diagnosis in order to understand that victims need all the help they can get? It is a disservice to victims to give them a diagnosis because they are suffering from the aftereffects of trauma. Evidence indicates that although they may be very troubled and deserve all available help, few of them are suffering from a mental disorder and fewer still have PTSD.

The long history of PTSD illustrates many of the shortcomings of DSM. By adopting a new diagnosis to identify the severe emotional problems suffered by Vietnam veterans, the developers of DSM opened a Pandora's box. Veterans fought hard for the inclusion of PTSD in DSM not because they were enthusiastic about identifying their problems as a mental disorder but because they needed recognition of the fact that war had done bad things to them and that they needed help in overcoming its aftereffects. The price they paid was to be identified as mentally ill.

However controversial this decision was, the repercussions of putting PTSD in the American Psychiatric Association's diagnostic manual went far beyond pathologizing the problems of war veterans. PTSD has become the label for identifying the impact of adverse events on ordinary people. This means that normal responses to catastrophic events often have been interpreted as mental disorders. Moreover, people must demonstrate how "sick" they are in order to get help; that is, assistance is offered to victims only after they demonstrate how mentally ill they have become. DSM is the vehicle for establishing this sickness. The diagnostic process makes it harder for victims to overcome problems they have not created and are trying to resolve.

5 THE DEFEAT OF MASOCHISTIC PERSONALITY DISORDER

We are scientists and not horse traders.
—Robert Spitzer, as quoted in *Time* magazine, December 1985

The relationship between women and the experts was not unlike conventional relationships between women and men. It was never an equal relationship. . . . But it was a relationship that lasted right up to our own time, when women began to discover that the experts' answer to the Woman Question was not science after all, but only the ideology of a masculinist society, dressed up as objective truth.
—Barbara Ehrenreich and Deirdre English, *For Her Own Good: 150 Years of the Expert's Advice to Women*

To the developers of DSM, it must seem, in retrospect, that their attempts to create a diagnostic category called Masochistic Personality Disorder was—well, masochistic. The origin of the attempt did not differ from the way many diagnoses come into existence. That is, a few influential insiders decided that a new category would be clinically meaningful and handy and lobbied for its inclusion. Usually, few mind the addition of a new category, and it is included with bureaucratic efficiency and no outside publicity. In the case of the proposal for Masochistic Personality Disorder, however, the developers—perhaps blinded by gender bias and misled by their beliefs about the quality and significance of their own research—were, in the end, publicly humiliated by their own professional association.

As with the homosexuality diagnosis, one of the issues behind the controversy over Masochistic Personality Disorder (MPD)—an issue that danced on the periphery of the dispute—was the coherence of the concept of mental disorder. Although the conflict raged over whether the criteria or the clinicians who used them were sex biased, whether all the scientific evidence was evenhandedly considered, and whether the APA's decision-making processes were fair and appropriate, the most fundamental question was not a technical or procedural one but, rather, one of conceptual integrity. Unlike the early controversy over the psychiatric status of homosexuality, which directly questioned the APA's ability to specify what constituted a mental disorder (a story told in chapter 3), the conflict over MPD never developed into a broad challenge regarding the nature of mental disorder. It remained a narrow dispute, an often bitter conflict between feminists and the male psychiatric establishment.

To the proponents of the diagnosis, the matter was relatively simple: some psychoanalysts reported clinical experience with patients who had nonsexual masochism, had some notion about its psychodynamic etiology, and thought that a label to describe a person who engages in this pattern of behavior would be handy. For Robert Spitzer and his DSM committees, creating a new diagnostic category was something of a house specialty; they had done it numerous times before. The recipe was easy: pick a label, provide a general description based on clinical wisdom, develop a menu of diagnostic criteria, check the proposed criteria with advocates for the new category, decide how many criteria must be met to use the diagnosis, counter opposition (if any), and—presto!—you have a new mental disorder.

For feminists, the proposal to add Masochistic Personality Disorder to DSM was offensive and regressive. They believed that it pathologized the experiences of many women, blamed female victims for trying to cope with an oppressive culture and oppressive relationships, and reflected the myopic views of dominating males and their powerful professional organizations. For feminists, much was at stake; they believed that if Masochistic Personality Disorder was accepted into DSM, women were very likely to be the recipients of the new label. DSM diagnoses have the power to transform everyday behaviors, even ones that are adaptive, into signs of internal deficits and dysfunction. Women beaten by their husbands could be viewed as seeking the abuse. Women passed over for promotions at work could be seen as lacking the desire to achieve. Mothers making enormous sacrifices for their families could be labeled as pathological. Women who, in the eyes of men, avoided opportunities for pleasure could be considered candidates for psychiatric treatment. In short, women from all walks of life who appeared not inclined to pursue narrowly defined self-interest could be suspected of suffering from a mental disorder. With the creation of a broadly defined new diagnosis that could be applied to millions of women, the pharmaceutical companies would not take long to pursue a chemical treatment for the supposed affliction. Feminists feared that a DSM-sanctioned diagnosis of Masochistic Personality Disorder would quickly find its way into arenas where decisions about divorce and child custody are made, where judgments about the validity of charges of spouse abuse are heard, and where the rights and opportunities for women are reviewed. Turning the struggles of women in society into a form of mental disorder was an outrage to the feminists. Most infuriating, the proponents of the new diagnosis tried to claim that DSM was a document containing scientifically validated categories. A struggle between the two camps was inevitable.

In this chapter we examine this struggle, which, like the conflicts over the Homosexuality and Posttraumatic Stress Disorder diagnoses, illustrates the power of a few psychiatric insiders and the political effectiveness of organized outside advocates. In this instance, however, the psychiatric establishment confronted a new, unanticipated interest group: feminist psychotherapists and their supporters. The story of this conflict reveals more than a rough-and-tumble political struggle for control of DSM. It also provides a glimpse of the quality of the thinking and the science that get pressed into service at times of crisis. Unlike the debates over the exclusion of Homosexuality, in which advocates for the diagnosis never tried to rely on scientific evidence, the proponents of Masochistic Personality Disorder marshaled their own research findings to support their proposal. We take this opportunity to critically examine how scientific studies are developed, implemented, and interpreted in the hothouse environment created by diagnostic battles.

THE EMERGENCE OF MASOCHISM IN DSM

The idea of a malady labeled Masochism has roots from the turn of the century. The earliest references are found in the psychoanalytic literature, where the term *masochism* was coined in reference to a psychosexual disorder.[1] Freud wrote of various types of masochism, some of them found in people who, as a result of a harsh conscience, incur failures or exhibit self-reproach. Other early psychoanalysts, such as Wilhelm Reich, talked about the masochistic character of those who have chronic subjective feelings of suffering, who continually complain and demand, and who engage in self-debasement and provocation. Karen Horney described those with a masochistic character as having a tendency toward feeling unattractive, helpless, insignificant, inefficient, turbid, and worthless; a clinging dependency on the benevolence of others; and a need to represent themselves as victimized and harmed.

Contemporary psychoanalysts and clinical psychologists share a concern about people who appear to submit passively to external force; to accept injury, blame, criticism, and punishment; or to seek and enjoy pain, punishment, and misfortune. In the seventies some therapists thought that a new diagnosis was needed to describe patients who feel guilty and are self-deprecating, doubtful, ruminative, obsessive, passive, depressed, and anxious.

A major proponent for the inclusion of Masochistic Personality Disorder in DSM was Richard Simons, a psychiatrist who presented an influential paper on the subject just before the APA announced the recommendation to include this new diagnosis in DSM-III-R.[2] Simons offered the following description of the proposed diagnosis:[3]

> Patients suffering from masochistic personality disorder have been vividly described in the psychoanalytic literature. . . . They are the patients who unconsciously provoke their therapists either to give up on them, or sadistically abuse them with premature and unempathic interpretations, or pejoratively dismiss them with the misdiagnosis of borderline personality disorder or passive-aggressive personality disorder.

Simons acknowledged that the unconscious motivating factors in each case may vary: some patients may be abused, others may fear separation from a loved one, and still others may feel a need for punishment. "But whatever the unconscious motives may be in an individual case," wrote

Simons, "the final behavioral outcome is the achievement of . . . 'victory through defeat,' and often the defeat is a failed psychiatric treatment."

DSM-II, published in 1968, devotes 2 1/2 short pages to a description of personality disorders ("disorders . . . characterized by deeply ingrained maladaptive patterns of behavior that are . . . life-long patterns, often recognizable by the time of adolescence or earlier"). In two or three sentences each, the manual briefly describes such maladies as paranoid, schizoid, obsessive-compulsive, and antisocial personality disorders. There is no mention of Masochistic Personality Disorder. The term *masochism* is mentioned only once, and that is under the heading Sexual Deviations, where it is explained that this "category is for individuals whose sexual interests are directed primarily toward objects other than people of the opposite sex, toward sexual acts not usually associated with coitus, or toward coitus performed under bizarre circumstances" (p. 44). Then, without the embellishment of any text, criteria, or definition, the terms *homosexuality, fetishism, pedophilia, transvestism, exhibitionism, voyeurism, sadism, and masochism* are listed. Each is assigned its own diagnostic code number.

DSM-III, published in 1980, is much more detailed but is similar to DSM-II in making no mention of Masochistic Personality Disorder among the 12 types described (see Table 5–1). Again, masochism is only mentioned under the category Psychosexual Disorders and within the subclassification (there are four) labeled Paraphilias. The text explains that the "essential feature of disorders in this subclass is that unusual or bizarre imagery or acts are necessary for sexual excitement" (p. 266). "The term Paraphilia," the manual continues, "is preferable [to the term *sexual deviations*] because it correctly emphasizes that the deviation (para) is in that to which the individual is attracted (philia)" (pp. 266–267). Described as paraphilias are fetishism, transvestism, zoophilia, pedophilia, exhibitionism, voyeurism, sexual sadism, and sexual masochism.

The manual recommends that the diagnosis of sexual masochism be made when the individual's preferred or exclusive mode of producing sexual excitement is to be humiliated, bound, beaten, or otherwise made to suffer or when the person has intentionally participated in activities that were physically harmful or life threatening in order to produce sexual excitement. Although there is no mention of Masochistic Personality Disorder in DSM-III (there is a listing for Sexual Masochism), apparently there were some members of the various APA committees involved in de-

TABLE 5-1

CHANGING PERSONALITY DISORDERS IN DSM (1968–1994)

DSM-II 1968	DSM-III 1980	DSM-III-R Draft, October 1985	DSM-III-R Draft, August 1986	DSM-III-R 1987	DSM-IV 1994
Paranoid personality	Paranoid	Paranoid	Paranoid	Paranoid	Paranoid
Cyclothymic personality					
Schizoid personality	Schizoid	Schizoid	Schizoid	Schizoid	Schizoid
Explosive personality					
Obsessive compulsive personality	Compulsive	Obsessive Compulsive	Obsessive Compulsive	Obsessive Compulsive	Obsessive Compulsive
Hysterical personality	Histrionic	Histrionic	Histrionic	Histrionic	Histrionic
Asthenic personality					
Antisocial personality	Antisocial	Antisocial	Antisocial	Antisocial	Antisocial
Passive aggressive personality	Passive Aggressive	Passive Aggressive	Passive Aggressive	Passive Aggressive	
Inadequate personality					
Other personality disorders	Atypical, mixed or other	Personality disorder NOS	Personality disorder NOS	Personality disorder NOS	Personality disorder NOS
	New Disorders				
	Schizotypal	Schizotypal	Schizotypal	Schizotypal	Schizotypal
	Narcissistic	Narcissistic	Narcissistic	Narcissistic	Narcissistic
	Borderline	Borderline	Borderline	Borderline	Borderline
	Avoidant	Avoidant	Avoidant	Avoidant	Avoidant
	Dependent	Dependent	Dependent	Dependent	Dependent
		New Disorders	*New Disorders*	*Appendix A*	*Appendix B*
		Masochistic	Self-Defeating	Self-Defeating	Depressive
			Sadistic	Sadistic	Passive-aggressive

veloping the manual who were proponents for it. Allen Frances, a personality disorder expert who would later chair the task force to develop DSM-IV, wrote in a commentary in the *American Journal of Psychiatry* that he would have preferred to include Depressive or Masochistic Personality Disorder in DSM-III.[4]

The absence of official recognition of Masochistic Personality Disorder ended abruptly when the group working to revise DSM-III proposed to create such a disorder.[5] This proposal was made at the same time that two other controversial categories were proposed—Premenstrual Dysphoric Disorder (popularly known as "premenstrual syndrome," or PMS) and Paraphilic Rapism—and they all appeared in the first draft of DSM-III-R, which was published in October 1985. Feminists thought that each of these proposals was a disadvantage to women, and they fought them all, although each disorder eventually had a different fate. Here we will focus only on Masochistic Personality Disorder.

In the first draft of DSM-III-R, sold by the APA for $10 to anyone re-

TABLE 5-2

INITIAL DSM DESCRIPTION OF MASOCHISTIC PERSONALITY
DISORDER (OCTOBER 1985)

301.89 Masochistic Personality Disorder [UNDER CONSIDERATION]
Feelings of martyrdom and Self-Defeating behavior as indicated by at least six of the following:

(1) remains in relationships in which others exploit, abuse or take advantage of him or her, despite opportunities to alter the situation

(2) believes that he or she almost always sacrifices own interests for those of others

(3) rejects help, gifts or favors so as not to be a burden on others

(4) complains, directly or indirectly, about being unappreciated

(5) responds to success or positive events by feeling undeserving or worrying excessively

(6) always pessimistic about the future and preoccupied with the worst aspects of the past and present

(7) thinks only about his or her worst features and ignores positive features

(8) sabotages his or her own intended goals

(9) repeatedly turns down opportunities for pleasure

Reprinted with permission from *DSM-III-R in Development* by Work Group to Revise DSM-III, 1985, pp. 133–134. Copyright 1985 American Psychiatric Association.

questing a copy, no rationale or justification was offered for developing the new category Masochistic Personality Disorder. The 180-page draft contains only one sentence in the introduction that acknowledges that the developers were aware of some controversy about their proposal. In the body of the draft, nothing more on the controversy appears, and the proposed diagnostic criteria are listed (see Table 5–2).

DISORDER OR MALE BIAS?

The description of the new disorder in the first draft of DSM-III-R is provocative. Although the term *masochism* is used, its meaning bears little resemblance to its former definition, which referred to the achievement of sexual excitement through abuse or humiliation. In the DSM-III-R proposal, the purported disorder is desexualized (there is no mention of sexual excitement) and explicit references to physical abuse or pain are absent; thus, the potential applicability of *masochism* is greatly expanded. The description of the disorder also removes any reference to possible motivation for the behavior. Whereas sexual excitement is listed as the objective of Sexual Masochism in DSM-III, Masochistic Personality Disorder in the draft for DSM-III-R appears to involve no personal motivation. Instead, the description is of individuals who make no demands on others, are self-sacrificing, and uncomfortable with trying to achieve success or recognition, feel unworthy, and often neglect their own goals and pleasures for those of others. To the psychiatrists who manufacture diagnostic categories, these characteristics apparently sounded clinically familiar and were used as the operational definition of a new mental disorder. For feminists, the characteristics smacked of traditional female role socialization, in which women are taught to be subservient, to sacrifice their goals for those of their husbands and children, to suffer silently, and not to expect or seek pleasure or success.

More ominously, a decade of research had uncovered the dirty secret of family violence, particularly wife beating. It was well known among experts who studied victims of battering that they often exhibited the very characteristics that were now being used to define Masochistic Personality Disorder. Coincidentally, the APA's proposal for the new category occurred just as Paula Caplan, who was a prominent critic of MPD, published her book *The Myth of Women's Masochism.*[6] Feminists could not avoid the conclusion that the victim of wife beating was now in danger of being blamed, via a mental disorder, for encouraging or fabricating her own abuse. And what really galled the feminists was the fact that this diagnostic proposal was dressed up in the gown of psychiatric science.

A Conceptual Assessment

How well does the description of MPD meet the requirements for a mental disorder? Simply developing a list of diagnostic criteria to describe some people's behavior is insufficient. Characteristics of stinginess could be developed and individuals who possess them could be identified but that would not make stinginess a mental disorder. A list of characteristics merely describes a type of behavior. For a behavior to constitute a disorder, a particular mental dysfunction must be identified and it must be established that significant harm exists as a result. Do the diagnostic criteria for MPD offer such a convincing portrayal? This is the question that should have been at the heart of the issue of whether MPD is a valid mental disorder.

Let's examine the eight criteria that were eventually used to define MPD (see Table 5–3; the numbers in parentheses after each item in the following list correspond to numbered items in Table 5–3):

- Makes bad choices in people and situations (1)
- Rejects help (2, 7)
- Isn't appropriately happy (3, 5)
- Makes people angry (4)
- Doesn't achieve own goals (6)
- Makes sacrifices for others (8)

These characteristics, according to the proponents of MPD, are the signs of mental dysfunction. By examining them, one can infer the implicit assumptions about mental functioning. The proponents of the MPD proposal appear to assume that our mental mechanisms are designed to make us wise and happy, to enable us to accept help and achieve our own goals, and to prevent us from unduly sacrificing ourself or making others angry. This description does not identify specific mental mechanisms that have failed to function properly. Instead, it presents a specific concoction of American mass culture, with elements of hedonism, individualism, and achievement. There is an expectation that normal people make good choices that help them get ahead, enjoy their achievements and other op-

TABLE 5–3

FINAL DSM-III-R DESCRIPTION OF SELF-DEFEATING PERSONALITY
DISORDER(1987)

A. A pervasive pattern of Self-Defeating behavior, beginning by early adulthood
and present in a variety of contexts. The person may often avoid or undermine
pleasurable experiences, be drawn to situations or relationships in which he or
she will suffer, and prevent others from helping him or her, as indicated by at
least five of the following:

(1) chooses people and situations that lead to disappointment, failure, or
    mistreatment even when better options are clearly available

(2) rejects or renders ineffective the attempts of others to help him or her

(3) following positive personal events (e.g., new achievement), responds with
    depression, guilt, or a behavior that produces pain (e.g., an accident)

(4) incites angry or rejecting responses from others and then feels hurt, de-
    feated, or humiliated (e.g., makes fun of spouse in public, provoking an
    angry retort, then feels devastated)

(5) rejects opportunities for pleasure, or is reluctant to acknowledge enjoy-
    ing himself or herself (despite having adequate social skills and the ca-
    pacity for pleasure)

(6) fails to accomplish tasks crucial to his or her personal objectives despite
    demonstrated ability to do so, e.g., helps fellow students write papers,
    but is unable to write his or her own

(7) is uninterested in or rejects people who consistently treat him or her
    well, e.g., is unattracted to caring sexual partners

(8) engages in excessive self-sacrifice that is unsolicited by the intended re-
    cipients of the sacrifice

B. The behaviors in A do not occur exclusively in response to, or in anticipation
of, being physically, sexually, or psychologically abused.

C. The behaviors in A do not occur only when the person is depressed.

Note: For coding purposes, record: 301.90 Personality Disorder Not Otherwise
Specified (Self-Defeating Personality Disorder).

Reprinted with permission from the *Diagnostic and Statistical Manual of Mental Disorders* (Third Edition-Revised),
Copyright 1987 American Psychiatric Association.

portunities for pleasure, and know how to accept help from others without unduly sacrificing their own personal ambitions. This is an image of
normality that fits the historical freedoms and opportunities of men
much more closely than the realities of the lives of many women. The diagnostic criteria for MPD also appear to be behaviors that don't suffi-

ciently exhibit the American enthusiasm for narrow self-interest. Apparently, according to this DSM proposal, if you can't be all that you can be, "go for the gusto," and "just be happy," you are failing to live up to an American creed and therefore, have a mental disorder. In this light, MPD is not just a dysfunction, it is anticapitalist.

Continuing our examination, we can ask, What significant harm is done and to whom by the behaviors listed in MPD? The following harmful consequences are suggested by the eight criteria (the numbers in parentheses after each item in the following list correspond to the numbered items in Table 5-3):

To self
    Feels disappointment; experiences failure or mistreatment (1)
    Suffers depression, guilt, hurt, or pain (3, 4)
    Avoids pleasures (5, 7)
To others
    Makes others angry (4)
    Rejects their help or sexual advances (7)

The first criterion suggests that the harm might consist of feelings of disappointment because of poor choices. This harm is purportedly self-inflicted, although reference to mistreatment suggests that the harm is due to the behavior of others. With this criterion, the harm does not appear to be significant (or at least its severity is not required or described). It is also unclear whether the people and situations chosen unexpectedly lead to unpleasantness or whether individuals intentionally choose some situation because they desire that result. The motivation and expectations of the individual are crucial, but they are left ambiguous by this criterion. There is also the avoidability condition: "even when better options are clearly available." Are the better options known to the individual at the time or only later? Are they known to the individual or only to others? Deciding whether a person chooses to be disappointed involves the application of a series of complex inferences.

The second criterion involves not allowing others to help. Although accepting assistance can at times be beneficial, there are frequently costs and obligations incurred in accepting help. It is invalid to assume that the act of rejecting help is itself harmful without understanding the motivation of the individual or the possible positive and negative consequences of the rejection. Rejecting help can be a sign of independence, of a willingness to be accountable for one's behavior, or a desire to go it alone. By itself, rejecting help is not necessarily a harmful dysfunction.

The third criterion is equally confusing: the individual is unhappy following some positive accomplishment. This is neither uncommon nor necessarily significantly harmful. At times, positive as well as negative life events can cause stress. Achieving a goal can be stressful. Getting a promotion or a new job, getting married, graduating from school, having a baby, and so on can produce unfamiliar circumstances and confront the individual with new uncertainties. For women who have been socialized to be less competitive, assertive, and obsessed with personal achievement than men, obtaining success can create mixed feelings.

The fourth criterion involves making people angry and then feeling humiliated. This is a complex series of interpersonal exchanges involving the individual as part of some interpersonal network of expectations that apparently get violated. To the extent that the harm is the result of the actions of others toward the individual, the locus of the difficulty appears not to be the individual's mental mechanism but the angry responses of others that prove to be hurtful.

The fifth criterion devalues the act of avoiding pleasure, a behavior that has a long, proud tradition in American culture. In fact, the Protestant ethic of hard work and dedication to personal achievement has been viewed as an important ideology that supports the development of capitalism in industrialized countries. Historical, religious, and cultural traditions suggest that this criterion is neither necessarily harmful nor a dysfunction of a mental mechanism.

The sixth criterion places a positive value on the accomplishment of personal tasks. The failure to achieve personal objectives is thus the implicit harm. There is no description of the severity of this harm nor any specification of what mental mechanism has gone wrong in this failure. The example offered as an illustration seems trivial; many students (and professors) can provide others with advice on writing but have some difficulty doing their own. Although this may suggest that the individual is not functioning at optimum capacity, it hardly signifies a serious harmful dysfunction. Furthermore, for many women, helping a husband and children with schooling, careers, and life tasks often takes precedence over pursuing their own goals.

The seventh criterion implies that there is a natural mental mechanism that makes people interested in those who express interest in them, make offers of help to them, or desire sexual relations with them. The precise mental mechanism that is supposed to accomplish this is unspecified. Moreover, the harm that is caused appears to be the disappointment to the helper or suitor, not to the individual. From the standpoint of many women, men often make overtures to help or to have sexual relations with them, but these are hardly unconditional offers and they often are not what the women necessarily desire. From the traditional male viewpoint, a woman is expected to allow a man to help her, to accept his offers, and not to reject his sexual advances; the man may perceive his behaviors as evidence of caring, but the woman may not. This criterion suggests that men may know best what women need.

The final criterion involves the placing of personal needs and interests behind those of others. This quality is sometimes viewed as altruism, unselfishness, and commitment to the well-being of others. What makes such behavior "excessive" is not specified, nor is the harm that is alleged to result. Implicitly, if individuals sacrifice less for others, they would be able to accomplish their own goals. The potential costs of not making sacrifices for others is ignored. For example, what are the potential costs to some families if a parent ignores all household chores to pursue personal interests? Although self-sacrifice may not be explicitly solicited, it is often expected as part of gender role socialization.

The diagnostic criteria for MPD fail to specify the nature of the mental dysfunctions or the significant harms that are required to establish a condition as a mental disorder. They constitute an ad hoc collection of behaviors that do not conform with late-20th-century notions of how to relate to others to maximize one's self-interest. Apparently, to the proponents of the MPD diagnosis, it appeared self-evidently pathological for people to underachieve, to not use others for their own benefit, to feel or be defeated, or to put the interests of others above their own: in a culture that places high value on pleasure, short-term gain, and using other people, the behavior of many women seemed inexplicable. It may not be a coincidence that this "disorder" emerged during the 1980s from the work of successful male psychiatrists in New York City—during the decade of greed in the city that relished it. Women's subservience, however beneficial it had been for men, was now viewed by the APA as problematic for women. Although many feminists may have agreed that it was problematic, they were reluctant to conclude, as the APA did, that this problem should be seen as a mental disorder. Where feminists offered so-

cial criticism for the predicament of women, the men of DSM offered a
psychiatric diagnosis.

REACTION TO THE PROPOSAL

Reaction to the proposal of the Work Group to Revise DSM-III was swift
and relentless, but it was not anticipated by the developers.[7] Objections
to MPD and the other new diagnoses began with Jean Hamilton, a psychiatrist who was participating in drafting DSM-III-R. In revising DSM,
the strategy of the developers was to encourage wide participation from
the entire APA membership while retaining control. This strategy was
largely successful in reducing controversies in the initial production of
DSM-III, but it backfired in producing DSM-III-R when Hamilton resigned in protest from the work group. Many psychotherapists and researchers had been unaware of the suggested changes until Hamilton
alerted them to the proposals.[8]

Teresa Bernardez, then chair of the American Psychiatric Association's
Committee on Women (which was supposed to be consulted on matters
affecting women), was not even told of the proposal for Masochistic Personality Disorder—or of the other proposed new diagnoses affecting
women. Nor was anyone else on her committee contacted. Bernardez
learned of the proposal from a colleague as the work group was nearing a
vote on the MPD diagnosis.[9] She quickly sent a letter to Spitzer detailing
her concerns. Other feminist psychotherapists were soon alerted to the
proposals, and a campaign to oppose them began.

Major hearings were scheduled to debate what had now emerged as
controversial diagnoses: a hearing in New York City in November 1985,
another hearing the following month in Washington, D.C., and a third
one at the APA annual convention in Washington the following May.
Members of both sides in the controversy worked tirelessly to promote
their views and to influence the final decisions, which would be made
through the complex decision-making structure of the APA and then reported in the mass media.

The November 1985 Hearing and Its Aftermath

Because of the clamor that was beginning to be raised by the women,
the APA Assembly suggested that hearings be held. Spitzer, who chaired

both the revision work group and the special committee assigned to deal with personality disorders, invited representatives from both the APA's own Committee on Women and the American Psychological Association's Committee on Women in Psychology.[10] He also lined up defenders for the new diagnoses. The ad hoc committee for the one-day hearing was mostly male; the only woman on it was Spitzer's wife, a social worker, who had been heavily involved in the development of both DSM-III and DSM-III-R. The committee allowed only six female critics to speak.[11]

Spitzer opened the hearings by explaining that they were trying through the DSM revision to make diagnosis more scientific. Then he offered as evidence his study of eight patients of psychiatrists in his department of psychiatry at Columbia University.[12]

Richard Simons, the president of the American Psychoanalytic Association and a longtime proponent of Masochistic Personality Disorder, then presented a historical overview in which he argued that similar diagnoses had been used in the past and were therefore valid. Spitzer also presented the results of a survey of psychiatrists who supported the inclusion of Masochistic Personality Disorder in DSM (this study is reviewed later in this chapter).

Then the women critics were allowed to speak. Lenore Walker, a psychological researcher who had done extensive research on battered women, explained to the panel that domestic violence often causes women to behave in the very ways that were now being considered as evidence of Masochistic Personality Disorder. She explained that the reason battered women do not strike back or leave their husbands is that they fear even worse battering and the possibility of being murdered, not that they seek punishment. She based her remarks on her research. Lynne Rosewater, a forensic psychologist who was chair of the Steering Committee of the Feminist Therapy Institute, described how each of the proposed criteria was a behavior typical of victims of violence. The proposed diagnosis, she suggested, would cause irreparable injury and violate the civil rights of women who are victims of abuse. She indicated to the panel that her institute would file a lawsuit against the APA if they passed the proposed diagnosis.[13]

The panel members were not impressed. They told the women that they had never looked at any of their studies and that the domestic violence research presented was "irrelevant."[14] The hearing ended at noon, although it was scheduled to last all day. Spitzer said that he had heard enough from the women, that the panel would start drafting diagnoses, and that the women should leave. The women protested their dismissal, and they were allowed to stay—but only if they did not speak.[15] In the afternoon session the panelists discussed among themselves how to define masochism; they made little reference to research. Diagnostic criteria were discussed and keyed into a computer. Lynne Rosewater recalled that during the discussion of a criterion of Masochistic Personality Disorder, Spitzer's wife said, "I do that sometimes," and Spitzer said, "Okay, take it out." "You watch this," said Rosewater, "and you say, 'Wait a second, *we* don't have a right to criticize *them* because this is a "science"?' It was really frightening."[16]

The hearing was not a meeting of people who agreed on very much. The women critics and the mostly male panel disagreed on the motivations for and possible consequences of the proposed diagnosis of Masochistic Personality Disorder, on what constituted credible scientific evidence for the validity of it, and on the appropriate process for including it in the official diagnostic manual. In response to this erupting dispute, the work group made several cosmetic changes to mollify the critics and to prepare for an important meeting in December 1985 at the APA headquarters in Washington, D.C. The first change was to drop the term *masochistic* and thus avoid, the panel hoped, the historical meaning of seeking pleasure through inviting abuse. The name of the proposed disorder was changed to Self-Defeating Personality Disorder (SDPD). In response to the strong opposition of the critics, the panel also decided to add an exclusionary clause that specified that the diagnosis was not for those individuals who were responding to physical, sexual, or psychological abuse or for those who were depressed. (Other changes in the specific criteria were also made by the time the next draft was published the following August.)

In the course of these ongoing debates with the feminists another new category was proposed—Sadistic Personality Disorder—for those who have a pervasive pattern of cruelty to others. The category emerged rather suddenly, as part of an attempt to mollify the opponents of Masochistic Personality Disorder by adding a disorder that would apply to the men in abusive relationships. Although the feminists were not mollified, Sadistic Personality Disorder was often swept up in the whirlwind of controversy; eventually, it was buried with other battle casualties.

The December 1985 Hearings

As soon as the November hearing was over, the work group began preparing for another one to be held on December 4 at the headquarters of the APA in Washington, D.C.[17] This hearing was convened by an ad hoc committee of the APA's board of trustees chaired by Robert Pasnau, president-elect of the APA. This ad hoc committee, set up to manage disputes arising in the revision of DSM-III, was responsible for making a recommendation to the full board, which would be the final arbiter in any dispute. The December 1985 hearing was the first time Spitzer's work group met with the ad hoc committee. The meeting covered many controversies in addition to those involving the feminist critics.

The ad hoc committee's hearing on December 4 was a replay of the November hearing. Testimony was invited from those for and against the three controversial diagnoses. (Masochistic Personality Disorder, Premenstrual Dysphoric Disorder, and Paraphilic Rapism). Spitzer, as chair of the work group that was making the proposals, defended the recommendations. Representatives from the APA's Committee on Women restated their opposition. Time was spent on each of the three diagnoses, and after listening to the testimony, members of the ad hoc committee and members of Spitzer's work group adjourned to the private "Freud room" to decide what to do with the three controversial diagnoses. The women critics were excluded from these discussions and were not told about the results of the deliberations for several days. In fact, they were not told until 30 minutes before the topic came up on the board of trustees' meeting agenda on December 7. At that meeting the board agreed to the ad hoc committee's (and Spitzer's) recommendation to conduct a field test to examine the new criteria for the proposed disorder (now called SDPD) and to establish its prevalence.[18]

Spitzer was delighted with the outcome of the hearing. A few days later (on December 11, 1985), he sent a short note to those of his work group colleagues who had helped him, informing them of the success of their efforts, and telling them that several members of the ad hoc committee had not expected them to succeed with the three controversial diagnoses:

> Because of your splendid efforts (and the efforts of our critics), we actually were successful in getting four out of four (Sadistic Personality being the fourth Category).

My impulse following the meeting was to squander Work Group funds and send each of you a rose, but better judgment prevailed. . . .

The Board also approved a field trial of the criteria for Self-Defeating Personality Disorder to help determine the threshold of the diagnosis. Fred Kass and I will be planning this field trial shortly.

On the same day, Spitzer wrote a much longer memo to all members of the work group, whom he referred to as "the Revisionists," appraising them of the current status of the issues that had been handled by the ad hoc committee. His bitterness toward the feminists was evident:

[I]t became quite clear to the members of the Ad Hoc Board/Assembly Committee that our critics kept repeating themselves and had little more to say than that these categories had a potential for being abused. Dr. Paul Fink, one of the Committee members, made it quite clear from the outset that this argument was not going to be decisive, since virtually all psychiatric disorders hold a similar potential for abuse.

Because of the very fine showing of our group and the often outrageous remarks of our critics (one of them virtually admitted having lied to a *Time* magazine reporter . . .), the Committee approved the inclusion of the four controversial categories . . . in DSM-III-R! . . . we were actually successful in four out of four.

The victory was short-lived, for the feminist critics would not be dismissed so easily by the actions of the male-dominated APA committees.

The Spring of Feminist Discontent

The feminist critics of the proposed diagnoses continued to organize in opposition to Spitzer's group by using the media, existing feminist groups, and other professional organizations. Many supporters were mobilized. Letters and petitions against the new categories were drafted. The anger of the women expressed itself in many ways. For example, Linda Gay Peterson, a psychiatrist at the University of Massachusetts Medical Center, sent Spitzer a proposal (on December 3, 1985) for several new diagnostic categories that she thought needed to be added to the manual to complement his advocacy for rapism and masochism. With bitter satire she suggested "castrationism" as a psychiatric legal defense for women who strike back, a diagnosis to match "rapism." She called for other categories for male behavior, such as pansyism, assaultism, and murderism. She pointedly asked that Spitzer "give all of these equal consideration with the inclusion of rapism and masochism." Letters of objection from women were the least of Spitzer's worries. He had a proven track record of managing controversy. He had negotiated a settlement between gays and the psychoanalysts over the diagnosis of homosexuality in the 1970s (see chapter 3), had fought back the Freudians on his proposal to drop the term *neurosis,* had defeated the psychologists on the definition of mental disorder, and had successfully maneuvered behind the scenes through dozens of disputes in the development of DSM.[19] A few missives from feminists did not appear to him to be a big problem.

Appearances can be deceiving. In March 1986, the Association for Women in Psychology met in Oakland and discussed the threat of the new diagnoses. The group voted to join a new "Coalition Against Ms . . . Diagnosis," a coalition that included representatives from the Feminist Therapy Institute, battered women, the American Psychological Association, the American Psychiatric Association, the National Association of Women and the Law, and the National Association of Social Workers. Petitions were circulated among women's groups nationwide.[20] Opposition to the new diagnoses began to build among powerful professional groups. At a meeting convened by the surgeon general on violence and public health, a working group on spouse abuse condemned Masochistic Personality Disorder as a victim-blaming diagnosis. In January the Institute for Research on Women's Health issued a statement of protest against the three proposed diagnoses. In February the American Psychological Association's Council of Representatives supported the opposition to the new categories. The U.S. Justice Department opposed Paraphilic Rapism because of concern that the diagnosis might provide a defense in criminal trials. In May 1986, the National Association of Social Workers protested the inclusion of the three controversial diagnoses.

The American Orthopsychiatric Association, the most prominent interdisciplinary organization in mental health, weighed in against the new diagnoses. Failing to get a response from an earlier letter, Claire Fagin, the president of the association, wrote Spitzer on March 27, 1986, expressing grave concern about the new diagnostic categories. She wrote that her association was concerned, about "how social and cultural biases affect systems of classification of mental disorders" and about how these suggested categories were "being considered for inclusion without any sound epidemiological data from which to draw inferences." With regard to Self-Defeating Personality Disorder, she wrote the following:

> The criteria described culturally accepted personality and behavior patterns which have been assigned to women. If this cluster of traits is added to the DSM-III it will be equating culturally induced behavior patterns with a psychiatric diagnosis of mental illness. There is no proposed parallel diagnosis for the aggressive, power-driven, exploiting personality and behavior patterns fostered by the culture in men. Neither one should be categorized as mental illness. Of particular concern are women who are victims of family violence and develop clinging behavior in response to terror. Studies show that the attachment of a victim to a victimizer is a frequent sequel to intimidation and fear of death. This behavior pattern is not a personality disorder but an effort to survive.

Psychologist Paula Caplan was particularly active in mobilizing opposition to the three categories. The author of the just published book *The Myth of Women's Masochism,* Caplan was particularly concerned that there was now a proposal to officially recognize as a mental disorder a behavior pattern she had argued was merely a myth used to oppress women. Among her many efforts that spring was her attempt to influence the way the health insurance industry viewed these new categories. Caplan realized that if insurance companies accepted the new categories and reimbursed psychotherapists for treating individuals who were given such diagnoses, these "disorders" would become institutionalized into the medical lexicon. She knew that reimbursement for services was the fiscal foundation for mental health services and that if the insurance industry refused to pay for treating these alleged disorders, therapists would lose interest in them and the APA would have less reason to include them in DSM.

The purpose of the spring campaign against the new categories was to mobilize broad opposition to Spitzer's recommendations so that the proposals would be defeated when the APA board of trustees voted on them on June 28. An important part of this campaign was a women's Speak Out protest at the APA annual meeting in Washington, D.C., just six weeks before the crucial vote of the trustees.

The Meetings of May 1986

The annual meetings of the American Psychiatric Association have become in recent years an odd mixture of scientific presentations, backstage politicking, pharmaceutical company emporium, and grass-roots protest. They are also largely a gathering of white men. As the meetings opened on May 12 in Washington, D.C., they were met by a protest march organized by individuals who had become all too familiar to Spitzer and the proponents of the controversial categories. The organizers included Lenore Walker, Laura Brown, Virginia O'Leary, Judy Sprei, Renee Garfinkel, Lynne Rosewater, Barbara Hart, Adrienne Smith, Joan Cummerton, Teresa Bernardez, and Beverly McGain.[21]

On the following day the "official" APA symposium, scheduled by Spitzer, on Premenstrual Dysphoric Disorder and Self-Defeating Personality Disorder began. (Rapism was not a focus of this debate.) The symposium was structured like a debate, with speakers selected to argue either for or against the new categories. At the symposium Jean Baker Miller and Paula Caplan had a combined total of 16 minutes to speak against Self-Defeating Personality Disorders. Frederic Kass and Richard Simons spoke in defense of it.[22] Amid the academic debate about the existence and validity of SDPD were signs of tension and anger. The female critics felt that despite what they had to say, despite the petitions and protests, and despite their reasoned attempts to marshal scientific evidence for their position and to point out the weaknesses of the scientific data that purportedly supported the new diagnosis, they were at a disadvantage in the struggle to influence the powerful APA and its committees.

Board of Trustees' Meeting, June 1986

The campaign against the proposed diagnostic categories subsequently focused on the meeting of the APA's board of trustees on June 28, where action was to be taken on the three categories. On June 23, 1986, Paula Caplan sent a letter to the board summarizing the major points that critics had been making: the insubstantial scientific basis for the categories; the fact that there was no known effective psychiatric treatment for any of them; the sharply divided opinions among personality specialists about the wisdom of the new categories; and the bias and subjectivity that would affect how the diagnoses would get used to disadvantage women. And she reminded the board of the embarrassing publicity the APA had been getting from the national media.

A petition with over 2,800 signatures—and endorsed by organizations with many more members—against the recommendations of Spitzer's work group proposals was sent to the APA's new president, Robert Pasnau. The National Organization of Women (NOW) voiced its objections, and women in positions of influence within the APA—including Carol Nadelson, the past president of APA, and Elissa Benedek, who would become president several years later—continued to raise objections and to speak out against the proposals.[23]

Surprisingly, the board voted 10 to 4 against Spitzer's recommendation to place the new categories within DSM. But this was only a partial victory for the women: Self-Defeating Personality Disorder and the ever-changing label for PMS were to be placed in an appendix to the revised manual; that is, the intention was to not list them as regularly approved categories but to nevertheless make them available in some form. Sadistic Personality Disorder, conceived as some kind of counterweight to Self-Defeating Personality Disorder, also was to be placed in the appendix. Paraphilic Rapism was dropped completely. To the women who had criticized the proposed categories, this was a "stunning victory";[24] not one of the categories had been fully approved. On the other hand, the meaning of placing them in an appendix was unclear and something to be watched closely.

Spitzer was quick to react to this defeat of his work group's recommendations. On July 2, a few days after his setback at the board, he wrote to members of the Advisory Committee on Paraphilias and relayed the disappointing news about what had transpired at the board meeting. While Spitzer appeared willing to let the rapism diagnosis be discarded, he continued to argue on behalf of the other controversial categories. He wrote to Robert Pasnau, the president of the APA, on July 9 and told him of the dismay that members of his work group felt at the board's rejection of their proposals. He also wrote, "the Work Group was dismayed that the concept of 'an appendix,' which had been discussed in great detail with the Ad Hoc Committee on two occasions, was endorsed by the Board for the new categories of Sadistic and Self-Defeating Personality Disorders and Perilutial Phase Dysphoric Disorder [the relabeled PMS disorder]." In the same letter, Spitzer complained that even when he polled board members themselves after the vote, they disagreed about what inclusion in an appendix meant. He accused the board of making a decision that was not "thoroughly thought out." Since he recognized that the board was unwilling to accept the new categories as regular di-

agnoses but was unclear about what exactly to do with them, he proposed a "compromise for the Board that we would like considered at its
September meeting."

Spitzer's compromise (as expressed in the letter to Pasnau on July 9)
was to have the board reverse its decision and include the new categories
in the main body of the manual but with the following disclaimer immediately after the name of the new category:

> Note: This category has been added to the DSM-III-R although there is con-
> troversy about its validity. This category has a high potential for missapplica-
> tion [sic]; therefore, the diagnosis should only be given after a careful
> differential diagnosis and when the diagnostic criteria are clearly met.

Spitzer thought that this compromise allowed the board to flag these diagnoses as "different from the other DSM-III-R categories" but would
allow "both researchers and clinicians to use these categories, but with
caution." In fact, of course, he was offering very little, since the board had
final authority in these matters. Furthermore, his work group's disclaimer
urging that a careful differential diagnosis using the official criteria be
used with these categories implied that this was not expected with every
diagnosis. Apparently to increase the pressure for the compromise,
Spitzer told Pasnau that his work group voted unanimously not to accept
the board's decision of an appendix. Clearly, Spitzer and the work group
were still prepared to argue that the three remaining new categories be included in the main body of the manual.

The work group's objection to the board's decision and its proposed
compromise to move the new categories into the main text failed quickly.
In less than two weeks, on July 22, Spitzer forwarded to the officers of the
board of trustees a memo conceding that the three diagnoses would appear in an appendix called "New Controversial Categories." He persisted
in proposing that Self-Defeating Personality Disorder and Sadistic Personality Disorder be listed in the section of the manual with the other personality disorders and given an official code number. They would be
placed in brackets, however, to signify their special status. This was, in
fact, exactly the way they were listed in the second draft of DSM-III-R,
published the following month.[25] Behind the scenes that fall, negotiations continued about what to call the new appendix and about whether
the controversial diagnoses should continue to carry code numbers.[26]
Women's groups continued to monitor the persistent efforts of Spitzer's

work group to undo the action of the board, efforts that led to a final vote on the matter in December 1986.[27]

A year later, when DSM-III-R was published, Self-defeating Personality Disorder, PMS (called Late Luteal Phase Dysphoric Disorder), and Sadistic Personality Disorder were to be found in a new appendix titled "Proposed Diagnostic Categories Needing Further Study." They were listed without code numbers. In addition, contrary to the board's decisions and popular belief, Spitzer had also managed to sneak these controversial diagnoses, with code numbers, into the other regular sections of the DSM and make them available to clinicians.[28] An entirely new type of appendix had been created, a holding tank for controversies and for diagnoses that could officially be used with caution. Self-defeating Personality Disorder was in the manual, but it did not yet enjoy full official status. Spitzer may not have described the process as horse-trading, but it was certainly a hard-fought political, not scientific, compromise.

In a prophetic conclusion in the 1987 paperback edition to her book *The Myth of Women's Masochism,* Caplan warns: "The second reason we cannot relax about these categories is that Spitzer or someone else can propose moving them into the main part of the book, thereby giving them full status, in DSM-IV, which is due to be published in 1990. And so the struggle must go forward."[29] And so it did.

DIAGNOSING SCIENCE

"Science had once attacked entrenched authority, but the new scientific expert himself became an authority himself. His business was not to seek out what is *true,* but to pronounce on what is *appropriate.*"

　—Ehrenreich and English, *For Her Own Good: 150 Years of the Expert's Advice to Women*

One of the much-touted achievements of DSM-III was its purported reliance on scientific evidence. No such claims had been made about earlier editions of DSM. In fact, the relative absence of a scientific rationale for previous editions of DSM was one of its primary vulnerabilities; it allowed Spitzer and his hand-picked committees to discard the older version of the manual in favor of a very different approach to diagnosis. Using the appeal of scientific standards, empirical investigation, and hard data, Spitzer and the DSM committees renovated the manual, claiming that henceforth the diagnostic categories would be created not on the basis of clinical whim or theoretical bias, but, rather, on objective evidence that would enable proposed categories to withstand empirical scrutiny.

During the process of revising DSM-III, the emergence of the proposal to create Masochistic Personality Disorder posed an uncomfortable problem. On the one hand, psychoanalytic theory had long included the idea of masochism, and its practitioners claimed that they treated patients who suffered from it—although the outcomes were often not very good.[30] The DSM-III-R committee thought it would be convenient to have an official diagnostic category that reflected this psychoanalytic tradition and that could be used to identify problem patients.

On the other hand, the proposed diagnosis had none of the rigorous scientific evidence that was supposed to be the foundation for new diagnostic categories. The psychoanalytic literature on female masochism had come under attack on many grounds: it confused learned behaviors with inherent biological phenomena, mistakenly interpreted women's self-sacrifice as pain seeking, ignored the fact that women often endure pain in order to achieve some later expected gratification, and viewed some women's strengths (being nurturing, caring, and altruistic) as signs of personality disorder.[31] Moreover, a particular vulnerability of this literature was that it was based only on anecdote and case studies, and was devoid of the methodological polish that was becoming the gloss of the new scientific psychiatry.

Into this scientific void stepped Spitzer and his band of data makers. How could the committee charged to revise DSM-III propose a new, possibly controversial, diagnostic category that was not defended by any supportive scientific evidence? For years the developers of DSM had perfected the relatively simple, quick methods of generating scientific evidence that served as the basis for their decisions. As they had done with Borderline Personality Disorder (see chapter 6), they used their ready access to patients and therapists at the New York State Psychiatric Institute, affiliated with the Columbia University Department of Psychiatry, when they needed evidence quickly.

There is no better way to understand the uses of science in creating diagnoses than to review research articles published in psychiatric journals. In the struggles over Masochistic Personality Disorder, claims were made and disputed about the meaning of the available research. Since the studies in question are few, relatively accessible to the lay reader, and salient in some of the debates, they provide a fine opportunity (not so readily available in other diagnostic disputes) to examine DSM science in action.

The Ten Traits Study

Spitzer and psychiatrists Frederic Kass and Roger MacKinnon, all members of the APA's Advisory Committee on Personality Disorders, which was developing the recommendation for Masochistic Personality Disorder, conducted a small study after the proposal for the disorder first emerged in the advisory committee but before it was widely known to outsiders. The study was apparently conducted in 1984 and published in February 1986.[32] By the time the study was published, however, the initial decision to include the new category in the manual had already been made. When this article appeared, the battle between the feminists and Spitzer's work group was well under way, and this little study had already come under attack because it was virtually the only evidence that was advanced by the DSM developers to support the new category.

The study is intriguing because it reveals how important issues concerning the nature of mental disorder get transformed by the gatekeepers of DSM into minor issues of the consistency of diagnostic criteria. This transformation is a process the gatekeepers had used before and would use again. It is how they invent diagnoses.

The title of the article—"Masochistic Personality: An Empirical Study"—promises much more than it delivers. The article is only three pages long and contains two tables of data and 16 references. Only two of the works referred to have publication dates within a decade of the article's own date, and a majority of the citations are to psychoanalytic works published more than 30 years earlier. If there was a recent empirical scientific literature on which to rest this new category, its proponents appeared not to be aware of it. It is probably safe to say that such a body of evidence did not exist. In this scientific vacuum, this brief article took on added significance. Not only did the article constitute one of the few pieces of evidence offered for the controversial category, but it was coauthored by the main architect of DSM and one of the major proponents of MPD. This study represented what was accepted as respectable psychiatric science.

The study was conducted as follows: The authors prepared a preliminary list of 10 traits that they thought characterized Masochistic Personality Disorder. The list was presented to the advisory committee, which modified and reworded them (the list was similar to the criteria listed in Table 5–2). Then the authors picked "a sample from the ongoing psychotherapy practices" of 15 psychiatrists or residents in their own academic department. The authors do not explain how or why these 15 psychiatrists were selected, if they were selected from some larger group, whether they were representative of other clinicians, or whether they were only a sample of convenience. Normally, information about the selection of the sample is contained in research articles.

The authors asked each of the clinicians to select "three to five patients, choosing from a list of their patients' last names and starting at the beginning or end of the alphabet." They do not explain what this procedure was designed to accomplish. On what basis were the clinicians instructed to choose the three to five patients? Were the patients to be selected in sequence? Any patients or only those with personality disorders? Perhaps the researchers assumed that the first or last patients listed would constitute a representative sample and that it didn't matter which ones were chosen by the therapists. Thus, in a paragraph whose ostensible purpose is to describe the sampling methods, thereby providing some information about the potential generalizability of the study, little useful information about sampling is actually provided.

The 59 patients selected in this nonspecific manner are described as 64 percent female and 88 percent white; the average age was 35. For each of the patients selected, the clinicians were asked to do four things: First, they were to rate the patients on each of the 10 masochistic traits by indicating whether the trait was present, absent, or unknown because of insufficient information. Second, they were asked to make a DSM-III diagnosis. Third, they were asked to rate each patient on each of the 11 DSM personality disorders on a 4-point severity scale ("no traits," "some traits," "almost meets DSM-III criteria," and "meets DSM-III criteria"). Fourth, "using their own respective personal criteria," the therapists then rated each patient for masochistic personality on the same 4-point scale.

The article does not indicate how the purpose or focus of the study was explained to the clinicians. In studies of clinical judgment, the purpose is often disguised to ensure that the researchers do not influence the judgments of the clinicians. There is no indication in the article that any such precautions were taken. Furthermore, since the three authors were known members of the DSM-III revision committee examining personality disorders and were soliciting information from their own colleagues in the department of psychiatry, it is reasonable to assume that the clinicians knew the purpose of the study. If they did not know in advance, it would certainly not have been difficult for them to figure it out once they received the researchers' checklists. Since they first had to complete a checklist of masochistic traits; then make a formal diagnosis; then rate the patient on each of 11 personality diagnoses; and, finally, using whatever criteria they wanted, rate the patient for Masochistic Personality Disorder, it would hardly take a psychiatrist to figure out what was going on.

Scientifically, what was going on is less certain. One of the major intentions of the researchers was to examine the relationships among the therapists' responses to these four tasks. Was there any pattern to their ratings of their own patients? There are two implicit assumptions in such research that are crucial to the integrity of the study. The first assumption is that the multiple ratings that each clinician makes are independent of their other ratings. The second is that none of these ratings is affected by the respondent's knowledge of what the researchers want to study. In this study both assumptions are invalid.

Clearly, the therapists made their "different" assessments with a full knowledge of their own prior responses, not "independently." Cognitive consistency, if nothing else, would probably lead to some pattern of responses quite apart from the actual objective characteristics of the patients. Rather than a rating of patients, the study was perhaps more accurately a test of the ability of psychiatrists to create consistency among their impressions of patients. It would be nearly impossible, given the study's methodology, for there *not* to be bias in their responses.

Moreover, the therapists had every indication that the researchers were in fact looking for a particular pattern, namely, one that justified the inclusion of Masochistic Personality Disorder in DSM. It is reasonable to assume that the implicit, if not explicit, message from the researchers to the clinicians was this: "Here are ten characteristics of Masochistic Personality Disorder; please tell us which of your patients has this disorder."

The clinicians complied with the request. According to the article, 44 (75%) of their patients were diagnosed with some personality disorder. This proportion is considerably higher than that usually reported for most clinical samples, indicating either deliberate selection of clinicians who had patients with personality disorders (although this was never mentioned in the sampling design) or the willingness of the therapists to find personality disorders in patients when asked to do so.

The therapists labeled eight of their patients as having Masochistic Personality Disorder, the second most frequent personality diagnosis made and the third most frequent diagnosis of *any* kind made for these 59 patients. This is a truly remarkable result. At the time of this study, Masochistic Personality Disorder was *not* an official psychiatric diagnosis, and there was no agreed-upon definition or diagnostic criteria. Nevertheless, some of these 15 therapists (we are not told how many) found masochism virtually as common as anxiety disorder among their patients. The researchers report that this unofficial disorder "was diagnosed frequently by clinicians," making it sound as if the study had "discovered" a heretofore unrecognized but prevalent disorder. This was about as scientific as asking born-again Christians if they had ever been born again and then acting surprised by the extent of positive responses.

In fact, although documenting the prevalence of masochism was not the explicit purpose of the study, it was one of its important political effects. What if the therapists had said that none of their patients suffered from masochism or its traits? The study would have fallen flat and, no doubt, would not have been published. Thus, being able to report that masochism was one of the most common diagnoses in this sample gave the authors the advantage of appearing to be studying something real, common, and unexplored. The report was presented as if the researchers themselves had played no role in creating this phenomenon or in influencing the therapists; and as if it only conveyed what was found.

Having established these important impressions, the article swiftly moves to the details. It reports that most of the 10 masochistic traits were rated as present in about half the patients (45% to 60%) and that the traits had a Cronbach's alpha of .78 (alpha is a common measure of the extent to which a series of characteristics "hang together" empirically). If items measure the same concept (e.g. masochism), the alpha measure is relatively high (approaching 1.0), which in this case it does; a low alpha implies that the items are not measuring the same thing.

If the alpha is high, however, the conceptual validity of the phenomenon itself is not established. For example, if you asked rabid anti-Semites to rate Jews on characteristics such as clannishness, wealth, communist sympathies, and the extent to which they control international finance, you might achieve a high alpha with those traits; they might hang together empirically and have good internal consistency. But that finding would not tell you whether characteristics of Jews were accurately measured; it would merely capture the prejudicial belief system of anti-Semites. Showing that masochistic traits hang together is not a definitive method of determining whether masochism exists or whether it is a mental disorder.

The explicit purpose of the study, however, was to test how well the 10 traits measure masochism and distinguish it from other disorders. The major findings from the study are reported in one large table, which shows the 120 correlation coefficients between each of the 10 traits and 12 personality disorders. The precise type of correlation coefficient used is not stated, either in the text or the table, constituting another surprising oversight for a research article in a major journal.[33] In general, the correlations were low between each of the 10 traits and the 11 existing personality disorders. However, there were modest correlations with the diagnosis of masochism (the range was .19 to .68). What this means is pretty simple: there was a greater tendency for the clinicians to find the 10 masochistic traits in patients they thought had Masochistic Personality Disorder than in patients they diagnosed otherwise. This was viewed as good, confirmatory news, evidence worth disseminating in the profession's leading journal.

Often when reporting correlations based on data from samples drawn randomly, researchers will report tests of statistical significance. Such tests assess to what extent the correlations could occur by chance alone as part of sampling error. This is particularly important with small samples, where sampling error is a much more serious problem. In this study, the sample size was relatively small (N=59), making the correlations potentially unstable. Significance tests might have been used to indicate which correlations were unlikely to be due to sampling error, but no such tests were reported for these 120 correlations.

Again, significance tests are handy when data come from random samples of clinicians and patients, a condition that may or may not apply to this study (it isn't known if the samples were randomly selected, since the description of the sampling methods is so incomplete). One rationale for why the authors did not report significance levels would be that the samples were not random (in which case the results are not necessarily generalizable). This explanation, however, is not given (in fact, no explanation is offered); had it been offered, however, it would have defeated the purpose of the study.

Revealingly, significance tests *were* used with some of the data, but for another purpose altogether. When the authors report that eight patients were diagnosed with Masochistic Personality Disorder, they make a special point of indicating that six of the eight were women. The gender distribution for no other diagnosis is offered. Why offer this information? By this time, sensitive to the criticism of feminists about this new diagnostic category, the authors were quick to report that the correlation between gender and masochism "was not statistically significant (r -.15, p = .12)." Making this observation was completely gratuitous.[34]

More importantly, using any statistical test of significance to compare scores between a small sample of six women and two men is practically doomed to nonsignificance, unless the magnitude of the differences on masochism is truly enormous. In short, where the authors chose to report significance tests was precisely where they were statistically meaningless—but politically important. They wanted to say that women are *not* more likely to be diagnosed as masochistic, as the feminists critics were arguing, even though six of the eight patients diagnosed with MPD were women. Using this little meaningless test of statistical significance allowed the authors to counter the women with data, albeit irrelevant data.

The final data reported in the article only confirm what the authors already show in several other ways. They explain that the greater the number of masochistic traits the clinicians saw in their patients, the more likely they were to diagnose them as having Masochistic Personality Disorder. This statement concludes the authors' report of their findings.

In the brief discussion section the authors reported that the advisory committee of which they were a part decided on the basis of these findings to delete several traits; reword some items; and add one new trait, namely, "repeatedly turns down opportunities for pleasure." The newly constructed diagnostic category was ready for the draft of DSM-III-R. In the minds of the researchers, the achievements of the little study were considerable, since they conclude:

> Eight of the 10 draft items for defining the disorder had higher correlations with clinical ratings of masochistic personality than with any existing axis II personality disorders, indicating that the masochistic personality dimension of personality disturbance, as defined by the items, is not redundant with

the existing axis II personality disorders. The high correlation of the items with clinical judgments of masochistic personality, the high internal consistency of the item set, and the generally high correlations of items with the mean scores of the other nine items indicate that the items reflect a robust dimension of psychopathology.

There is little doubt that the authors viewed their study as a major step forward in recognizing a new malady; in their words, they were well on their way to a new "robust dimension of psychopathology." What their study reflects, more accurately, is that if you give psychiatrists a checklist of masochistic traits and ask them to rate their patients using those traits and then ask them which patients may have Masochistic Personality Disorder, there is some association between who they say have the traits and who they say is masochistic. What is robust about the study is not the results themselves—they are hardly surprising—but the manner in which the DSM advisory committees manufactured and used "scientific" evidence to make diagnoses.

The proponents of MPD used the study to forge ahead with their proposal, data in hand, with very little credible evidence about the validity of the category and virtually no developed argument that it constituted a mental disorder. The latter question was assumed a priori to be true.

More Studies, Mixed Evidence

Buoyed by the results of their first study, Spitzer and his research group immediately launched two other studies. They, too, took place amid growing controversy and objections from feminist critics. This was hothouse research, conducted with the expectation that results would be scrutinized critically by friend and foe alike. Rather than remaining abstractions in a journal article, these results would be used immediately. Spitzer was, after all, chairing the committee considering Masochistic Personality Disorder for inclusion in the APA's diagnostic manual, and he and other proponents of the new category desperately needed some data to support their cause.

In December 1985, Spitzer achieved a preliminary victory at the meeting of the APA's board of trustees when the board approved a national field trial of the proposed criteria for what had just been relabeled Self-Defeating Personality Disorder (SDPD). (Although the word masochism, used to denote a personality problem, was decades old, with a rich clinical tradition, it was dropped in an unsuccessful attempt to placate the women critics). With the APA go-ahead, Spitzer and the datamakers went to work again. In early 1986, just as the first study was appearing in print, they conducted two more studies. Both studies were described in a single article titled "National Field Trial of the DSM-III-R Diagnostic Criteria for Self-Defeating Personality Disorder." The results did not appear in print until December 1989, two years *after* DSM-III-R had been published.[35] This pattern of late publication was not uncommon. With many revisions of DSM, the relevant studies often were not published until after key decisions had been made and the new version of the manual had been published.[36]

The first study involved mailing a questionnaire to "2000 psychiatrists who had indicated a special interest in personality disorders in APA's *Biographical Directory*."[37] Whether these 2000 psychiatrists represented a sample drawn in some systematic manner is not explained in the journal article. The researchers went directly after the evidence they wanted. The questionnaire was sent with a letter (on APA letterhead) that noted the controversy surrounding SDPD and asked the respondents to provide data that would be helpful to the researchers, who everyone knew were major proponents of the attempt to include SDPD in DSM. The questionnaire included the following:

> Now we would like to know if you believe that the diagnosis of Self-Defeating Personality Disorder should be included in DSM-III-R. An answer of YES would mean both of the following:
>
> You have seen patients with a pattern of Self-Defeating behavior that is characterized by some of the eight items that are listed in question 5. This pattern began by early adulthood and did not occur only in response to, or in order to avoid, being physically, sexually, or psychologically abused, or only when the individual was feeling depressed.
>
> You believe that none of the Personality Disorders currently in DSM-III is adequate for describing and understanding this Self-Defeating pattern of personality disturbance. (Other Personality Disorders, such as Borderline, however, may coexist.)
>
> If YES (you think there is a need for the diagnosis of Self-Defeating Personality Disorder in DSM-III-R), check here————and continue.
>
> If NO, check here————and return questionnaire in enclosed envelope.[38]

The manner of soliciting information in the study was unusual for survey research. Normally, the beliefs of the researchers are unknown to the respondents and great care is taken to inquire about controversial matters in a carefully worded, neutral way so that the respondents are not subtly and unintentionally influenced to respond one way or the other. There is, in fact, a substantial body of evidence that demonstrates how easy it is for researchers themselves to affect the responses of the people they are studying.[39] In this context, it is noteworthy that the researchers chose to word their inquiry in declarative sentences ("You have seen . . .", "You believe . . .", "You think there is a need . . .") rather than in interrogative sentences ("Have you seen . . . ?" or "Do you think there is a need . . . ?"). More surprising is the last sentence, in which those who do not think there is a need for SDPD in DSM-III-R are told to return the questionnaire and not complete the section that asks them to describe their patients. Those who answered in the affirmative were instructed to select two patients whom they knew well; one was supposed to be "a good example of someone with Self-Defeating personality disorder and the other (a control) a patient with any of the DSM-III personality disorders." Spitzer et al. justify their exclusion of the psychiatrists who answered in the negative (the nonbelievers) this way: "Since it made little sense to ask a respondent who had not seen patients with the pattern of Self-Defeating behavior described in the criteria to describe a patient with the diagnosis, respondents who checked 'NO' were asked to return their uncompleted questionnaires."[40]

Apparently the researchers decided that there was nothing of importance concerning SDPD that they could learn from those who did not agree with them that the diagnosis was needed, even though these individuals constituted half of those who returned questionnaires. The investigators did not ask the nonbelievers why they saw no need for the new category, how they viewed or interpreted the behaviors described in the criteria, or how they would describe the clinical profiles of the patients they treated. The nonbelievers were simply dismissed from the study.

The believers, who were the only ones from whom data were collected, were asked to examine the list of eight criteria of SDPD and to indicate for each one of them whether it characterized their patient who had SDPD and their patient who did not. This was not a tricky task for the believers. As with the assigned tasks from the earlier study, the respondents were easily capable of such a quiz; after all, these were MDs and board-certified psychiatrists. They were presented with eight criteria of SDPD and asked to identify one patient who has the disorder and one who does not. Then they were asked to rate these two patients on the presence or absence of the eight criteria. This was not a daunting task. In fact, it required nothing more than short-term memory and some minimal capacity for cognitive consistency. It would have been truly astounding, given the methods of this study, if these highly trained psychiatrists could not provide the data Spitzer wanted.

There were no major surprises, but there was disappointment. Only 620 (31%) psychiatrists responded to the questionnaire, only 12% of them were women, and only 222 of the original 2,000 completed the rating of two patients. The result is that the data are based on only 11% of the sample; this small subgroup of respondents had been deliberately screened into the study by the researchers and, one can assume, were among those most supportive of the proposal for SDPD. None of these problems was emphasized by the authors of the report.

The results were as anyone would expect. Psychiatrists reported that those patients who had SDPD were more likely to have characteristics of SDPD than those patients whom they identified as not having SDPD. Each of the SDPD traits was used to describe from 70% to 92% of the SDPD patients. But these same traits were *not* absent as characteristics of the other patients; each trait was judged present in 29% to 51% of the non-SDPD patients.

This simple, predictable result was presented with all the scientific trimmings: two tables of data; odds ratios, calculations of sensitivity, specificity, and predictive values; and talk of discriminating power, maximization of the total predictive value of the criteria, and logistic regression. An uncritical reader of the journal article might be led to believe that something of enduring importance was discovered in this "national field trial" of ony 222 carefully screened and self-selected respondents.

The second study reported in the same article used a similar methodology but was slightly different in focus. A separate sample of 5,000 psychiatrists who had a special interest in personality disorders was drawn from the same source used in the previous study. A questionnaire was sent with an accompanying letter asking for help in exploring the relationships among personality disorder diagnostic criteria. No explicit mention was made of SDPD, although it seems reasonable, given the national media reports of the DSM controversy that had appeared, that many psychiatrists were aware of the conflict and of Spitzer's role in it. Still, only

28% of the psychiatrists who had indicated a special interest in personality disorders (the topic of the survey) returned the questionnaires.

The questionnaire listed 32 diagnostic criteria: all of the proposed criteria for Borderline Personality Disorder, Dependent Personality Disorder, and Self-Defeating Personality Disorder, as well as seven additional criteria from other types of disorders. Psychiatrists were asked to choose their first patient who "came to mind" who had a personality disorder—a questionable method of generating information about patients. They were then asked to indicate which of the 32 criteria described the patient and to note the patient's DSM-III personality disorder. The intent of the study was to gauge the degree of overlap among the three personality disorders.

Using the computer to extract the DSM-III-R diagnoses on the basis of which combination of diagnostic criteria the psychiatrists checked, Spitzer et al. reported how many male and female patients were classifiable as having one of the three personality disorders. For each of the three disorders, they found that female patients were more likely than male patients to be diagnosed. Women were 1.5 times more likely to meet the criteria for SDPD than were men—a finding that makes the conclusion reached by Kass, MacKinnon, and Spitzer in the earlier study (namely, that there is no significant difference in the prevalence of SDPD in men and women) seem premature. Other analyses were reported as well. The internal consistency, as measured by alpha, of the criteria for SDPD was .61, a modest (not high) level. More problematic was the finding that SDPD was not particularly independent of the other two disorders.[41] The high degree of overlap greatly weakened the case for SDPD—but, of course, by the time this article appeared in print, SDPD was already safely ensconced in the special appendix of DSM-III-R.

Finally, the researchers subjected the pool of diagnostic criteria to factor analysis, a complex statistical procedure that also identifies whether the criteria that are supposed to distinguish the three disorders from each other actually do so. The results, the authors admitted, "indicate that the factorial structure of the total criteria set did not match the clinical hypothesis of three distinct personality domains."[42] This final study was the only one of the three in which the respondents were not coached explicitly about what the researchers wanted to hear, and it was the only one that clearly suggested that the new SDPD category seemed visible only to those who already believed in it.

There are other limitations of these studies, pertaining both to the samples used and to their methodologies, but such problems will add little to the central point: *at the time the APA developed, proposed, and approved SDPD for inclusion in DSM-III-R, there was precious little evidence of any kind that the new diagnosis represented a distinct mental disorder or that it was broadly supported by practicing psychiatrists.* The data were generated in ways that hardly achieved a minimum level of scientific rigor. Despite these limitations, a new diagnosis was created in DSM, against organized and strong opposition. With the DSM committees and decision makers, a little data went a long way.

THE DEFEAT OF MASOCHISTIC PERSONALITY DISORDER

From the pattern established during the development of DSM-III and continued to this day, one can see that the APA's process of creating diagnoses never really ends. Adding new categories, revising diagnostic criteria, and unmaking diagnoses appear to go on constantly, between the periodic revisions of the official manual. Although Self-Defeating Personality Disorder had garnered enough political support to fight its way into the special appendix of DSM-III-R in 1987, by the following year, when the work began on DSM-IV, the battle was rejoined.

Three factors made a new struggle over SDPD inevitable. First, as a political compromise the new category had been placed in an appendix titled "Proposed Diagnostic Categories Needing Further Study." SDPD had not achieved tenure in the manual, but it had a novel, probationary status. It was expected that SDPD would either find enough support among clinicians and researchers to be promoted into the regular part of the manual, where Spitzer's group wanted it, or it would be dropped altogether. Second, since one of the dominant themes of the DSM-IV Task Force was its commitment to scientific assessment as a method of making decisions about diagnoses, it was inevitable that sooner or later the flimsy scientific evidence that had been used to justify SDPD would be seen as inadequate. New data were needed that would be more convincing. Third, the women critics were preparing to launch an embarrassing public fight to prevent this offensive category from slipping into the manual. During the development of DSM-IV, Self-Defeating Personality Disorder would have to fight for its life.

The Ideology of Decision Making

Early in the development of DSM-IV, the signal was given that scientific data were going to be more important in making decisions about DSM than they had been in previous versions. In part, this was a rhetorical position (and a safe one) to reassure critics that the next version would not be the product of fads and fashions and would bolster psychiatry's image as a branch of medical science.

Allen Frances, who had been a member of the DSM-III-R Task Force and was an expert on personality disorders, was selected to head the DSM-IV Task Force, ensuring that the personality disorders in DSM-IV would get considerable attention. That attention was further ensured by the appointment of Thomas Widiger, a psychologist, as the research coordinator of DSM-IV. Widiger had also written extensively on personality disorders.[43]

Work groups were set up to address different diagnostic categories or issues. During 1988, Susan Fiester, a psychiatrist with Northeast Psychiatric Associates in Nashua, New Hampshire, was assigned the task of reviewing issues related to SDPD. Paula Caplan was directed by Allen Frances to contact Fiester and to serve as an outside consultant. Caplan eagerly followed through on Frances's suggestion by writing to Fiester (on October 24, 1988) and explaining that she had planned to review the relevant literature on SDPD and "would be pleased to do this as a consultant to the Work Group."[44] It was an innocent beginning to what later became a problematic relationship between Caplan and the DSM decision makers, a relationship that eventually led her to abandon her role as a consultant to the work group. But along the way, Caplan discovered just how difficult it was to know who was doing what, and when or how it was being done, in the purportedly open scientific process of developing the diagnostic manual. Because Caplan has written about her experience and has also made her correspondence available, we are able to get a glimpse of what the process looked like from the standpoint of a DSM critic and opponent of a particular category.

Putting the Cap on Caplan

In telephone calls and letters to Frances and Fiester, Caplan was enthusiastic about helping to assess the scientific literature, but she was often frustrated in her attempts to find out how she could get involved. Six months after she had contacted Fiester, Caplan had not received any copies of the material the SDPD work group had gathered about SDPD, had not been given Fiester's mailing address, and had not received instructions about what she could do to be helpful. Caplan wrote Fiester on May 2, 1989 to express concern. She reminded Fiester that she had been prepared to do an extensive literature review herself about SDPD and make it widely available to those who were likely to oppose inclusion of that diagnosis in DSM but that in response to Frances's invitation she had indicated her willingness to work with the work group rather than against it. Caplan reminded Fiester of the adverse publicity and embarrassment suffered by the APA when those who opposed SDPD and other diagnoses went to the media. She told Fiester that she had found little empirical research that warranted the permanent establishment of SDPD as an official diagnosis. Caplan's letter was also a warning that she was feeling excluded from the work group; she stated that if the work group chose not to involve her in its deliberations, she was prepared to go directly to the public and the media, as she and others had done three years before in order to push SDPD out of the manual's main text and into a special appendix. She sent a copy of the letter to Frances, who wanted to avoid the public confrontations that had plagued his predecessor, Spitzer.

Since Caplan was only a consultant, there was no commitment by Fiester to keep her posted on the timetable for decision making. Fiester was certainly willing to receive information from the consultants and to periodically send them material to review, but the role of consultant was very different from that of work group member. This difference led Caplan to feel out of the loop, and indeed she was. As she had promised, Caplan completed for publication a manuscript reviewing the evidence for SDPD and sent it to John Gunderson, the chair of the major DSM-IV personality disorders work group. Gunderson thanked her for the review but informed her that it had arrived too late for the work group to consider and that the group thought the existing evidence was "insufficient to move . . . [SDPD] in either direction." Since the personality work group was not yet persuaded to include or exclude SDPD from DSM-IV, said Gunderson, it would take new evidence to tip the balance.

Frances acknowledged receiving Caplan's review article. Although he thought it was "too polemical," he revealed to her for the first time that he was pleased that the personality work group did not seem enthusiastic about SDPD. In a letter dated October 26, 1989, Frances told Caplan that he preferred "that the SDPD diagnosis be withdrawn because a dispassionate review of the evidence fails to demonstrate sufficient empirical support," adding that he saw no need for "heated controversy." Amazingly, just two years after Spitzer had fought passionately for the inclusion of SDPD as a regular category, his former lieutenant and now the task force chair, Allen Frances, was signaling that his preference was to discard the diagnosis and avoid renewed controversy. And he was admitting this to Caplan, who clearly was not going to allow SDPD into DSM without a fight (and a public one if necessary). Frances wanted to assure her that even without her opposition the category might die for lack of scientific evidence. It was a minor peace offering, a show of solidarity.[45]

Caplan continued to express her concerns to Frances about the SDPD work group, and Frances continued to reassure her (in a letter of February 7, 1990) that her voice was being heard and that he doubted that SDPD would be a controversial topic with DSM-IV. On November 8, 1990, Caplan wrote Frances severing her ties with the SDPD group and requesting that her name not be listed among those who consulted on DSM-IV. In a letter to Caplan dated November 27, 1990, Frances admitted being "puzzled" by Caplan's "continued misunderstanding of the careful methods being applied in DSM-IV." He accepted her resignation.

In fact, Frances had a better sense of where SDPD was headed than Caplan did. She had spent six years observing how the men of the APA manufactured data, overlooked counterevidence, and generally got their way—unless strong, vociferous, public opposition forced them into some compromise. And she had reason to believe that the DSM-IV work groups did not want her too close to the center of action but just close enough so that they could later claim they had solicited advice from many experts, including the women critics. Co-optation in the service of DSM had been used many times before to contain controversy before it reached the news media.

The Final Disposition

By the time Fiester published her review of the empirical evidence regarding SDPD, her conclusions were not very different than those Caplan had reached five years earlier, namely, that little scientific evidence existed to indicate a need to add Self-Defeating Personality Disorder to the diagnostic manual. Although other studies had been conducted after the little field trial studies of Spitzer and his associates, the findings were mixed. Fiester reported as follows:

> Although there has been progress in the attempt to elucidate the nature of Self-Defeating personality disorders, the small body of research that has been carried out over the past several years has significant limitations. . . . Few data are available to address the issue of external validity, for example, associated features, impairment, complications, predisposing factors, family history, and biological markers. . . . There are no formal data on the potential harmful effects of the use of the disorder in clinical, forensic, or other settings. There is little or no information about whether the diagnosis implies something about the course of illness, prognosis, or helps inform decisions regarding treatment as no studies of course, prognosis, or treatment outcome have been carried out. . . . In addition, significant concerns exist about the potential negative consequences of including the disorder in DSM-IV.[46]

Fiester concluded that the data were lacking to support the inclusion of SDPD in DSM-IV. She suggested that the diagnosis be either included in an appendix of disorders requiring further study, as it had been in 1987, or left out of DSM altogether, as the feminist critics had been arguing since 1985. These conclusions are an indication of how meager the supporting evidence had been four years earlier when Spitzer and the diagnosis makers successfully used it to convince various high-level committees of the APA that SDPD was just what the doctor ordered.

In September 1991, the APA began selling a book (for $10) that provided the first awkward glimpse of DSM-IV. The book contains suggested changes in DSM-III-R and reflections on the options that were under consideration. In the section on personality disorders, there is one page devoted to SDPD, and the discussion opens bluntly: "Because of insufficient evidence, this disorder will not be included as an official diagnosis in the classification."[47] If SDPD remains in the appendix, the text states, it will be necessary to make various modifications that have been suggested for the diagnostic criteria. These minor modifications, which seem to be responses to various criticisms of the criteria listed in the appendix of DSM-III-R, are then provided. Thus, there appeared to be little enthusiasm remaining for the diagnostic category SDPD.

By March 1993, the next draft of DSM-IV was made available (for

$17.50). In this book there is absolutely no mention of Self-Defeating Personality Disorder in the section on personality disorders. There is a listing of diagnoses that were intended for an appendix, and the following explanation is given: "The Task Force determined that there was insufficient information to warrant inclusion of these proposals as official categories in DSM-IV. Text and criteria will be provided to facilitate systematic clinical research."[48] But even in this listing of failed diagnostic proposals, SDPD is not mentioned. The proposal that had brought controversy to the APA and the DSM in the mid-eighties did not earn so much as a courtesy footnote in the final draft of DSM-IV. The defeat of Self-Defeating Personality Disorder was almost complete.

Some groups within the APA, however, were not ready to concede defeat. At the annual meeting of the APA in San Francisco in May 1993, where action was to be taken by the APA assembly on DSM-IV, a formal amendment was made to retain SDPD in DSM-IV. After spirited debate, the amendment was defeated by a 63% to 37% vote, although DSM-IV itself gained approval from the Assembly.[49] Two months later, the APA board of trustees gave final approval to DSM-IV. As DSM-IV moved toward publication in 1994, SDPD was finally abandoned after a decade of controversy.

MASOCHISM GETS A MATE: DELUSIONAL DOMINATING PERSONALITY DISORDER

In the midst of the struggles to defeat Self-Defeating Personality Disorder, Paula Caplan and Margrit Eichler, a sociologist, wrote a letter to Allen Frances (dated May 8, 1989) proposing for inclusion in DSM another new diagnosis: Delusional Dominating Personality Disorder (DDPD). They explained that their proposal conformed to the standards set forth in DSM by Spitzer; that is, it was descriptive and atheoretical and was based on research that documented its pervasiveness and harm. Caplan and Eichler noted that DDPD constituted a personality disorder because it was maladaptive in terms of having healthy, loving relationships; they pointed out that DDPD could, like sociopathy, be "adaptive for some high-paying, high-prestige positions." They encouraged the APA to seize the opportunity to educate mental health professionals and the public about the harm DDPD can cause. They offered to form or participate in a review committee to work on developing the proposal further, and they sent copies of the proposal to 43 prominent individuals who had an interest in this topic.

In the letter Caplan and Eichler enclosed a list of 14 diagnostic criteria for DDPD, including the following:[50]

- Inability to identify and express a range of feelings
- Inability to respond appropriately . . . to the feelings and needs of close associates
- Tendency to use power, silence . . . and avoidance . . . in the face of interpersonal conflict
- Having excessive need to inflate the importance . . . of oneself
- a tendency to feel inordinately threatened by women who fail to disguise their intelligence
- the presence of . . . delusions that women like to suffer . . . ; that pornography and erotica are identical; that physical force is the best method of solving interpersonal problems
- a need to affirm one's social importance by displaying oneself in the company of females who . . . are conventionally physically attractive, younger than oneself, shorter in stature, weigh less and are more submissive than oneself

The proposal (later expanded and published by Kaye-Lee Pantony and Paula Caplan) obviously constituted a frontal assault on traditional masculine socialization and its harmful effects, effects largely unrecognized because DDPD *"characterize[d] so many of the powerful people in our society."*[51] Pantony and Caplan indicated in their proposal that DDPD was "most commonly seen in males" and that it tended "to characterize leaders of traditional mental health professions, military personnel, executives of large corporations, and powerful political leaders of many nations." They admitted that their primary aim was "to use the DDPD as a hub for efforts to rethink what is normal and what is healthy."[52] Although DDPD was initially proposed in an effort to raise the consciousness of the APA committees that were considering the inclusion of Self-Defeating Personality Disorder, it took on a life of its own because its logic appeared to parallel that of other diagnostic categories that the APA had supported.

In 1991 Pantony and Caplan discussed the multiple purposes of developing the diagnostic category DDPD. On the one hand, they wanted to demonstrate how unexamined assumptions about sex role stereotypes (particularly about women) were being pathologized in DSM; at that

time, both Self-Defeating Personality Disorder and Premenstrual Dysphoric Disorder were being given serious consideration for inclusion in
DSM-IV. Pathologizing stereotypically male behavior allowed Pantony and
Caplan to cleverly make this point. For example, they offered the following criterion (among others) for DDPD: "A tendency to feel inordinately
threatened by women who fail to disguise their intelligence."[53] What
could a predominantly male committee do with this suggestion by obviously intelligent, assertive women? Reject it out of hand? Angrily dismiss
it? Deny that the behaviors associated with DDPD occur? Claim that the
"diorder" is unimportant? What could they do that did not smack of their
feeling inordinately threatened by the proposal? Many of the other criteria
for DDPD called for a similar level of critical self-reflection about sex role
stereotypes and how they influence views of mental disorder.

On the other hand, Pantony and Caplan went a step further in their
proposal for a DDPD diagnosis than just pointing to sex bias. They argued that some typically male behaviors are themselves harmful and dysfunctional for men and women. This aspect of their proposal was the
more profound one, because it could not be addressed simply by tinkering with the criteria of existing diagnostic categories. It required a more
concentrated examination of the concept of mental disorder. Pantony and
Caplan knew that if, in fact, common male behaviors could be shown to
be dysfunctional and harmful, a theoretical case could be made for including them in the diagnostic manual. In their article, Pantony and Caplan set out to make that case.

The first task in the Pantony–Caplan article was to establish that
DDPD exists. Their argument was tentative and incomplete. They described a study that was under way, but they provided no results. They indicated that they had developed a 75-item checklist, composed of all the
criteria items from DDPD as well as items from six other personality disorders, and were distributing the checklist not only to therapists, who
would describe their clients, but also to other people, who could choose
to describe themselves or their partners. After collecting these questionnaires, they planned to examine whether the DDPD criteria clustered together coherently or whether DDPD overlapped too greatly with existing
personality disorders, such as Narcissistic Personality Disorder or Antisocial Personality Disorder.[54]

The second task was to describe DDPD's basic nature and varieties. In
this section of their article, Pantony and Caplan described the proposed

diagnostic criteria and culled evidence from the social science literature that men were more likely to have these traits than women. For example, for the criterion concerning the inability to establish and maintain meaningful interpersonal relationships, they cited authors who have suggested that male socialization often hinders the development of relational abilities and teaches men to be detached and self-reliant, to need power over others, to avoid emotional intimacy with same-sex friends, and to base their sense of masculinity on how well they compete with, not relate to, other men. For the criterion pertaining to the inability to identify and express a range of feelings in oneself and others, they cited reports that suggest that men regard inexpressiveness as manly and use anger to cut off feelings of vulnerability, fear, helplessness, and sadness.

Pantony and Caplan marched through all fourteen of their criteria in this way, citing works in the literature that suggest that socialization is more likely to produce these characteristics in men than in women. At times, the literature cited is slight and circumstantial; at other times the point being made has considerable validity (as does, for example, the observation that men are more likely to have the delusion that physical force is the best method of solving interpersonal problems).

The third task undertaken by Pantony and Caplan in the article was to document the harm that the characteristics of DDPD cause. Here the authors argued that men are more likely to embrace masculine stereotypes because the behaviors are considered more desirable than behaviors traditionally associated with being female. They argued that this causes harm to the men themselves, although this is not easily recognized. They observed, for example, that men reveal less information about themselves than women do, are more guarded and tense, and are less able to talk about their problems. The resulting stress, they argued, may explain the higher rates among men of ulcers, hypertension, heart attacks, chronic diseases, and criminal activity and may account for their greater tendency to be victims of crimes, homicide, and suicide and to indulge in drug and alcohol abuse and other dangerous behaviors. Men also have a shorter life span than women. Men have more difficulty achieving intimacy and using the social support that is available in their environment. Men also are excessively competitive and aggressive and appear to adopt maladaptive patterns of coping with stress.

Pantony and Caplan suggested that the harms men suffer affect others as well: women and children who live with DDPD sufferers are made to feel uncomfortable at best and are subjected to anger and violence from these men at worst. They concluded that their formulation of DDPD was a first step toward redressing the sexist imbalance in DSM, and they suggested that before a psychiatrist uses the label Self-Defeating Personality Disorder for a woman, it is important to determine whether the woman is living and coping with a man who suffers from DDPD.

The analysis by Pantony and Caplan was hardly encouraged by those working on the DSM-IV task force. In fact, not only was the task force reluctant to open a Pandora's box to establish what is normal and healthy—DSM developers had been trying valiantly to keep the lid on that topic since the controversy over homosexuality in the early 1970s—but they simply could not fathom what Caplan and her associates were trying to do. Allen Frances wrote to Caplan on June 12, 1989, expressing his puzzlement and offering paternal advice:

> I really wasn't sure what to make about your "delusional dominating personality disorder." How serious are you about it? We intend to be stringent in our requirements for new diagnoses in DSM-IV in a way that I am sure you would endorse. I am very doubtful that DDPD has the kind of empirical support necessary for serious inclusion in DSM-IV. I think a more useful approach to the problem you are probably trying to highlight would be to suggest specific ways of modifying those criteria sets (especially dependent and histrionic) that may have lack of gender balance and also to document data to support those changes.

In questioning Caplan's seriousness, Frances indicated that the proposal was likely to get nowhere, implied that he was knowledgeable about the empirical support available and believed it to be woefully inadequate, and advised her to work within the established diagnostic categories and help the DSM developers tidy up any inadvertent gender imbalances in the diagnostic criteria. For Frances, the proposal was dead on arrival.

In a reply to Gunderson written on June 23, 1989, Caplan said she was "extremely serious." She claimed that the empirical base for DDPD was in fact "far, far better than the empirical bases of some of the categories . . . kept in the DSM-IV." Frances again issued a strongly discouraging and defensive response to Caplan in a letter of July 24, 1989:

> We cannot apply the same level of empirical support to diagnoses already within the system, especially since there has been insufficient time for these

to be studied systematically and it is disruptive to constantly tinker with the classification. Thus the argument that a new diagnosis is just as well (or poorly) supported as existing diagnoses does not carry very much weight. New diagnoses must meet much higher standards.

Frances chose not to deny Caplan's assertion that DDPD had better empirical support than some existing diagnoses; instead, he claimed that it didn't matter. For Frances, as for his predecessor, this was an uncomfortable argument to make, since he had repeatedly emphasized the primary importance of empirical evidence for any changes in the diagnostic manual. He attempted to resolve this apparent inconsistency by making two astounding claims: that there was insufficient time to study existing diagnoses and that constantly tinkering with the diagnostic system was disruptive. Apparently, Frances thought that new diagnoses should be given more time and attention than existing ones, even though those diagnoses in use were having profound effects on patients. Furthermore, some existing DSM diagnoses had been in the manual for decades, allowing plenty of time to study their validity. His claim that he was trying to avoid tinkering constantly with DSM was false: the American Psychiatric Association had been deliberately and constantly tinkering with DSM since the 1970s, when the development of DSM-III began. There have been six major revisions of DSM since it was first published, and the APA has announced plans to publish a seventh revision in the next few years.[55]

To counter Caplan's report of support from some constituencies, Frances personally dismissed it in the letter written to her on July 24, 1989: "I also do not give much weight to enthusiastic endorsements—empirical support is a sine qua non." Yet a few sentences earlier, Frances had claimed that existing diagnoses did not need empirical support and that the simple endorsement of being in the manual was justification enough. Perhaps sensing that he was making contradictory arguments, Frances conceded that an empirical review for DDPD should be the first step; despite his opinion that the research on attitudes toward women was not pertinent, he offered to review the material if she was prepared to do the initial work. But he concluded, "If this sounds discouraging, I'm afraid it is meant to." Few readers of his letter would misread it as encouragement.

Later, in a letter of October 16, 1989, Frances told Caplan that she was headed for disillusionment because now the standards were higher than before for the inclusion of categories, because there was "neither a widespread clinical tradition nor a significant clinical literature" to support DDPD; and, finally, because time was running out for considering any new categories. Frances had raised more hurdles for the proponents of DDPD. Now, on top of his previous assertion that enthusiastic endorsements were not enough and his insistence that the empirical base must be more substantial for new than for existing disorders, he added the requirement of an established clinical tradition and clinical literature and the threat of time pressure. These were daunting challenges. A new diagnosis, almost by definition, does not have a clinical tradition or literature. In fact, it is often the inclusion of a new diagnostic category in DSM that allows a clinical tradition to develop and research to be conducted to support it. Frances's call for the existence of a clinical tradition before ratification of a new diagnosis, whatever the reasonableness of the requirement, was virtually impossible to meet.[56]

Caplan persisted. In February 1990, she learned that the DSM-IV Task Force was seeking money to conduct field trials on some diagnostic categories, and she inquired of Frances how she and her research group on DDPD could apply for funds to assist them in developing their proposal. The tone of Frances's response in a letter to Caplan on March 13, 1990, was strident. No funds were going to be devoted to DDPD, he said, adding that he didn't know what procedure would be used to review her proposal; that he was very much against adding any new personality disorders, particularly DDPD; and that he would not recommend that the work group devote any of its resources to DDPD. Apparently, the developers of DSM had enough from this woman who did not heed their advice, which, they perhaps did not recognize, had been contradictory.

Other disappointments followed for Caplan and her associates. Without assistance, funding, or any encouragement from the DSM-IV Task Force, they faced the enormous task of assembling published evidence that would support the legitimacy of DDPD as a mental disorder.[57]

The Mate Perishes, Too

There is no indication that any of the DDPD material was ever seriously considered by the APA work groups. No mention was ever made in any subsequent DSM publication that DDPD had ever been proposed. It was not mentioned in the first or the second draft of DSM-IV or even in the appendix that listed disorders that might be worth studying in the future.

Unlike SDPD, which was championed by DSM insiders and received prompt attention by the work groups, who tried, albeit unsuccessfully, to furnish a comfortable home within the DSM for it, DDPD was never invited into the house or even given a handout. The door was quickly slammed shut, as soon as the DSM developers discovered that Caplan and her associates were serious. Eventually, Caplan quit and went public with her critique of how the APA makes diagnoses.[58]

The death of Delusional Dominating Personality Disorder can be easily misinterpreted. The moral of the story is not that a proposal for a valid new diagnostic category was made and unfairly rejected simply as a result of sex bias. The proposal for DDPD was underdeveloped, as Caplan and her associates were quick to acknowledge. As Frances had pointed out, there was no clinical tradition regarding DDPD. The review of the proposal was clouded by the fact that it was, in part, a response to the political battle over Self-Defeating Personality Disorder. Furthermore, critical information regarding DDPD's conceptual coherence, the stability of its diagnostic criteria, and the precise ways in which it may be considered a mental disorder was not complete. Nevertheless, with some time and resources, a credible case could have been made for DDPD, certainly a case as credible as, and perhaps even more credible than, the one supporting SDPD or Borderline Personality Disorder (to which we turn in the next chapter) or some of the other personality disorders in DSM.

The moral is to be found in the different ways in which DDPD and SDPD were handled by the DSM-IV Task Force. SDPD made it quickly into the draft of DSM-III-R, virtually without review. When SDPD was ushered into the DSM process by prominent insiders, there existed only a scattered clinical literature and little credible scientific evidence of its coherence as a disorder. It was only because of the ruckus raised by feminists both inside and outside the psychiatric establishment when they learned about what had been sneaked into the manual that hearings were held to debate the legitimacy of the diagnostic category. Eventually, the continuing opposition and the flimsy underlying scientific evidence led to the defeat and exclusion of SDPD from DSM-IV.

The proposal for Delusional Dominating Personality Disorder was handled very differently, because it was championed by outsiders who raised questions about the gender bias of DSM. The DSM-IV Task Force initially viewed the proposal for DDPD as a clever hoax concocted by feminist outsiders merely to cause trouble. From the very beginning, the proposal was discouraged, even before any evidence had been reviewed. No assistance or guidance was offered to Caplan and her associates, no specific suggestions were made about how they might prepare the most persuasive evidence, and little information was proffered about how or when the review of the proposal would occur. The proposal for DDPD never had a chance, despite the evidence; the proposal for Masochistic Personality Disorder had a good chance, despite the paucity of evidence.

6 BORDER WARS

Borderline Personality Disorder (or, How Patients Seduce Their Therapists)

The battles over the inclusion and exclusion of diagnoses in DSM have consequences for prospective patients and for psychotherapists. Once a diagnosis is placed in DSM, it is given professional legitimacy and scientific respectability and takes on an unsupervised life of its own, often one not fully anticipated by its developers. The long battles over a homosexuality diagnosis, the new and unexpected uses of Posttraumatic Stress Disorder, and the uses that might have been made of Masochistic Personality Disorder illustrate the need to monitor what the APA committees do in revising DSM. In light of the wavering, invalid, or inconsistent criteria that are used to identify mental disorders and of the shabbiness of the scientific evidence that is often accepted in deciding which mental disorders to create, it should come as no surprise that once a diagnosis is created it is vulnerable to misuse. In fact, in the case of a diagnosis that is itself invalid as a disorder or that cannot be used reliably by clinicians, it is nearly impossible to even distinguish use from deliberate or unintentional misuse.

Personality disorders in DSM are mental disorders that are characterized by conditions and patterns of behavior that are defined as enduring, inflexible, and maladaptive, as distinct from disorders, such as Posttraumatic Stress Disorder, that imply a temporary condition. Because person-

176

ality disorders are defined as continuing throughout life, once such a diagnosis is applied to a patient, it can have wide-ranging implications for that individual for decades to come. This chapter describes the creation and use of one such diagnostic category: Borderline Personality Disorder. We first describe its creation by the diagnosis makers. Then we examine how the diagnosis has been used by psychiatrists to undermine the credibility of women who complain about their male psychotherapists. We describe the truly remarkable lengths to which some will go to blame a patient for a psychiatrist's misbehavior.

DIAGNOSES FROM THE LAB

When DSM-III was published in 1980, a number of new diagnoses were included in the manual. One was Borderline Personality Disorder (BPD). At the time, its evolution was a prototype for a new method that research psychiatrists would use to create new diagnoses, a method that relied on sophisticated statistical techniques. The story of BPD also illustrates some of the important, but not necessarily new, purposes that diagnoses serve.

The recognition of Borderline Personality Disorder as an accepted diagnosis was signaled in 1979 when the American Medical Association's *Archives of General Psychiatry* published an article by Robert Spitzer and his associates titled "Crossing the Border into Borderline Personality and Borderline Schizophrenia."[1] In their article, the inventors of the new diagnosis explained how it evolved. Previously, the term *borderline* had been used for psychiatric diagnoses in two principal ways. One was for a condition that the authors identified as borderline schizophrenia, a condition they eventually called Schizotypal Personality Disorder (STPD). The other application was for those patients with "unstable" personalities. It is this latter phenomenon that was finally named Borderline Personality Disorder. When the two new diagnoses appeared in DSM-III, they joined ten other ailments within the larger class of what is called Personality Disorders. (See Tables 6-1 and 6-2 for descriptions of these two disorders.)

Although both these conditions had been discussed in the psychiatric literature, neither was mentioned explicitly in earlier editions of DSM. The American Psychiatric Association traced Borderline Personality Disorder to a predecessor diagnosis in DSM-II, namely, latent schizophrenia. Now, however, BPD was not considered part of the schizophrenia spectrum (DSM-III, p. 379). This amoeba-like splitting of conditions, with

TABLE 6-1

DIAGNOSTIC CRITERIA FOR SCHIZOTYPAL PERSONALITY DISORDER

The following are characteristic of the individual's current and long-term functioning, are not limited to episodes of illness, and cause either significant impairment in social or occupational functioning or subjective distress.

A. At least four of the following:

(1) magical thinking, e.g., superstitiousness, clairvoyance, telepathy, "6th sense," "others can feel my feelings" . . .

(2) ideas of reference [i.e., an idea, held less firmly than a delusion, that events, objects, or other people have a particular meaning specifically for the person]

(3) social isolation, e.g., no close friends or confidants, social contacts limited to essential everyday tasks

(4) recurrent illusions, sensing the presence of a force or person not actually present (e.g., "I felt as if my dead mother were in the room with me") . . .

(5) odd speech (without . . . incoherence), e.g., speech that is digressive, vague, overelaborate . . .

(6) inadequate rapport in face-to-face interaction due to constricted or inappropriate affect, e.g., aloof, cold

(7) suspiciousness or paranoid ideation

(8) undue social anxiety or hypersensitivity to real or imagined criticism

B. Does not meet the criteria for Schizophrenia.

Reprinted with permission from the *Diagnostic and Statistical Manual of Mental Disorders, Third Edition.* Copyright 1980 American Psychiatric Association.

their migration from one class of mental illness to another, is a common phenomenon throughout the many revisions of DSM. Since BPD was no longer on the border of schizophrenia, or anything else, the term had lost its literal meaning. Nevertheless, effacing the common understanding of a diagnostic term has its advantages in the development of psychiatric nomenclature; the importance of the word or phrase as a technical term is enhanced, since only professionals with special training can understand the peculiar way in which it is being transformed.

Here is how Spitzer and his associates, the developers of BPD, went about their work: First, they reviewed the literature and consulted various researchers who had investigated BPD. From these sources, they identified behaviors that they reformulated as a preliminary list of nine diag-

TABLE 6-2

DIAGNOSTIC CRITERIA FOR BORDERLINE PERSONALITY DISORDER

The following are characteristic of the individual's current and long-term functioning, are not limited to episodes of illness, and cause either significant impairment in social or occupational functioning or subjective distress.

A. At least five of the following are required:

    (1) impulsivity or unpredictability in at least two areas that are potentially self-damaging, e.g., spending, sex, gambling, substance use, shoplifting, overeating, physically self-damaging acts

    (2) a pattern of unstable and intense interpersonal relationships, e.g., marked shifts of attitude, idealization, devaluation, manipulation (consistently using others for one's own ends)

    (3) inappropriate, intense anger or lack of control of anger, e.g., frequent displays of temper, constant anger

    (4) identity disturbance manifested by uncertainty about several issues relating to identity, such as self-image, gender identity, long-term goals or career choice, friendship patterns, values, and loyalties, e.g., "Who am I?", "I feel like I am my sister when I am good"

    (5) affective instability: marked shifts from normal mood to depression, irritability, or anxiety, usually lasting a few hours and only rarely more than a few days, with a return to normal mood

    (6) intolerance of being alone, e.g., frantic efforts to avoid being alone, depressed when alone

    (7) physically self-damaging acts, e.g., suicidal gestures, self-mutilation, recurrent accidents or physical fights

    (8) chronic feelings of emptiness or boredom

B. If under 18, does not meet the criteria for Identity Disorder.

Reprinted with permission from the *Diagnostic and Statistical Manual of Mental Disorders, Third Edition*, Copyright 1980 American Psychiatric Association.

nostic criteria that embodied the following concepts: "identity disturbance, unstable and intense interpersonal relationships, impulsive and self-damaging behavior, anger dyscontrol [sic] and affective instability, problems tolerating being alone, chronic feelings of emptiness, and poor work or school achievement."[2] After they identified these characteristics, the researchers asked a group of therapists to apply the criteria to one of their patients, a patient identified by each therapist as suffering from borderline personality organization. The therapists were also asked to apply the same set of criteria to a nonborderline, nonschizophrenic patient whom they knew well. The study procedures resulted in a sample of 18 borderline patients and 15 control cases.

The objective of this research was to develop a set of diagnostic criteria that would allow clinicians to identify those patients with BPD and would exclude those patients who did not have BPD. This is a fundamental requirement in developing a classification system like DSM.[3] The result of the initial study of Borderline Personality Disorder was that all of the borderline patients met at least three of the nine criteria and only three of the fifteen nonborderline control cases exhibited behaviors that satisfied three or more of the criteria. The investigators also completed a small second study that yielded similar results.

When they had completed these procedures for Borderline Personality Disorder and a similar set of investigations for Schizotypal Personality Disorder, Spitzer and his associates reported, "The results of these developmental studies . . . suggested that each procedure seemed able to identify individuals characterized as belonging to either of the two major types of borderline categories."[4] But this was not the end of their work. They decided that they wanted to assess how these criteria would be used by a large number of psychiatrists and patients and whether the criteria would identify separate and mutually exclusive disorders. In a sense, they were checking to see if there was broad agreement among clinicians about what BPD was.

The researchers selected a random sample of 4,000 members of the American Psychiatric Association and sent them a questionnaire that listed all of the behavioral criteria they had developed for both STPD and BPD, as well as five additional items that had often been linked to the borderline concept. The selected psychiatrists were each asked to identify one of their own patients with some form of borderline diagnosis and control case who was not a borderline. The participating psychiatrists were asked to exclude any patients who had ever received a diagnosis of chronic schizophrenia. Of the 4,000 psychiatrists in the random sample, 808 responded.

Participants were asked to check off which of the 22 criteria were present in each case and to identify any other borderline behaviors. All of the responses were subjected to a series of statistical analyses. On the basis of their analysis, the researchers decided that they had operationally defined the overall borderline concept. Among the cases that participants identified as borderline, 93% met the new operational criteria for STPD or BPD. However, 25% of the control group also met the criteria for one of the borderline disorders, even though these patients were deliberately selected because they supposedly did not have a borderline disorder. This finding—that is, that those presumably without the disorder still meet the criteria—is a common problem with DSM criteria sets. Nevertheless, Spitzer and his colleagues reported, "Given the ambiguities of the borderline concept . . . , the sensitivity and specificity obtained in these studies is quite high, and certainly satisfactory for clinical purposes."[5]

The researchers also felt confident that they had identified two subsets of the borderline concept, as they had hoped, even though more than half of the borderline cases met the criteria for *both* STPD and BPD. Their conclusion was that these diagnoses were independent but not mutually exclusive. They then defined BPD in terms of eight criteria. One of the initial criteria for BPD—poor work history or school achievement—was dropped from the final list because the statistical analysis did not provide strong support for its inclusion.

Although the statistical evidence for two separate borderline disorders was not particularly persuasive, Spitzer and his colleagues maintained that the distinction was valid. Despite the weakness of the data, their journal article ushered in a new era in the creation of psychiatric diagnosis. Heretofore, new diagnoses were usually introduced by the presentation of a clinical case that illustrated the disorder; other clinical case descriptions followed, until there was general acceptance of the disorder among clinicians and researchers. Seldom had new disorders been presented without colorful illustrations, and even less often had they been justified by complex statistical analyses. The 1979 journal article by Spitzer and his associates appeared to signal to the mental health community that new diagnoses would need empirical support in order to obtain official recognition. The irony is that, as was illustrated by the history of Masochistic Personality Disorder in chapter 5, neither the diagnostic criteria nor the empirical support that needed to be assembled had to be very convincing. As with so much of DSM, symbols are at least as important as substance. Diagnostic criteria and "data" were important symbols of science.[6] Regardless of the label adopted or how the criteria were chosen, once BPD became ensconced in DSM, psychiatrists found many uses for it, although many of its applications were not for their patients.

DR. GUTHEIL'S HYPOTHESES

The new diagnosis of Borderline Personality Disorder has attracted the attention of psychiatrists like moths to a flame. Since its inclusion in DSM-III, there has been extraordinary interest in Borderline Personality Disorder. Recently, the American Psychiatric Association's Press announced, "At this time Borderline Personality Disorder is the most researched [personality] disorder and is beginning to rival the major psychoses for space devoted to the topic in prominent journals.[7]

In much that is written about Borderline Personality Disorder, there is far greater concern about the boundaries of appropriate behavior and relationships than about the borders between different disorders. Psychiatrists claim to be experts on identifying the boundaries where normal behavior shades into pathological behavior. One of the important tasks of psychotherapists is to help patients recognize and respect those boundaries. Patients with BPD are often viewed by clinicians as difficult patients to treat precisely because they are said to have many problems with boundaries in interpersonal relationships. In fact, patients with BPD have been accused of inducing boundary violations in other people, including their psychotherapists. A vivid example of how the DSM diagnosis of BPD has been used to discredit patients and rationalize the inappropriate behavior of therapists is in an article published in 1989 in the *American Journal of Psychiatry* by a Harvard psychiatrist, Thomas Gutheil, and titled "Borderline Personality Disorder, Boundary Violations and Patient–Therapist Sex: Medicolegal Pitfalls."[8]

Psychiatric diagnoses are often used to explain the behavior of patients. The remarkable thesis of Gutheil's article is that the BPD diagnosis of *female patients* is an explanation of the inappropriate sexual behavior of their *male psychiatrists*. Furthermore, according to Gutheil, if a female patient complains about her psychiatrist's behavior, it is taken as additional evidence of the accuracy of the diagnosis BPD and increases the likelihood that her accusation will be perceived by others as false. This is such a novel use of psychiatric diagnosis that it is worthy of examination.

According to Gutheil, the reason therapists have sex so often with borderline patients is that "psychotic patients are not perceived as attractive and . . . neurotic patients are clear enough to know better than to become sexually involved. Thus, the field may be left to patients with borderline personality disorder through a kind of diagnostic default, as it were."[9]

Not completely content with the sex-by-default explanation, because it does not explain how borderline patients seduce their psychiatrists, Gutheil describes in his journal article the dynamics of the process. Borderlines, in Gutheil's words, "are particularly likely to evoke boundary violations of various kinds, including sexual acting out" (p. 597). Gutheil attributes to BPD four features that supposedly explain how borderline patients incite sexual behavior in their psychiatrists. These are borderline rage, neediness and/or dependency, boundary confusion, and manipulativeness associated with entitlement.

Perhaps Gutheil's most novel assertion is that intense rage, a particularly unattractive characteristic attributed to borderlines, is a major reason why therapists sleep with their borderline patients. "Borderline rage," he explains, "is an affect that appears to threaten or intimidate even experienced clinicians to the point that they feel or act as though they were literally coerced—moved through fear—by the patient's demands; they dare not deny the patient's wishes" (p. 598). In other words, bullied by their borderline patients, psychiatrists are coerced into having sexual relations with them.

Therapists do not respond only to the rage of their borderline patients. Even the anticipation of an angry response can prompt a therapist to violate boundaries. According to Gutheil, therapists "may feel actually trapped or pressured by the patient's *potential* rage into unusual and inappropriate degrees of social interaction with the patient or of self disclosure, such as discussing their own marital difficulties" (p. 598; emphasis added). The intimidation of psychiatrists may be further reinforced by suicide threats, even if they are not direct but are only "latent and implicit."

Although rage does not seem to us to be an aphrodisiac, Gutheil claims that it works for psychiatrists who are trapped into succumbing to their borderline patients. He maintains that therapists are psychologically overpowered and coerced into submission. We usually refer to sexual intercourse under these circumstances as sexual abuse or rape, but Gutheil only goes so far as to argue that therapists are the victims of their abusive patients.

Borderlines have other arrows in their romantic quiver that can induce psychiatric sexual misconduct, according to Gutheil. One is neediness and/or dependency. Gutheil claims, "The rescue fantasy—common if not universal in trainees—appears to me to occur particularly frequently in treating those patients with borderline personality disorder who manifest a helpless or waif-like demeanor." Although DSM does not list these traits as characteristic of those with Borderline Personality Disorder, Gutheil includes them in the diagnostic category. According to Gutheil, these borderline patients seem to have personalities that are quite different from the wrathful, vengeful sex-coercers just discussed, but the outcome is the same, namely, sexual transgressions by the therapist; he claims that some borderline patients "cherish a related wish," which another psychiatrist has called "the golden fantasy: the wishful belief that the therapist will gratify all needs, not just the therapeutic ones." In this fantasy, the psychiatrist appears to be cast as Daddy Warbucks the Stud, offering satisfaction to an erotic, seductive Orphan Annie.

In addition to rage and neediness, another factor that leads to patient–therapist sex is boundary confusion, and once again it is the patient's Borderline Personality Disorder that triggers the problem: "Under stress, patients with borderline personality disorder may lose sight of the me–thee boundary, and . . . may induce similar confusion in therapists. This confusion may derive from patients' own boundary blurring interpersonal manner" (p. 598). Boundary confusion is apparently contagious, and Gutheil warns that "if the therapist colludes with the patient," perceptions "may be powerfully influenced and distorted by the intense affects, longings, and wishes common in patients with Borderline Personality Disorder" (p. 599). That is, the patient's intense feelings are transmitted to the therapist, who, in this description, is the passive corespondent.

The last reason that Gutheil offers for patient–therapist sex is that borderline patients are so powerfully manipulative that therapists become addicted to them. "Clinicians have rejected early sexual advances from patients with borderline personality disorder, pleading professionalism, only to succumb later, like the alcoholic who, flushed with success at passing a bar, goes back to toast the victory" (p. 599).

Gutheil reports that, at conferences and consultations, offending therapists often repeat key phrases. He has decided that admissions such as "I ordinarily don't do this" or "Although I really didn't think I should be doing this" are indications of a psychological "troublespot with a probably borderline patient, since the latter appears to generate and invite 'not my usual' behavior" (p. 599). Of course, it would be hard to imagine psychiatrists confessing to their colleagues that sex with patients was their usual form of behavior, but this argument does not daunt Gutheil, who concludes as follows:

> This situation appears to draw some of its force from the narcissistic entitle-ment and consequent sense of specialness of the patient with borderline personality disorder, in which the therapist may wish to share. This special-ness may tempt the therapist to make exceptions for both the patient and himself or herself . . . . The doctor, already idealized, is further invited to share in the patient's specialness through a narcissistic seduction. (p. 599)

Gutheil's theory about the impact of Borderline Personality Disorder on patient–therapist sex was criticized as an example of blaming the vic-tim. Critics of Gutheil's hypotheses were offended by his contention that borderlines "seduce, provoke, or invite therapists into boundary viola-tions" (p. 600). They compared these charges to "the kind of vilification we see of rape victims for behavior that provokes attack or of sexually abused children for being seductive"[10] and related his article to the "his-tory in the field of psychiatry of this kind of verbal and diagnostic abuse of women patients, beginning with labeling patients' early attempts to speak of sexual misconduct by therapists as 'psychotic transference' and including Freud's suggestion that hysterical patients imagined incidents of incest."[11] Critics also contended, "The implication that patients who are sexually abused by therapists have a borderline diagnosis also should be examined; it is not our experience that this is true."[12] They feared that Gutheil's thesis would be used by male psychiatrists to justify their own misbehavior and that the BPD diagnosis would be used to suggest that fe-male patients are partially to blame for their psychiatrists' misdeeds.

Gutheil's response was unyielding. He testily replied to one critic, who had written a letter to the editor of the *American Journal of Psychia-try*, "The mark of the mature intellect is that it can entertain two contra-dictory ideas and still continue to function. I hoped for such intellects . . . However, it appears that I must push clarification to the pellucid limit." He informed the letter writer that her position offended him "as a feminist." The pellucid conclusion he offered was, "Although the doc-tors were culpable and the patients were not, both were voluntarily in bed."[13] Gutheil was equally disparaging toward others. He informed them, "As a teacher who takes his teaching seriously, I become depressed whenever even one student in my class fails to get the point." He con-fessed that his critics had left him disheartened, and he asked, "[Can my critics] accept the complex possibility that the physicians I described committed ethical and legal violations, malpractice, breaches of the fiduciary relationship, and abuses of a power asymmetry and that the patient played some role in this—a role that can be studied without shifting the slightest culpability from the doctor?" Gutheil challenged his critics "to put aside their outrage."[14]

What response can be made to Gutheil's challenge? One is to do as he asks: Look carefully at how he has studied the problem and examine the data he used to make his case. On the following pages we evaluate the evidence for Gutheil's two hypotheses: (1) that borderline patients seduce their therapists and (2) that they are the majority of those who make false accusations of patient–therapist sex. Is his evidence strong enough to sustain his position?

Examining the Evidence

The first question to ask in evaluating Gutheil's hypotheses is, Where did he get his information? How many cases did he examine? Gutheil does not tell us very much. In his 1989 article he writes, "To illustrate the points in this paper I will use actual but disguised cases that I reviewed in the context of either malpractice litigation (28 cases) or forensic consultations (dozens) to clinicians or patients" (p. 599). Thus, we do not know the total number of cases; we know only that it is more than 28. It is unlikely, however, that the group of cases Gutheil studied is representative of the thousands of patients who have sexual relations with their therapists. One reason for potential bias is the way he selected cases (or the cases selected him). Gutheil's cases are ones in which the patient complained about the therapist. Even among those patients who have sex with their therapists, most do not publicly report it. Those who do make reports are likely to be different from those who do not. It seems reasonable to assume that those who complain publicly are probably more likely to be angry than those who do not. Since anger is the subject of one criterion for BPD, it is easy to see how complainers can be conveniently labeled as borderline patients.

There are other potential sources of bias in Gutheil's selection of cases. Given the nature of his views that patients are partially to blame for their psychiatrists' inappropriate behavior, Gutheil is probably much more likely to be retained as an expert witness by an accused psychiatrist than by the accusing patient in malpractice cases. Although he does report that he has consulted with individuals on both sides, we are not told in what proportion. If, as we suspect, most of his cases have been on behalf of psychiatrist-defendants, his data are likely to be biased because it is to be expected that defendants would offer pejorative descriptions of their patient-victims as angry, unstable, and seductive, all characteristics attributed to Borderline Personality Disorder. Once again, we do not know how great the bias may be, because Gutheil did not report any systematic attempt to identify or control for it in his selection of cases.

So, with regard to Gutheil's evidence, we do not know how many patients he studied, how they were selected, how he obtained information about them, how he made the diagnoses, what methods he used to analyze his information, or whether any tests were used to determine if his generalizations are warranted. From all indications, his report relies principally on unsystematic, anecdotal information that he received directly from psychiatrists or from their case records. Thus, one can assume that the cases he presents to document his thesis are biased in his favor and constitute the strongest, most persuasive evidence he has to support his hypotheses. Gutheil offers ten cases to illustrate his arguments. Illustrations, of course, are not the same as proof but they can be illuminating and, indeed, they are in this case. All of the cases involve male psychiatrists and female patients. Since these cases represent the only concrete evidence that Gutheil offered in his article, they should be examined carefully.

PATIENT–THERAPIST SEX

Gutheil presents only two cases that involve actual patient–therapist sex. The first one illustrates his argument about therapists succumbing to a needy, waif-like patient and might be called "Orphan Annie's Anatomy Lesson." The following is Gutheil's complete description:

> A psychiatrist responding to the alleged sexual naïveté of a patient with borderline personality disorder gave her anatomy lessons on both their naked bodies. He reasoned that as long as they stopped short of intercourse, the behavior was not really sex and thus acceptable. Over time, predictably, the relationship eventually came to include sex. (p. 601)

If it strains credulity to believe that the mental disorder of the patient in this case induced the misconduct of a physician trained as a therapist, the second case indicates even less about how Borderline Personality Disorder contributed to the psychiatrist's downfall. This case may be called "The Midnight Therapist":

> Rationalizing the press of scheduling, a psychiatrist saw a patient with borderline personality disorder in the hospital daily for 2- and 4-hour appointments, sometimes running from 2:00 to 6:00 A.M. The relationship eventually became sexual. (p. 601)

In this case we are presented with nothing more than a diagnosis; there are no characteristics of the patient that indicate why or how the nocturnal therapist wound up in bed with her.

Although neither of these cases includes a description of how the patient seduced her therapist, Gutheil maintains that there is an obvious connection. When therapists violate boundaries, they start down a "slippery slope" that ends up in the patient's bed (or on the psychiatrist's couch). The slippery slope remains an implicit connection, as the following examples illustrate.

BOUNDARY VIOLATIONS

Most of Gutheil's vignettes are not about patient–therapist sex but are simply examples used to describe boundary violations. Gutheil attributes these infractions, at least in part, to "the ability of patients" with Borderline Personality Disorders "to seduce, provoke or invite therapists" into these transgressions. One example:

> In addition to doing therapy, a psychiatrist gave a patient with borderline personality disorder hundreds of dollars; gave her medication from a supply he had prescribed to himself, and had her stay, at his invitation in his own house—in a spare bedroom—during a housing "crisis." The psychiatrist slept on the floor in front of the spare bedroom so that the patient could not leave without his knowing it. All of the actions were rationalized as being a response to the patient's needs. (p. 600)

In this case, as in others, Gutheil gives enough information to convince us that the conduct of the psychiatrist is inappropriate, if not completely deranged. He provides no information about the patient to indicate what she did to provoke or invite this behavior, other than to receive a diagnosis of Borderline Personality Disorder.

In the following two cases Gutheil offers a clue—fear of the patient's rage—to help explain the psychiatrist's motivation. However, neither report provides the slightest evidence to support his conjecture. We are simply asked to accept his judgment without any information to indicate how he formed his opinion. Of one case, Gutheil writes, "A psychiatrist invited a hospitalized patient to stay rent free at a guest house on his property as a halfway step to discharge to outpatient status" (p. 600). In another vignette, a psychiatrist offered extra appointments as compensation to a patient after he was away for a week. He claimed that he "did not want to disappoint her," but Gutheil contends that he was afraid of incurring the patient's wrath.

The last two illustrations of "boundary violations" seem to have even less to do with the patient's personality dynamics or needs than do the previous cases. One vignette includes a description of late-night telephone calls between a psychiatrist and a patient with Borderline Personality Disorder while the psychiatrist's family slept. According to Gutheil, the psychiatrist "remained blind to the erotic potential of his habit" and "shared many personal, marital and financial troubles of his own" (p. 600). The one-sentence report in the other vignette is this: "A psychiatrist asked an editorially gifted patient to work with him on improving his professional articles for publication" (p. 600). Gutheil finds "similar dynamics" between these last two cases and the previous two; all "appear to foster the exchanging of gifts, real and symbolic, between the patient and therapist."

Gutheil warns that even if psychiatrists do not yield to borderline patients' seductive blandishments by sleeping with them, nonsexual boundary violations can still lead them down the slippery slope. If therapists are not very careful about boundary violations, they risk false accusations. The last three vignettes illustrate another characteristic that Gutheil associates with a borderline's rage, namely, the tendency of these patients to seek revenge with false accusations of patient–therapist sex.

FALSE ACCUSATIONS

The hypothesis about patients with Borderline Personality Disorder that has the most serious ramifications is that such patients are the majority of those who make false accusations of patient–therapist sex. This is significant because it provides powerful evidence to assail the credibility of any plaintiff with a diagnosis of Borderline Personality Disorder. If most of the false charges are raised by these patients, then the diagnosis casts a cloud over any complaint that any borderline patient makes about patient–therapist sex. (We'll ignore the serious problem of ex post facto diagnosing, where Gutheil in some instances seems to determine after the fact and because a case was brought to his attention by a defendant in a lawsuit that the patient had a Borderline Personality Disorder.)

Gutheil's hypothesis is almost impossible to test. It is a daunting challenge to find out how many cases of false accusation exist. Only those cases of false accusation that are discovered can be evaluated. There is no way to know how many cases of undiscovered false accuation there are. The best that Gutheil can do is prove that most of the accusations that are discovered to be false are made by borderline patients. As we have already observed, Gutheil's anecdotes are inadequate to yield any substantial conclusion. How, then, does he propose to support his hypothesis? He offers the following guidelines: "To bring some validity to the often complex issue of which allegations are true and which are false, I have identified . . . as false those cases in which either the patient retracted the claim and identified it as false, or the patient admitted to a disinterested third party that the claim was specious" (p. 599).

Gutheil does not report how many cases he has identified, but he does offer three examples that provide some insight into how he arrived at his conclusions about false accusations. The first example follows:

> A patient with borderline personality disorder became enraged at her physician because she felt he was treating her in a disrespectful manner: in her words, "like a welfare case." She later brought suit against him for sexual molestation. During the discovery phase of the lawsuit, an investigator, who was not known to the patient, visited her under false pretenses and obtained (probably illegally) a tape recording of her admitting that she had been furious with the physician and had fabricated this story in a scheme to "get him good." (p. 599)

The undercover investigator in this case is not a disinterested third party. As Gutheil points out, the patient's illegally taped admissions probably would be inadmissible in court. Does Gutheil believe they are valid as scientific evidence that the patient made a false accusation? Perhaps there is more to this story, but what has been presented would be considered tainted evidence.

In the next example, there is a similar problem. A psychiatrist rejected the request of a patient to see him on a major holiday, pleading family commitments. The enraged patient initiated litigation for "sexual abuse and other specious claims but confided in a fellow patient, who revealed the deceit to the attorney" (p. 599). As in the previous case, we can ask whether the evidence meets Gutheil's own test that the accuser admitted to "a disinterested third party" that the claim was false. It is doubtful whether any researcher would consider the statement allegedly made to a fellow patient to be a credible admission to a "disinterested" person. There may be other relevant facts, but the information in the vignette does not provide the kind of evidence that supports Gutheil's theory about false accusations. As in the first case, he relies on evidence provided by the defendant-psychiatrist.

The third vignette involving false accusations is a description of a "tumultuous, out of control" session to terminate treatment of "a patient with very primitive borderline personality disorder" who had "a history of major psychotic regressions, confusion of fact and fantasy, and of intimacy and sexuality, sexual abuse by her family in childhood, and, on one occasion, she had fabricated sexual accusations for attention" (p. 600). In the course of treatment, the psychiatrist and other staff members had given this patient many hugs as rewards, including "social hugs," "reassurance hugs," "goodbye hugs," and "congratulatory hugs." At the end of the termination session, the patient requested and received a good-bye hug. She began to breathe heavily and thrust her pelvis, and she drew a vibrator from her purse. After calming her down, the psychiatrist drove the patient home at her request and offered to see her again, because of the possibility of misunderstandings. She subsequently accused the psychiatrist of sexual relations in the office and the car but eventually retracted her complaint.

The aforementioned vignettes—two case descriptions that involve sexual encounters and three vignettes that purport to describe false accusations—constitute all the evidence Gutheil offers in his article in the *American Journal of Psychiatry* to support his dual claims that patients with Borderline Personality Disorder seduce, provoke, or invite psychiatrists into sexual relations and that they are the majority of those who make false claims of sexual relations with their therapists.

In a later article, Gutheil strengthens his claim about false accusations by asserting, "This subset of false complainants of abuse is almost totally dominated by borderline patients." Using pseudoscientific jargon, he actually strays further from serious empirical investigation. He also offers a different diagnosis for men who are involved in sexual relations with their male therapists: "In the author's experience with male patients victimized by male clinicians, the males were isolated and somewhat schizoid, often sexually undifferentiated despite being married and clearly lacked charismatic paternal figures with whom to identify."[15]

Once again, Gutheil offers no evidence for his new generalization except a one-sentence anecdote that consists of a single quote from a tearful patient who reported that his therapist called him "my little blue-eyed beach boy." Gutheil asserts that this terminology indicates "the (essentially exploitative) possessiveness and relegation of the patient to the child position."[16] He appears to find male patients to be more passive than their female counterparts in sexual relations with male psychiatrists.

Even if we leave aside the flimsiness of the evidence and the circularity of his argument and give Gutheil the benefit of the doubt about each case, we have nothing that any serious investigator will accept as evidence to substantiate his hypotheses. If we take the cases at face value, they indicate very little about the seductive capabilities of the patients and far more about the misbehavior of the therapists. What is most astounding about these articles is that they were not written by a kooky preacher or salesman turned psychological guru peddling nonsense in the drugstore book rack. It was authored by a respected Harvard-trained physician and a board-certified psychiatrist who is currently professor of psychiatry at Harvard Medical School. He is the author of more than 100 publications, and his credentials are impeccable. Furthermore, Gutheil's initial article was printed in the premier publication of the American Psychiatric Association. Articles are accepted for this journal after they have been subjected to peer review by experts in the field. In addition to this article, Gutheil has repeated his claims in other articles in this journal and in other respected publications, including the *Harvard Medical School Mental Health Letter,* *Psychiatric Annals,* and the APA's *Review of Clinical Psychiatry and the Law.*[17]

Other therapists have defended Gutheil's position. One psychiatrist reported, "My experience as a member of the APA Ethics Committee supports the idea that a majority of complaints about sexual involvement come from patients with borderline personality disorder or traits and mostly concern therapists who are unskilled in treating such patients or who disregard their more usual ways of practice."[18] One of Gutheil's supporters wrote, "Dr. Gutheil's unflinching description of the role that some women patients play in becoming their own oppressors can be viewed as strengthening feminist arguments. He should be celebrated rather than scorned."[19]

Gutheil claims that he does not excuse psychiatrist offenders and that his objective is to educate his unwary colleagues. He maintains that if his article "keeps even one fragile, insecure, ignorant, or disturbed clinician" from abusing a patient, the piece has justified its publication.[20] He acknowledges that his "dynamic, instructional approaches are, moreover, of no avail with consciously exploitative, predatory therapists," asserting that "fortunately, those individuals are comparatively rare. . . ."[21] This is a rhetorical claim, since few of those in the helping professions are likely to acknowledge to themselves or others that their actions are exploitative or predatory. However, there is evidence that patients often consider sexual relations with their therapists to be exploitative and harmful.[22]

On the other hand, most psychiatrists who responded to a survey about patient sexual contact, published in the *American Journal of Psychiatry,* did not claim they were seduced by their patients.[23] When a random sample of psychiatrists was questioned anonymously, 6.4% admitted to sexual relations with patients, and one-third of this group reported that they had had sexual encounters with more than one patient. Respondents who had sexual relations with patients were asked about their most recent experience, and less than a third (31.7%) said that their patients had initiated the sexual contact. Most (57.3%) claimed that both they and the patient had initiated the relationship, and another 11% indicated that they had taken the initiative. Questioned about their motives, 73% of the therapists said that they had engaged in sexual contact for love or pleasure. A small minority indicated that they became involved sexually because of "a loss of control," "a judgment lapse," or "impulsivity." Thus, even among psychotherapists who admit to engaging in sexual relations with patients, most do not reach for the Gutheil defense, namely, "the patient made me do it."

THE LEGAL DEFENSE FOR THE ACCUSED THERAPIST

If Gutheil's articles about patient–therapist sexual relations do not meet minimal scientific standards to support the empirical claims he has made, why have they received widespread recognition and support in the profession? Is it because Gutheil's claims about Borderline Personality Disorder provide justification for therapists' misdeeds? They appear to be useful in mitigating the impact of attacks that are often aired in the media and in courtrooms against psychiatrists who are charged with sexual abuse of their patients.

Despite his explicit denials, Gutheil subtly (and sometimes not so subtly) helps to construct an apology for therapists. He contributes to their defense implicitly by his unsubstantiated conclusions about the role of patients with Borderline Personality Disorder in sexual relations with their therapists. A review of this defense appears in a coauthored chapter of the APA's *Annual Review of Psychiatry* (1992) that illustrates the complex justification Gutheil helped to develop for erring psychiatrists. The chapter, entitled "Expert Opinion: A Case of Therapist–Patient Sexual Misconduct," consists of a brief history of a fictionalized case. The chapter includes a description by the patient of an increasingly eroticized relationship with her therapist that culminated in sexual intercourse; another version of the story by the therapist, who denied that he had engaged in sexual intercourse with the patient but acknowledged that she had convinced him to hug her at the end of sessions and that she had once kissed him when he drove her home in a snowstorm; an "argument for the plaintiff" by Gutheil; and an "argument for the defendant" by Robert Sadoff, another well-established authority on forensic psychiatry.[24]

Gutheil's argument for the plaintiff is a remarkable contribution. His assignment in this fictional case is to argue for the plaintiff, to make a persuasive case that the patient should prevail in her lawsuit against the psychiatrist. But in his attempt to construct his argument for the patient, it is often difficult to tell whether Gutheil is advocating for the psychiatrist or for the patient. For example, he frequently follows condemnations of the therapist with mitigating arguments for the therapist. One of his principal points is that patients with Borderline Personality Disorder have the capacity to make decisions, including deciding to sleep with their therapists. "For every patient heinously taken advantage of while drugged, unconscious, or psychotic, there are dozens of patients who enter into sexual relations in a competent, though clearly misguided and usually unduly influenced, way" (p. 337). Gutheil acknowledges that the physician is always blameworthy, and he suggests that the basis for the patients' lawsuits is that they are subjected to undue influence. "However," he later concludes, "both parties are usually relatively competent adults and are responsible for their behaviors as any other adults" (p. 342).

As Gutheil knows, it is hard for a patient who voluntarily agrees to sexual relations to win damages, even if the psychiatrist violates professional prohibitions. Furthermore, if a woman seduces her therapist, as Gutheil has claimed is often true of borderline patients, then her contribution to the sexual affair is even more likely to diminish her chances of convincing a court to award her damages.

As Gutheil also knows, it is not enough to prove that the therapist has committed a breach of professional conduct. The patient must also show that the psychiatrist's breach of professional ethics has caused damage. What damage is done? Choosing his words carefully, Gutheil asserts that all sexual contact is inherently harmful, "because it constitutes bad therapy, wastes time, compromises objectivity, and imperils future therapy," and that, furthermore, "often preexisting disorders are exacerbated and new ones may appear" (p. 337). But he then undercuts the patient's case by saying that "actual trauma is far less common." Although he acknowledges that sexual misconduct may be abusive because it exploits a patient, he differentiates it from situations where there is "unconsented violence directed against the patient" (p. 337). What trauma may exist, he argues, is not necessarily from the sexual misconduct of the psychiatrist but "arises when the relationship is ended, and its true exploitative nature is revealed" (p. 337). In other words, the sexual relationship itself does not necessarily lead to trauma; it is the abandonment by the psychiatrist when he ends the relationship that is so hurtful to patients.

Another example of Gutheil's sympathy for therapists is evident in his observation that they are often misjudged because they commit boundary violations, even when they draw the line at sexual misconduct: "I have seen cases settled by insurers where I felt no misconduct had occurred, simply because the insurer despaired of having a jury believe that a therapist who had violated many other boundaries had drawn the line at the bedroom door" (p. 338). Gutheil admonishes psychiatrists to toe the line even though he understands that "some boundary violations are innocuous." In fact, he says, "Minor violations may be appropriate or even necessary under some circumstances" (p. 339). Furthermore, he warns, "Predictably the complexity of analysis required for case-by-case assessments is usually trampled in litigation by simplistic characterizations by plaintiff's attorneys" (p. 339).

After this prologue, the chapter continues with an analysis of the hypothetical case, but Gutheil cannot resist providing the psychiatrist with defenses. Although he concludes that the elements of malpractice may be demonstrated by the plaintiff's story, his tepid argument is far from compelling. His opponent in this psychiatric moot court does not suffer from the same constraints. Sadoff's sympathy is clearly on the side of the therapist. He makes the case for the psychiatrist, often using arguments that are familiar from his "opponent's" writings.

Although little is new in his basic analysis, Sadoff adds some interesting embellishments. One is that sometimes a psychiatrist's legal difficulties occur because of misdiagnosis. He reports that after their lawsuits were over, "several experienced therapists . . . confessed that they had never considered the diagnosis of borderline personality disorder, but had diagnosed the patient as having histrionic or anxiety disorder." The therapists claimed that had they recognized that the real diagnosis was borderline personality disorder, "they would never have allowed the liberties that they did in boundary violations" (p. 343). Apparently, to some psychiatrists, taking liberties with patients may be legitimate, depending on their diagnosis.

Another embellishment begins with Sadoff's commenting that "it is well known that rejection and abandonment are the two worst fears of borderline patients" (p. 345) and ends with his observation that "by instituting a lawsuit, the patient can re-establish a relationship with the doctor and is not totally abandoned" (p. 345). Sadoff maintains that such a patient looks forward to depositions and hearings because these afford an opportunity to see the former therapist; he asserts that the patient's motive is not retaliation but a desire to continue the relationship. Where is Sadoff's evidence for this claim? He reports that "the evidence for this scenario lies in the statements of a number of patients who have been evaluated after filing similar lawsuits" (p. 345).

We have come full circle, since Sadoff, like Gutheil, does not offer a hint about who made the evaluations, how many patients were evaluated, or any of the other data that we expect from scholars who make empirical generalizations. But, as we have seen, there are different standards of evidence for psychiatric patients once they are assigned a DSM label, particularly when they make claims against their doctors. It may be true that Sadoff or others have interviewed one or more clients who made these assertions, but to move from individual reports to a generalization about patients who may or may not share a diagnosis is a big, unwarranted leap.

THE PROBLEMS WITH BORDERLINE PERSONALITY DISORDER

The flimsiness of the evidence provided for Gutheil's hypotheses and for Sadoff's embellishments is not the most serious issue in this controversy. What is far more important is the fact that the profession, aided by the scientific mystifications provided by DSM, has accorded respectability to these claims. Their publication in articles in the leading research journals gives these opinions an aura of science.

One of the problems is Gutheil's basic assumption that Borderline Personality Disorder is a clearly identifiable, distinct diagnosis and that clinicians can reliably agree on which patients have this type of disordered personality. The early research by the developers of DSM did not establish the validity of BPD, nor did they ever demonstrate that psychiatrists can independently recognize it. On the contrary, there is little evidence that this is a diagnosis that can be made reliably, and considerable evidence exists suggesting that diagnoses of personality disorder with DSM are made unreliably in general. These reliability problems are exacerbated still further by the willingness of psychiatrists to depart from the DSM criteria when they make a diagnosis. For example, two of the main characteristics of Borderline Personality Disorder that Gutheil and his colleagues identified were waif-like dependency and seductiveness. Neither of these features was listed among the criteria for the disorder in DSM-III-R. Waifs and seductresses may be major subgroups of the borderline population, but the criteria for BPD in the then-current version of DSM (DSM-III-R) did not acknowledge them.

Accurate use of the diagnosis may be further compromised, as suggested in the chapter by Gutheil and Sadoff in the 1992 *Review of Clinical Psychiatry and the Law*. In that chapter Gutheil appears to make the "correct" diagnosis of Borderline Personality Disorder only after the patient makes an accusation against the unsuspecting psychiatrist. The late recognition of the disorder may be entirely self-serving. The accused therapist can conveniently use Gutheil's hypotheses to defend himself. According to Gutheil, patients who induce their therapists to have sex with them probably have Borderline Personality Disorder, and borderlines are likely to make false accusations against therapists. Thus, an accused therapist can label the patient as borderline and, by doing so, can undermine her credibility. The patient whose therapist had sex with her and who wants to press charges has a predicament. By virtue of the therapist's misbehavior, according to Gutheil, the patient is likely to have a Borderline Personality Disorder. But if she has BPD, the accusation may be fabricated. This is wonderful reasoning, only topped by Joseph Heller in the famous passage that gave the title to his novel *Catch-22*. If the patient makes an accusation, it is used as evidence that she is a borderline. If she is a borderline, there is a likelihood that she is lying and the accusation is false. For the offending psychiatrist, this is a crafty defense.

As we have seen, the validity of Borderline Personality Disorder as a diagnosis has been questionable ever since Spitzer legitimized it and included it in DSM-III. From the start, it has been hard to support it as a distinct mental disease. It is still harder to distinguish it from Schizotypal Personality Disorder. It is also hard to distinguish it from Histrionic Personality Disorder and Narcissistic Personality Disorder and from various classes of diagnoses, such as depression and anxiety.

These scientific debates about Borderline Personality Disorder appear not to trouble Gutheil and his colleagues, who seem to have no difficulty recognizing those who are borderline. And with their guidance, the rest of us can identify them, too. They are likely to be women (76% of those who are given a diagnosis of Borderline Personality Disorder are estimated to be women).[25] If a woman is very angry, she is more likely to be borderline. If an angry woman has a history of sexual abuse, the likelihood increases. If she accuses her psychiatrist of improper sexual conduct and seeks revenge by suing her psychiatrist, she must definitely have Borderline Personality Disorder.

The diagnosis of Borderline Personality Disorder has replaced the need for objective evidence and reasoned argument. As with so many of the entries in DSM, this diagnostic label is inappropriately used as an explanation for behavior—when, in fact, it can carry no such burden. The causes of most mental disorders are unknown. Psychiatric diagnostic labels do not explain why people behave the way they do. A label is simply an attempt to identify a cluster of behaviors, yet it is accepted as a claim that those behaviors constitute a mental disorder. Consequently, using a diagnosis as an explanation for behavior is circular. For example, we don't increase our understanding one iota by saying that someone is sad because he or she is depressed. Similarly, if impulsivity is used as a criterion for BPD, it gets us nowhere to say that a person is impulsive because he or she has Borderline Personality Disorder. And saying that a patient has

BPD certainly cannot explain impulsivity in the patient's therapist. Nevertheless, Gutheil would have us believe that a patient's diagnosis causes the therapist's sexual misbehavior. Perhaps Gutheil is cleverly proposing a new diagnosis for DSM-V. He seems to be suggesting that therapists are seduced by patients because the patients have Therapist Seduction and False Accusation Disorder. As one therapist has summarized the situation to us: "Borderline is a wastebasket diagnosis; the diagnosis is given to patients who therapists don't like, or are troublesome or are hard to diagnose and treat. Many of those who are diagnosed as Borderline have histories of sexual abuse and incest."[26] *Borderline* is a code word for trouble for the therapist. Instead of dealing with the real source of trauma, it is easier to talk about the patient's pathology and make a diagnosis of Borderline Personality Disorder.

Diagnoses with shaky empirical support and vague, flexible boundaries lend themselves easily to distortion and misuse. In the case of the creation of Borderline Personality Disorder, there were no inside or outside advocacy groups questioning the evidence or identifying the misuses or harms that might stem from a diagnosis used primarily as a label for patients, particularly women, who can be difficult to treat. There was no pressure group asking tough questions about the nature of the personality "border"—or, for that matter, raising the troubling question of how a patient can have an unstable personality when *personality* is defined by DSM-IV as "an enduring pattern of inner experience and behavior" that is "pervasive and inflexible" and "stable over time" (p. 629). One of the results of this lack of scrutiny has been the creation of a new mental disorder that purports to explain how difficult and angry women seduce their unsuspecting therapists. Such reasoning is not foreign to the history of psychiatry, as we shall see in the next chapter, which deals with the legacy of racism in diagnosis.

7 THE ENDURING LEGACY OF RACISM IN THE DIAGNOSIS OF MENTAL DISORDERS

Since the founding of the republic, racial issues have been a preoccupation in its response to mental illness, and diagnosis—in the broadest sense—has been pivotal in the continuing controversies. Defenders of slavery, proponents of racial segregation, and advocates for the exclusion of more recent immigrants have consistently attempted to justify oppression by inventing new mental illnesses and by reporting higher rates of abnormality among African Americans or other minorities. Avowed racists have not been the only ones who have created new diagnoses and attributed abnormally high rates of insanity to minority groups. Innovations in diagnostic and treatment techniques are often proposed by those who claim to be committed to helping African Americans and other minority groups, but these innovations often perpetuate or increase racist thinking and lead to solutions that intensify persecution. The enduring legacy of racism in the identification of mental disorders persists in the latest edition of DSM. Its origins can be traced to the founding fathers, and its development can be identified in many of the major innovations in psychiatric diagnosis.

BENJAMIN RUSH

Benjamin Rush, the father of American psychiatry and a signer of the Declaration of Independence, was a committed abolitionist. He wrote anti-slavery tracts, and in 1795 he served as the first president of the American Convention for Promoting the Abolition of Slavery and Improving the African Race. Rush did not confine himself to abolitionist activities: he participated in events in the African American community in Philadelphia, and he attempted to secure financial assistance for free Negroes to build churches and to establish a farming community in Pennsylvania. As a physician, Rush wrote about the adverse effects of slavery on the mental health of Negroes. He countered pro-slavery assertions that Africans had less mental capacity than Europeans by arguing that it was necessary to differentiate free Negroes from slaves. He maintained that it was not possible to accurately evaluate the mental capacity of slaves whose moral faculties and understanding were rendered torpid by bondage.[1]

Rush was not entirely free of racist thinking. He compromised on the question of integration and recommended segregated institutions. He also had some strange ideas about the medical condition of Negroes. For some time he believed that they were immune to yellow jaundice, until examination of their eyes revealed that they were susceptible. He never corrected his belief that their color was caused by a type of leprosy; he felt that a cure, which would remove blackness, would contribute to the unity of the human race. Nevertheless, when his work as a whole is taken into account, Rush is considered the preeminent contributor to the improvement of race relations in the history of American psychiatry.[2] Unfortunately, his continuing attempts to explain putative deficiencies of African Americans established an approach that has been followed by his psychiatric heirs, and his well-intentioned remedy, separatism, was the precursor of the "separate but equal" doctrine that led to two centuries of racial segregation.

THE INSANE CENSUS OF 1840

The first major controversy over racial bias in the identification of mental disorders occurred just before the Civil War, when the struggle over slavery was a preoccupation in American political life. Simultaneously, a concern for the mentally ill was becoming increasingly important, and asylums were emerging as the primary solution to the problem of insanity. It is not surprising that when issues of race and mental illness converged, the result had lasting influence in both areas.

In this country the first official system to count the mentally ill was developed for the Sixth Decennial Census of the United States in 1840. Two groups of the mentally ill were identified, namely, idiots and lunatics, but they were merged and reported as a single category—the insane. Insanity had been identified as a leading social problem soon after the founding of the republic. The decision to measure the extent of insanity for the first time was the inevitable outcome of decades of discussion about the problems of mental illness. The increased concern about insanity was not the result of a rise in the incidence of mental disorders in the population.[3] As the United States moved from a rural to an urban economy, many of the ills that beset society were interpreted as the result of urban life. The well-ordered agrarian society that Jefferson envisioned quickly gave way to an industrial economy with a rapidly growing urban population. This social reorganization led, during the first half of the 19th century, to a major transformation in the concept of social deviance.[4] New city dwellers, who were either from foreign countries or from rural areas of the United States, were considered to be at risk of becoming insane as a result of the disruption of the orderly agrarian existence they were accustomed to.

For a time, mental illness was believed to be triggered by the social environment. In 1848 Edward Jarvis, a founder of both the American Psychiatric Association and the American Statistical Association, observed, "Society establishes, encourages or permits these customs out of which mental disorder may and frequently does arise." Jarvis insisted that society has "a duty to heal the wounds it inflicts."[5] The way to meet this duty, according to the medical superintendents of institutions for the insane and their allies among the social reformers, including the famous Dorothea Dix, was to build mental hospitals. The institutions were not thought of as dumping grounds to warehouse the untreatable but as well-ordered asylums to which those at risk were to be committed at the first sign of illness. The reformers believed that if those who were at risk were committed soon enough to asylums that offered regular routines and simple work, it was possible to restore them to health.

The response to this view of deviance and its cure was a steady increase in the number of mental hospitals in the 1830s and 1840s.[6] Two sources of information contributed to the impetus to build new asylums: First, dramatic stories were publicized by reformers about mistreatment in jails and almshouses, where the insane often were kept chained in basements. Second, statistics about the extent of insanity were used to make the case for more asylums, since justification for building institutions also depended on finding out how many people needed hospitalization. The decision to count the insane in the 1840 census was envisioned as a method of obtaining authoritative information to assist in planning remedies for the pressing social problem of insanity.

Many of the insane who were counted in the 1840 census were already in institutions, but an effort was made to identify mentally ill people who were not institutionalized. Marshals were instructed to count the inhabitants of each household, both white and colored. They were told to identify lunatics and idiots and to determine their source of support. These reports were forwarded to Washington, where the returns were published in 1841, with the notation that they had been corrected at the Department of State, which was in charge of the census. The report concluded that there were 17,069,453 people in the United States and that 2,960,467 were Negroes. According to the census, 17,456 inhabitants were lunatics and idiots; of that number, 14,521 were white and 2,935 were Negroes. This ratio of insane to the population at large was approximately 1 out of every 978 residents. Among Negroes, the ratio of insane to the total number was actually a little better than it was for the country as a whole: 1 out of 1009. But the fact that mental illness was not more frequent among the Negro population was overlooked, and regional contrasts in mental disorders became the source of a major international controversy.

Although there were only 171,894 free Negroes in the northern states, 1,191 were counted as insane. The ratio, 1 in 144, compared unfavorably to the ratio in southern states of one insane Negro out of every 1,558. The difference of 11 to 1 in the ratios of sane to insane Negroes in the two sections of the country was the figure that interested Southern politicians, and they broadcast it to the rest of the world. There were other figures that were even more extreme: in Maine 1 out of 14 Negroes was reported to be insane, and in Michigan 1 out of 28. This was in contrast to the ratios in South Carolina (1 out of 2,477 Negroes) and Louisiana (1 out of every 4,310 Negroes). It appeared that the farther north Negroes went, the more likely they were to be insane and the farther South, the more likely they were to be sane.[7] In a letter to a New York journal, an observer attempted to explain the disparity in the rates of insanity by attributing it to climate: northern winters had "no influence on the temperaments of whites," who were used to them, but harsh winters affected "the cerebral organs of the African race," who came from a tropical climate. This theory was later developed in a book by a French scientist, and after the turn of the century it was resurrected again by American psychiatrists.[8]

Southerners offered another explanation, one that rapidly overshadowed the climatic theory. They believed that slavery made the difference! In June 1843, an article in *The Southern Literary Messenger* (an important periodical that had been edited shortly before this time by Edgar Allan Poe) discounted the climatic explanation, attributed the sectional differences to "moral causes," and concluded that Negroes fared far worse in places where slavery was prohibited. The article did not attempt to extol slavery but claimed to do quite the opposite:

> We are not friendly to slavery. We lament and deplore it as the greatest evil that could be inflicted on our country. We lament it not for the sake of the black race but of the white. The former, who are slaves, are not only far happier in a state of slavery than of freedom, but we believe the happiest class on this continent.[9]

The article warned of the potential disaster that would be a consequence of emancipation: there would not be enough penitentiaries or lunatic asylums to house dangerous Negroes, making it impossible to live in a country where "maniacs and felons met the traveler at every cross road."[10] The article concluded with an admonition:

> Whenever it can be shown to us of the South that the free blacks of any of the "free states" are as happy as the slaves, the subject of general emancipation will be entitled to more consideration. But as long as they furnish little else but materials for jails, penitentiaries and madhouses; warned by such examples, we cannot desire to be the destroyers of the dependent race.[11]

Thus was another argument added to the traditional justifications offered for the South's "peculiar institution." Not only was slavery necessary for the economy and essential to the social order of the South, but it was required to assure the well-being of Negroes, who would otherwise go mad. It was an ironic version of the white man's burden to argue for the perpetuation of slavery to preserve the sanity of black people while recognizing bondage as a great evil.

Southern politicians quickly exploited the argument that slavery was a benevolent institution. Foremost among them was John C. Calhoun (ex–vice president of the United States and, at the time of the following comments in 1841, a senator), who proclaimed, "Here is proof of the necessity of slavery. The African is incapable of self-care and sinks into lunacy under the burden of freedom. It is a mercy to give him the guardianship and protection from mental death."[12] When he was appointed secretary of state in 1844, Calhoun responded to pressures from Britain to abolish slavery in Texas by using the 1840 census to argue for its merits, even though the data had been thoroughly discredited by then. He informed the British ambassador as follows:

> The census and other authentic documents, show in all instances in which the states have changed the former relation between the two races, the condition of the African, instead of being improved, has become worse. They have been invariably sunk into vice and pauperism, accompanied by the bodily and mental inflictions incident thereto—deafness, blindness, insanity, and idiocy—to a degree without example; while in all other states which have retained the ancient relation between them, they have improved greatly in every respect—in number, comfort, intelligence, and morals.[13]

The flood of speeches and articles that used the census to justify slavery and to attack "the weeping philanthropists of the North" did not go unchallenged.[14] The counterattack was initiated by Edward Jarvis, an influential psychiatrist who at first agreed with southern orators that the census provided evidence that slavery had "a wonderful influence upon the development of moral facilities and the intellectual powers."[15] But the extraordinarily high rate of insanity reported for Northern Negroes suggested to Jarvis that something was wrong. By undertaking a careful reanalysis of the census figures, he discovered that there were major errors in the reports. Using the data from the census, Jarvis contrasted general population figures with statistics on the insane, and he demonstrated that the reports were inconsistent and often contradictory. For example, Northern towns with no black freedmen were credited with having insane Negroes, and in other towns the number of insane Negroes exceeded the total number of Negro residents.[16]

The errors were not minor ones. In Ohio there were 165 cases of insanity; 88 of them were located in towns whose total Negro population was 31.[17] In Worcester, Massachusetts, Jarvis discovered that the census report of 133 colored lunatics and idiots really represented the number of white patients in the state hospital located in that community. In Maine, towns that had no African American inhabitants were credited with insane Negroes and in others the number of insane Negroes was greater than the total number of black freedmen; with a little more than a hundred insane Negroes in Maine, the obvious errors in these towns alone had a major impact on the frequently cited 14 to 1 ratio of sane to insane.

When Jarvis compared four different printings of the census, he found that they contradicted each other in major ways. He also used other data besides the census to corroborate his findings. Comparing the federal census to more accurate ones compiled by the states, he uncovered substantial errors. He summed up his findings by reporting, "Such a document as we have described, heavy with its errors and its misstatements, instead of being a messenger of truth to the world to enlighten its knowledge and guide its opinions, is in respect to human ailment, a bearer of falsehoods to confuse and mislead." Jarvis then sounded an ominous warning about the future use of the census when he predicted, "So far from being an aid to medical science, as it was the intention of government in ordering these inquiries, it has thrown a stumbling-block in its way which it will require years to remove."[18]

Jarvis campaigned vigorously to rectify the errors of the census, and other commentators added their criticisms in the popular press and other periodicals.[19] A number of scientific journals published Jarvis's reports,[20] and he helped to draft a study that the American Statistical Association presented to Congress. The protesters wanted a government investigation in order to officially correct the census figures. John Quincy Adams, who became a member of Congress after his term as president, demanded an investigation and charged that the United States had almost found itself at war with Great Britain and Mexico on the basis of the errors. Initially, Calhoun, now secretary of state, resisted congressional pressure. The secretary acknowledged that errors could be expected in an undertaking as ambitious as the census, but he claimed that they canceled each other out.[21] Eventually, he agreed to an investigation; in a move that anticipated Watergate and the Iran–Contra affair in the next century, he appointed a Southerner who had been superintendent of the census of 1840 "to give the subject a thorough and impartial investigation."[22] It was a foregone conclusion that the investigation would not find serious flaws in the census, and when the results of the inquiry were forwarded to Congress, Calhoun declared unwavering support for the census:

> On a review of the whole, two conclusions, it is believed, will be found to follow inevitably. The one is, that the correctness of the late census, in exhibiting a greater prevalence of the diseases of insanity, blindness, deafness and dumbness, stands unimpeachable.
> The other conclusion, not less resistible, is, that so far from bettering the condition of the Negro or African race, by changing the relation between it and the Europeans as it now exists in the slave holding states, it would render it far worse. It would be indeed, to them, a curse instead of a blessing.[23]

With this report from the "impartial investigation," the matter was officially closed, and further efforts to obtain a retraction were rebuffed. Although there has never been formal clarification of the reasons for the distortions in the 1840 census, two major hypotheses have been offered. One source of statistical bias has to do with the reluctance of masters to identify their chattel as insane. According to this theory, mentally ill slaves were undercounted because plantation owners would not tolerate deviant behavior that interfered with work and would not commit slaves to asylums, and thus incur the cost of the confinement. (Many Southern institutions would not even accept Negro patients, although this was also true in some Northern asylums.)

These factors may have accounted for some of the disparity in the 1840 rates of insanity between Northern and Southern Negroes, but the principal explanation that has been offered is deceit in the preparation of the census. The problem with this theory is that no evidence has been uncovered to explain how the fraud was arranged or who was responsible for the deception. No one has added substantial new information to Jarvis's path-breaking analysis. His conclusion is still the most convincing one, namely, that the Sixth Decennial Census of the United States failed to provide an accurate enumeration of insane people in the United States and gravely distorted the situation of African Americans. The comment of one observer puts the matter in perspective: "It was the census that was insane, and not the colored people."[24]

THE MEDICAL RESPONSE TO PSYCHIATRIC
DISORDERS AMONG NEGRO SLAVES

An objection can be made that distortions in the 1840 census do not bear directly on the problem of racism in the diagnosis of mental disorders by mental health workers. One can argue that the census was, after all, a government document that became a weapon in a deadly political struggle and that, if anything, the episode reflects positively on the medical profession, since it was a physician, Jarvis, who exposed the miscount. Although Jarvis's contribution is important, there were many other physicians who insisted on the susceptibility of freed Negroes to mental illness. Physicians in both the North and the South continued to accept the findings of the census, even after Jarvis exposed them. In 1851 the *American Journal of Insanity* (AJI) reprinted the following newspaper account:

> It is obvious, from the following schedule (taken from the 1840 census), that there is an awful prevalence of idiocy and insanity among the free blacks over the whites, and especially over the slaves. Who would believe, without the fact in black and white before his eyes, *that every fourteenth* colored person in the State of Maine is an idiot or lunatic?[25]

Jarvis responded quickly to the resurrection of the controversy, but the myths generated by the census persisted.[26] Despite the vigor with which he disputed the claims of the beneficial emotional effect of slavery, even Jarvis contributed to the myth that Negroes were less mentally disordered because they were less civilized. In the April 1852 issue of the AJI, Jarvis published a detailed discussion of the new ways that civilization contributed to insanity. He analyzed the available data in order to demonstrate that insanity increased in civilized countries at a greater rate than the growth of the general population. Because he found the statistical evidence inconclusive, he was forced to rely on statements by the French psychiatrist Esquirol and the German naturalist Humboldt and on "the general opinion of writers, travelers and physicians" to support his conclusion that insanity "is seldom found in the savage state while it is known to be more frequent in the civilized state."[27] Although Jarvis rejected the idea that slavery prevented insanity, his comments helped reinforce the belief that there are differences between primitive groups and civilized ones in their susceptibility to insanity.

Other physicians offered arguments directly in support of the theory that slavery was beneficial for Negroes because it controlled insanity. Long after Jarvis and others published their objections to the 1840 census reports, the superintendent of the Louisiana State Asylum lectured Northerners as follows:

> It is exceedingly seldom that our slaves ever become insane . . . you will agree with me that this fact is a striking commentary on the *pseudo philanthropy* of some of our Northern brethren. . . . [The slaves'] great exemption from insanity is due to their situation, the protection the law guarantees them, the restraint of a mild state of servitude, the freedom from all anxiety respecting their present or future wants, the withholding (in a great degree) of all spirituous and drugged liquors, and all other forms of excess into which the free Negroes plunge.[28]

Fourteen years after Jarvis's exposé of the 1840 census, Stanford Chaillé, a prominent New Orleans physician, wrote in support of the contention that slaves were less susceptible to insanity than freed African Americans. He expressed indignation at criticisms by Northerners, particularly because prejudice existed against insane Negroes in Northern asylums.[29] Even after the Civil War, psychiatrists, physicians, and other mental health workers continued to argue that Negroes benefited from slavery by receiving special care and supervision, which in turn reduced the incidence of insanity. In 1887, Andrews raised the issue and in the 1890s, similar claims were made. In 1914, O'Malley repeated them, as did Bevis in 1921.[30]

THE MENTAL DISORDERS OF SLAVES

With no apparent sense of the contradiction, some antebellum physicians argued that slaves were particularly immune to insanity even as others were identifying mental deficiencies and new disorders that afflicted slaves. In 1843, Samuel Cartwright, another prominent Southern physician, described cranial inadequacies of African Americans:

> The brain being ten percent less in volume and weight, he [the Negro] is, from necessity more under the influence of his instincts and animality than other races of men and less under the influence of his reflective facilities. His mind being thus depressed, nothing but arbitrary power, prescribing

and enforcing temperance in all things, can restrain the excesses of his mental nature and restore reason to her throne.[31]

These assertions were used by Calhoun to buttress his claim that slavery
was necessary for Negroes. Even after emancipation, these supposedly
scientific findings provided the basis for craniological theories about
racial inferiority.

Although census data and craniological theories were used to explain
why slavery was beneficial for Negroes, some of the same people argued
that Negroes also were at risk of becoming mentally ill as a result of slavery. In 1851, Cartwright published an essay in the prestigious *New Orleans Medical and Surgical Journal* on two new mental disorders peculiar to
Negroes. One was drapetomania and the other was dysaesthesia
aethiopis. Cartwright minted the term *drapetomania* from *drapetes,* the
Latin word for "runaway slave," and *mania,* meaning "mad" or "crazy."
He observed that the disease was previously unknown to medical authorities although "its diagnostic symptom, the absconding from service, is
well known to our planters and overseers." He concluded that what "in-
duces the Negro to run away is as much a disease of the mind as any
other species of mental alienation, and much more curable." The measure he recommended to prevent slaves from developing the disease was
"whipping the devil out of them." He cautioned owners that patients
should be "treated like children, with care, kindness, attention and dig-
nity." He warned that overly severe whipping *or* too lenient treatment
would induce drapetomania; brutality and permissiveness both had to be
avoided. He assured his readers, "With the advantages of proper medical
advice strictly followed, this troublesome practice that many Negroes
have of running away can be almost entirely prevented, although the
slaves be located on the borders of a free state, within a stone's throw of
the abolitionists."[32]

Escaping slavery was not the only behavior attributable to a mental
disorder. "Paying no attention to property," which led a slave to destroy
things; "breaking the tools he works with"; and self-indulgence leading to
"idleness and sloth" were symptoms of dysaesthesia aethiopis.
Cartwright expressed less respect for the views of plantation managers in
regard to this disease: "The term rascality when given to this disease by
overseers, is founded on an erroneous hypothesis and leads to an incorrect empirical treatment which seldom or never cures it."[33]

Cartwright believed that dysaesthesia aethiopis, which was "peculiar to Negroes," resulted from respiratory weakness that led to a lack of oxygen in the system and that the remedy was to stimulate the liver, skin, and kidneys in order to assist in decarbonizing the blood. To do this, Cartwright prescribed hard work in fresh air—chopping wood, splitting rails, sawing, and lifting and carrying heavy weights—in order to expand the lungs and increase breathing: "The compulsory power of the white man, by making the slothful Negro take active exercise, puts into active play the lungs, through whose agency the vitalized blood is sent to the brain, to give liberty to the mind."[34] Another part of the decarbonizing treatment was "whipping in," which consisted of lightly oiling the skin and gently whipping the surface so that the oil would penetrate and break up the carbon in the system.

Cartwright's diagnostic formulations of the mental illnesses of Negroes were publicized throughout the English-speaking world. His "discoveries" were not always interpreted as an apology for slavery. They received international acclaim when they were publicized by Daniel Tuke, whose famous English family established the York Retreat, a 19th-century model for moral treatment in asylums.[35]

The Morphology of Evil: Racism and Mental Illness After the Civil War

No one will be surprised that racism in the identification of psychiatric disorders did not end with the Emancipation Proclamation. Concerns about the mental illnesses of African Americans were overshadowed after the Civil War by new fears of insanity among other "races." In order to identify these threats, it was first necessary to expand the concept of race. Races were no longer considered to be groups having different skin pigmentation; now they were identified on the basis of religious preferences, class, or country of origin. The population of Europe itself was divided into three races: the Nordic, the Alpine, and the Mediterranean.[36] The Nordic "master race" was further subdivided into Anglo-Saxons and Teutons.

Biological differences were identified among the races, and these were linked to cultural and intellectual ones. Craniologists invented a "cephalic index," which measured differences in head size. Nordics were identified as longheaded dolichocephalics and Alpines as roundheaded brachycephalics. Theories were advanced that dolichocephalics from Protestant northern Europe were more adept at urban living, had a greater aptitude for success, and were more enterprising and imaginative than brachycephalics, who were Catholics from middle and eastern Europe. Although it was not long before these theories were scientifically discredited, they continued to be used for more than a century as the justification for laws and practices that advanced racial discrimination.[37] Immigration of poor eastern and southern Europeans led many of the nation's leaders and intellectuals, as well as ordinary citizens, to fear the dilution of the hereditary advancement that had been made by the Nordic race, which originally colonized the United States. Arguments were made that the newer "races" entering the United States were more prone to mental illness, criminality, and other forms of social deviance.

The hopes of early-19th-century reformers that the insane asylum would be the centerpiece in the elimination of mental illness were shaken by the exposure of misleading reports of highly inflated cure rates by superintendents of many mental hospitals. Overcrowding and abuses of patients added to public dissatisfaction with many institutions. Widely publicized conflicts between neurologists and medical superintendents of insane asylums about the identification of mental disorders and about their etiology contributed to the disenchantment with mental health care.[38]

There were increasing demands for reform. A growing perception that many mental patients were incurable led to the creation of institutions that separated the feebleminded from the insane, and those who suffered from chronic illnesses from those who could be returned to society after treatment. Sterilization laws, marriage restrictions, and other regulations were introduced to stop the spread of insanity and feeblemindedness. A major strategy to deal with mental disorders was to restrict immigration. Many new laws were introduced, which included "racial" exclusions and quotas.[39]

Once again, proponents of various theories about insanity and mental illness looked to the census as a source of data. In order to gather information about insanity for the 1880 census, a new classification system was devised that consisted of seven subclasses: mania, melancholy, monomania, paresis, dementia, dipsomania, and epilepsy. The census included a separate volume on the problems of deviance, including mental illness: "Report on the Defective, Dependent and Delinquent Classes as

Returned at the Tenth Census (June 1, 1880)." This volume was written by a leading reformer, Frederick H. Wines, who declared that "there is a morphology of evil" and made the following recommendation: "For the information of legislatures, it is important that the whole extent of the evil to be contended against shall be known and that it may be accessible in a single report, in order that they may make adequate provision for its care or alleviation." Wines believed that environmental factors were the primary consideration in the development of mental disorders. Although he attempted to demonstrate this in his report on the census, his view did not prevail.[40]

The belief that inheritance is the major factor in insanity grew stronger throughout the second half of the 19th century. This belief was fueled by an increasing fear of immigration and by the great increase in the number of people in mental hospitals, an increase equated with a rise in insanity. Biological explanations for the adverse effects of undesirable characteristics were drawn from the theories of Darwin, Mendel, Malthus, and especially Galton, who studied the influence of heredity on human beings, a subject to which he gave the name *eugenics*.

Whether they attributed insanity to social conditions or to population growth among the genetically defective, most commentators believed that the inferior "races" then entering the country were the primary source of the rapid increase in mental illness. Organizations were formed to stem the tide of immigration, to exclude mental defectives, and to deport those who were found to be insane after immigration. Starting in 1882, Congress passed bills excluding known criminals, lunatics, idiots, polygamists, epileptics, beggars, prostitutes, anarchists, persons suffering from loathsome or dangerous contagious diseases, and those likely to become public charges, but these measures still did not decrease the amount of poverty and dependency, reduce the number of people in mental hospitals, or remedy the other threats that worried many people. Nor did Asian exclusion laws and a 1907 gentlemen's agreement that stopped Japanese immigration make a noticeable difference.

A major force behind the agitation was the Immigration Restriction League, an organization founded by wealthy Harvard graduates who were deeply committed to a belief in Anglo-Saxon superiority and to the view that other races would contaminate the hereditary preeminence of the old settlers. They supported legislation sponsored by a former professor of theirs—Senator Henry Cabot Lodge. The basic strategy of the Immigration Restriction League was the adoption of a literacy bill, which members believed would serve as a method of excluding defectives.[41] Although a literacy law was finally passed in 1917 and even more stringent measures were added during the 1920s, mental hospitals continued to be overcrowded.

Throughout this period, scientists in many fields contributed to the growing racist sentiment. The eugenics movement became the focus for investigations on the impact of heredity on human problems. A major organization that promoted research on heredity was the American Breeders Association, which established a committee on eugenics whose members included Alexander Graham Bell, David Starr Jordan, Luther Burbank, and many illustrious university professor.[42] Adolf Meyer and Emil Southard, eminent psychiatrists, also participated in a committee established by the American Breeders Association to study the influence of heredity on insanity. The most active member was Charles Davenport, a famous biologist who established the Eugenics Records Office, where specially trained field workers traced the lineage of thousands of American families in an effort to identify the effects of heredity. This effort, supported by contributions from the Harriman family and from the Carnegie Foundation, provided continuous examples of the ill effects of bad breeding and of the positive benefits when families were well bred. The scientific and political activities of the period, which did not end until the 1930s, made Hitler's Aryan campaign seem less like the aberrant rantings of a mad man and more like the direct result of a century of scientific and political thought in which scholars, scientists, and philanthropists from the United States played a major role.

The history of scientific racism, and especially of the eugenics movement, in this country has been obscured for many reasons, not the least of which is its contribution to the Holocaust. Although there have been historical accounts of these developments, they have not been linked to the expression of hereditarian views in recent studies about the nature of psychiatric disorders. Even those who object to genetic explanations of mental disorders have neglected the historical background for these ideas. We can do no more at this moment than to draw attention to the growing popularity of biological theories, especially those that rely on genetics to explain such mental disorders as schizophrenia in adults and attention deficit disorder (hyperactivity) among children.[43] These assertions are made even though their proponents acknowledge that they do not yet have the scientific evidence to directly substantiate their claims. Because of the dramatic advances in research technology, we are assured, it is only a matter of time until the scientific proof is available. Similar claims have been made repeatedly for more than a century, with the same vigor.

Although they were absorbed in studying the biological threats from new races that were coming to America in increasing numbers, and although large importations of Africans had ended prior to the Civil War, scientists, physicians, and mental health workers did not ignore the mental problems of blacks. The beneficial effects of slavery and the deterioration in the mental health of African Americans after emancipation were periodically reasserted. Each new development in the treatment of mental illness was accompanied by new theories on the biological causes of the mental illness of African Americans; likewise, every new scientific advance was occasion for a new theory on the biogenetic basis for their psychiatric problems. In 1886, a psychiatrist from a Mississippi asylum analyzed the increase in insanity among Negroes from 1 out of 5,799 (as reported by the 1860 census) to 1 out of 1,096 (according to the 1880 census). He attributed this rise in part to the poor living conditions that existed after emancipation and to the effects of physical illnesses, especially tuberculosis, which were believed to contribute to insanity. He also noted that there were links between insanity and civilization. He added some new ideas to this theory and suggested that Negroes would never be able to reach the level of civilization of whites because of biological deficiencies "owing, as some pathologists maintain, to the fact that the cranial sutures close much earlier in the Negro than in other races." Echoing the theories of the craniologists, he reported that "the growth of the brain is arrested by premature closing of the cranial sutures and the lateral pressure of the frontal bones."[44]

The most important contribution to the scientific study of heredity in the 19th century, the theory of evolution, also was used to explain why African Americans were vulnerable to insanity. Darwin's theory of the survival of the fittest was the foundation for the lead article in the July 1901 issue of the *American Journal of Insanity*. Charles Woodruff, an army doctor, presented a long essay on the development of the brain and its relation to the advancement of civilization. Combining evolutionary theory, craniology, and xenophobia in a fascinating amalgam, he explained the intellectual superiority of northern European Christians. In this wide-ranging essay, he accounted for the lack of emotional and intellectual development of blacks in terms of "nigressence." Woodruff arrived at the following conclusion:

> As civilization and brain development have gone hand in hand, the lower races which have not taken part in it are forever unfit for it. . . . The Negro is a survival of men who migrated too soon and whenever he is left alone he invariably reverts to ancestral life as in Haiti. His color and physique bar him from the best parts of this country where he quickly perishes, and the struggle in a civilized environment is causing such degeneration that he is producing a tremendous crop of degenerates in the south from bad food, bad habits and exposure. Crime, consumption, and insanity increase and hasten the inevitable extinction. He is sure to become extinct and is not an exception to the rules of acclimatization.[45]

FREUD COMES TO AMERICA

Advances in psychiatry, psychology, and related social sciences were inevitably accompanied by analyses of the mental disorders of blacks. This was true of the introduction of psychoanalytic theory at the turn of the century, a watershed in the development of American psychiatry. Freud's 1911 visit to give the Clark lectures signaled a dramatic change in the mental health movement in the United States. In 1914 the first volume of the *Psychoanalytic Review* was published, and it contained three articles about Negroes.

In one of the articles, Evarts, a physician at the government hospital (St. Elizabeth's), in Washington, D.C., argued that mental diseases had a phylogenetic origin. He interpreted mental illness as a regression to earlier stages of racial development and asserted that "because the colored patient already lives on a plane much lower than his white neighbor, actual deterioration in the individual must be differentiated from the supposed loss of a racial period he has not yet attained" (p. 394). Evarts used Theodore Roosevelt's descriptions of Negroes he encountered during his African safaris to paint a picture of the primitive state of the "colored race." He reasserted the theory that their experience in America had little effect on Negroes. He reported that "bondage in reality was a wonderful aid to the colored man" and warned that under conditions of freedom his "upward progress" would become "infinitely harder" (p. 394).

Evarts claimed that the colored race because of the "vicissitudes of its history" was particularly prone to dementia praecox, which we now call schizophrenia. He used admission rates to St. Elizabeth's Hospital, which were higher for blacks than for the population as a whole, to demonstrate their susceptibility to the disease. However, he cautioned that there were differences in the manifestations of the disorder in other, more advanced, races. For example, according to Evarts, "Voluntary attention, the staying power which carries a disagreeable or difficult task to completion, is already deficient in the race. Hence its impairment under a psychosis is usually more apparent than real" (p. 396). On the other hand, because most Negroes did manual labor that was repetitive and directed by others, they were more likely, claimed Evarts, to continue working until the disease reached an advanced stage. That is, "Whereas in the Caucasian race [inability to work at a job or profession] is often the earliest and perhaps for some time the only manifestation, in the Negro race, when the ability of the patient to carry on his daily task is impaired, the disease is no longer in its incipiency" (p. 396).

Evarts further claimed that some mental disorders that were found among more developed races were lacking among Negroes. He asserted that because sexual instincts were unrestrained among Negroes, their desires were usually fully satisfied and "the ordinary sexual perversions" (p. 397), including female masturbation, were less frequent. Even though Freudian theories emphasized the impact of life events on the development of mental disorders, and thus contributed to the shift away from the theories of biological determinism that were widely accepted at the time, a commitment to a psychodynamic approach did not reverse racist thinking about Negroes.

A second article ("The Dream as a Simple Wish-Fulfillment in the Negro") in the same volume of the *Psychoanalytic Review* was written by Evarts's colleague at the government hospital, John E. Lind. Freud had urged the study of children's dreams in order to understand abnormal adult psychology, but, Lind noted, "[In Freud's country] there is no such race as we have here whose psychological processes are simple in character and so readily obtainable." Lind asserted that the mind of "the so-called pure-bred Negro" was simpler than that of a white and similar to that of the savage. He speculated that "perhaps to the American investigator the Negro might prove as valuable and more accessible than the child."[46]

Lind analyzed the dreams of 100 Negroes admitted to the government hospital and concluded that 84 had wish fulfillment dreams of a juvenile nature. An 87-year-old man dreamed that he was going to get a pension, and several prisoners dreamed that they were free. The dreams were direct expressions of wishes, Lind claimed, uncomplicated by the activities of an inner censor; the absence of the inner censor confirmed his hypothesis about the simple, savage-like character of the Negro. Other articles by Evarts and Lind in the first and in subsequent volumes of the *Psychoanalytic Review* echoed these themes, and other physicians published confirming reports.

Lind was not the only one interested in the dreams of Negroes at St. Elizabeth's. When he accompanied Freud to the United States in 1911, Jung analyzed the dreams and statements of 15 blacks at the government hospital. He reinforced the phylogenetic theory of the primitive nature of the Negro mind by claiming that "the different strata of the mind correspond to the history of the races." He reported that the Negro "has probably a whole historical layer less than the white man." He added a special twist to the discussion by suggesting that Negro childishness was contagious, and he named the infectious disorder "the American Complex." He found the influence of Negroes on whites in America in everything from the way they swayed their hips to Teddy Roosevelt's infectious laugh. Jung explained the sexual repressions of Americans as a defensive maneuver against Negroes. Even before his visit to St. Elizabeth's, he made the following statement to the Second International Psychoanalytic Congress in 1910:

> The causes for the repression . . . can be found in the specific American Complex, namely to the living together with lower races, especially with Negroes. Living together with barbaric races exerts a suggestive effect on the laboriously tamed instinct of the white race and tends to pull it down. Hence, the need for strongly developed defensive measures, which precisely show themselves in those specific features of American culture.[47]

Although Jung had second thoughts about some of his earlier racist sentiments after the Holocaust, he did not entirely repudiate them. At the time they were published, they contributed important authority to the evolving racism in the identification of mental disorders.

Another article about Negroes, written by Mary O'Malley, also a psychiatrist at the government hospital, appeared in the same year (1914) in the

American Journal of Insanity. In her report of a five-year study of 880 Negro and white women at the institution, she assumed without question that there were deficiencies in the evolutionary advancement of the colored race:

> A psychosis in an obviously lower race such as the colored race really is, must necessarily offer some features from a mental standpoint which distinguish it in a general way from a psychosis in a higher race. This is so apparent that it requires no further discussion. The lower psychic development of the colored race, under certain pathological conditions, offers some phenomena which are observed to approach more nearly the general features and characteristics of children.[48]

O'Malley found that the differences between Negro and white women at St. Elizabeth's were not all negative. She reported that Negroes were not as filthy and disgusting and were not as likely to soil, wet, or expose themselves as were white inmates. According to O'Malley, Negroes had not evolved as far and therefore did not deteriorate as much; moreover, because of their limited evolutionary advancement, Negroes did not suffer from depression.

In another journal published in 1914, E. M. Green, the clinical director of the Georgia State Sanitarium, also reported the infrequency of depression among Blacks:

> It appears that the Negro mind does not dwell upon unpleasant subjects; he is irresponsible, unthinking, easily aroused to happiness, and his unhappiness is transitory, disappearing as a child's when other interests attract his attention. Depression is rarely encountered even under circumstances in which a white person would be overwhelmed.[49]

The theme of the happy, irresponsible savage can be traced in psychiatric literature and teaching up to the 1960s.

In 1921, as part of an overall reorganization of the American Psychiatric Association, the *American Journal of Insanity* changed its name to the *American Journal of Psychiatry*. For the first volume of the renamed journal, W. M. Bevis, another physician from St. Elizabeth's, the government hospital, wrote an article titled "The Psychological Traits of the Southern Negro with Observations of Some of His Psychoses." The article repeats the phylogenetic theory and other themes of earlier articles from physicians at St. Elizabeth's and elsewhere: "The Negro race evinces certain phylogenetic traits of character, habit and behavior . . . these psychic characteristics have their effect upon and are reflected in the psychoses most frequently seen in the Negro" (p. 69). Bevis noted that Negroes had been cannibals and savages until recently and were unwillingly brought to America "into an environment for which biological development of the race had not made adequate preparation" (p. 69). He explained that because of "the black man's talent for mimicry," he was often able to imitate whites, but he warned readers that this apparent similarity could "delude the uninitiated into the belief that the mental level of the Negro is only slightly inferior to that of the Caucasian" (p. 69). He pointed out that although Negroes were often bright and lively as children, their development froze at puberty and they entered a life of sexual promiscuity, petty thievery, and debauchery. These depredations, he claimed, produced many mental diseases, the principle one being dementia praecox (schizophrenia). Bevis concluded, "This is not surprising, when their racial character make-up and the atmosphere of superstition in which they move are considered. Much of their usual behavior seems only a step from the simpler types of this classification" (p. 74).

Although the newly named *American Journal of Psychiatry* may have helped to launch the profession into the modern age, the Bevis article is a distillation of a century of misinformation and racism.

THE FEEBLEMINDED, PSYCHOLOGICAL TESTING, AND RACISM

In the first half of this century, psychiatry was not alone among the mental health professions in making increasingly racist representations that were routinely presented as scientific studies. If anything, social scientists from other disciplines were more active in spreading prejudiced and damaging information. In fact, psychiatrists often were criticized for their isolation from and indifference to major social policy debates.

Psychology was just emerging as a discipline at the beginning of the 20th century, but the profession made substantial contributions to the scientific literature about the biological inferiority of immigrants and Negroes. It is important to note that one of the characteristics that distinguished psychologists from other mental health workers was their use of psychometrics, principally intelligence tests. The development of IQ tests was inextricably linked to the way they were used to demonstrate the inferiority of blacks and immigrant groups. The claims do not need to be repeated here; most readers are familiar with the continuing assertion (e.g., in *The Bell Curve,* by R. J. Herrnstein and C. Murray) that differences in IQ scores reflect hereditary differences among the "races."[51] Even though the standings of various groups have changed, the arguments about inherited differences that contribute to the scores have not. When Jews first came to America, their poor scores were seen as a sign of racial inferiority, and when their economic and educational level improved and they began to score higher than the norm on IQ scores, the argument was made that their scores reflected the hereditary intellectual superiority of Jews.

What is most remarkable is how far distinguished psychologists were willing to go to prove racial inferiority. Many of the major figures in the development of IQ testing—Terman, Burt, and others—contributed to the myth of the inferiority of the Negro IQ. Probably the most disturbing story involves the English psychologist Cyril Burt, "the father of educational testing," who was made a knight for his contributions to the field. Burt falsified data, invented assistants who collected it, and wrote reports under their names to substantiate his claims. He created his falsifications with such abandon that even Arthur Jensen, the Berkeley psychologist who championed the assertion of the intellectual inferiority of blacks, became suspicious (the data Burt generated looked like textbook descriptions of statistical distributions, rather than the imperfect data that are likely to be produced in field experiments). The fraud in Burt's case, like that in the 1840 census, was exposed because the statistics were too good to be true.

The psychologists' contributions to the myth of black inferiority went far beyond the field of mental health. Probably the greatest damage was done in the schools, where differences in IQ were used to segregate black students, a decision that deprived them of the educational resources available to whites. Racism in IQ testing also had a major impact in the mental health field. This occurred in two ways: First, blacks were often misidentified as mentally retarded, and their problems were overlooked or attributed to intellectual inferiority. They were inappropriately classified and assigned to programs for unsalvageable patients, in which they often deteriorated. Second, even when black patients were appropriately identified as mentally retarded, they were assigned to programs that had the fewest resources. IQ scores were used to make a priori judgments about the ability of patients to function, and a low score was given as the rationalization for denying resources that might have improved a patient's life. Findings of mental retardation also were used as a justification for involuntary sterilization and other draconian measures.

IQ scores are the principal data used to identify mental retardation, even in psychiatric classifications such as the *Diagnostic and Statistical Manual of Mental Disorders*. The belief in the importance of intelligence, as measured by IQ tests, is pervasive in American society, and it is reinforced by mental health professionals who administer the tests and who continue to be involved in the care and custody of those who are diagnosed as mentally deficient.[52]

The recent publication of *The Bell Curve* has revived interest in IQ scores. The widespread publicity given to the book indicates how important IQ is in determining attitudes about African Americans and other racial minorities. An examination of the shortcomings of *The Bell Curve* would take us far from the subject of psychiatric diagnosis.[53] However, it is important to recognize that IQ testing is an indispensable feature of certain psychiatric diagnoses and that this in turn has led to certain attitudes toward African Americans and other groups, attitudes that have resulted in a restriction of opportunities, resources, and programs for them.

MODERN TIMES

A complete history of racism in the diagnosis of mental disorders would include an examination of the repeated manipulation of epidemiological data to demonstrate the psychological vulnerability of African Americans and almost every immigrant group except those who came from northern Europe. Further scrutiny of the historical record would include an analysis of the periodic census reports on insanity during the early part of the century and of other research on psychiatric epidemiology up to the 1960s. For example, even after the beginning of the civil rights movement, the claim was made in the *American Journal of Psychiatry* that the increasing commitment rate of African Americans to Virginia's mental hospitals was due to agitation by labor organizers and Communist agents who promoted desegregation after the 1954 Supreme Court decision in *Brown v. Board of Education*.[54] This claim (a reincarnation of the pre–Civil War myth that manumission caused insanity) and others that have already been described illustrate how the identification of mental disorder has been used to promote stereotypes and how such thinking continues to be used to reinforce bigotry long after it has been scientifically discredited. There is a long history of misuse of census data and other official research reports to perpetuate racist myths, and more examples may add to the evidence, but the basic point is this: Psychiatric diagnoses have been used frequently as tools to promote racial injustice. Let us now turn to the post–World War II period to analyze the impact of psychiatric diagnosis on racism today.[55]

DSM, EPIDEMIOLOGY, AND RACISM

The last time the federal government placed a major emphasis on investigating the extent of mental illness in the United States was during the administration of Jimmy Carter, who established the President's Commission on Mental Health (PCMH) in order to assess the nation's mental health problems and to plan future services. The commission found that it did not have sufficient information about the frequency of mental illnesses or about the prevalence of specific mental disorders to plan rationally for the development of an effective mental health system. Without knowing how many people needed mental health treatment or how many were receiving it, policymakers could not answer questions about the need for facilities or determine whether it was necessary to increase the number of (and consequently the training initiatives for) mental health professionals.

Government officials were dealing with essentially the same problem that confronted Edward Jarvis and his peers 150 years ago. The major distinction between the concerns of contemporary policymakers and those who were involved in these issues in the first half of the 19th century is that the scope of the problem and the dimensions of the solution have broadened. Mental illness is understood to be much more pervasive than the insanity that worried early proponents of psychiatric hospitals; 19th-century reformers were concerned about those who would now be considered acutely psychotic or suffering from a profound organic disorder. Those who are less severely afflicted now are counted as mentally ill, and the concept of mental illness now includes behaviors, such as drug addiction or agoraphobia, that would not have been considered evidence of it 150 years ago. Solutions for these more recently recognized mental disorders are also different. The earlier response to mental illness was to calculate how many asylums were needed. Today it is necessary to figure out what personnel must be trained and what training they need. Information is needed not only on the number of hospital beds for the acutely ill but on board and care facilities, outpatient programs, educational programs for severely emotionally disabled children, and an endless variety of other resources that may be used by those who have different mental illnesses. Furthermore, policymakers want to establish the right mix of psychiatrists, psychologists, nurses, social workers, and other mental health professionals to address these problems.

The President's Commission on Mental Health evaluated the existing data and decided that they could not adequately answer questions about epidemiology, resource utilization, manpower needs, or planning for additional facilities. The various studies completed since World War II used different criteria for mental disorders and produced estimates that ranged from a lifetime prevalence rate of 90% in one survey to a low of 11% in another. Each study looked for something different. After a careful review of the major epidemiological studies of mental disorders in the country from 1950 to 1980, the PCMH concluded as follows:

> These widely differing results clearly did not address the questions posed by the PCMH, which asked how the mentally ill are being served, to what extent are they underserved and who is affected by such underservice. Deficits were found not only in the standardization of mental disorder definitions and case identification methods, but also in the linkage of available prevalence data with assessments of need for and use of mental health services.[56]

To answer these questions, the National Institute of Mental Health organized and funded what was considered to be the largest epidemiological study of mental illness ever undertaken (obviously ignoring the history of the census). This new initiative was named the Epidemiological Catchment Area (ECA) study. Surveys were conducted at five sites: one in North Carolina, which included both a rural and an urban population, and one in each of four urban areas—New Haven, St. Louis, Baltimore, and Los Angeles. Approximately 20,000 people were interviewed, and an effort was made to assure that there was an adequate representation from all population groups, including minorities. Unusual efforts were made to collect information about African Americans.[57]

Careful attention was paid to methodological issues in the ECA studies in order to avoid the problems encountered in earlier surveys. To deal with the problems of reliability, a data-gathering instrument was devised that used the Diagnostic Interview Schedule (DIS), an instrument that was based on the newly published DSM-III, designed to elicit valid information; and purported to assure consistent, reliable diagnoses. In their description of the study, the principal investigators reported that "the DIS content and face validity . . . [were] high as facilitated by the explicit DSM-III criteria and certified under contract by the principal authors of that diagnostic system (J. Williams and R. Spitzer)."[58] Among epidemiologists the ECA project is considered to be a major achievement in the design of scientific studies. The ECA surveys represent the state of the art in the field of epidemiology. In the next chapter, we will examine the ECA studies more broadly; here we wish to focus attention on the identification of mental disorders among African Americans.

In dealing with the issue of racial differentials in psychiatric disorders, the ECA investigators were caught on the horns of a dilemma. They were aware that institutional racism can unconsciously bias even the best-intentioned social scientists. They were also aware that certain statistics show an overrepresentation of racial minorities in public psychiatric facilities, which are the only ones in which information is accessible. One part of the dilemma was how to avoid overreporting the incidence of psychiatric disorders among minorities who are overrepresented in state mental hospitals and other public programs because of biases in the way they are treated in the mental health system. The other problem was how to avoid the charge that severe pathology in minority groups is often ignored or is considered to be criminal behavior rather than mental illness.

Other problems in relation to race and class also affected the study. For example, during the time that the ECA studies were conducted, Ronald Reagan was in office and the political climate was increasingly conservative. William W. Eaton and his associates, who helped design the studies, described the constraints that resulted from the political climate:

The survival of the ECA program during the early budget cuts of the Reagan administration may be partly a result of its medical orientation. Some of these cuts were directed specifically at research on "Social Problems" defined as research which attempted to study the way that society itself was flawed or might be changed. Research on racism and socioeconomic stratification was deemphasized as a result, for example. But the ECA program was portrayed as strictly medical, counting persons with diseases. The design is very weak in the study of risk factors, such as racism for example, because so much room in the questionnaire was devoted to diagnoses. This narrowness of focus may have helped it obtain relatively stable funding through 1983.[59]

Although the ECA report described significant differences between blacks and whites at individual sites for some disorders, the overall conclusion was that when the results were aggregated, variations in mental illnesses were due to chance rather than to major racial differences. As the researchers put it, "Differences between blacks and others in rates of psychiatric disorders are generally modest and rarely statistically significant."[60]

The initial ECA findings included data from only three of the test sites, and it wasn't until later that results from the other two areas, North Carolina and Los Angeles, were published. In 1987 the first report was circulated that dealt with a specific mental health problem of African Americans.[61] In an article titled "Alcohol Abuse and Dependence in the Rural South," Blazer, Crowell, and George conclude that there were "elevated odds" of alcohol abuse or dependence among rural black men at the North Carolina study site. Although they found a statistically significant correlation between race and alcoholism, the authors acknowledge that there is no way their data can yield information about the reasons why the rural blacks in their survey showed higher rates of alcohol dependence. Despite this disclaimer, they offer a hypothesis:

> Nevertheless, a number of explanations for this association can be suggested. One of the more intriguing is the possibility of increased consanguinity in the rural countries. Clinically, consanguinity is an infrequent finding in families with inherited disorders in the United States. This is because the background rate of consanguinity in the general population is very low. Nevertheless, intermarriage in rural counties of North Carolina is known to be higher than in urban areas, and given the partial hereditary explanation of alcoholism this possibility cannot be overlooked. If one accepts a genetic predisposition to alcohol abuse and/or dependence and if the genes for such a predisposition are concentrated in rural families, then some families may have higher prevalence of these disorders.[62]

The authors used an empirical finding of variation in rates of alcohol abuse and dependence as an opportunity to introduce a hypothesis built on a house of cards, a hypothesis that included undocumented assumptions about consanguinity and genetic predisposition to alcoholism. The authors admit being "intrigued" by this explanation, which echoes many of the old themes of sexual licentiousness and genetic deficits, although they recognize that "no data are available to test this hypothesis."

Blazer, Crowell, and George offer other ideas on the elevated rates of alcohol abuse or dependence reported in their article, including the thought that the rural African Americans in the study lived in pockets of poverty and that "such pockets in rural areas may be especially conducive to excessive alcohol use, possibly because of isolation."[63] They suggest that blacks in their survey area who are alcohol prone may drift to the rural areas. This migration theory also echoes explanations that were first used to account for why Northern blacks showed higher rates of mental disorder than Southern slaves. Another theory they offer—that alcohol abuse is more accepted among rural Southern blacks than among others in their study—also is reminiscent of 19th-century attitudes.

Almost as an afterthought, Blazer, Crowell, and George mention some data that they neglected to discuss earlier, namely, that the rate of alcohol abuse among rural blacks is the same as that reported for all races at other study sites in New Haven, Baltimore, and St. Louis. In other words, the real difference was that African Americans as well as whites in urban North Carolina showed lower rates of alcohol abuse and dependence than whites and blacks at all the other sites.

The report "Alcohol Abuse and Dependence in the Rural South" repeats the enduring pattern of racism in the identification of mental disorders. For the ECA investigators from North Carolina, the important finding was that there are higher rates of alcoholism among rural African Americans in their sample, not that there are lower rates among urban blacks as compared with whites and blacks at the other sites, an intriguing finding they offer no hypothesis to explain. Their final conclusion is, "The ECA data provide a rich source for exploring complex environmental and individual interactions that may complement our clinical understanding of the peculiar problem of increased alcohol abuse and/or dependence in the rural south."[64]

These researchers were not dealing with the "peculiar institution" of slavery, but with the "peculiar problem" of black alcoholism, and they were still determined to tease out of their meager data whatever deficits they could find and to ignore positive information. Skeptics can say that a single report that may have racist connotations does not demonstrate pervasive bias in the diagnosis of mental disorders. We analyzed this article to illustrate how racist stereotypes are introduced into discussions about mental disorders even when modern mental health workers claim to be free of prejudice. The ECA report from North Carolina does not demonstrate the pervasiveness of racism in diagnosis, but other data do.[65]

RACISM IN PRACTICE

An equally important question is how racism affects diagnosis of individual African Americans and other minority group members. In a study of diagnostic prejudices, Loring and Powell surveyed 488 psychiatrists, who composed a stratified random sample of members of the American Psychiatric Association and two state psychiatric associations.[66] The psychiatrists were distributed almost evenly among four groups: white males, white females, black males, and black females. The survey instrument consisted of two case studies for which participants were asked to either apply one of six DSM diagnoses or indicate that none was appropriate. Although all other information on the questionnaire was kept constant, the client's race and gender were altered so that an equal proportion of the psychiatrists of each race and gender evaluated cases of white males, black males, white females, and black females (the race and gender of both cases on each questionnaire were the same). Approximately one-fifth of the questionnaires had no identifying information about race or gender.

The results indicated that generally "when the sex and race of the psychiatrist and of the case study coincided the psychiatrist tended to choose the same diagnosis as he or she probably would choose if there were no information about the client's sex or race" (p. 17).[67] The only exception was that a majority of the white women psychiatrists chose the least severe diagnosis for white female clients. The most striking finding was that each group of clinicians tended to identify black male clients as more severely disordered than any of the other racial and sexual subgroups. The investigators reported, "Black males are most likely to be diagnosed by each type of psychiatrist as having a paranoid schizophrenic disorder."[68] Furthermore, both black males and black females were more likely than their white counterparts to be given a diagnosis of Paranoid Personality Disorder. The report concluded, "Clinicians appear to ascribe violence, suspiciousness, and dangerousness to black clients even though the case studies are the same as the case studies for the white clients."[69]

One of the ramifications of the kind of variation in clinical response indicated by this study is that racial and sexual biases in the identification of mental disorder lead to differential treatment. But there is another:

> Equally (if not more) important, if diagnoses are influenced by such characteristics as sex and race, these different standards will change our perceptions of mental health. The "reality" of psychopathology is derived increasingly from hospital and epidemiological reports on mental disorders. If women and men (and blacks and whites) are seen differentially even if they exhibit the same behavior, these differences will be reflected and legitimized in official statistics on psychopathology.[70]

Loring and Powell have identified the dynamic involved in the enduring legacy of racism. When a diagnostic system, such as DSM, that appears to be free of racism actually permits the introduction of racial biases, a sequence of events is triggered that influences public perception about the incidence of mental disorders among minority groups. These perceptions confirm, then reinforce, and finally expand the system of beliefs about racial inferiority.[71]

IN THEIR OWN VOICES: AFRICAN AMERICAN VIEWS ABOUT MENTAL ILLNESS

Thus far, our discussion of racism in psychiatric diagnosis has focused principally on a white perspective. Most of the voices have been those of white racists who made scientific claims about the mental defects of African Americans (there have been instances—although surprisingly few—where whites have objected to such claims). It is not that African Americans have ignored these issues; they have responded forcibly and repeatedly, but their complaints are not acknowledged. Even when the history of these controversies is told, African American voices are rarely included. The following examples illustrate what happens when African Americans attempt to participate in these controversies. These episodes retrace some of the ground we have covered:

The first instance involves the efforts of James McCune Smith, an African American physician. Smith drafted a petition to the United States Senate in which he objected to the 1840 census. He spoke eloquently about the issues in his petition at a mass meeting of African Americans in New York City in 1844. Although the assembly adopted the petition, their pleas were ignored.[72] Even when the story of the census was rediscovered in this century, it was Jarvis's efforts that became the focus of attention and little was said about the efforts of Smith and other African Americans. Smith's relentless and eloquent opposition to scientific racism in antebellum America is not generally known. In addition to crusading against the 1840 census, Smith forcefully challenged the theories of Samuel Cartwright and other craniologists in public speeches in New York. He also opposed the movement favored by Benjamin Rush and many others sympathetic to African Americans to create separate African American communities.

A second example occurred almost a century later, when E. Franklin Frazier, the distinguished African American sociologist, published an article, "The Pathology of Race Prejudice," in the June 1927 issue of the *Forum,* a liberal periodical that addressed social policy issues. In the article Frazier attempted to redirect attention to the psychology of whites who promote discrimination. His thesis was simple: "The behavior motivated by race prejudice shows precisely the same characteristics as that ascribed to insanity." He argued, "Race prejudice is an acquired psychological reaction and there is no scientific evidence that it represents the functioning of inherited behavior patterns."[73] In order to demonstrate the link between prejudice and insanity, Frazier used the leading psychological concepts of the period, especially Freudian theories. He identified dissociation of consciousness as the basic mechanism underlying racial prejudice and made the following observations:

> Southern white people write and talk about the majesty of law, the sacredness of human rights, and the advantages of democracy,—and at the next moment defend mob violence, disenfranchisement, and Jim Crow treatment of the Negro. White men and women who are otherwise kind and law-abiding will indulge in the most revolting forms of cruelty towards black people.[74]

Frazier explained, "The whole system of ideas respecting the Negro is dissociated from the normal personality and,—what is more significant for our thesis,—the latter system of ideas seems exempt from the control of the personality." He identified the emotional component of this mechanism of dissociation as "the Negro Complex," and he commented that this complex had "the same intense emotional tone that characterizes insane complexes."[75]

Frazier noted that one aspect of the Negro Complex was the existence of delusions, equivalent to those of the insane. He also observed that those who were delusional distorted facts to maintain the consistency of their delusions; an example was the Southerner who even when presented with authoritative statistical evidence to the contrary insisted that nine-tenths of Negroes had syphilis. Frazier also observed that delusional thinking prompted racists to defend lynching as a measure that was needed to protect white women and that it even justified mob action against white jurors who voted to acquit Negroes accused of crimes. Other psychological mechanisms that Frazier identified among racists were defense mechanisms, projection, and hallucinations. Frazier pinpointed one difference between the delusions of the insane and those of Southern whites: madmen were judged to be insane by the general population whereas the delusions of Southern racists were supported by their community. This distinction led Frazier to conclude, quoting Nietzsche, "Insanity in individuals is something rare,-but in groups, parties, nations and epochs, it is the rule."

Frazier's thesis did not go unnoticed. In the furor that ensued, he was dismissed as the director of the Atlanta University School of Social Work. He fled the city at night, with a gun in his belt for protection. Although Southern bigots were willing to take him very seriously, Frazier found little encouragement among psychiatrists and psychologists who were concerned with identifying different types of psychopathology. Frazier went on to receive great acclaim—he was the first African American to be elected president of the American Sociological Association—but his groundbreaking work on the pathology of racism is not among the contributions for which he is generally remembered.[76]

The demand for recognition of the pathology of racism did not die with Frazier. In 1975 the Committee of Black Psychiatrists recommended the inclusion of racism as a mental disorder in DSM.[77] Spitzer approached the matter obliquely by focusing on the meaning of the concept of mental disorder. He informed the black psychiatrists that his group was "still struggling with the problem of defining what is a mental disorder"; citing the task force's current working definition, he argued, "Racism would not meet the criteria for a mental disorder since it is only in certain environments that it is associated with distress." He concluded that racism should be regarded as "a vulnerability," like male chauvinism or religious fanaticism, and that "in certain environments patients with this condition will evidence subjective distress."[78]

The black psychiatrists also asked for representation on the DSM-III task force, but the request was denied. Spitzer reported that the qualification for becoming a member of the task force was "special expertise in problems of classification of mental disorders." Adding insult to injury, he informed them, "I applied what I regarded as principles of affirmative action in considering minority group members who had such expertise. In so doing several women are members or consultants to the Task Force." Apparently, Spitzer saw no problem in lumping African Americans together with women to satisfy his affirmative action standards. As a consolation, Spitzer offered to maintain contact with the black psychiatrists: "Although there is no black psychiatrist on the task force, we would be glad to meet with representatives of your group to further discuss this or any other matter relevant to DSM-III."

Spitzer acknowledged that the black psychiatrists had provided useful illustrations of "the special environments" where racism becomes symptomatic, and he informed them that he anticipated that the APA would, in the discussion of what is a mental disorder in DSM-III, "list racism as a good example of non-optimal functioning which renders a person vulnerable in certain environments to manifesting signs of disorder." This prediction did not materialize; there is no discussion of racism in DSM-III or any subsequent edition.

The omission was not for want of trying. During the preparation of the latest edition of DSM, W. T. Hamlin proposed that Racist Personality Disorder be included in the manual.[79] He argued that it met the standards for a mental disorder, listed potential diagnostic criteria; and described some of the psychological mechanisms involved, including projection, repression, and suppression. He observed that sufferers often experience dramatic personality changes and extreme lability and have a tendency to form pathological cliques. Although it would be easy to criticize shortcomings in Hamlin's formulations, his proposal suffered a worse fate: it was ignored.[80]

Racism has been a source of every imaginable kind of pathological behavior on a group and individual level, yet it is outside the psychiatric frame of reference. Neither lynching nor genocidal rape nor racially motivated bombings nor any of the other forms of racist mayhem that fill the daily papers is a proper subject for inclusion in the compendium of symptoms found in DSM.

CULTURAL VARIATIONS AND CULTURE-BOUND SYNDROMES

It is not that the APA has completely neglected ethnic and cultural issues in its diagnostic manual of mental disorders. In the latest edition of the manual, DSM-IV, the APA has responded to long-standing criticism by including (1) a discussion of "cultural variations in the clinical presentations" in the description of each of the official diagnoses and (2) an appendix that contains both an "Outline for Cultural Formulation" and a "Glossary of Culture-Bound Syndromes." These contributions illustrate how the APA deals with the problems of racism. Overall, there has been remarkably little change in its approach since the 19th century.

Here is how DSM-IV presents ethnic and racial issues: When it is available, information about racial and cultural variations is included in a separate section of the description of each disorder. In general, these sections consist of admonitions to clinicians to avoid the identification of a given behavior as pathology when it may be acceptable within a person's culture. In the manual's introduction, one finds the following statement: "Diagnostic assessment can be especially challenging when a clinician from one ethnic or cultural group uses the DSM-IV classification to evaluate an individual from a different ethnic or cultural group."

The problem is more complex then the DSM formulation suggests. There is an implicit assumption that the clinician is from the dominant culture and the client is a member of a minority group. A typical example is the following discussion of "specific culture features" in the diagnosis of Paranoid Personality Disorder:

> Some behaviors that are influenced by sociocultural contexts may be erroneously labeled paranoid and may even be reinforced by the process of clinical evaluation. Members of minority groups, immigrants, political and economic refugees or individuals of different ethnic backgrounds may display guarded or defensive behaviors due to unfamiliarity (e.g., language barriers or lack of knowledge of rules or regulations) or in response to the perceived neglect or indifference of the majority society. These behaviors can, in turn, generate anger and frustration in those who deal with these individuals, thus setting up a vicious cycle of mistrust, which should not be confused with Paranoid Personality Disorder. Some ethnic groups also display culturally related behaviors that can be misinterpreted as paranoid.

Although there are often racial or cultural differences between clinicians and clients, the interpretation of behavior quoted above is not necessarily accurate. Very often, appropriate behavior is misconstrued by suspicious clinicians who are fearful of their clients. It is just as likely that the clinician will display guarded and defensive behavior but attribute it to the client and explain that the difficulty is due to the client's "cultural" orientation.

Another difficulty is that racial and cultural issues may be harder to identify when a diagnosis is made by a clinician of the same race as the client. The following clinical vignette may illustrate this point:

Bigger was born in a small Southern town where racial prejudice is rampant. Although formal rules of segregation were abolished before he was born, Bigger found that integration often heightened the tensions in school; at sporting events; and, when he reached adulthood, on the job. His family was incensed over racial conflicts in the community, and they encouraged him to stand up for himself when antagonisms developed. Throughout his life Bigger participated in fights triggered by real or imagined racial slurs, and he carried a weapon in anticipation of trouble. Local politicians consistently exploited racial tensions, and the media dramatized the conflicts. When Bigger was arrested for a series of unprovoked racial attacks, he claimed that his victims were thinking disparaging thoughts about him and would "get" him if he did not "get them first." After he was arrested, a psychiatrist examined him and made a diagnosis of Paranoid Personality Disorder on the basis of the diagnostic criteria in DSM-IV (see Table 7-1). The psychiatrist found that criteria 1, 4, 5, and 6 were applicable.

If Bigger is an African American, few people would object to identifying his acts of violence as pathological behavior. He would be seen as a latter-day incarnation of Richard Wright's Bigger Thomas, a person involved in the pathology of violence. It would be much more difficult to make the same diagnosis of a white Bigger whose violent activities occurred while he was participating in cross burnings, church bombings, and lynchings conducted by the Ku Klux Klan. This clinical vignette points to the difficulty of discriminating between socially sanctioned brutality and violent behavior driven by internal pathology. DSM-IV does not provide adequate tools to distinguish between pathology and so-called normal behavior that is violent or otherwise objectionable.

TABLE 7-1

DIAGNOSTIC CRITERIA FOR PARANOID PERSONALITY DISORDER

A. A pervasive distrust and suspiciousness of others such that their motives are interpreted as malevolent, beginning by early adulthood and present in a variety of contexts, as indicated by four (or more) of the following:

  (1) suspects, without sufficient basis, that others are exploiting, harming or deceiving him or her

  (2) is preoccupied with unjustified doubts about the loyalty or trustworthiness of friends or associates

  (3) is reluctant to confide in others because of unwarranted fear that information will be used maliciously against him or her

  (4) reads hidden demeaning or threatening meanings into benign remarks or events

  (5) persistently bears grudges, i.e. is unforgiving of insults, injuries or slights

  (6) perceives attacks on his or her character or reputation that are not apparent to others and is quick to react angrily, or to counterattack

  (7) has recurrent suspicions, without justification, regarding fidelity of spouse or sexual partner

Reprinted with permission from the *Diagnostic and Statistical Manual of Mental Disorders, Fourth Edition*, Copyright 1994 American Psychiatric Association.

A final criticism of the "specific culture" features in DSM-IV is that the descriptions do not refer to specific cultures. The entries are broad admonitions that involve few references to specific cultures other than the dominant white culture in America, as the entry on Paranoid Personality Disorder indicates. This same myopia can be seen in the second innovation in DSM-IV that deals with cultural differences, namely, the "Outline for Cultural Formulation." In addition to augmenting the general information about the client, the cultural formulation is "to address difficulties that may be encountered in applying DSM-IV criteria in a multicultural environment" (p. 843). A brief page of instructions directs the clinician to provide a narrative summary for each of the following categories: the cultural identity of the client, cultural explanations of the illness, cultural factors related to the client's psychosocial environment and level of functioning, cultural elements of the clinician–client relationship, and overall cultural assessment for diagnosis and care (pp. 844–45). DSM-IV does not describe how this information will be used to diagnose clients. In fact, in the main body of the manual, eight examples illustrate how to record a DSM-IV evaluation (pp. 33–35), but there is no mention of a cultural formulation in any of them.

Unarticulated assumptions about culture are even more apparent in the "Glossary of Culture-Bound Syndromes." There are entries for 25 conditions from different regions of the world. Five are from China, and an equal number are from Latin America. One or two are included from each of a number of other large geographical areas, from Malaysia to the Caribbean, but there is no attempt to be exhaustive or systematic in the selection of entries or cultures. Nor is there information about the process for selecting entries. All DSM-IV tells us is that the entries are "some of the best-studied culture-bound syndromes and idioms of distress that may be encountered in clinical practice in North America" (pp. 844–45). The glossary is a hodgepodge of exotic, and sometimes titillating, human idiosyncrasies, including *koro,* a fear reported in various Asian countries of disappearing penises, and brain fag, mental exhaustion experienced by West African schoolchildren.[81] The most apparent feature of these culture-bound syndromes is that they have been ripped out of context and shorn of their cultural meanings.

Culture-bound syndromes are defined in DSM-IV as "recurrent, locality-specific patterns of behavior and troubling experience that may or may not be linked to a particular DSM-IV diagnostic category" (p. 844). The specific locality may be as large as Asia or Latin America, but culture-bound syndromes are somehow different than DSM-IV disorders. The manual offers the following explanation of how they differ:

> Although presentations conforming to the major DSM-IV categories can be found throughout the world, the particular symptoms, course, and social response are very often influenced by local cultural factors. In contrast, culture-bound syndromes are generally limited to specific societies or culture areas and are localized, folk, diagnostic categories that frame coherent meanings for certain repetitive, patterned, and troubling sets of experiences and observations. (P. 844)

This formulation implies that there is a universal quality to DSM-IV diagnoses that is not to be found in culture-bound syndromes, even if certain examples of the latter occur in areas of the world that encompass a billion or more people and many cultures. On the other hand, even though certain DSM-IV disorders, such as Anorexia, Agoraphobia, and many Sexual

Dysfunctions, are not applicable to all cultures, they are nevertheless not considered culture-bound syndromes.

AND WHAT ABOUT RACISM?

Whatever the virtues of the new culturally oriented features of DSM-IV, they do not solve the problem of racial bias. The manual does not even acknowledge the difference between race and culture. It does not take notice of the repeated finding that identical behavior by patients of different races who share the same culture will be interpreted differently. Poor Southern sharecroppers who are white are no less different from middle-class therapists than are African American sharecroppers, but there will be differences in the way these clients' symptoms are interpreted and their diagnoses are formulated. On the basis of repeated and convincing empirical evidence, we can predict that African Americans will be diagnosed as more severely disturbed than whites who manifest the identical symptoms. In short, there has been no significant correction of the biases incorporated into DSM diagnoses.

8 DIAGNOSING THE PSYCHIATRIC BIBLE

On April 23, 1996, the Senate of the United States unanimously passed the Health Insurance Reform Act, a bill similar to one passed by the House of Representatives one month earlier. The original and major intent of the proposed legislation was to make health insurance coverage "portable," a widely popular bipartisan provision that would allow workers to change jobs without jeopardizing continuing health insurance coverage. Just before the Senate passed the measure, Senators Domenici and Wellstone added an amendment to the bill that made headlines, created a firestorm of controversy across the country, and jeopardized the possibility that the House–Senate conference committee would reach a compromise on their different versions of the legislation.

The Domenici–Wellstone amendment simply proposed that mental health care insurance coverage should be the same as (that is, should have "parity" with) coverage for physical care in regard to such things as copayments, treatment limitations, lifetime benefit limits, and so forth. Congressional advocates came from both ends of the political spectrum and included conservatives such as Senator Alan Simpson. The common denominator for this strange coalition was that many legislative backers had family members who suffered from severe mental illness. The parity proposal also enjoyed the strong support of mental health professional associations and mental health consumer organizations, who had sought such provisions for many years.

The proposal was strongly opposed by business, and the conflict spilled out on the editorial pages of the nation's press. Some unsympathetic critics described parity legislation as nothing more than a full employment plan for psychotherapists. Why such controversy? The easy answer, the one used immediately by the insurance and business lobbyists, was that it would cost too much. Health costs were already too high, as almost everyone agreed, and any mandated extension of coverage would raise the costs even further. It was feared that small businesses that could barely afford minimal coverage for their employees would be forced to drop all medical insurance coverage rather than be saddled with the added mental health parity coverage. Consequently, the opposition suggested, overall insurance coverage might decline for the American public rather than expand.

This easy answer, that it would cost too much, is not a complete explanation. Why, in the first place, is mental health insurance coverage different from physical health coverage? Why does mental illness present special problems of cost that are not presented by physical illness? Why is it feared that mental health coverage will break the bank? Why would a popular health reform initiative become endangered by including reference to mental illness? Why would the insurance and business communities fear a flood of claims from the mentally ill? A partial answer to these questions is found in the weaknesses of DSM and the ways in which it has expanded the definition of mental illness and the opportunities for misuse of psychiatric diagnosis.

THE SYMPTOMS OF FAILURE

A good physician begins by noting the patient's obvious symptoms, makes inferences about the likely underlying causes and the probable consequences, and then proposes a remedy. The purpose of revising DSM was ostensibly to take mental illness out of the realm of superstition, opinion, and ideology and place it firmly in the antiseptic medical world of science. The earlier chapters of this book provide a rich array of examples of how and where DSM has failed to accomplish this.

From Anita Hill's experience (see chapter 1), one understands the potential destructive power of psychiatric diagnosis and how it was marshaled at the highest levels of our political system to defend Clarence Thomas by skewering his accuser. In her story one sees the enormous discretion that DSM permits in placing people in mental illness categories and how newly minted proposals for new categories can rapidly be pressed into political service. We showed how leading psychiatrists were used as hired guns or eager volunteers ready to quickly draw DSM from their holsters to defend or attack a person's character and veracity and how the psychiatric establishment obsessed over the proper diagnosis for the woman while it completely ignored the equally significant question about the mental health of her tormentor. Hidden biases about gender and race are embedded in DSM, and they are important elements in the diagnostic potshots fired at Anita Hill.

We explained that DSM is at the core of so many controversies not only because it attempts to construct diagnostic categories out of everyday behaviors but also because it has grown to encompass more and more behaviors that are less and less abnormal. Furthermore, the construction process itself, which has become much more elaborate, has also become much more public—and political. We showed that proposals are made, alternatives are suggested, and compromises are hammered out and that final decisions are made by committee vote. Although the decision process is more visible than in previous eras, it now has a new rationale: that it be based on science and hard data. However, this rhetoric of science so often fails to match what is done, and the data that are used are often no more substantial than ordinary opinion.

At the center of many controversies is the faulty core of the DSM enterprise, the definition of mental disorder. This core was directly attacked in the controversy over homosexuality as a mental disorder. In this episode, we revealed how political factions campaigned and maneuvered to construct and deconstruct a diagnosis that potentially affects millions of well-functioning people.. But with this diagnosis the debates were not just among small select groups of psychiatrists but in the streets. The diagnosis of mental disorder was revealed to be susceptible to external pressures and contemporary culture in a way that the diagnosis of, say, influenza, TB, or cancer is not.

The example of external pressure forcing the diagnostic category of homosexuality out of DSM is matched by the story of Posttraumatic Stress Disorder, where external pressure forced a new category to be adopted.

Although the label is new, PTSD is not so much a new category as one re-created to manage the casualties of war. Nevertheless, the story illustrates the politics of making diagnoses. Despite opposition from within the psychiatric establishment, external forces prevailed. Like that of a hot new initial public offering on Wall Street, the value of PTSD to the psychiatric establishment skyrocketed, and it has achieved a secure, if constantly revised, place in the diagnostic bible. Ironically, the new category has become one of DSM's success stories: PTSD is now applied to a broad range of problems resulting from very different kinds of trauma. PTSD also serves as a lesson to insurers: external political pressure can create popular new disorders whose applicability can spread rapidly.

Not all proposals for new illness categories fare so well, as we learned from the saga of Masochistic Personality Disorder. Here the developers of DSM attempted, with hardly any credible evidence, to create a disorder that had broad applicability. Once more, external pressure—from a variety of feminist and mental health organizations—was decisive, this time in beating back the proposal. The stinging lesson here is how easily common, if tired, assumptions about social roles—this time about the role of women—can be fashioned into a list of "scientific" diagnostic criteria. The relative ease with which prominent psychiatrists could manufacture a diagnosis out of a few uncritical assumptions about the "pathology" of what may be adaptive or culturally sanctioned behaviors was widely broadcast as a warning about the potential expandability and gender bias of DSM. The controversy surrounding MPD did not improve the scientific respectability of the psychiatric establishment.

In striking contrast was the dismissive manner in which the DSM developers handled the question of whether the role behavior of powerful men could possibly be evidence of mental disorder. The proposal for Delusional Dominating Personality Disorder had no clinical tradition, although it certainly captured social tradition. But because such male behavior is not viewed as pathological, because men are not treated for it, and because there is no organized constituency able to muscle it into psychiatric legitimacy, the proposal for DDPD died quickly and quietly, under the dominance of the male psychiatric establishment.

The consequences of making diagnoses, as well as the gender biases they may express, are aptly illustrated by the case of Borderline Personality Disorder. A diagnostic category, once enshrined in DSM, offers therapists and others considerable discretion in deciding how it should be applied. And often the applications proposed are astounding: for example, a well-respected psychiatrist used BPD to explain how patients induce the sexual misbehavior of their therapists. Thus, a diagnosis can be not just a shorthand rubric for identifying mental disorders but an elaborate justification for unethical conduct by professionals.

The misuses of psychiatric diagnosis are nowhere more evident than in the history of racism against African Americans. The government's attempt to count the insane as part of the 1840 census provided the quantitative foundation for arguments about the superiority of slavery for the well-being of African Americans. This early, grossly flawed example of epidemiology illustrates the misuses of data. The strategy of misinterpreting data to defend white superiority continued in slightly altered guises in the eugenics movement and in anti-immigration efforts; it is present today in the continuing controversies about the inheritability of IQ. The rhetoric of science and the illusion of hard data have continued to provide a cover for that ugly impulse that we call racism, which is born of fear and self-doubt and nurtured by social and economic self-interest.

The illusion of science in psychiatry is still evident, and it has very real consequences in how this country determines how many people are mentally ill and how resources should be allocated to treat them. The difference between the census of 1840 and today, however, is that it is much more difficult to identify the errors being made, buried as they are in technical decisions. Nevertheless, it is crucial to an understanding of mental illness in America and of the vast policy implications in such legislation as the parity amendment to know how the U.S. government counts those it considers mentally ill and how those counts, based on the flaws of DSM, affect us all.

MAKING AMERICA SICK

"Thus 24.1 percent of the population, or 48.2 million Americans, have some kind of mental disorder within a 12-month period."[1] Bold pronouncements like this are issued regularly by the National Institute of Mental Health and have become common in the media and in mental health literature, but their veracity is almost never questioned. The public has no easy way to examine these conclusions. People either ignore the implications or conclude that they live amid a vast disturbed population. Such statistics come from studies that are based on DSM's inadequate definition of mental disorder. These numbers not only shape mental health policy and the allocation of federal and state revenues but also undoubtedly scare the business and insurance industry into working against legislation such as the parity amendment. DSM is used to directly affect national health policy and priorities by inflating the proportion of the population that is defined as "mentally disordered."

As mentioned in the last chapter, during the 1980s the National Institute of Mental Health sponsored an expensive epidemiologic study.[2] This much-acclaimed study was the most sophisticated epidemiologic research on mental disorders ever undertaken in this country; its purpose was to estimate the number of mentally ill in the United States. Called the Epidemiologic Catchment Area (ECA) study, it has been praised as "a rich lode of new information on the natural history of psychiatric disorders" and as "the soundest fundamental information about . . . psychiatric disorders ever assembled."[3] It has been referred to by prominent psychiatric researchers as an impressive achievement; a recognized hallmark; the largest and most sophisticated study undertaken in the U.S., if not the world; an outstanding scientific and scholarly report; a storehouse of valuable data; and as a major milestone in the development of psychiatry and medicine.

Five university-affiliated research teams interviewed in person almost 20,000 randomly selected adults. All the research teams used an interview protocol (the Diagnostic Interview Schedule, or DIS) that probed for the presence or absence of specific mental disorders by following very closely the diagnostic criteria listed in DSM-III, which had just been published before the study began. Diagnoses were made by computer, using algorithms based on DSM-III.[4]

On the basis of the ECA study, a parade of assertions about mental disorders in America has appeared: that 32% of American adults have had one or more psychiatric disorders in their life; that 20% have a disorder at any given time; and that there are higher lifetime prevalence rates among men (36%) than women (20%), among the young (37%) than the old (21%), among African Americans (38%) than others (32%), among those with less education (36%) than more (30%), among those in institutions (65%) than those in households (32%), and among those who are financially dependent (47%) than the wealthier (31%). And with all these we hear about distributions by age, gender, ethnicity, specific disorder, and so on. We are even told how many Hispanic women between the ages of 45 and 64 have ever had an antisocial personality (1.3%).

It is just such use of the data that should cause us concern. Given the magnitude of this study, its sponsorship by NIMH, and the outstanding reputations of the researchers, these data provide the definitive word on psychiatric disorders in America for years to come. When government officials, advocacy organizations, or enterprising program developers want to document the prevalence of a particular disorder or the disproportionate suffering among some demographic subgroup, they go to the ECA reports to find the fact that supports their cause. Little thought is given to the meaning of the statistics in those tables or to how they were derived.

Why should one be concerned about the national DSM-based count of the mentally ill? First, because of the constant revisions of DSM, many definitions of specific disorders used in the ECA were obsolete years *before* the ECA study was published. The Diagnostic Interview Schedule was explicitly tied to the definitions of disorders given in DSM-III (published in 1980), but in 1987 a revised version of DSM was published that altered the criteria for all of the major disorders. Furthermore, the appearance of DSM-IV in 1994 made the DIS criteria two generations out of date. Although some of these changes are minor and do not greatly affect gross prevalence rates, other alterations in diagnostic criteria can have a major impact. For example, for obsessive-compulsive disorder the ECA study, using DSM-III criteria, reports a lifetime prevalence rate of 2.6%, a figure that was 50 times greater than earlier estimates; but if one uses the criteria specified in DSM-III-R, which provides greater specification of the disorder, the prevalence rate is considerably lower. Since the survey, hundreds of articles based on the ECA study have been published and have confidently offered assertions about mental disorders in the United States, yet all the ECA study estimates were based on diagnostic criteria that were in varying stages of obsolescence. By simply altering slightly the wording of a criterion, the duration for which a symptom must be experienced in order to satisfy a criterion, or the number of criteria used to establish a diagnosis, the prevalence rates in the United States will rise and fall as erratically as the stock market.

Second, one should be concerned about the ECA study because the ECA definitions of seemingly simple but fundamentally crucial terms such as *age of onset, lifetime prevalence,* and *current presence of an active disorder* shape all the ECA reports. A casual reader might assume, for example, that the age of onset of a disorder is the person's age when he or she first had the disorder, that is, when the person simultaneously met all the criteria for the disorder as defined by DSM. This appears to be the meaning of the term for some conditions (e.g., Affective Disorders) but not for others. For Schizophrenia, Alcoholism, and Anxiety Disorders, the age of onset is defined as the age when the first symptom occurred in those people who later meet the other criteria for the disorder. For example, for a lifetime diagnosis of Alcohol Abuse, there must be evidence of the occurrence of two symptoms, *but they need not be present at the same time.* If one symptom occurred in a person's youth and the second appears 30 years later, the person could be diagnosed as having an Alcohol Abuse disorder despite the fact that there was no time period in which the two required criteria were met simultaneously. Not only does this raise serious conceptual questions about the operational definition of a mental disorder, but it makes the meaning of the term *age at onset* troublesome. If, for example, the diagnosis of flu requires evidence of a fever and an upset stomach, would a person who had a fever for a few days at age 19 and an upset stomach at age 35 be designated as someone who has had flu? And was the onset of the disease at age 19? Conceptual confusions such as these help to explain why 24 percent of American men were determined to have a lifetime diagnosis of Alcohol Abuse or Alcohol Dependence. For drug abuse and dependence, a different meaning of *age of onset* was used—the age when the illicit drug *use* began, not when the abuse or dependence began. Beginning of illicit drug use is a very different concept than the beginning of illicit drug abuse.

The way in which active cases (for one-year prevalence rates) were determined also deserves scrutiny. The intuitive sense of an active case is one in which the person currently meets the minimum criteria for a specific disorder. This is generally *not* the meaning used in the ECA study; for that study, an active case was one in which the person met the minimum criteria sometime in his or her life and had at least one symptom at the time of the study. Again, as with the term *age of onset,* one has to read carefully to determine what the term *active case* means with respect to a given condition, since the definition varies. For some conditions an active case is one in which the diagnostic criteria were met "at some time in the person's life" and in which there was "some sign of the disorder" within the year before the interview. Having "some sign of the disorder," which presumably means meeting at least one diagnostic criterion during the past year, is certainly different from having the disorder during the past year, particularly since many single "symptoms" consist of everyday behaviors, like insomnia, restlessness, or tension, experienced by a majority of the population. Consequently, defining *active case* as the presence of a single symptom means abandoning any defensible definition of mental disorder. Indeed, the ECA study authors candidly suggested how this method of inflated counting could be used: "A count of active disorders is useful information for purposes such as the development of annual budgets for the provision of mental health services." Using the occurrence of one symptom to establish the presence of an active case of a disorder may do wonders for budget justifications by inflating prevalence rates and may allow for claims that 20% of all American adults currently suffer from that disorder, but it doesn't represent good, or even defendable, science.[5]

The ECA study, based on DSM definitions, will be used for years because it is a treasure trove of statistical information. We suspect, however, that the data will be misused and misinterpreted almost as frequently as they are cited. Many readers of the ECA statistics will be impressed by the illusion of exactitude conveyed by reams of data and will fail to appreciate the conceptual and operational foibles that some of these numbers represent.

Americans may be told that 20% of adults in this country currently have mental disorders, but they are not warned that the figure is based on outdated diagnostic criteria, on methods of untested accuracy and reliability, on a selective choice of disorders, on wavering definitions of *age of onset*, and on an inflated concept of what an active case of a disorder is. What will be most enduring about the ECA study in the future will not be the numbers it provides about mental disorders in America but what it reveals about the state of diagnosis in American psychiatry. And what it reveals, in part, is how psychiatry has been captured by the illusions of science provided by the psychiatric bible.

THE SCIENTIFIC ILLUSIONS OF DSM

At the close of the 19th century, Sigmund Freud tried to demonstrate that intensive case analysis of an individual's dreams could yield an understanding of the causes and mechanisms of a patient's psychopathology.

Freud's science of dreams produced a revolution in our thinking. Now, at the close of the 20th century, a revolution of similar proportions is re-shaping our thinking. It is a revolution that de-emphasizes case analysis in favor of using checklists of everyday feelings and behaviors to identify and classify disorders. There are many sources of this descriptive approach, but its primary goal is to make psychiatric diagnosis scientific. This dream of science is embodied in the last three editions of the DSM, which are strikingly different from earlier versions. We are not referring merely to the enormous weight and page gain but to its very transformation. DSM-I and DSM-II made no pretense of being scientific documents. They were administrative codebooks put out by a small, obscure committee. In contrast, today's DSM is viewed as a major repository of knowledge of mental disorders, as a distillation of the major literature reviews and field trials, and as the product of more than a thousand consultants and as many committee meetings, and it is promoted by endless journal articles and promotional newsletters.[6]

There is no dispute that the latest editions of DSM have been smashing successes. And DSM has firmly embedded itself in all aspects of the mental health enterprise. Its approach and definitions are required for those seeking research funding from the National Institute of Mental Health or writing textbooks about abnormal behavior. It is used by attorneys in various matters bearing on competence and culpability. It is used in schools, prisons, welfare offices, and other social agencies grasping for labels and rationales. And, of course, it is on the desks of almost all mental health clinicians. It has been an enormously successful financial investment for the American Psychiatric Association. In its first 10 months, DSM-IV alone is reported to have brought in $18 million.[7]

The essence of DSM's scientific contribution is a method of identifying mental disorders through the use of checklists of specific behaviors, the diagnostic criteria. These diagnostic criteria for over 300 categories of disorder, criteria created by subcommittees of experts, are DSM-III's solution to the many problems confronting psychiatry. These criteria are an attempt to end the confusion in diagnostic practice and to uplift psychiatry's faltering reputation as a branch of medicine. DSM's dreams of science rest on this structure of diagnostic criteria. Surprisingly, the developers of the recent DSMs have relatively little to say about the meaning of these hundreds of lists of everyday behaviors. In the introduction to DSM-III (1980) only the following explanation is offered:

Since in DSM-I, DSM-II, and ICD-9 explicit criteria are not provided, the clinician is largely on his or her own in defining the content and boundaries of the diagnostic categories. In contrast, DSM-III provides specific diagnostic criteria as guides for making each diagnosis since such criteria enhance interjudge diagnostic reliability. It should be understood, however, that for most of the categories the diagnostic criteria are based on clinical judgment, and have not yet been fully validated by data about such important correlates as clinical course, outcome, family history, and treatment response. Undoubtedly, with further study the criteria for many of the categories will be revised. (p. 8)

For DSM-IV these modest, cautious assertions were removed, and all that is said about diagnostic criteria comes on a strange separate page under the bold heading "Cautionary Statement" (apparently intended to ward off the use of DSM by mischievous attorneys):

The specified diagnostic criteria for each mental disorder are offered as guidelines for making diagnoses, because it has been demonstrated that the use of such criteria enhances agreement among clinicians and investigators. . . .

These diagnostic criteria . . . reflect a consensus of current formulations of evolving knowledge in our field. (p. xxvii)

DSM-IV is more assertive, claiming that the diagnostic criteria are based on knowledge and consensus and that their use "enhances agreement."

In recent DSMs, the diagnostic criteria are described in ways that lead one to conclude that they serve three different and wavering functions.[8] DSM suggests that the criteria may define and describe the disorder itself, that is, "the content and boundaries" of the pathology. Or they may be only the "indicators" of the disorders, that is, the observable symptoms or manifestations of the pathology, not the disorders themselves. Or they may be only guidelines that enhance agreement among clinicians but may not be direct expressions of either the pathology or the symptoms. These are very different meanings. Thus, at the very heart of the DSM revolution lies an ambiguity about what these lists of behaviors, the diagnostic criteria, constitute. Regardless of their precise functions, their usefulness rests entirely on their ability to help clinicians identify all those persons with a particular disorder (this is the sensitivity criterion) and to exclude all those who do not have the disorder (the specificity criterion). If the diagnostic criteria do not accomplish that, DSM's aspirations toward scientific excellence are only illusions. The APA's aspirations for the diagnostic criteria are that they will (1) produce valid categories of mental disorder, (2) improve the reliability of diagnosis, and (3) control how clinicians use diagnosis. Earlier in this book, we addressed aspects of all of these claims, especially in relation to particular diagnostic categories. Here we seek to recap these concerns and to suggest that these problems are generalizable to the entire manual.

Validity: Are You Sure It's a Mental Disorder?

DSM makes no claim of achieving a valid classification system. Nevertheless, the sheer enormity of the undertaking; the endless pages with the names of hundreds of expert contributors; the NIMH and foundation funding; the conferences and committees; the extensive literature reviews; the field trials; the reanalysis of data sets; the constant promises that decisions about DSM will be governed by fact, not fancy; and the official imprimatur of the highest governing bodies of the American Psychiatric Association—all this grand display of intricate process and authority strongly suggests that the diagnostic system is valid.

Of course, in this era of skepticism, we know that lists of experts, promotions by professional organizations, and sheer bulk have little bearing on whether something makes conceptual sense. And, certainly, the work of dozens of disparate committees is no more likely to produce a document of elegant conceptual coherence than blind men touching an elephant.

Assessing the conceptual validity of DSM is cumbersome, because its own formal definition of mental disorder is not used consistently to include or exclude disorders or to guide the selection of diagnostic criteria. One must examine the manual category by category to assess how well the diagnostic criteria distinguish mental disorders from other human problems that could be better described as normal, nonpathological variation; general unhappiness and distress; normal inabilities; social deviance; and the like. As we have demonstrated throughout this book, one doesn't have to read very far to question whether the diagnostic criteria actually identify valid mental disorders.

Let us illustrate the problem. When we needed an example at this point, we pulled DSM-IV from the shelf, opened it, and immediately found a disorder we had not examined before—code 302.71 Hypoactive Sexual Desire. This diagnosis is accompanied by the standard diagnostic information: the disorder's "features," subtypes, associated features, course, and differential diagnosis. All these are written in an authoritative voice and appear in a format that provides the illusion that what is being described is a real medical disorder:

Diagnostic criteria for 302.71 Hypoactive Sexual Desire Disorder

A. Persistent or recurrently deficient (or absent) sexual fantasies and desire or sexual activity. The judgment of deficiency or absence is made by the clinician, taking into account factors that affect sexual functioning, such as age and the context of the person's life.

B. The disturbance causes marked distress or interpersonal difficulty.

C. The sexual dysfunction is not better accounted for by another . . . disorder (except another Sexual Dysfunction) and is not due exclusively to the direct physiological effects of a substance (e.g., a drug of abuse, a medication) or a general medical condition.

How do these three diagnostic criteria—diagnostic criteria being the essence of DSM—make clinical diagnosis more scientific? Let's apply DSM to two cases.

Case 1: Mary, a 33-year-old successful real estate agent, developed less and less sexual desire for her husband as her career blossomed. He complained bitterly to their family therapist about the absence of sexual activity in their marriage.

Case 2: Ronald, a 45-year-old truck driver, lives alone and has never married. He masturbates occasionally, but has little interest in having sexual intercourse. He has little distress or concern about his sexuality, but the women he gets involved with complain about his lack of interest in intercourse.

Both Mary and Ronald appear to meet the three diagnostic criteria for Hypoactive Sexual Desire Disorder. They have deficient sexual desire or activity, it has caused difficulty in their relationships, and it is not due to some other disorder or medical condition. According to DSM-IV, clinicians would be on solid ground in diagnosing a mental disorder. What is wrong with this DSM-styled "science"? What's wrong is not sexual deficiency in Mary or Ronald but the obvious deficiency of the diagnostic criteria themselves. The first and primary criterion is deficient sexual fantasies, desire, or activity. This criterion goes no further than restating the name of the disorder. There is no information about what standard one would use to distinguish a pathological deficiency from normal variation. The text accompanying this disorder recognizes this problem by admitting that there is a lack of normative age- and gender-related data on frequency or degree of sexual desire. It suggests that "clinical judgment" be used "based on the individual's characteristics, the interpersonal determinants, the life context, and the cultural setting" (p. 496). How the clinician should use the person's life context to determine deficiency in sexual fantasies, desire, or activity when there is an admitted lack of knowledge about the norms in these matters is unclear.

The second diagnostic criterion for Hypoactive Sexual Desire Disorder is that the "disturbance causes marked distress or interpersonal difficulty." Again, there is no information on the type or amount of distress or difficulty that is relevant. Both concepts cover immense conceptual terrain: distress can range from mild discomfort to suicidal despair, and "interpersonal difficulty" covers subtle rudeness to murderous assaults. Certainly there may be a point and a life context where sexual deficiency causes problems, but this DSM criterion hardly tells us where that may be.

The third and final criterion instructs clinicians to use this category only if they can't use another category or find some physiological explanation for the deficiency. This is not particularly helpful, because it does not describe any aspect of the disorder itself but instead makes it a residual category.

It is difficult to see how these diagnostic criteria produce a valid diagnosis. These particular criteria, which are broad and vague, may meet the requirement of identifying all those with some pathological sexual deficiency, but they also identify many, many people who are not disordered. The criteria are overinclusive and pathologize too many behaviors as expressions of mental illness. *The failure to adequately distinguish mental disorder from other problems that manifest in the same behaviors is the central failure of DSM's diagnostic criteria for many disorders.*

Even though both Mary and Ronald meet the diagnostic criteria for Hypoactive Sexual Desire Disorder, a good clinician would probably ignore DSM and would not give them a psychiatric diagnosis. In these cases, common sense and clinical judgment would provide better guidance than the DSM diagnostic criteria. Unfettered clinical judgment, of course, is exactly what the DSMs attempted to minimize, yet the newest edition, DSM-IV, allows clincians to ignore the diagnostic rules, thus defeating the purpose of introducing the criteria in the first place.

The developers of DSM assume that if a group of psychiatrists agree on a list of atypical behaviors, the behaviors constitute a valid mental disorder. Using this approach, creating mental disorders can become a parlor game in which clusters of all kinds of behaviors (i.e., syndromes) can be added to the manual. For example, why not add Excessive Motorized Speed Disorder. The criteria might read as follows:

1. Persistent or recurrent excessive motorized speed activity. The judgment of excessive is made by a clinician, taking into account factors that affect driving, such as age and the context of the person's life.
2. The disturbance causes marked distress, interpersonal difficulty, or the threat of disability.
3. The speeding is not better accounted for by another disorder.

Every sports car enthusiast, speed boat operator, and motorcyclist would be mentally ill. Illustrations such as this should make us uneasy about the fact that the diagnostic criteria in DSM appear very often to be insufficient to distinguish cases of mental disorder from other phenomena. One of the unavoidable problems with the diagnostic criteria is that they often describe behaviors, feelings, and cognitive states that are rather ubiquitous, for example, depressed mood, insomnia, inflated or deflated self-esteem, fears, and anxiety. Under some circumstances these phenomena may indeed indicate some mental problems, but the essential task for a diagnostic manual is to enable the clinician to determine when they are the result of a mental disorder and when they are the result of the vicissitudes of life. DSM and its diagnostic criteria fail at this essential task.

Reliability: How Come Psychiatrists Disagree?

DSM makes a second, more mundane, claim: that the diagnostic criteria will greatly improve reliability of diagnosis. If the goal of validity of the diagnostic criteria was implicit and hazy, the goal of reliability was explicit, vivid, and central to the developers of DSM-III. Great emphasis was given to attempts to improve reliability. Having emphasized the goal of reliability, the developers of the manual had little choice but to claim repeatedly that DSM had attained that goal. Even though the evidence offered for this claim was lacking—an issue we review at great length in another book[9]—few commentators seemed to notice. The evolution of that illusion involved the pressing political need to solve the reliability problem, the sudden and convenient lowering of standards of what constitutes "good reliability," and the effective use of the rhetoric of science in promoting DSM.[10] Why did the development of DSM's diagnostic criteria fail to solve its reliability problem?

The adoption DSM's diagnostic criteria was an attempt to limit the discretion of clinicians. Since discretion was viewed as the breeding ground for diagnostic unreliability, the developers of DSM sought to control discretion by using checklists, structured interview schedules, and formal decision rules. This was all supposed to work, but even in the research settings that served as the incubators for diagnostic criteria, investigators complained that the criteria were not specific enough.[11] It is easy to demonstrate that the criteria for many disorders may indeed by ambiguous to clinicians. For example, the criteria for Dysthmic Disorder in DSM-IV include poor appetite, low energy, low self-esteem, poor concentration, and difficulty making decisions (p. 349). Although these criteria are more specific than the term *depression,* they are still vague. Moreover, good psychotherapists do not agree on when, for example, a person's appetite or concentration is "poor" or when the person's energy or self-esteem is "low."

At first glance, the solution appears to lie in establishing even greater specificity for the diagnostic criteria (which later editions of DSM do). For example, poor appetite can be defined by the exact amount of food consumed, the number of times per day the person feels hungry, or the amount of weight loss; insomnia can be defined more precisely by the amount and quality of sleep per day; and so forth. This approach assumes that DSM has just not gone far enough in specificity, and that greater specificity of diagnostic criteria would increase reliability among users. This kind of obsession about reliability can become silly and can actually reduce validity. Increasing the specificity of the diagnostic criteria is unlikely to improve DSM's reliability, because clinicians must make many complex causal inferences over and above judgments about whether the diagnostic criteria for a given disorder are met.

Let us illustrate this important, but largely neglected, problem. Conduct Disorder in children (DSM IV, p. 85–91) is defined by a list of 12 diagnostic criteria that includes threatening others, fighting, using a weapon, being cruel to people or animals, setting fires, running away from home, theft, and truancy from school. The clinician must determine that at least three of these criteria were present during the 12 months preceding the diagnostic interview, with one of them being present during the last 6 months. Let's review a case:

Vin is a 14-year-old Vietnamese refugee who lives in Los Angeles. His family is war ravaged and poor. He is referred to the school psychologist because he was caught stealing from and threatening other children. He belongs to a gang, and recently he has been truant from school.

Assume that clinicians agree that three diagnostic criteria—stealing, threatening, and truancy—are present. Does that result in perfect diagnostic agreement? Probably not, because identifying the diagnostic criteria is just the beginning of the inferences clinicians are required to make to use the diagnosis Conduct Disorder. DSM cautions clinicians that Conduct Disorder should "be applied only when the behavior in question is symptomatic of an underlying dysfunction within the individual and not simply a reaction to the immediate social context" (p. 88). So Vin's clinician is required to make some judgment about whether there is an underlying dysfunction within Vin (i.e., a disorder) or whether his behavior is a reaction to his social context (i.e., not a disorder). Identifying the three minimum diagnostic criteria is insufficient to make this judgment. Stealing from others, for example, could be motivated by Vin's family's need for food, could be the boy's response to peer pressure, or could be his way of settling scores for attacks against him; in short, there could be any number of reasons for his stealing that do not necessarily indicate an internal dysfunction. Similarly, truancy could be the result of Vin's fear of retribution from a rival gang at school, of his desire to avoid taking a test for which he feels unprepared, or of lack of reliable transportation. Since Conduct Disorder is supposed to exclude behaviors that are merely "reactions to the immediate social context," the clinician must determine whether Vin's behavior is caused by, for example, his poverty status, his family environment, his cultural milieu, his neighborhood norms, or peer influences. Only when these possible causal circumstances are ruled out does the diagnosis of Conduct Disorder remain viable. And if they are not ruled out, Vin cannot be diagnosed with Conduct Disorder. Unfortunately, DSM provides no guidance for making these essential and complex inferences. Will different clinicians sort through all these considerations in exactly the same way and arrive at the same conclusions, thereby producing diagnostic agreement? Not likely.

Furthermore, the diagnostic process in this case is even more complicated, because the DSM criteria also require the clinician to determine if Vin's mental disorder is behind the behaviors that cause significant impairment in his social, academic, or occupational functioning. That is, the clinician must determine whether Vin's mental disorder—and not something else—has caused impairments. For example, if Vin is getting low grades in school, the clinician must rule out that the low grades are due, for example, to malnutrition, family disorganization, difficulty with the English language, lack of interest in school, or racial discrimination. Only if the low grades are caused by the internal dysfunction, and not by any combination of these factors, can the clinician establish that the disorder caused the impairment. DSM provides little guidance for this complex task.

Lack of guidance for making these assessments is not an isolated problem in the diagnostic category Conduct Disorder; throughout the manual clinicians must make these complex inferences. For example, the most common criterion across all diagnostic categories is that each disorder *causes* "clinically significant distress or impairment in social, occupational [academic], or other important areas of functioning." The introduction to DSM-IV stresses the importance of this criterion in distinguishing between nonpathological conditions and mental disorders but concedes that it is "an inherently difficult clinical judgment" (p. 7). Thus, at the heart of every diagnosis is a clinical judgment that a mental disorder and not some other factor directly causes the person's distress. Given the multiplicity of roles people occupy, the multiple factors that can lead to problems in those relationships, and the absence of any guidelines about how to make those complex inferences, it is not surprising that researchers and clinicians have plenty of room to arrive at different diagnostic conclusions (unreliability) based on the same information. It is impossible to determine whether (and to what extent) clinicians attempt to make these complex inferences or simply rely on the DSM checklists of diagnostic criteria that pathologize everyday behaviors.[12]

In the case of Vin, no matter how specific DSM makes the diagnostic criteria, clinicians are forced to make extraordinarily complex, contingent causal inferences. In the absence of any guidelines or comprehensive knowledge about how to make those inferences, it is understandable that clinicians have plenty of room to arrive at different conclusions. Diagnostic criteria, some 900 pages of them, do not prevent clinicians from mak-

ing conflicting, often contradictory, diagnoses—as they did in the celebrated case of John Hinckley, who shot President Reagan.

Managed Care and Diagnostic Distortions

The opening paragraph of DSM-IV (p. xv) states that the highest priority
of its developers was to make the manual useful and user-friendly for clinicians. Given that priority, it is astounding how little research was conducted on how clinicians use DSM.[13] Has DSM actually made diagnosis
more accurate? Has it greatly reduced misdiagnosis in clinical settings?
Has DSM made routine diagnosis more scientific? Unfortunately, there is
limited information about these issues. From a few surveys, several
ethnographic studies, and a sketchy literature, there are indications that a
substantial number of clinicians do not think that DSM accurately reflects
clients' problems or clarifies individual differences or that it is very helpful for treatment planning.[14] Many clinicians think that DSM is more a
management than a clinical tool, that is, that it is used to control client
flow into and out of agencies. Psychiatric diagnosis, as one author put it,
is "malleable and ambiguous, often valued more for its strategic than its
medical purposes."[15] Furthermore, for many years (before DSM-III) clinicians used "mercy diagnoses" for clients, where less stigmatizing diagnoses were used in official records rather than the more clinically accurate
ones. But this form of misdiagnosis pales in comparison to what is apparently happening now in mental health practice, when the primary strategic purpose of diagnosis is very often not accuracy or even the minimizing
of stigmatization but financial reimbursement.

Until recently, diagnosis was only marginally related to the economics
of mental health practice. In this era of health care cost containment,
DSM is, in the words of one commentator, "the authoritative guide for
defining 'medical necessity,' without which there would be no third-party
reimbursement for any health care for anybody for any reason."[16] We are
witnessing a strange de facto institutional marriage between a diagnostic
enterprise widely heralded as a major triumph of modern psychiatry and
a new reimbursement system widely feared as the potential nemesis of
humane mental health care. That potential nemesis is managed care. As
one therapist remarked, "If DSM didn't exist, managed care would have
had to invent it."[17]

Clinicians are now routinely trying to fit their clinical impressions to both the complexities of DSM and to the requirement of some managed care corporation in an ethically challenged game of cat and mouse among therapists, clients, and payers. In countless clinics, private practices, and supervisory sessions, the game is how to fit a diagnosis to the presumed preferences of a managed care corporation and its faceless bureaucrats not to the client's mental disorder.

To illustrate this phenomenon is an account of the experiences of a new intern at a mental health clinic, which includes a report on the uses made of DSM:[18]

The clinic is a nonprofit, community-based mental health center that provides affordable . . . treatment for children and their families. Often children come to the attention of the clinic when they are experiencing significant impairment in functioning at school that interferes with their ability to learn. Seven-year-old Alice is a typical case.

Alice has been suspended from school twice for using obscene language with her teacher and with peers. At home and at school, she often loses her temper, is easily annoyed by others, and often actively defies or refuses to comply with adults' requests or rules. Her initial assessment [at the clinic] characterized her as someone who is spiteful, deliberately annoys people, and blames others for her mistakes.

Prior to my first scheduled session with Alice, I had only a few minutes to scan the myriad of forms in her chart. In that brief moment, I wanted to acquire a snapshot of her difficulties and flipped to the Initial Assessment form to read her DSM-IV diagnosis: 313.81 Oppositional Defiant Disorder. An image of the second grader I was about to meet formed in my mind's eye. New to clinical work, I pictured Alice as a hellion, greeting my arrival in her young life with obvious hostility. I knew she had refused to participate in the intake interview eight days prior to this appointment. I was filled with apprehension.

When it was three o'clock, I walked to the reception area and scanned expectant faces for a biracial girl. The receptionist on duty directed me toward Alice and her mother, a disheveled, heavyset woman in her mid-thirties. Alice looked up at me with inquisitive brown eyes and said, "You're pretty!" Good, I thought, she's curious about me. I was grateful for any advantage I might have with this child.

My first meeting with Alice and her mother can only be described as chaotic. I suggested to the mother that we meet for a few minutes, alone, when she gestured to her entourage: her elderly mother with Alzheimer's; her two-year-old toddler; and Alice's severely disturbed older brother, who was exchanging four-letter words with another child's mother.

After warring parties were separated and tempers calmed, I was able to meet jointly with Alice and her mother, but not without the toddler in tow. While I was in the midst of establishing good rapport with Alice, the older brother burst into the room demanding his mother's attention. I firmly directed him out of the room. "This is Alice's time. You need to leave," I said. I suggested that the mother return to the waiting room with her toddler and son while I finished with Alice. I looked at the slender girl before me, now engrossed in playing with the dollhouse, and wondered how she even managed to get her needs met in such a chaotic family.

Alice and I continue to meet every week for play therapy. I offer her a choice of activities, and she invariably asks me to join her in each. She is polite, cooperative, and responsible during our time together. However, when I return her to her mother, her whole demeanor changes. Alice becomes oppositional and sullen, barely acknowledging my departure. This is our parting ritual, for as soon as I have nearly reached my office door, she runs after me to wave and smile and say good-bye. Sometimes she grabs my arm and hugs me. I am always moved by her honesty, innocence, and innate goodness.

Over a five-week period, the clinical intern soon learned of the extent of Alice's family chaos. Alice's home was a small apartment in which she, her two siblings, mother, grandmother, and an uncle resided. The family was living on $700 per month in public assistance, of which more than half went for rent. The mother was recently separated from Alice's father, an angry, volatile man who was emotionally abusive. He had recently had a stroke that left him paralyzed and confined to a wheelchair. In the presence of Alice, he had threatened suicide. There was an allegation being investigated by child welfare officials that Alice's older brother was sexually molesting her. Alice's mother, who had been a victim of childhood sexual abuse, had minimal parenting skills and a penchant for involvement in an ongoing series of crises. Currently, she was fighting with her father and brother for custodial care of the grandmother afflicted with Alzheimer's, because they all wanted to benefit from the grandmother's disability check. The older brother was so disturbed that he could only function in the most restrictive settings. Family life was perpetual chaos.

The clinic diagnostic and treatment procedures, the intern noted, "follow a model of individual pathology or disorder." After the extensive gathering of information about the child's family and developmental history, DSM-IV was used to arrive at a specific diagnosis. "For children like Alice, a typical outpatient case," wrote the intern, "it means disregarding family or systemic dysfunction in favor of pathologizing the child. Seven of eight pages of bio-psycho-social assessment painstakingly recorded on the Assessment Form—mandated for our use by the County—are ignored to arrive at the DSM-IV diagnosis." The intern arrived at the following diagnosis: "Alice's constellation of symptoms and behaviors are indeed troublesome; however, given the circumstances of her family, they are adaptive rather than pathological responses to a chaotic environment." She quoted approvingly from well-known critics of psychiatry:

> Children who are in conflict with their families, schools, and society rarely have anything wrong with their brains, and when they do suffer from brain dysfunction, it does not by itself make them unruly or dangerous. Children in trouble are typically the victims of emotional, physical, and sexual abuse. If we include neglect, abandonment, poor parenting, inadequate schooling, and the effects of poverty, sexism, and racism, then almost all children seen by mental health professionals are victims of child abuse.[19]

How can we understand why clinics would diagnose Alice's problems as an internal mental disorder when her difficulties are primarily external and environmental? Here is how the intern answered this question:

> Why, then, would social and environmental factors be ignored or, at best, minimized when they so profoundly impact the lives of young children who come to the clinic? The answer is, simply, money. Funding and the need for accountability to the funding sources that support the agency have shaped service delivery. . . . The clinic receives 80% of its funding from public money, particularly Medicaid and county grants. . . . There are no outpatient clients for whom the clinic does not partially or wholly subsidize the cost of therapy. . . . To be eligible for services at the clinic, a child must have a DSM-IV diagnosis. [Many diagnoses do not qualify for reimbursement], such as sibling or parent–child relational problems, which provide more accurate descriptions of the dysfunctions in the lives of my young clients than do the diagnoses with which they have been—and are required to be—la-

beled. . . . Clinicians at the clinic are forced to manipulate diagnoses in order to secure reimbursement from third-party payers. . . . Nearly one-third of the clinic's clients are diagnosed with Oppositional Defiant Disorder. . . . Are those diagnoses accurate portrayals of client dysfunction, or does the diagnosis of Oppositional Defiant Disorder serve as an agency 'cash cow' to garner funds for the clinic?

We know relatively little about the extent or magnitude of these practices, about how clinicians think about and cope with them, or about the ways they may be distorting not just diagnoses but all of mental health practice. The limited evidence suggests that individuals are given DSM diagnoses when family, marital, and social interrelationships are clearly the problem; that treatments are shaped to adhere to what is reimbursable, rather than what may be needed; and that troubled individuals are getting more severe and serious diagnoses than may be warranted.[20] And it is in this context that Alice, Mary, Ronald, and Vin might receive a psychiatric label when none is justified.

These distortions of diagnosis are not the fault of DSM. DSM is simply an instrument infused with scientific respectability that is being used to distort the delivery of mental health and social services. In this struggle, which takes place every day in the real world, DSM is used by managed care companies and by clinicians in ways that hardly fulfill the APA's dreams about the science of diagnosis.

Michael First, one of the developers of DSM-IV, recently was quoted as saying that DSM "provides a nice, neat way of feeling you have control over mental disorders," but he confessed that this is "an illusion."[21] There are indeed many illusions about DSM and very strong needs among its developers to believe that their dreams of its scientific excellence and utility have come true, that is, that its diagnostic criteria have bolstered the validity, reliability, and accuracy of diagnoses used by mental health clinicians. But in our assessment the rhetoric of science that surrounds the publication of each new version of DSM inflates how much is known, exaggerates the certainty and precision with which it is known, and tries to persuade by authority and process rather than by argument and evidence.

Freud's science of dreams began as a controversial undertaking, gained a stronghold in the heart of American psychiatry, but collapsed because it promised much more than it could ever deliver. DSM's dreams of science are on a similar path in pursuing the illusions of diagnostic criteria.

THE BITTER MEDICINE

Ann Linehan, a Boston woman in her early sixties, was in the throes of a very stressful family matter.[22] She was attempting to gain access to an out-of-wedlock grandchild. She assumed that her discussions with her psychiatrist, in which she had talked about this struggle, were completely confidential. She was mistaken. She was dismayed to learn that detailed notes on every session with her psychiatrist were stored in computerized medical records and were easily available to anyone within her health care organization—and, perhaps, beyond. Why should this be so troubling to Ms. Linehan or to us?

Certainly, one element of our concern is the decline of confidentiality in psychotherapy.[23] State laws and court decisions have altered the therapist–client relationship, making the relationship less a sanctuary for the emotionally distressed than a new arena for state surveillance. There is an expanding list of third parties (state legislatures, regulatory agencies, courts, licensing boards, insurance companies, child welfare authorities, police, etc.) demanding information about the private details of the therapeutic relationship. Therapists are mandated to report a presumed instance of child abuse, to warn a possible victim of a violent crime, to protect the innocent lover of an HIV positive client, and so on. Although each of these breaches of confidentiality has a compelling justification, the trend of requiring reporting to third parties erodes therapists' primary responsibility to the individual client and redirects them toward serving the needs of the state and the health care industry.

A second element of our concern involves the transformation of the health care industry, through which so much mental health care is delivered. At one time, therapists had to do little more than file simple insurance forms indicating that the insured person was being treated and perhaps stating a provisional, vague diagnostic label. But now therapists are frequently required to reveal details about a patient and the treatment to cost-effectiveness clerks of managed care companies.

The loss of therapeutic confidentiality, however, should be considered as only a part of the general decline of privacy in American life. Who believes that anything is private any longer? Medical records, financial transactions, electronic communications, travel itineraries, and the rest are apparently readily available to anyone with a modem and a motivation. Government and corporate intrusions into private space and affairs are so commonplace and the recording and transmittal of information so silent and rapid that it should not be surprising that the 50-minute hour has failed to remain sacred. (Psychotherapy is not alone in its declining power and significance. Many other formerly revered professionals—such as physicians, lawyers, elected officials, ministers, and professors—have lost their pristine public image of altruistic service. Professionals are simply not trusted as much as they once were to provide selfless service.)

Ann Linehan's discovery goes beyond the matter of confidentiality. It is one thing for you to find that information about your recent bladder infection, heart palpitations, or influenza is electronically recorded and accessible, but you have an increased sense of personal violation when you discover that information obtained from your psychotherapist about your drinking habits, depression, sexual difficulties, marital problems, or personality quirks is accessible to everyone. What is the nature of the difference, which you naturally and immediately sense?

Having a bladder infection does not call your character into question. It does not jeopardize your job, your right to vote, your right to have a driver's license, and your ability to manage your own legal and financial affairs. A bladder infection does not lead to involuntary commitment to a state hospital, to removal from normal educational programs, to disqualification for public office, or to stigmatization or employment discrimination, and it does not affect your claim to custody of your children or grandchildren. In short, diagnoses for physical ailments rarely have the social consequences that diagnoses for mental illnesses do. This is because how you think, feel, and behave is what you believe constitutes your "real" self; it is your essence as a human being. To know another person means to be familiar with their thoughts, emotions, and patterns of relating to others, not with how well their heart, kidneys, or lungs function. Accordingly, people are rightfully protective of the secrets they tell psychotherapists, because those secrets reveal their essence in a way not matched by a measure of their blood pressure or cholesterol level.

In fact, what people reveal to psychotherapists is often not medical at all. And this is a central point. Psychotherapists learn about their patients' despair and fears, about their low self-esteem, unfulfilling relationships, and unmet expectations for themselves and others. They hear about their patients' friends and associates, their parents and children, and their partners. Therapists, at their best, are not just observers of their patients' mental condition; they are witnesses to the full texture of their lives. In the process of that exposure, therapists and patients attempt to fashion some remedies, some palliatives; they attempt to make a little progress in slightly altering significant relationships, changing personal viewpoints, or holding in check unruly emotions. This is usually not information that people want on the World Wide Web, and they properly object when they discover that managed care companies are now demanding such personal details from therapists. Therapists are rightfully concerned about violating the patient–therapist relationship by providing previously undisclosed details to faceless, low-level reviewers in managed health care corporations. Your internist may be able to convey only that you had a bladder infection and the name of the antibiotic she prescribed for you; your character will be left out entirely. But your psychotherapist may have to describe the details of your abusive relationship and what she hopes you will do about it and when. Moreover, your psychotherapist has incentives to retell your story in the most unflattering way in order to ensure that your difficulties will be viewed by your insurer as extremely serious and as something you can't handle without therapy. Otherwise, your claim for insurance reimbursement will be denied.

The bitter medicine for American psychiatry is that, in the decades-long redevelopment of its psychiatric bible, it has unsuccessfully attempted to medicalize too many human troubles. Managed care companies increasingly distrust psychiatric diagnoses, and so should the rest of us. Managed health care companies are responsible for approving treatment that is "medically necessary," but they do not feel compelled to reimburse therapists to help their clients with problems in living, no matter how serious they may be. That is why they demand detailed information about the patient's problems and the intended treatment. Managed care companies recognize what the psychiatric bible has labored to conceal: not all human troubles contained in DSM are mental disorders of a medical nature. Ms. Linehan's custody battle for a grandchild, Alice's school difficulties, your neighbor's marital problems, your friend's drinking habits, and your anxiety about an upcoming speech may cause great pain and be worthy of help from a psychotherapist, but that pain and that need for assistance require no psychiatric diagnosis to understand and no specific medical therapy to treat.

We are not selling some alternative diagnostic system, nor are we suggesting that diagnosis in psychiatry is without redeeming value. But we have suggested throughout this book that DSM is seriously flawed and that those flaws are largely ignored by the American Psychiatric Association and are unrecognized by DSM's diverse users. We have several recommendations that would begin to remedy these problems, although these will be bitter medicine for the APA. First, DSM should narrow its definition of mental disorders and the accompanying diagnostic criteria to those conditions where there is substantial scientific consensus that there is evidence of an internal mental dysfunction. We have demonstrated how easily the existing criteria can be and are misused to label as mentally ill people who are troubled but who probably have no mental disorder. Second, even with this narrowed scope, DSM and its sponsors should be much more modest in their proclamations about the scientific foundations for the manual. DSM's definition of mental disorder is flawed, the claims of validity and reliability of the manual as a whole are shaky, and the causes of most mental disorders are unknown. Researchers may have uses for such an underdeveloped classification system, but no manual should be foisted on clinicians or the public or used for purposes of reimbursement unless there is substantial evidence for its reliability and validity. Third, clinicians should use DSM honestly, refusing to compromise their integrity and their clients' medical records and avoiding the practice of forcing personal and social troubles into ill-fitting categories of mental disorder. Finally, if these first three recommendations are taken seriously, we as a society would be forced to develop services to assist troubled children, adults, and families without labeling so many of them as mentally ill, squeezing their difficulties into medical diagnoses, or treating them within medical systems of care. There is nothing inherent in the troubles of many individuals who seek help in mental health clinics that requires *medical* insurance or *medical* reimbursement systems. Just as problems are being distorted and fitted into categories of mental disorder, so too are the systems of financing assistance to those with such problems being distorted and misused. DSM should not be used to promote this duplicity.

It is not that there are no such phenomena as mental disorders, that their existence is all a myth or psychiatric hoax. The point is that mental disorders constitute a small part of what is described in the current *Diagnostic and Statistical Manual of Mental Disorders*. Clearly, as we have shown in this book, psychiatrists and other mental health professionals benefit from DSM's unrelenting expansion of domain, its attempts to sweep all manner of personal troubles under the medical umbrella and to rationalize those moves on the basis of research and science. The public at large may gain false comfort from a diagnostic psychiatric manual that encourages belief in the illusion that the harshness, brutality, and pain in their lives and in their communities can be explained by a psychiatric label and eradicated by a pill. Certainly, there are plenty of problems that we all have and a myriad of peculiar ways that we struggle, often ineffectively, to cope with them. But could life be any different? Far too often, the psychiatric bible has been making us crazy—when we are just human.

POSTSCRIPT

In 1996, the American Psychiatric Association published a slim volume entitled *DSM-IV Coding Update*, which contains hundreds of changes in the code numbers for DSM diagnoses that are the key to reimbursement for psychotherapy from insurance companies and the government. Few users are aware that DSM-IV, still distributed with obsolete codes, is out of date.

The coding update contains an important announcement:

A text revision of DSM-IV is planned for publication in 1999–2000. No changes to the diagnostic categories or criteria sets will be made. The only changes will be to update those text sections that provide information regarding prevalence, course, associated features and so on (p.16)

Deja vu? Very shortly after the publication of DSM-III, a revision was announced and users were assured that it was to be a minor midcourse correction to incorporate new findings and rectify errors. When DSM-III-R appeared, most of the diagnoses had been changed, new ones had been added, and other substantial alterations had been adopted. The protests described in chapter 5 prevented even more significant changes. The announcement of the plan to revise DSM-III was hauntingly similar to the one in the *DSM-IV Coding Update*. Whatever the outcome of the next revision of DSM may be, we can be assured that the APA is continuing its unrelenting effort to make us crazy.

NOTES

PREFACE

1. "Man in Charity Fraud Case Pleads No Contest," *New York Times*, 27 March 1997, Sec. A, p. 14; "U.S. Says Mental Impairment Might Be a Bar to Citizenship," *New York Times,* 19 March 1997, p. 1; "Citizenship Rules for Disabled Unveiled," *Los Angeles Times*, 19 March 1997, Sec. B, p. 1; Serge Schmemann, "Madness Meets Politics: Gunmen Can Act Alone, but Not Entirely," *New York Times*, 16 March 1997, Sec. E, p. 3; Letter to the editor, "Shine Depicts False View of Mental Illness," *New York Times*, 15 March 1997, p. 18; Denise Grady, "Manual Is Faulted on Overdoses," *New York Times*, 5 March 1997, Sec. B, p. 13; "Gateway to Madness," *New York Times*, 29 March 1997, p. 18; T. Lewin, "Suit Focuses on Rights of Learning Disabled," *New York Times*, 8 April 1997, Sec. A, p. 9.

2. L. J. Davis, "The Encyclopedia of Insanity: A Psychiatric Handbook Lists a Madness for Everyone," *Harper's*, February 1997, 61–66.

CHAPTER 1. DOUBTING THOMAS: PSYCHIATRIC DIAGNOSIS AND THE ANITA HILL CONTROVERSY

1. A. Rosenthal, "Psychiatry's Use in Thomas Battle Raises Ethics Issues," *New York Times,* 20 October 1991.

2. T. Phelps and H. Winternitz, *Capitol Games: Clarence Thomas, Anita Hill, and the Story of a Supreme Court Nomination* (New York: Hyperion, 1992).

3. Rosenthal, "Psychiatry's Use in Thomas Battle."

4. See "1,189 Psychiatrists Say Goldwater Is Psychologically Unfit to Be President," *Fact Magazine,* September-October 1964. For more on the American Psychiatric Association's reaction to the survey and the adoption of the Goldwater rule, see "Psychiatrists' Interaction with Media Said to Be Serious Ethical Responsibility," *Psychiatric News,* 16 July 1993, pp. 6, 21.

5. J. Danforth, *Resurrection* (New York: Viking, 1994), 175.

6. B. Vobjejda, "Who's Telling the Truth? Experts Say Answer May Never Be Known," *Washington Post,* 13 October 1991, Sec. A, p. 30.

7. Ibid.

8. "Use of Psychiatry in Thomas Battle Raises Ethics Issue," *New York Times,* 20 October 1991, p. 1.

9. Ibid.

10. American Psychiatric Association, *Diagnostic and Statistical Manual of Mental Disorders,* 3rd. ed. (Washington, D.C.: American Psychiatric Association, 1980).

11. R. Spitzer, S. Kaplan, and D. Pelcovitz, "Victimization Disorder" (unpublished draft manuscript, 9 February 1989).

12. Letter from Laura Brown to Robert Spitzer, March 28, 1989, p. 1.

13. American Psychiatric Association, *Diagnostic and Statistical Manual of Mental Disorders,* 4th ed. (Washington, D.C.: American Psychiatric Association, 1994).

14. American Psychiatric Association, *Diagnostic and Statistical Manual of Mental Disorders,* 3rd ed., rev. (Washington, D.C.: American Psychiatric Association, 1987).

15. A. Stanley, "Erotomania: A Rare Disorder Runs Riot—in Men's Minds," *New York Times,* 10 November 1991, Sec. E, p. 2.

16. Several years after Thomas's confirmation, his principal patron, Senator John Danforth (see Danforth, *Resurrection*), wrote a detailed account of the confirmation proceedings that added even more evidence for those looking for psychiatric disturbance. The book jacket announced, "It can now be told: Thomas collapsed emotionally under the onslaught." Danforth reported that in the months before the confirmation hearings Thomas was convinced that someone was going to kill him; he was afraid to go near windows and insisted that the shades be drawn. In the face of Hill's accusations, Thomas was unable to sleep in his bed and curled up on the floor in a fetal position. As the hearings progressed, Thomas continued to decline until the day of his final testimony, which he turned into a full-scale attack on the Senate Judiciary Committee.

Danforth, an ordained Episcopal minister, does not dwell on any possible pathological aspects of Thomas's behavior, although he was one of those who most persistently broadcast allegations about Anita Hill's psychiatric disabilities. "Reverend Jack," as he was referred to in the Senate, where he was widely respected for his integrity, is much more concerned about theology when it comes to his protégé. His interpretations of Thomas's conduct are not based on the work of Freud, Kraepelin, or de Clérambault. Danforth's text is the Bible, and he concludes that Thomas died and was reborn spiritually. He compares Thomas to Jesus Christ, and the ordeal is seen as a modern-day reenactment of the resurrection!

17. M. Lejoyeuz et al., "Phenomenology and Psychopathology of Uncontrolled Buying," *American Journal of Psychiatry* 153 (1996): 1524–29.

18. D. Wallis, "Just Click No," *New Yorker,* 13 January 1997, 28–29.

19. See L. N. Robins and D. A. Regier, *Psychiatric Disorders in America: The Epidemiologic Catchment Area Studies* (New York: Free Press, 1991) and R. Kessler et al., "Lifetime and 12-Month Prevalence of DSM-III-R Psychiatric Disorders in the United States," *Archives of General Psychiatry* 51. (1994): 8–19.

20. D. Goleman, "Helping Family Doctors Spot Psychiatric Problems," *New York Times,* 14 December 1994, Sec. B, p. 8.

21. Ibid.

22. R. Spitzer et al., "Utility of a New Procedure for Diagnosing Mental Disorders in Primary Care: The PRIME-MD 1000 Study," *Journal of the American Medical Association* 272 (1994): 1749–56.

23. S. A. Kirk and H. Kutchins, *The Selling of DSM: The Rhetoric of Science in Psychiatry* (Hawthorne, N.Y.: Aldine de Gruyter, 1992).

24. American Psychiatric Association, *Diagnostic and Statistical Manual of Mental Disorders,* 2nd ed. (Washington, D.C.: American Psychiatric Association, 1968).

CHAPTER 2. EVERYDAY BEHAVIORS AS PATHOLOGY

1. Lest we be accused of exaggeration, we refer the reader to an article in a highly regarded journal that reports that one-third of us have "excessive anxiety" when asked to speak to large audiences and may be suffering from a mental disorder; see M. Stein, J. Walker, and D. Forde, "Public-Speaking Fears in a Community Sample: Prevalence, Impact on Functioning, and Diagnostic Classification," *Archives of General Psychiatry* 53 (1996): 169–74.

2. American Psychiatric Association, *Diagnostic and Statistical Manual of Mental Disorders* (Washington, D.C.: American Psychiatric Association, 1952), 31.

3. American Psychiatric Association, *Diagnostic and Statistical Manual of Mental Disorders,* 2nd ed. (Washington, D.C.: American Psychiatric Association, 1968), 39.

4. For measurement, see F. N. Kerlinger, *Foundations of Behavioral Research* (New York: Holt, Rinehart & Winston, 1986) and J. C. Nunnally, *Psychometric Theory* (New York: McGraw-Hill, 1978); for diagnosis, see D. H. Barlow, ed., "Special Issue on Diagnosis, Dimensions, and DSM-IV: The Science of Classification," *Journal of Abnormal Psychology* 100, no. 3 (August 1991): 243–412; and R. E. Kendell, *The Role of Diagnosis in Psychiatry* (Oxford, U.K.: Blackwell Scientific Publications, 1975).

5. M. Foucault, *Madness and Civilization: A History of Insanity in the Age of Reason* (New York: Random House, 1965).

6. T. S. Szasz, "The Myth of Mental Illness," *American Psychologist,* 15 February 1960, 113–18; T. S. Szasz, *The Myth of Mental Illness* (New York: Hoeber-Harper, 1961; rev ed. Harper & Row, 1974).

7. T. J. Scheff, *Being Mentally Ill: A Sociological Theory* (Chicago: Aldine, 1966).

8. See B. Liptzin et al., "An Empirical Study of Diagnostic Criteria for Delirium," *American Journal of Psychiatry* 148, no. 4 (1991): 454–457, and L. N. Robins and D. A. Regier, *Psychiatric Disorders in America: The Epidemiologic Catchment Area Studies* (New York: Free Press, 1991).

9. R. Spitzer and J. Endicott, "Medical and Mental Disorder: Proposed Definition and Criteria," in *Critical Issues in Psychiatric Diagnosis,* ed. R. Spitzer and D. Klein (New York: Raven Press, 1978), 15–39.

10. Even though the published paper was not an official product of the DSM-III Task Force, the proposal from the man who headed it was widely interpreted as representing its intent. The president of the psychologists' organization exchanged heated letters with the president of the psychiatrists' group and complained that since most mental disorders have no known organic cause, they should not be considered as medical disorders; see S. Kirk and H. Kutchins, *The Selling of DSM: The Rhetoric of Science in Psychiatry* (Hawthorne, N.Y.: Aldine de Gruyter, 1992), 111–16.

11. The italicized words are the only changes/additions made between DSM-III-R and DSM-IV, pp. xxi–xxii.

12. Many authors have struggled with these matters — see, for example, Spitzer and Endicott, "Medical and Mental Disorder," and R. E. Kendell, *Role of Diagnosis in Psychiatry* —but have generally failed to provide the conceptual coherence really needed to guide the development of DSM. J. C. Wakefield's analyses, on which some of the following discussion is based, illuminate the promise and failures of the DSM definition of mental disorder; see J. C. Wakefield, "Disorder as Harmful Dysfunction: A Conceptual Critique of DSM-III-R's Definition of Mental Disorder," *Psychological Review* 99, no. 2 (1992): 232–47; J. C. Wakefield, "The Concept of Mental Disorder: On the Boundary Between Biological Facts and Social Values," *American Psychologist,* 47, no. 3 (1992), 373–88; and J. C. Wakefield, "The Limits of Operationalization: A Critique of Spitzer and Endicott's Proposed Operational Criteria for Mental Disorder," *Journal of Abnormal Psychology* 102 (1993): 160–72.

13. See, for example, the influential review by R. E. Kendell, *Role of Diagnosis in Psychiatry;* see also R. E. Kendell, "The Concept of Disease and Its Implications for Psychiatry," *Journal of Psychiatry* 127 (1975): 305–15.

14. J. C. Wakefield, "Disorder as Harmful Dysfunction: A Conceptual Critique of DSM-III-R's Definition of Mental Disorder," *Psychological Review* 99, no. 2 (1992): 238.

15. Ibid.

16. Ibid.

17. J. Brody, "Quirks, Oddities May Be Illnesses," *New York Times,* 4 February 1997, Sec. B, pp. 9, 11.

18. "Mild Depression Common and Harmful, Study Finds," *Los Angeles Times,* 1 November 1996, p. 1.

19. See F. G. Alexander and S. T. Selesnick, *The History of Psychiatry* (New York: Harper & Row, 1966), and G. Zilboorg, *A History of Medical Psychology* (New York: Norton, 1941).

20. The context of this evolution is the linguistic legacy of 19th-century epidemiology, which pursued the causes of infectious diseases by plotting morbidity and death among various populations of people; see J. Mirowsky and C. Ross, "Psychiatric Diagnosis as Reified Measurement," *Journal of Health and Social Behavior* 30 (1989): 11–25, and J. Mirowsky and C. Ross, *Social Causes of Psychological Distress* (Hawthorne, N.Y.: Aldine de Gruyter, 1989). As epidemiology developed, it spawned a variety of methods of counting and sorting people who had or were at risk of having some disease. These methods presupposed that people could be sorted into two groups: those with the disease and those without. Psychiatry, mimicking the approach of medicine, adopted this basic concept of "caseness" and pursued systems of classification into which cases of psychiatric disorders could be placed.

But psychiatry was slow to become enamored with diagnostic classification, in part because psychiatrists recognized that any classification of disease based on symptomatology rather than etiology presented formidable problems. Furthermore, while there were vigorous discussions about etiology in the 1800s, there was not enough consensus about the causes of insanity to produce a nosology; see G. N. Grob, "Origins of DSM-I: A Study in Appearance and Reality," *American Journal of Psychiatry* 148, no. 4 (1991): 421–31. Nevertheless, at the end of the 19th century, Emil Kraepelin, working with patients at his clinic in Heidelberg, developed a system of identifying diseases by focusing on certain groups of symptoms and tracking their eventual outcomes.

21. See chapter 7 and Grob, "Origins of DSM-I."

22. Grob, "Origins of DSM-I."

23. Ibid.

24. Ibid.

25. See R. Spitzer and J. B. W. Williams, "Classification in Psychiatry," in *Comprehensive Textbook of Psychiatry*, ed. H. I. Kaplan and B. J. Sadock (Baltimore: Williams & Wilkins, 1983), 591–613.

26. Grob, "Origins of DSM-I."

27. Ibid.

28. The eighth edition of the ICD was approved in 1966 and became effective in 1968. American psychiatrists who had been directly involved in working with ICD committees during the early and mid-1960s played key roles in the APA's Committee on Nomenclature and Statistics, which produced DSM-II in 1968. Thus, the international manual exerted some direct control over the making of DSM-II.

29. R. L. Spitzer and P. T. Wilson, "A Guide to the American Psychiatric Association's New Diagnostic Nomenclature," *American Journal of Psychiatry* 124 (1968): 1616–29; R. L. Spitzer and P. T. Wilson, "DSM-II Revisited: A Reply," *International Journal of Psychiatry* 7 (1969): 421–26.

30. Spitzer and Wilson, "A Guide to the American Psychiatric Association's New Diagnostic Nomenclature."

31. American Psychiatric Association, *Diagnostic and Statistical Manual of Mental Disorders*, 2nd ed. (Washington, D.C.: American Psychiatric Association, 1968), viii.

32. See Grob, "Origins of DSM-I," and M. Wilson, "DSM-III and the Transformation of American Psychiatry: A History," *American Journal of Psychiatry* 150 (1993): 399–410.

33. N. Sartorius, Introduction in *Sources and Traditions of Classification in Psychiatry*, ed. N. Sartorius et al. (Lewiston, N.Y.: Hogrefe & Huber, 1990), 1–6.

34. F. D. Chu and S. Trotter, *The Madness Establishment* (New York: Grossman, 1974).

35. T. Millon, "On the Past and Future of the DSM-III: Personal Recollections and Projections," in *Contemporary Directions in Psychopathology: Toward the DSM-IV*, ed. T. Millon and G. L. Klerman (New York: Guilford, 1986), 29–70.

36. Ibid., 39.

37. Ibid.

38. Ibid., 39–40.

39. R. Bayer and R. Spitzer, "Neurosis, Psychodynamics, and DSM-III: A History of the Controversy," *Archives of General Psychiatry* 42 (1985): 187–95.

40. Ibid., 193.

41. The new manual included a multiaxial system. Instead of limiting a diagnosis to a single word or phrase, clinicians were asked to evaluate five dimensions or "axes" of human behavior. Axis One, titled Clinical Syndromes, included the type of descriptive words (e.g., *schizophrenia, agoraphobia* or *pyromania*) we usually associate with psychiatric diagnosis. Two groups of diagnoses, Personality Disorders and Specific Developmental Disorders of Childhood and Adolescence, were listed on Axis Two. Medical conditions related to the patient's mental disorder were to be reported on Axis Three. Axes Four and Five were each eight-point scales. Axis Four assessed psychosocial stressors, and Axis Five rated the person's highest level of adaptive functions during the previous year. These numerical scales added to the sense of scientific precision the new manual conveyed, although they were not required to complete an "official" diagnosis.

42. Millon, "On the Past and Future of the DSM-III"; Work Group to Revise DSM-III,

DSM-III-R in Development, draft, 5 October 1985 (Washington, D.C.: American Psychiatric Association, 1985).

43. D. Franklin, "The Politics of Masochism," *Psychology Today,* 21, no. 1 (January 1987): 52–57.

44. For a discussion of this controversy, see chapter 5 and H. Kutchins and S. Kirk, "DSM-III-R: The Conflict over New Psychiatric Diagnoses," *Health and Social Work* 34, no. 4 (1989): 91–103.

45. See Task Force on DSM-IV, *DSM-IV Options Book: Work in Progress* (Washington, D.C.: American Psychiatric Association, 1 September 1991), Introduction.

46. Ibid.

47. M. Zimmerman, "Why Are We Rushing to Publish DSM-IV?" *Archives of General Psychiatry* 45 (1988): 1135–38; M. Zimmerman, "Is DSM-IV Needed at All?" *Archives of General Psychiatry* 47 (October 1990): 974–76.

48. R. E. Kendell, "Relationship Between the DSM-IV and ICD-10," *Journal of Abnormal Psychology* 100, no. 3 (1991): 297–301.

49. T. A. Widiger, "DSM-IV Methods/Applications Conference Synopsis" (November 29 & 30, 1988, mimeographed); T. A. Widiger, "DSM-IV Literature Reviews: Synopsis of Purpose and Process" (December 22, 1988, mimeographed).

50. The process of revision was described as rigorous and open by T. Widiger et al., "Toward an Empirical Classification for the DSM-IV," Journal of Abnormal Psychology 100, no. 3 (1991): 280–88, a claim that some found strained, for example, C. E. Dean, "Development of DSM-IV," *American Journal of Psychiatry* 148, no. 10 (1991): 1426 (letter to the editor), and H. Kutchins and S. Kirk, "DSM-IV and the Hunt for Gold: A Review of the Treasure Map," *Research on Social Work Practice* 3, no. 2 (1993): 219–35.

51. Kirk and Kutchins, *Selling of DSM.*

52. R. Spitzer, J. Forman, and J. Nee, "DSM-III Field Trials: I. Initial Interrater Diagnostic Reliability," *American Journal of Psychiatry* 136 (1979): 815–17; R. Spitzer and J. Forman, "DSM-III Field Trials: II. Initial Experience with the Multiaxial System," *American Journal of Psychiatry* 136 (1979): 818–20.

53. S. Hyler, J. Williams, and R. Spitzer, "Reliability in the DSM-III Field Trials," *Archives of General Psychiatry* 39 (1982): 1275–78.

54. J. Cohen, "A Coefficient of Agreement for Nominal Scales," *Educational and Psychological Measurement* 20 (1960): 37–46; R. Spitzer and J. L. Fleiss, "A Reanalysis of the Reliability of Psychiatric Diagnosis," *British Journal of Psychiatry* 125 (1974): 341–47.

55. J. D. Matarazzo, "The Reliability of Psychiatric and Psychological Diagnosis," *Clinical Psychology Review* 3 (1983): 103–45.

56. G. Klerman, "Historical Perspectives on Contemporary Schools of Psychopathology," in *Contemporary Directions in Psychopathology: Toward the DSM-IV,* ed. T. Millon and G. Klerman (New York: Guilford, 1986), 25; see also G. Klerman, "The Advantages of DSM-III," *American Journal of Psychiatry* 141 (1984): 539–42.

57. R. Michels, "First Rebuttal," *American Journal of Psychiatry* 141 (1984): 548–51; R. Michels, "Second Rebuttal," *American Journal of Psychiatry* 141 (1984): 553; G. Vaillant, "The Disadvantages of DSM-III Outweigh Its Advantages," *American Journal of Psychiatry* 141 (1984): 542–45.

58. R. C. Carson, "Dilemmas in the Pathway of the DSM-IV," *Journal of Abnormal Psychology* 100 (1991): 302–7.

59. Kirk and Kutchins, *Selling of DSM.*

60. J. B. Williams et al., "The Structured Clinical Interview for DSM-III-R (SCID): II. Multi-Site Test–Retest Reliability," *Archives of General Psychiatry* 49 (1992): 630–36.

CHAPTER 3. THE FALL AND RISE OF HOMOSEXUALITY

1. The first DSM borrowed heavily from the biopsychosocial approach of Adolph Meyer of Johns Hopkins University, the leading academic psychiatrist in the United States at that time. Although he was hostile to classical psychoanalysis, Meyer agreed with Freud that certain early childhood experiences contributed to later psychological difficulties. This orientation is evident in the first DSM.

2. The second edition of DSM was published in order to bring the manual into conformity with the *International Classification of Disease,* the compendium of illnesses published each decade by the World Health Organization to standardize the reporting of all medical conditions including mental disorders.

3. American Psychiatric Association, *Diagnostic and Statistical Manual of Mental Disorders,* 2nd ed. (Washington, D. C.: American Psychiatric Association, 1968), 44.

4. Attacks on psychiatric diagnosis from the general public and from professionals were increasing, and DSM became a focus of those attacks. Critics complained that diagnoses led to stigmatization and that DSM was a tool used to blame victims for society's problems. A mounting number of research studies by psychologists, sociologists, and others challenged the validity of psychiatric diagnosis. Many serious social scientists questioned the existence of some psychiatric diagnoses, and some challenged the validity of the entire system.

Even in the heart of the psychiatric establishment, rapidly accumulating evidence increased dissatisfaction with diagnosis. The issue centered around reliability, which meant, to research psychiatrists concerned with the problem, the level of agreement among clinicians about the diagnosis of a patient. Study after study consistently demonstrated that diagnostic agreement among therapists was unacceptably low. It was in the midst of this ferment that the fight over homosexuality arose.

5. B. Hansen, "American Physicians' Discovery of Homosexuals, 1880–1900: A New Diagnosis in a Changing Society," in *Framing Disease,* ed. C. Rosenberg (New Brunswick, N.J.: Rutgers University Press), 104–33.

6. D. Greenberg, *The Construction of Homosexuality* (Chicago: University of Chicago Press, 1988), 400–434.

7. J. Katz, *Gay American History,* rev. ed. (New York: Meridian, 1992).

8. G. Schmidt, "Allies and Persecutors: Science and Medicine in the Homosexuality Issue," *Journal of Homosexuality* 10 (1984): 127–40.

9. C. Dorman, "Are Gay Men Born That Way?" *Time,* 9 September 1991, 60–61.

10. R. Bayer, *Homosexuality and American Psychiatry: The Politics of Diagnosis* (New York: Basic Books, 1981), 72. The following discussion is also based on Bayer.

11. Ibid., 97.

12. Ibid., 96.

13. P. Conrad and J. W. Schneider, *Deviance and Medicalization: From Badness to Sickness* (St. Louis: Mosby, 1980), 200.

14. E. White, "Gender Uncertainties," *New Yorker,* 17 July 1995, 75.

15. E. Marcus, *Making History: The Struggle for Gay and Lesbian Equal Rights* (New York: Harper Collins, 1992), 251.

16. There had been a number of protests against psychiatrists at meetings across the country since the 1968 meeting of the American Medical Association, but the 1970 APA meeting in San Francisco was different. The tactics the protesters used were much more disruptive; the demonstration was more like street theater than a carefully orchestrated plan. It reflected the growing confrontational approach of the demonstrators, an approach that was typical of antiwar and civil rights activists of the period and that was now embraced by the newly empowered post-Stonewall Gay Liberation Front.

17. M. Spector, "Legitimizing Homosexuality," *Society* 14 (July/August 1977): 52–56.

18. Spector, "Legitimizing Homosexuality"; Bayer, *Homosexuality and American Psychiatry.*

19. It is hard to believe that Spitzer's decision to take a leading role in the struggle was as casual as has been portrayed; his psychoanalytic opponent, Charles Socarides, has a different interpretation of how it came about.

20. Spector, "Legitimizing Homosexuality," 54.

21. Bayer, *Homosexuality and American Psychiatry,* 103.

22. Ibid., 126.

23. Ibid.

24. R. L. Spitzer, "A Proposal About Homosexuality and the APA Nomenclature: Homosexuality as an Irregular Form of Sexual Behavior and Sexual Orientation Disturbance as a Psychiatric Disorder," *American Journal of Psychiatry* 130, no. 11 (1973): 1214–16.

25. Spector, "Legitimizing Homosexuality," 54.

26. The trustees also approved a civil rights resolution drafted by Spitzer and Gold that placed the APA on record as being opposed to criminal sanctions against private consensual homosexual sexual activity and to discrimination against gay men and lesbians.

27. Spector, "Legitimizing Homosexuality," 55.

28. Several years earlier the APA had adopted a referendum policy as a reaction to the unwillingness of the association's executives to allow a debate about the Cambodian invasion and the Kent State massacre at the business meeting of the 1970 annual convention. Since the adoption of the policy, the only referendum that had been conducted was about the Vietnam War.

29. Spector, "Legitimizing Homosexuality," 55.

30. Of the 18,000 members of the APA, 10,000 cast a ballot; 58 percent were in favor of deleting homosexuality from DSM, while only 37 percent voted against the proposal. Those familiar with voting patterns among large groups of people would characterize this as a landslide.

31. C. Socarides, *Homosexuality: A Freedom Too Far* (Phoenix, Ariz.: Adam Margrave Books, 1995), 162.

32. Ibid., 164.

33. Ibid., 165.

34. Bayer, *Homosexuality and American Psychiatry.*

35. M. Scott, "Chronicles of a Past President: Alfred M. Freedman, M.D." (Part 1), *Psychiatric News* 15 March 1996, pp. 7–9; M. Scott, "Chronicles of a Past President: Alfred M. Freedman, M.D." (Part 2), *Psychiatric News,* 19 April 1996, pp. 11–13.

36. Spector, "Legitimizing Homosexuality," 56.

37. C. Socarides, *Homosexuality: A Freedom Too Far,* 158.

38. After they lost the referendum in 1974, Socarides and his allies among the psychoanalysts withdrew from the field, and they played no visible part in the reintroduction of the diagnosis. Gay activists and their psychiatric allies opposed it. Judd Marmor, the

president of the APA in 1974–75 and a key proponent in the later fight for the approval of DSM-III by the APA, was a principal opponent of inclusion of the new homosexuality diagnosis. He and the gay activists did not want a change unless it was the deletion of the earlier compromise diagnosis, Sexual Orientation Disturbance.

39. There are three principle sources for information about the inclusion of Ego-dystonic Homosexuality in DSM-III. Spitzer published an article titled "The Diagnostic Status of Homosexuality in DSM-III: A Reformulation of the Issues," *American Journal of Psychiatry* 138, no. 2 (1981): 210–15, which presents his justification for the changes that occurred. A second source is an article by Bayer and Spitzer titled "Edited Correspondence on the Status of Homosexuality in DSM-III," *Journal of the History of the Behavioral Sciences* 18 (1982): 32–52. This article includes 25 letters and memos, including eight communications from Spitzer and correspondence from six opponents and two supporters; communications from Spitzer's opponents constitute less than one-third of the text, and they are carefully edited. The third source is a chapter in Bayer's *Homosexuality and American Psychiatry,* which describes the controversy in detail, but, as we indicated in the discussion about the fight over homosexuality in DSM-II, Bayer's account is heavily influenced by his close association with Spitzer. Although none of these accounts is free of Spitzer's strong influence, they reveal enough to provide some sense of how the dispute was managed. One important aspect of the conflict is that there is no mention of an empirical study of homosexuality in any of the three historical accounts.

40. Green had been one of the principals in the 1974 struggle to delete the homosexuality diagnosis from DSM-II; Bayer and Spitzer, "Edited Correspondence," 35.

41. This select group included Harold Lief, editor of *Medical Aspects of Human Sexuality,* a psychoanalyst who was an authority on clinical aspects of human sexuality, sexual and marriage counseling, and sex education; Paul Gebhard of the Kinsey Institute at Indiana University, a psychiatrist and an anthropologist who was a specialist "in the extensive variability of human sexuality, including sex offenses"; Diane Fortney-Settlage, an obstetrician-gynecologist whose subject was sexual dysfunctions; and Green, who claimed special knowledge in the area of gender identity development, both typical and atypical, including homosexuality. Green also identified Richard Freedman, a psychoanalyst from Spitzer's institution, as another one of the original members.

42. Green probably was referring to the Advisory Committee on Sexual Disorders as the "task force."

43. Bayer and Spitzer, "Edited Correspondence," 36. In a memorandum to Green dated December 27, 1976, Spitzer insisted that the new name did not reflect a change in the conception of the disorder, but he claimed that it was "more accurate and far more acceptable to the profession than the original term" (Bayer and Spitzer, "Edited Correspondence," 36).

44. The conflict became more intense several months later, in March 1977, after publication of a draft of DSM-III that included Dyshomophilia, the latest name Spitzer coined for the category.

45. Winokur's motto "No new words without new data" was reported in a memo from Pillard (Bayer and Spitzer, "Edited Correspondence," 39). Winokur's warning that the creation of new words would leave the APA open to the epithet "clown" appears in Bayer, *Homosexuality and American Psychiatry,* 172. The information about the poll comes from Memorandum from Richard Green, M.D., to DSM-III Colleagues, June 27, 1977, reprinted in Bayer and Spitzer, "Edited Correspondence," 41.

46. Bayer and Spitzer, "Edited Correspondence," 42.

47. Ibid., 45.

48. This position was favored by at least one task force member—Donald Klein.

49. Bayer and Spitzer, "Edited Correspondence," 52.

50. Bayer, *Homosexuality and American Psychiatry,* 171, quoting the newsletter of the Gay, Lesbian and Bisexual Caucus.

51. Ibid., 170.

52. Ibid., 181.

53. Ibid., 176.

54. Bayer and Spitzer, "Edited Correspondence," 52.

55. DSM-III, 282.

56. DSM-III-R, 426.

57. R. Bayer, *Homosexuality and American Psychiatry: The Politics of Diagnosis,* 2nd ed. (New York: Basic Books, 1987), 210.

58. This explanation is a bit thin. At the same time that EDH was dropped from DSM, a strenuous argument was being made to include Sadistic Personality Disorder, even though there were no articles in the scientific literature about the proposed new diagnosis and it was never recognized in clinical practice. Sadistic Personality Disorder was included in an appendix to DSM-III-R but was dropped from the next edition of the manual. Almost the same reason was given for dropping SPD as was offered for deleting EDH, namely, that there was neither research nor clinical interest in the diagnosis. Apparently, this is an acceptable, rational explanation for invalidating a diagnosis, but it is not a persuasive argument when there is adequate political pressure either from outsiders or from influential insiders to include a diagnosis in the psychiatric manual.

59. Bayer, *Homosexuality and American Psychiatry,* 2nd ed., 210.

60. During the course of the controversy over these diagnoses, the names changed over a dozen times. Masochistic Personality Disorder became Self-defeating Personality Disorder when it was finally included in DSM-III-R (it was subsequently dropped from DSM-IV, see chapter 5). Paraphilic Rapism was dropped early in the battle and was replaced by Sadistic Personality Disorder, which was later deleted from DSM-IV. Premenstrual Dysphoric Disorder is the only one that has survived, albeit in an appendix, after a number of transformations.

61. See chapter 5 for a fuller discussion of the conflict with feminists.

62. R. L. Spitzer, "The Diagnostic Status of Homosexuality in DSM-III," 214.

63. Bayer, *Homosexuality and American Psychiatry,* 2nd ed., 211.

64. Ibid., 215.

65. The chapter, written by a member of the DSM-III-R Advisory Committee on Sexual Disorders, was subsequently dropped.

66. In a memo to Spitzer on January 15, 1986, Harold Lief, a committee member who supported the decision to retain EDH in the manual but nonetheless objected to Spitzer's conclusion that homosexuality is abnormal, wrote the following:

> I believe it [EDH] should be retained because it is clinically useful. Despite the clinical usefulness of the diagnosis, I do believe, however, that homosexuality is a normal variant; the nearest analogy is that of left-handedness. Recent data by Heinz Meyer-Bahlburg and Anke Ehrhardt studying the children of the women who have been prenatally exposed to DES have come up with the first direct "proof" that the changes in fetal brain programming are etiologically related to homosexual fantasies and/or behavior. This is why the analogy of left-handedness makes sense to me.

An evident flaw in his logic is that left-handedness is not a mental disorder; by analogy, if homosexuality is a normal variant, it should not be considered a mental disorder. Lief offered a non sequitur to justify his position: "Despite its being a normal variant, I still consider it useful to keep the category [EDH] in DSM-III-R. I suppose it could be argued that ego-dystonic left-handedness might be included in our list of diagnoses, but that is a problem that doesn't carry the significance of ego-dystonic homosexuality." Lief didn't spell out what he meant by "significance." Many left-handed people suffer because of their condition. How significant must the suffering be before a natural variant becomes a mental disorder? There isn't a clue in Lief's memo.

67. Bayer, *Homosexuality and American Psychiatry* (2nd ed.), 215.

68. Ibid., 217.

69. DSM-IV, 538.

70. "Gay Psychiatrists Break New Ground Internationally," *Psychiatric News*, 18 October 1996, p. 1.

71. Letter from Joseph Nicolosi, NARTH secretary-treasurer, to all participants in the 1995 NARTH Conference, April 24, 1995.

72. Reverend Sheldon, a white minister, organized a group of African American pastors to demonstrate for Clarence Thomas during his confrontation with Anita Hill. He also appears frequently on television as a pro-life spokesman in abortion debates.

73. Brochure of NARTH, 1995.

74. J. Nicolosi, "Pedophilia Not Always a Disorder," *NARTH Bulletin* 3, no. 1 (April 1995): 1–3.

75. The contemporary discovery of a biological and perhaps genetic basis for homosexuality is similar in many ways to the medicalization of homosexuality that occurred at the end of the 19th century. See B. Hansen, "American Physicians' 'Discovery' of Homosexuals, 1880–1900: A New Diagnosis in a Changing Society," in *Framing Disease: Studies in Cultural History*, ed. C. F. Rosenberg and J. Golden (New Brunswick, N.J.: Rutgers University Press, 1992), 104–33.

76. A recent scientific report states that the chance of being gay is statistically greater for men with more older brothers—even if some or all of a man's older brothers died before he was born. There is great speculation as to why this is the case, but the new data weaken the theory that homosexuality is genetically determined. Observers have offered both biological and psychological hypotheses to explain the new scientific finding, reported in R. Blanchard and A. Bogaert, "Homosexuality of Men and Number of Older Brothers," *American Journal of Psychiatry* 153 (1996): 27–31.

77. "Gay Survey," *NARTH Bulletin* 7, no. 3 (December 1994): 13.

78. Although this argument has grown more popular, there are still many gay and lesbian leaders and scholars who take issue with this view, including a growing group of writers who object to the underlying assumptions. For this newly emerging group, the idea that people are either homosexual or heterosexual belies the fundamental bisexual nature of human existence. Curiously, these authors remind us that this concept was espoused by Sigmund Freud and that it is a central assumption in his theory of human development. This assumption of basic human bisexuality is not embraced by either NARTH members, the psychoanalytic opponents of a genetic basis for homosexuality, or the gay-oriented proponents of it, who accept instead a bimorphic interpretation of sexuality and gender identity (i.e., one is either gay or straight). Those who are concur-

rently bisexual may be classified as either gay or straight, depending on who is doing the classifying.

79. D. J. Kevles, "The X Factor: The Battle over the Ramifications of a Gay Gene," *New Yorker,* 3 April 1995, 85.

80. Reverend Sheldon of the Traditional Values Coalition is one such opponent.

81. This is made clear by columnist Mona Charen, who writes: "While it may very well be true that we are born with genetic predispositions to certain kinds of behavior (who doubts that a bad temper can be inherited?) we do not know how many people with the same kind of predisposition learn to control it. . . . We are born with countless innate tendencies . . . that we are socialized to control." From "More Questions on the Brain Study," *NARTH Bulletin* 7, no. 1 (March 1994): 3.

82. Another voice from the past, Green, a lawyer and psychiatrist, was the member of the Advisory Committee on Sexual Disorders who first raised the cry against the introduction of Ego-dystonic Homosexuality in DSM and resigned in protest over its inclusion. In fact, his leadership in the battles over the diagnosis of homosexuality predates this episode; Green had a prominent role in the initial efforts to remove the diagnosis of homosexuality from DSM in the early 1970s.

83. Kevles, "The X Factor," 87.

84. *Romer v. Evans,* U.S. Supreme Court 94-2039, May 20, 1996.

85. Kevles, "The X Factor," 88.

86. Although the majority of American psychiatrists seem to be in favor of depathologizing homosexuality, psychiatrists throughout the rest of the world are far less sympathetic.

87. The fear that Hawaii would legalize gay and lesbian marriages led to the adoption of the Defense of Marriage Act by Congress, and President Clinton's effort to eliminate discrimination against gays in the military resulted in the adoption of the questionable "don't ask, don't tell" policy (even this unfortunate compromise has backfired: newspapers report that more people in the military are being persecuted for being gay and that there are more discharges related to homosexuality now than before the policy was adopted).

88. For example, in 1980 the majority of psychiatrists in the United States subscribed to a Freudian or related psychodynamic approach. In less than a decade they had shifted to a biological orientation. The influence of DSM-III was one important reason for the shift.

CHAPTER 4. BRINGING THE WAR BACK TO DSM

1. W. J. Scott, "PTSD in DSM-III: A Case in the Politics of Diagnosis and Disease," *Social Problems* 37, no. 3 (1990): 294–310.

2. S. Bentley, "A Short History of PTSD from Thermopylae to Hue," *Veteran* 11, no. 1 (January 1991): 13. Much of the history of war trauma in this chapter is taken from this article.

3. Ibid., 13.

4. R. A. Gabriel, *No More Heroes: Madness and Psychiatry in War* (New York: Hill and Wang, 1987).

5. J. Brunner, "Psychiatry, Psychoanalysis and Politics During the First World War," *Journal of the History of the Behavioral Sciences* 27 (October 1991): 353.

6. Ibid.

7. Ibid., 354.

8. Ibid., 356.

9. Ibid., 358.

10. Scott, "PTSD in DSM-III," 296.

11. Ibid.

12. G. Grob, *The Mad Among Us: The History of the Care of America's Mentally Ill* (New York: Free Press, 1994), 192.

13. A different psychological problem was the hallmark of this conflict: brain washing. Because there was no clearly understood mission in this war and also because soldiers were rotated in and out of combat individually and not in companies, group solidarity broke down when troops were captured by the Chinese. Americans were very susceptible to the mind-control techniques perfected by the Chinese. For the first time in American history, large numbers of American prisoners of war denounced their country or collaborated with the enemy. To correct this, a number of steps were taken, including the adoption of the Uniform Code of Military Justice.

14. R. J. Lifton, *Home from the War* (New York: Simon & Schuster, 1973).

15. A. Kardiner, *War, Stress, and Neurotic Illness* (New York: Paul B. Hoeber, 1947); R. Grinker and J. Spiegel, *Men Under Stress* (Philadelphia: Blakiston, 1945).

16. D. Goleman, "In Gulf War, Many Wounds Will Be Mental," *New York Times,* 22 January 1991, Sec. C, pp. 1, 8.

17. Ibid.

18. B. L. Green et al., "Risk Factors for PTSD and Other Diagnoses in a General Sample of Vietnam Veterans," *American Journal of Psychiatry* 147, no. 6 (June 1990): 729–35.

19. Scott, "PTSD in DSM-III," 298.

20. Ibid.

21. Ibid., 299.

22. Ibid., 303.

23. Ibid., 104.

24. J. Talbott, "An Inch, Not a Mile: Comments on DSM-II," *International Journal of Psychiatry* 7 (1969): 382–84.

25. Scott, "PTSD in DSM-III," 298.

26. Ibid., 304.

27. B. Latour, *Science in Action: How to Follow Scientists and Engineers Through Society* (Cambridge, Mass.: Harvard University Press, 1987).

28. She is now the editor-in-chief of the APA's leading publication, the *American Journal of Psychiatry.*

29. Scott, "PTSD in DSM-III," 307.

30. L. Gordon, "Killing in Self-Defense," *Nation,* 24 March 1997, 25–28. Gordon describes the evolution of psychological theories about the behavior of victims of abuse, starting with the introduction of Battered Woman Syndrome by Lenore Walker in 1978.

31. J. Ziskin, "Challenging Post-traumatic Stress Disorder," in *Coping with Psychiatric and Psychological Testimony,* vol. 2, 5th ed. (Los Angeles: Law and Psychology Press, 1995), 1248.

32. N. Andreasen, "Post-traumatic Stress Disorder: Psychology, Biology and Manichaean Warfare Between False Dichotomies," *American Journal of Psychiatry* 157, no. 7 (1995): 963–65; R. Yehuda and A. McFarlane, "Conflict Between Current Knowledge About Post-traumatic Stress Disorder and Its Original Conceptual Basis," *American Journal*

of Psychiatry 152, no. 12 (1995): 1705–13; R. Hales and D. Zatzick, "What Is PTSD?" *American Journal of Psychiatry* 154, no. 2 (1997): 143–45.

33. In DSM-III the qualifying trauma was described as "generally outside the range of usual human experience" (p. 236). DSM-IV expanded the description to "exposure to an extreme traumatic stressor involving direct personal experience of an event that involves actual or threatened death or serious injury, or other threat to one's physical integrity; or witnessing an event that involves death, injury, or a threat to the physical integrity of another person; or learning about unexpected or violent death, serious harm, or threat of death or injury experienced by a family member or other close associate" (p. 424).

34. J. von Tagle, "The New DSM-IV: Is It Easier to Prove Damages?" *California Trial Lawyers Association Forum* 25, no. 1 (January/February 1995): 13–19.

35. Wars have spawned mysterious physical diseases as well as psychological ones. In the Civil War a battlefield condition was described as Irritable Heart (DeCosta) Syndrome; in World War I it was called Effort Syndrome (and also called Soldier's Heart and neuro-circulatory asthenia). In World War II, Effort Syndrome was reconceptualized as a psychoneurosis rather than a medical disease, and it was classified with other psychological conditions, including acute stress reaction (also known as battle fatigue or combat exhaustion or operational fatigue). These conditions had somatic as well as psychological symptoms. Effort syndrome also contributed to the postwar conceptualization of a number of peacetime illnesses, including anxiety neurosis, manic-depressive illness, panic disorder, mitral prolapse syndrome, and chronic fatigue syndrome.

When veterans initially began to report illnesses after Vietnam, their problems were first called Vietnam War Syndrome. In addition to PTSD, another condition with more of a medical emphasis, Agent Orange Exposure, was identified. There has also been a major emphasis on the somatic aspects of Gulf War Syndrome. For an account of the development of the medical interpretations of war-generated illnesses, see K. Hymans, S. Wignall, and R. Roswell, "War Syndromes and Their Evaluation: From the Civil War to the Persian Gulf War," *Annals of Internal Medicine* 125, no. 2 (September 1996): 398–405.

36. "Possible Explanation for 'Gulf War Syndrome,'" *Psychopharmacology Update* 6, no. 12 (December, 1995): 5.

37. Ziskin, "Challenging Post-traumatic Stress Disorder," 1232–33. Citations in the original text are omitted here.

38. Ibid., 1234.

39. Ziskin, "Challenging Post-traumatic Stress Disorder," 1239.

CHAPTER 5. THE DEFEAT OF MASOCHISTIC PERSONALITY DISORDER

1. For a review on which the discussion in the text is based, see T. A. Widiger and A. J. Frances, "Controversies Concerning the Self-Defeating Personality Disorder," in *Self-Defeating Behaviors: Experimental Research, Clinical Impressions, and Practical Implications,* ed. R. Curtis (New York: Plenum, 1989), 289–309.

2. H. Kutchins and S. A. Kirk, "DSM-III-R: The Conflict over New Psychiatric Diagnoses," *Health and Social Work* 34, no. 4 (1989): 91–103.

3. R. Simons, "Psychoanalytic Contributions to Psychiatric Nosology: Forms of Masochistic Behavior," *Journal of the American Psychoanalytic Association* 35 (1987): 596.

4. A. Frances, "The DSM-III Personality Disorders Section: A Commentary," *American Journal of Psychiatry* 137 (1980): 1052.

5. Work Group to Revise DSM-III, *DSM-III-R in Development*, draft, 5 October 1985 (Washington, D.C.: American Psychiatric Association, 1985).

6. P. Caplan, *The Myth of Women's Masochism* (New York: Signet, 1985).

7. See reviews of these events in P. J. Caplan, *They Say You're Crazy* (Reading, Mass.: Addison-Wesley, 1995); P. J. Caplan, *The Myth of Women's Masochism*, 2nd ed. (New York: Signet, 1987); S. Faludi, *Backlash: The Undeclared War Against American Women* (New York: Crown, 1991); and Kutchins and Kirk, "DSM-III-R: The Conflict over New Psychiatric Diagnoses."

8. L. Walker, "Masochistic Personality Disorder, Take Two: A Report from the Front Lines," *Feminist Therapy Institute Interchange* (January 1986): 1–2.

9. Faludi, *Backlash*, 357.

10. Caplan, *Myth of Women's Masochism*, 257.

11. Faludi, *Backlash*.

12. Ibid., 359. Six of the long-term patients were women, and all eight patients had been diagnosed by their psychiatrists as masochists. Apparently, this study was supposed to demonstrate that masochism exists. When one of the women critics asked Spitzer how many of the female patients were battered women or victims of violence, Spitzer was unable to provide an answer. None of the psychiatrists had bothered to find out!

13. Caplan, *Myth of Women's Masochism*, 257.

14. Faludi, *Backlash*, 360. *Time* magazine reported that at least one psychologist who attended the hearing was distressed by the DSM panel's thinking. According to *Time*, psychologist Renee Garfinkel, a staff member of the American Psychological Association, said, "The low level of intellectual effort was shocking. Diagnoses were developed by majority vote on the level we would use to choose a restaurant. You feel like Italian, I feel like Chinese, so let's go to a cafeteria. Then it's typed into the computer. It may reflect on our naïveté, but it was our belief that there would be an attempt to look at things scientifically" (as quoted in Caplan, *Myth of Women's Masochism*, 258).

15. Faludi, *Backlash*, 360.

16. As quoted in Faludi, *Backlash*, 361.

17. Caplan, *Myth of Women's Masochism*, 259–61.

18. Caplan, *They Say You're Crazy*.

19. S. Kirk and H. Kutchins, *The Selling of DSM: The Rhetoric of Science in Psychiatry* (Hawthorne, N.Y.: Aldine de Gruyter, 1992), 111–16.

20. Caplan, *Myth of Women's Masochism*.

21. The protesters had planned a speak-out and a press conference that would receive national media coverage. At the request of the outgoing APA president, Carol Nadelson, the protesters scheduled their press conference for 10:30 A.M. to avoid a conflict with Nadelson's presidential address. Just as they were beginning their speak-out, they learned that Spitzer, with the aid of the APA staff, had also scheduled a press conference at another location to discuss the controversy. See Caplan, *Myth of Women's Masochism*, 265.

22. Caplan, *They Say You're Crazy*.

23. Caplan, *Myth of Women's Masochism*, 269.

24. Caplan, *They Say You're Crazy*.

25. Work Group to Revise DSM-III, *DSM-III-R in Development*, 2nd draft, 1 August 1986 (Washington, D.C.: American Psychiatric Association, 1986).

26. Memo from Fink to Ad Hoc Committee, September 1986.

27. Letter from Caplan to APA's board of trustees, December 5, 1986.

28. Under the regular Personality Disorders section of DSM-III-R are instructions for diagnosing Self-defeating Personality Disorder and Sadistic Personality Disorder as code "301.90 Personality Disorder Not Otherwise Specified" (p. 358). Similar provisions were made for PMS, which had been relabeled Late Luteal Phase Dysphoric Disorder: it could be coded as "300.90 Unspecified Mental Disorder" (p. 363).

29. Caplan, *Myth of Women's Masochism,* 271.

30. F. Kass, R. MacKinnon, and R. Spitzer, "Masochistic Personality: An Empirical Study," *American Journal of Psychiatry* 143 (1986): 216–18.

31. See, for example, Caplan, *Myth of Women's Masochism.*

32. Kass, MacKinnon, and Spitzer, "Masochistic Personality."

33. Usually, when a correlation coefficient is used without specification (there are many of them, and they have different assumptions and intended uses), researchers commonly assume that it is a Pearson's r coefficient. The potential problem in this case is that the data analyzed did not meet the requirements for using r, those requirements being that all the measures be continuous (interval) and normally distributed. The data they present, however, were clearly different in form. The 10 traits are rated dichotomously (absent versus present), and the 12 personality disorders are each rated on a four-point ordinal scale (from "no traits" to "meets all DSM-III criteria"). Technically, some nonparametric statistic should have been employed, and perhaps it was.

34. First, the authors used Pearson's r for data that apparently consisted of one dichotomous nominal variable (gender) and one concocted variable "of the mean of the 10 masochistic traits" (p. 217). They do not explain how this mean was derived from present versus absent ratings, nor do they give any information about the resulting distribution of mean scores. Given what limited information is presented, the data might more appropriately lend themselves to a t test or a nonparametric significance test, rather than an r correlation.

35. R. Spitzer, J. Williams, F. Kass, and M. Davies, "National Field Trial of the DSM-III-R Diagnostic Criteria for Self-defeating Personality Disorder," *American Journal of Psychiatry* 146 (1989): 1561–67.

36. Kirk and Kutchins, *Selling of DSM.*

37. Spitzer et al., "National Field Trial," 1562.

38. Ibid.

39. R. Rosenthal and R. Rosnow, *Artifact in Behavioral Research* (New York: Academic Press, 1969).

40. Spitzer et al., "National Field Trial," 1562.

41. This was revealed in several ways. First, those who met the criteria for SDPD also tended to meet the criteria for Borderline Personality Disorder or Dependent Personality Disorder, too ($r = .58$ and $.56$, respectively), indicating a relative lack of independence among what were expected to be distinct disorders. Second, SDPD was *rarely* diagnosed by itself when the computer, rather than the clinician, was making the judgment: only 4% of the 1,377 patients whom therapists had identified as having personality disorders had only SDPD, a third of the rate found in the 1986 article. More troubling, those with SDPD usually had characteristics qualifying them, according to computer analysis, for a diagnosis of either Borderline Personality Disorder or Dependent Personality Disorder.

42. Spitzer et al., "National Field Trial," 1565.

43. In an early memo (September 19, 1988) to the various work groups that had been set up to accomplish the next revision, Frances and the APA's director of research, Harold Pincus, signaled to these groups how they expected them to proceed: "Essentially we are undertaking a scientific assessment project . . . [which should] proceed in as systematic and scientifically based a manner as possible." They asked the groups to identify major issues by consulting with recognized experts. Each group was to determine which disorders were to be added or dropped, what the subtypes should be, and where they should be placed. Further, the groups were to develop systematic literature reviews to guide their decision making and to identify what relevant existing data were available and what kind of evidence needed to be considered in resolving issues. As much as possible, Frances and Pincus declared, the new manual would be based on scientific data.

44. We are grateful to Paula Caplan for sharing copies of her correspondence with us. Caplan's experiences with the DSM decision makers is recounted in Caplan, *They Say You're Crazy.*

45. Finally, a month after the work group meeting, after Caplan's complaints that she had been kept in the dark about the dates of meetings and deadlines, and after the deadline for comments, Fiester sent Caplan (on November 17, 1989) a copy of a draft of the SDPD literature review and solicited her comments. Caplan was surprised by what she thought was the poor quality of Fiester's review. Caplan wrote both Fiester and Frances (on November 28, 1989) to inform them that she found the Fiester review "shockingly sloppy and irresponsible." She didn't think that Fiester was methodologically sophisticated enough to critically evaluate the weaknesses of the research on which the SDPD diagnosis was based. She suggested that Frances would be embarrassed by the Fiester review unless it was improved, and she enclosed an 11-page critique of Fiester's review, pointing out weaknesses. Caplan had virtually no further contact with Fiester. Her role as a consultant to Fiester's group had never amounted to more than the guarded exchanges between professional adversaries.

Meanwhile, Caplan's own review of the literature was rejected as too polemical and harsh by the *American Journal of Psychiatry* and the *Journal of Personality Disorders,* periodicals edited by DSM insiders and bastions of pro-DSM scholarship. Eventually it was published in a more obscure new journal, where it was not likely to be seen by the men of the APA; Caplan's review is in P. Caplan and M. Gans, "Is There Empirical Justification for the Category of 'Self-defeating Personality Disorder'?" *Feminism and Psychology* 1, no. 2 (1991): 263–78. By contrast, Fiester's review was eventually published in a special edited section of the *Journal of Personality Disorders* created to present the literature reviews for some of the DSM-IV personality disorder categories: S. Fiester, "Self-defeating Personality Disorders: A Review of Data and Recommendations for DSM-IV," *Journal of Personality Disorders* 5 (1991): 194–209.

46. Fiester, "Self-defeating Personality Disorders," 207.

47. Task Force on DSM-IV, *DSM-IV Options Book: Work in Progress* (Washington, D.C.: American Psychiatric Association, September 1, 1991), R 18.

48. Task Force on DSM-IV, *DSM-IV Draft Criteria* (Washington, D.C.: American Psychiatric Association, March 1, 1993), W 1.

49. American Psychiatric Association, "Assembly Approves DSM-IV After Some Debate," *APA News,* 18 June 1993, 2.

50. Caplan and Eichler's proposal was later expanded and published as a journal article: K. Pantony and P. Caplan, "Delusional Dominating Personality Disorder: A Modest

Proposal for Identifying Some Consequences of Rigid Masculine Socialization," *Canadian Psychology* 32, no. 2 (1991): 120–33.

51. Ibid., 122; emphasis in the original.

52. Ibid., 123.

53. Ibid., 121.

54. The study, which was parallel to what Spitzer's groups had done, was never completed.

55. American Psychiatric Association, *DSM-IV Update* (Washington, D.C.: American Psychiatric Association, 1996).

56. A few days later, on October 26, 1989, Frances wrote Caplan again about SDPD and DDPD. He commented that he found it "paradoxical" that Caplan was actively trying to defeat the proposal for SDPD then under consideration while she was championing "a new diagnosis of . . . [her] own." Caplan was perturbed. In a letter of November 8, 1989, she asked Frances what was paradoxical and reminded him that she had never suggested that DDPD be held to a different or lower standard for inclusion in DSM. She also inquired why no one from the DSM-IV work groups had offered to assist her in preparing the empirical material that both he and Gunderson had requested. She also asked why they were being so "consistently discouraging and unsupportive" rather than being simply neutral until the evidence was in. She asked for the schedule of information gathering for DSM-IV decision making. She made the same request of Gunderson, in a letter of November 1, 1989, and asked when the empirical material needed to be submitted in order to be considered. "It is very important," she stressed, "for us to know *ahead of time* what the deadlines and process will be [emphasis in original]." Gunderson wrote another discouraging letter to her on November 14, 1989, stating that he was unable to give her an exact deadline for consideration of DDPD and explaining that the fact that DDPD was not "generally recognized" was the "most formidable obstacle," regardless of the empirical evidence she could assemble. A few days later (December 5, 1989), Frances also sent another bluntly discouraging letter to Caplan; it was marked by a rising tone of exasperation with her efforts and contained evidence of frustration with her failiure to heed their advice and turn her attention elsewhere.

57. Although Frances had given them until March 1990 to submit the material, it was not until July 1990 that Caplan sent a preliminary review of the evidence for DDPD. That review, Frances's response, and Caplan's rebuttal were published in *Canadian Psychology* the following year. See Pantony and Caplan, "Delusional Dominating Personality Disorder"; P. Caplan, "How Do They Decide Who Is Normal? The Bizarre, but True, Tale of the DSM Process," *Canadian Psychology* 32 (1991): 162–70; P. Caplan, "Response to the DSM Wizard," *Canadian Psychology* 32 (1991): 174–75; A. Frances et al., "DSM-IV: Toward a More Empirical Diagnostic System," *Canadian Psychology* 32 (1991): 171–73.

58. J. Larkin and P. Caplan, "The Gatekeeping Process of the DSM," *Canadian Journal of Community Mental Health* 11 (1992): 17–28; Caplan, *They Say You're Crazy*.

CHAPTER 6. BORDER WARS: BORDERLINE PERSONALITY DISORDER

1. R. Spitzer, J. Endicott, and M. Gibbon, "Crossing the Border into Borderline Personality and Borderline Schizophrenia: The Development of Criteria," *Archives of General Psychiatry* 36 (January 1979): 17–24.

2. Ibid., 20.

3. This is measuring the sensitivity and specificity of the criteria. These measurements are scientific procedures designed to identify chronic problems in psychiatric diagnosis, that is, the over- and underinclusion of patients in a diagnostic group. For more than a century, there have been recurrent complaints that patients are misdiagnosed. On many occasions, clinicians have overlooked disorders when assessing patients, and, possibly more often, they have given patients an unwarranted diagnosis. By measuring sensitivity and specificity of diagnostic criteria, the researchers hoped to reduce the possibility of misdiagnosis.

Spitzer and his associates provided the following descriptions of sensitivity and specificity in "Crossing the Border": "Sensitivity is the proportion of the total number of cases that are correctly identified as cases by the procedure. Specificity is the proportion of the total number of noncases that are correctly identified as noncases by the procedure" (p. 19). Thus, sensitivity reflects "cases correctly identified" and specificity is a measure of "noncases correctly identified."

4. Spitzer, Endicott, and Gibbon, "Crossing the Border," 20.

5. Ibid., 23.

6. One tradition Spitzer and his associates did continue was to provide confusing names for new disorders. Originally the researchers called this new diagnosis Unstable Personality Disorder. They finally rejected that term because clinicians who treated these patients felt the term was a misnomer. These clinicians believed that the personality of such patients "is in fact quite stably unstable." The researchers further claimed, "Clinicians will never abandon the term borderline in favor of the term unstable." Not content with this explanation, Spitzer and his associates added another rationale:

> Schizophrenia and conversion are both examples of terms whose original meaning has little to do with the current conception of the conditions they name. Similarly, borderline has been a useful metaphor, indicating that the patient had some features that were sometimes seen in patients with psychoses. It would now appear that the term "schizotypal personality disorder" can be applied to cases that previously have been called borderline schizophrenia, and that the term "borderline personality disorder" can be applied to the other patients previously referred to as borderline. There would be no need for the term "unstable personality disorder." ("Crossing the Border," p. 24)

To avoid confusion, Schizotypal Personality Disorder should have been called Borderline Personality Disorder and Unstable Personality Disorder should have continued to be the name of the diagnosis for those whose illness does not border on schizophrenia. Although the logic of Spitzer and his associates may be strained, it offers a revealing insight into psychiatric traditions.

7. American Psychiatric Association Press, *Fall Catalogue,* 1992, p. 109.

8. T. G. Gutheil, "Borderline Personality Disorder, Boundary Violations, and Patient–Therapist Sex: Medicolegal Pitfalls," *American Journal of Psychiatry* 146, no. 5 (May 1989): 597–602.

9. Ibid., 598. Actually, Gutheil adopted a suggestion by Alan Stone, a former president of the American Psychiatric Association, that borderlines become candidates for patient–therapist sex through a process of libidinal elimination because they are sufficiently attractive to therapists and do not "know better" than to participate.

10. J. Jordan et al., Letter to the Editor, *American Journal of Psychiatry* 147, no. 1 (January 1990): 129–30.

11. Ibid., 129–30.

12. Ibid., 130.

13. T. Gutheil, Reply to Letters, *American Journal of Psychiatry* 147, no. 1 (January 1990): 130.

14. Ibid.

15. T. Gutheil, "Patients Involved in Sexual Misconduct with Therapists: Is a Victim Profile Possible?" *Psychiatric Annals* 21, no. 11 (November 1991): 661–67.

16. Ibid.

17. T. Gutheil, "The Concept of Boundaries in Clinical Practice: Theoretical and Risk Management Dimensions," *American Journal of Psychiatry* 150, no. 2 (1993): 188–96; T. Gutheil, "Patient–Therapist Sexual Relations," *Harvard Medical School Mental Health Letter* 6 (1989): 46; T. Gutheil, "Patients Involved with Therapists: Is a Victim Profile Possible," *Psychiatric Annals* 21, no. 11 (1991): 661–67; T. Gutheil and R. Sadoff, "Expert Opinion: A Case of Therapist–Patient Sexual Misconduct," *American Psychiatric Press Review of Clinical Psychiatry and the Law* 3 (1992): 331–48.

18. K. Mogul, Letter to the Editor, *American Journal of Psychiatry* 146, no. 10 (1989): 1356.

19. P. Illingworth, Letter to the Editor, *American Journal of Psychiatry* 147, no. 9 (September 1990): 1259.

20. T. Gutheil, Reply to Letters, *American Journal of Psychiatry* 147, no. 1 (January 1990): 130.

21. Gutheil, "Borderline Personality Disorder, Boundary Violations, and Patient–Therapist Sex," 601.

22. N. Gatrell et al., "Psychiatrist–Patient Sexual Contact: Results of a National Survey: I. Prevalence," *American Journal of Psychiatry* 143, no. 9 (1986): 1126–31.

23. Ibid.

24. Gutheil and Sadoff, "Expert Opinion."

25. T. Widiger and M. Weissman, "Epidemiology of Borderline Personality Disorder," *Hospital and Community Psychiatry* 42 (October 1991): 1015–21.

26. Personal communication, April 1997.

CHAPTER 7. THE ENDURING LEGACY OF RACISM IN THE DIAGNOSIS OF MENTAL DISORDERS

1. Rush established the tradition of political psychiatry in America and was concerned about the impact of politics on women's mental health. According to a text on transcultural psychiatry, "The possibility that English society might be neurotic because it was 'decadent' (in a moral rather than in a racial sense) was an idea that appealed to American revolutionaries, and before long their leading physician, Benjamin Rush, was claiming (probably on the basis of clinical observation) that participation in the Revolution was curing women of hysteria, whereas traditional life under the monarchy was generating mental disorder"; from H. B. M. Murphy, "Historical Development of Transcultural Psychiatry," in *Transcultural Psychiatry,* ed. J. Cox (London: Croom Helm, 1986), 8. On the other hand, Rush and the other founding fathers were alarmed at the

prospect of too much power for common people. He created a new mental disorder called Anarchia for those who believed too fervently in the participation of the masses.

Among Rush's other contributions to American psychiatry was the invention of the "tranquilizer," a chair that rotated on a wheel. Agitated patients were strapped to it and spun around until they were pacified; see R. Smith and A. Wade, eds., *Madness, Insanity and Mental Illness: Documents and Readings in Social Policy* (Sacramento, Cal.: Self-published, 1978), especially Reading 2, "Dr. Benjamin Rush's Remedies" (pp. 30–32), an excerpt from Rush's 1794 work *Medical Inquiries and Observations on the Diseases of the Mind.*

Rush's most celebrated patient was George Washington. Rush administered to Washington, who had contracted a fever after being thrown from his horse, the preferred treatment of the time—bleeding the patient. Although Washington had been robust prior to his fall, he became weak from the loss of blood and died shortly afterward.

2. B. L. Plummer, "Benjamin Rush and the Negro," *American Journal of Psychiatry* 127, no. 6 (December 1970): 793–98; R. Takaki, *Iron Cages: Race and Culture in Nineteenth Century America* (New York: Knopf, 1979).

3. H. Goldhammer and A. Marshall, *Psychosis and Civilization* (Glencoe, Ill.: Free Press, 1953); see especially Part A, "A Century of Admissions Rates in Massachusetts."

4. D. J. Rothman, *The Discovery of the Asylum: Social Order and Disorder in the New Republic* (Boston: Little, Brown, 1971).

5. E. Jarvis, "On the Supposed Increase in Insanity," *American Journal of Insanity* (April 1852): 353–54. See the discussion in N. Dain, *Concepts of Insanity in the United States, 1779–1865* (New Brunswick, N. J.: Rutgers University Press, 1964), 88, 109.

6. Before 1800 there were only two public hospitals, in Virginia and Maryland, and a private, nonprofit one in Philadelphia. Starting in 1817, when another hospital was established in Philadelphia, there was a rapid increase in institutions, and by 1840 there were twenty-one hospitals in 13 states; from W. Barton, *The History and Influence of the American Psychiatric Association* (Washington, D.C.: American Psychiatric Press, 1987).

7. From "Table of Lunacy in the United States" in Hunt's *Merchants' Magazine and Commercial Review* 8 (1843): 460–61; cited in L. Litwack, *North of Slavery* (Chicago: University of Chicago Press, 1961).

8. R. B. Caplan, *Psychiatry and the Community in Nineteenth-Century America* (New York: Basic Books, 1969).

9. "Reflections on the Census of 1840," *Southern Literary Messenger* 9 (June 1843): 350.

10. Ibid., 347.

11. Ibid., 350.

12. Ibid.

13. Dain, *Concepts of Insanity in the United States,* 106.

14. Ibid., 105.

15. Litwack, *North of Slavery,* 43; see also B. Pasamanick, "Some Misconceptions Concerning Difference in the Racial Prevalence of Mental Disease," *American Journal of Orthopsychiatry* 33 (1963): 72–86.

16. This happened in eleven Northern states. In Ohio there were 37 towns where this happened; in New York, 16; and in Michigan, 12. Maine, which showed such high rates of insanity, had 9 towns where the number of insane Negroes exceeded the total number of Negro residents.

17. A. Thomas and S. Sillen, *Racism and Psychiatry* (New York: Brunner/Mazel, 1972).

18. A. Deutsch, "The First U.S. Census of the Insane (1840) and Its Use as Pro-Slavery Propaganda," *Bulletin of the History of Medicine* 15 (1944): 476.

19. Litwack, *North of Slavery*, 44–45, n. 25.

20. Dain, *Concepts of Insanity in the United States*, 104.

21. Litwack, *North of Slavery*, 45.

22. Deutsch, "The First U.S. Census of the Insane," 477.

23. John C. Calhoun to the Speaker of the House of Representatives, February 8, 1845, reprinted in *Niles' National Register* 67 (June 7, 1845): 218–19.

24. Litwack, *North of Slavery*, 46.

25. Deutsch, "The First U.S. Census of the Insane," 478. The *American Journal of Insanity* was once the name of the official publication of the American Psychiatric Association; it is now called the *American Journal of Psychiatry*.

26. Jarvis responded in an article published in the same journal in January 1852; Deutsch, "The First U.S. Census of the Insane," 478.

27. Dain, *Concepts of Insanity in the United States*, 89.

28. Ibid., 106.

29. Ibid.

30. J. B. Andrews, M.D. (president of the International Medical Congress), "The Distribution and Care of the Insane in the United States," in *Transactions of the International Medical Congress, Ninth Session*, ed. J. B. Hamilton (Washington, D.C.: International Medical Congress, 1887), 226–37. Similar claims were expressed by A. H. Witmer, M.D., in "Insanity in the Colored Race in the United States," *Alienist and Neurologist* 12 (1891): 19–30; by J. W. Babcock, M.D. (superintendent of the South Carolina Lunatic Asylum), in "The Colored Insane," *Alienist and Neurologist* 15 (1895): 423–47, and in "The Colored Insane," *Proceedings of the National Conference of Charities and Corrections*, 22nd Annual Session, May 24–30, 1895, ed. Isabel Barrows (Boston: Press of Geo. H. Ellis, 1895); by T. O Powell, M.D. (medical superintendent, State Lunatic Asylum, Milledgeville, Ga.), "The Increase in Insanity and Tuberculosis in the Southern Negro Since 1860 and Its Alliance and Some of the Supposed Causes," *Journal of the American Medical Association* 27 (1896): 1185–88.

The same themes were echoed by physicians at the U.S. Government Hospital for the Insane in Washington, D.C., in journal articles published in the early 20th century. See M. O'Malley, M.D., "Psychoses in the Colored Race: A Study in Comparative Psychiatry," *American Journal of Insanity* 71 (October 1914), and W. M. Bevis, "Psychological Traits of the Southern Negro with Observations as to Some of His Psychoses," *American Journal of Psychiatry* 1 (1921): 69–78.

During this period, other physicians at government hospitals also contributed racist theories about the mental status of African Americans. See, for example, J. E. Lind, M.D., "The Dream as a Simple Wish Fulfillment in the Negro," *Psychoanalytic Review* 1 (1914): 295–300; "The Color Complex in the Negro," *Psychoanalytic Review* 1 (1914): 404–14, and "Phylogenetic Elements in the Psychoses of the Negro," *Psychoanalytic Review* 4 (1917): 303–32; see also A. B. Evarts, "Dementia Praecox in the Colored Race," *Psychoanalytic Review* 1 (1914): 388–403, and "The Ontogenetic Against the Phylogenetic Elements in the Psychoses of the Colored Race," *Psychoanalytic Review* 3 (1916): 272–87. Other contributions to the development of racism in the diagnosis of psychiatric disorders were made by E. M. Green, M.D. (clinical director, Georgia Sanitarium), "Psychoses Among Negroes: A Comparative Study,"

Journal of Nervous and Mental Disorders 4 (1914): 697–708, and "Manic Depressive Psychoses in the Negro," *American Journal of Insanity* 73 (April 1917): 619–26.

Other authors—Thomas and Sillen, *Racism and Psychiatry;* S. Fernando, *Race and Culture in Psychiatry* (London: Croom Helm, 1988); and T. S. Szasz, "The Sane Slave," *American Journal of Psychotherapy* 25 (1971): 228–39, and "The Negro in Psychiatry," *American Journal of Psychotherapy* 25 (1971): 469–71—have traced the persistent reemergence of psychiatric theories about the benefits of slavery and the psychological deterioration of African Americans after emancipation.

31. S. A. Cartwright, *Essays* (Natchez: 1843), 12, quoted in W. S. Jenkins, *Proslavery Thought in the Old South* (Chapel Hill, N.C.: 1935), 251; the quotation is reprinted in Deutsch, "The First U.S. Census of the Insane," 471.

32. S. A. Cartwright, "Report on the Diseases and Physical Peculiarities of the Negro Race," *New Orleans Medical and Surgical Journal* 7 (1851): 707.

33. Ibid., 711–12.

34. Ibid., 714.

35. Fernando, *Race and Culture in Psychiatry,* 24.

36. W. Z. Ripley, *The Races of Europe* (London: Kegan, Paul Trench, Tubner & Co., 1899), 103 ff., cited in M. H. Haller, *Eugenics: Hereditarian Attitudes in American Thought* (New Brunswick, N. J.: Rutgers University Press, 1963), 55.

37. A. Chase, *The Legacy of Malthus* (New York: Knopf, 1977).

38. B. E. Blustein, "A Hollow Square of Psychological Science: American Neurologists and Psychiatrists in Conflict," in *Madhouses, Mad-Doctors and Madmen,* ed. A. Scull (Philadelphia: University of Pennsylvania Press, 1981), 241–70.

39. Caplan, *Psychiatry and the Community in Nineteenth-Century America,* 299–300.

40. G. Grob, "The Origins of American Psychiatric Epidemiology," *American Journal of Public Health* 75, no. 3 (1985): 231.

41. Administration of a literacy test in English was seen as a way of limiting the influx of members of the "inferior races," who came from non-English-speaking countries, and of barring immigrants from English-speaking countries who were not educated and affluent. The bill first passed Congress overwhelmingly in 1896, but it was vetoed by President Cleveland; it was blocked repeatedly during subsequent Republican and Democratic administrations. Although it was favored by Theodore Roosevelt, it was not finally adopted until 1917, during the Wilson administration.

42. Jordan, a biologist, was the first chancellor of Stanford University.

43. See E. F. Torrey, A. Bower, E. Taylor, and I. Gottesman, *Schizophrenia and Manic Depressive Disorder: The Biological Roots of Mental Illness as Revealed by the Landmark Study of Identical Twins* (New York: Basic Books, 1994), and S. Farrone and J. Biederman, "Genetics of Attention Deficit Hyperactivity Disorder," *Child and Adolescent Psychiatric Clinics of North America* (1994): 285–302.

44. J. M. Buchanan, "Insanity in the Colored Race," *New York Medical Journal* (July 17, 1886): 67–70, 68.

45. C. Woodruff, "An Anthropological Study of the Small Brain of Civilized Man and Its Evolution," *American Journal of Insanity* 5, no. 48 (July 1901): 171.

46. Lind, "The Dream as a Simple Wish Fulfillment in the Negro," 300.

47. Thomas and Sillen, *Racism and Psychiatry,* 14.

48. O'Malley, "Psychoses in the Colored Race," 310.

49. E. M. Green, "Psychoses Among Negroes: A Comparative Study," *Journal of Nervous and Mental Disease* 41 (1914): 703.

50. W. M. Bevis, "The Psychological Traits of the Southern Negro with Observations as to Some of his Psychoses," *American Journal of Psychiatry* 1 (1921): 69–78.

51. R. Herrenstein and C. Murray, *The Bell Curve: Intelligence and Class Structure in American Life* (New York: Free Press, 1994).

52. We hasten to add that other psychological tests have on occasion been used for the opposite purpose, that is, to measure the impact of racism on blacks. The most famous example is Kenneth Clark's doll tests, which were used to demonstrate the devastating effects of segregation on the self-image of African American children. (In these tests Clark asked children to choose either a brown doll or a white one as "the doll you like to play with," "the doll you like best," "the nice doll," "the bad doll," and "the doll that is a nice color." The majority of African American children tested indicated an unmistakable preference for the white doll and a rejection of the brown one.) The recognition of these tests by the Supreme Court in footnote 11 of *Brown v. the Topeka Kansas Board of Education* was a positive contribution in the fight against segregation. Although Clark's contribution and the work of many other psychologists have been important in efforts to dispel racist beliefs, they do not counterbalance the pervasive effect of racism in IQ testing and other psychological examinations in schools, in military settings, and in institutions that treat mental disorders and retardation.

53. S. J. Gould, "Curve Ball," *New Yorker,* 28 November 1994, 139–49.

54. See J. Fischer, "Negroes and Whites and Rates of Mental Illness: Reconsideration of a Myth," *Psychiatry* 32 (1969): 428–46. Fischer's efforts to correct such blatant prejudice took place in the context of the civil rights struggles of the sixties, and they were an important exposé of the racist views that affected the identification of mental disorders.

Even though Fischer made a major contribution to dispelling biased findings and conclusions among mental health workers, his efforts were subjected to the charge of racism. Whereas Fischer claimed that mental disorders were overreported, Dorothy Otnow Lewis raised the issue of the underreporting of mental disorders. See D. Lewis, D. Balla, and S. Shanok, "Some Evidence of Race Bias in the Diagnosis and Treatment of the Juvenile Offender," *American Journal of Orthopsychiatry* 49(1) (1979): 53–61. Although this issue was never resolved, there were, curiously, important elements of truth in both Fischer's critique and Lewis's, and both repeated aspects of the debate over the 1840 census. Fischer objected to overcounts of mental disorders among blacks in circumstances that degraded them. Lewis was concerned about circumstances where an identification of mental disorder might be helpful but is denied to a black person, as, for example, when a person is charged with a criminal offense for behavior that actually reflects mental illness; she assembled data to demonstrate that whites were more likely than blacks with comparable psychiatric histories and behavior to be treated as mental patients. The differences between the Fischer and Lewis positions reflect the different ways in which insanity in blacks was treated in the North and in the South in the 1840s as well as the 1960s. Southern slaves who were seriously mentally or emotionally impaired were undercounted because it would have been an economic and social burden for their masters to identify them as retarded or insane and place them in an institutition. The identification of Northern Negroes as insane was less of a problem, since no individual property holders were responsible for their care and since insane asylums were places to confine undesirable people, even those who had not committed a crime.

55. Theories about mental disorders are bound to reflect contemporary views, including racial attitudes. Many would argue that we cannot condemn, for example, the diagnostic misconceptions of Benjamin Rush because of his racism when he was, if anything, ahead of his time in combating prejudice against blacks; nor can we find fault, simply because they repeated common racial myths of their times, with Jarvis and those of his contemporaries who fought hard against pro-slavery distortions. Even Cartwright's bigotry had a positive side in that he attempted to prescribe more humane remedies and to discourage severe abuse of slaves who were unwilling to work or ran away. Although we may be less willing to excuse the shortsightedness of the Freudians at St. Elizabeth's, they also shared commonly held misconceptions during a time of virulent racism in this country. Even Cyril Burt's mendacious behavior has been explained as the result of great personal stress brought on in part by the London blitz in World War II, which destroyed his research, and of other events that led to his deterioration in old age (for more on Burt, see S. J. Gould, *The Mismeasure of Man* [New York: Norton, 1981]). Although these explanations are not an excuse for racial prejudice, they make it more understandable. But when we see the same charge of racism recur when the purpose of the commentator is to dispel racial prejudices, as happened in the case of Fischer's efforts, the problem seems almost unsolvable.

What these episodes demonstrate is that the intentions of psychiatrists and other mental health workers did not matter if their actions contributed to racism, even though they often saw themselves as providing assistance for those who were suffering from mental disorders or other emotional problems. They often contributed to racist sentiments despite—or, rather, because of—strong humanitarian commitments. There are two lessons in these examples. One is that attitudes toward African Americans and other minority groups, even those that appear to be most supportive, must be carefully examined in order to identify unfounded prejudices. The second is that often the assumptions that practitioners and theoreticians believe are unprejudiced involve inherent biases that lead to racial oppression.

56. D. A. Regier et al., "The NIMH Epidemiologic Catchment Area Program: Historical Context, Major Objectives and Study Population Characteristics," *Archives of General Psychiatry* 41 (October 1984): 936.

57. Regier et al., "The NIMH Epidemiologic Catchment Area Program," explained that "in order to have greater information on the possible effect of ethnic status, the nonwhite population was deliberately oversampled (stratified sample) in St. Louis, resulting in a sample that was 42% black in an area where the adult population is actually 19% black" (p. 938).

58. Ibid., 940.

59. W. W. Eaton, C. Ritter, and D. Brown, "Psychiatric Epidemiology and Psychiatric Sociology: Influences on the Recognition of Bizarre Behaviors and Social Problems" (paper presented at the Annual Meeting of the Society for the Study of Social Problems, New York City, July 1987), 37.

60. L. N. Robins et al., "Lifetime Prevalence of Specific Psychiatric Disorders in Three Sites," *Archives of General Psychiatry* 41, no. 10 (October 1984): 955.

61. D. Blazer, B. Crowell, and L. George, "Alcohol Abuse and Dependence in the Rural South," *Archives of General Psychiatry* 44 (1987): 736–40.

62. Ibid., 739.

63. Ibid.

64. Ibid., 740.

65. African American psychiatrists have commented on the inadequacies in epidemiological surveys, and they have criticized the ECA reports; see D. Williams, "The Epidemiology of Mental Illness in Afro-Americans," *Hospital and Community Psychiatry* 37, no. 1 (January 1986): 42–49. Williams reviewed many of the most important epidemiological studies of African Americans and made the following observations:

> There have been no studies of variation in mental illness in African-Americans of different backgrounds. The most sophisticated communitywide surveys of African-Americans have been of populations that are mostly Euro-Americans and utilized survey techniques suited to the study of the majority group. This is evident in the NIMH Epidemiological Catchment Studies currently underway.
>
> While the NIMH ECA studies are a major advance in communitywide field studies of Euro-Americans, they are seriously flawed and misleading as a national survey of mental illness in Afro-Americans. . . . The ECA studies have also failed to obtain a statistically significant sampling of middle and upper-income Afro-Americans. . . . As a result it will be impossible to use ECA data to obtain intraethnic comparisons of Afro-Americans or to contrast psychiatric illness among Afro-Americans and Euro-Americans of similar socioeconomic class. Thus it will be impossible to determine the impact, if any, of factors associated with racism and socioeconomic status upon the manifestations of psychiatric illness in Afro- and Euro-American populations.

Williams concluded, "The earliest American epidemiological studies of psychiatric illness distorted the rate of mental illness among Afro-Americans. One hundred and forty-five years later there is still no comprehensive, unbiased study of mental illness in the Afro-American population." Williams warned, "The present national policies may again create a climate of increased racial tension that will lead to misuse of epidemiological data about African-Americans."

66. M. Loring and B. Powell, "Gender, Race, and DSM-III: A Study of the Objectivity of Psychiatric Diagnostic Behavior," *Journal of Health and Social Behavior* 29 (March 1988): 1–22. The return rate for their questionnaire was 59.4%.

67. Ibid., 17.

68. Ibid., 14.

69. Ibid., 18.

70. Ibid., 19.

71. See B. Jones and B. Gray, "Problems in Diagnosing Schizophrenia and Affective Disorders Among Blacks," *Hospital and Community Psychiatry* 37 (1986): 61–65, for a review of the problems of overdiagnoses of schizophrenia and underdiagnosis of affective disorders among African Americans and a discussion of some of the major reasons for these problems, including faulty diagnostic criteria, cultural differences, and the reliance on racial myths and stereotypes.

72. H. Morais, *The History of the Negro in Medicine* (New York: Publishers Co. Inc., 1967), 32–33, Appendix B.

73. E. F. Frazier, "The Pathology of Race Prejudice," *Forum* (1927): 856–62.

74. Ibid., 857.

75. Frazier provided many examples that demonstrated the intensity of these dissociative responses. One was the white community's reaction to a white woman who called a Negro "mister." She was forced to listen to a diatribe against African Americans by other

whites who were offended, and she was asked if she would want her sister to marry a Negro.

76. A. Platt, *E. Franklin Frazier Reconsidered* (New Brunswick, N.J.: Rutgers University Press, 1991).

77. Committee of Black Psychiatrists, "Report to the Task Force on Nomenclature and Statistics," October 17, 1975.

78. Letter from Spitzer to Committee of Black Psychiatrists, December 29, 1975.

79. W. T. Hamlin, *The Chains of Psychological Slavery: The Mental Illness of Racism* (Maryland: ICFP, Inc., 1990), 17–25.

80. The APA boasted that it had raised the threshold for the acceptance of new disorders in DSM-IV, and to compensate for not including promising new candidates in the official classification system, it added an appendix for proposed diagnoses that were under consideration for adoption in future editions.

81. All of our graduate students, mostly white Americans, insist that they, too, suffer from brain fag syndrome.

CHAPTER 8. DIAGNOSING THE PSYCHIATRIC BIBLE

1. "Prevalence of Serious Mental Illness Among American Adults Estimated at 5.7 Percent in 12-Month Period," *Psychiatric Services* 47, no. 5 (May 1996): 546.

2. L. N. Robins and D. A. Regier, eds., *Psychiatric Disorders in America: The Epidemiologic Catchment Area Study* (New York: Free Press, 1991).

3. Daniel X. Freedman, in foreword to Robins and Regier, *Psychiatric Disorders in America*.

4. Every major research study is expected to confirm the obvious and perhaps provide some surprising findings. *Psychiatric Disorders in America* does both and in just about every chapter. We are not surprised to learn that there is not much abuse of illicit drugs by residents of nursing homes and that cognitive impairment is more prevalent in the elderly than the young. Examples of surprising data that beg for considerably more attention are the findings that 22% of those in psychiatric hospitals have never had a psychiatric disorder and that 27% showed no evidence of having one during the year preceding the study. Whether this peculiar finding is a commentary on the nature of psychiatric hospitals, an unexpected and discouraging test of the validity of the ECA study's epidemiological methods, or both is probably worth exploring.

5. Other numbers presented in *Psychiatric Disorders in America* raise other issues. Somatization Disorder, for example, was difficult to find in the population. A third of the 37 DSM-III criteria for this disorder must be met to make the diagnosis. Although this book on the ECA study aspired to present the major mental disorders, only a small fraction of 1% of the sample qualified for this diagnosis. Since many of the physical symptoms that characterize Somatization Disorder are experienced by many people (e.g., back pain, nausea, painful menstruation), the authors lowered the threshold number of criteria to four for men and six for women and relabeled it "somatization syndrome" instead of Somatization Disorder, thus artificially boosting the lifetime prevalence rate to 11.6%, or 100 times the rate of Somatization Disorder. They then had enough cases to perform the routine breakdowns with the demographic correlates. This example of taking liberties with the threshold number of criteria illustrates the sensitivity that prevalence rates have to technical decisions about diagnostic criteria and to the ambiguities inherent in a diagnos-

tic system with a wavering concept of disorder. *Psychiatric Disorders in America* is a gold mine of examples of how prevalence rates can be viewed as artifacts of shifting psychiatric operations.

6. There were many other dreams of science embodied in DSM, including the hope that psychiatric research would produce consensus about mental disorders and their classification and treatment; that a descriptive and detailed classification system would be much easier for clinicians to use; that science would somehow limit the political abuse of psychiatry, which was practiced in the Soviet Union and other countries, including the United States; that having many researchers involved in myriad scientific activities would ensure a scientific document; and that clearly differentiated categories would make treatment selection more accurate.

7. M.S. Wylie, "Diagnosing for Dollars?" *Family Therapy Networker* (May/June 1995): 23–69.

8. E. E. Gorenstein, *The Science of Mental Illness* (San Diego, Cal.: Academic Press, 1992), 71ff.

9. S. A. Kirk and H. Kutchins, *The Selling of DSM: The Rhetoric of Science in Psychiatry* (Hawthorne, N.Y.: Aldine de Gruyter, 1992).

10. Ibid.

11. See J. Helzer and W. Coryell, "More on DSM-III: How Consistent Are Precise Criteria?" *Biological Psychiatry* 18, no. 11 (1983): 1201–3; G. Winokur, M. Zimmerman, and R. Cadoret, "'Cause the Bible Tells Me So,'" *Archives of General Psychiatry* 45 (1988): 683–84; and P. McGorry et al., "Spurious Precision: Procedural Validity of Diagnostic Assessment in Psychotic Disorders," *American Journal of Psychiatry* 152 (1995): 220–23.

12. In the case of Vin, even if all these complexities are surmountable, the clinician must still puzzle over the contradiction between DSM's statement "Neither deviant behavior . . . nor conflicts that are primarily between the individual and society are mental disorders" (DSM-IV, p. xxii) and the equally explicit description of Conduct Disorder as the youthful violation of the rights, norms, or rules of others.

13. Certainly during the selected field trials attention was given to how supervised clinicians in research settings used a few of the over 300 categories. But generalizing from those special circumstances to the immensely diverse world of clinical practice is hazardous.

14. See Kirk and Kutchins, *Selling of DSM*; H. Kutchins and S. A. Kirk, "The Business of Diagnosis: DSM-III and Clinical Social Work," *Social Work* 33 (1988): 215–20.

15. L. Rhodes, *Emptying Beds: The Work of an Emergency Psychiatric Unit* (Berkeley: University of California Press, 1991), 93.

16. Wylie, "Diagnosing for Dollars?" 24.

17. Ibid., 24–25.

18. This case narrative was provided by Kelly D. Warner. It has been edited and used with her permission. The identity of the clinic and client are disguised.

19. P. Breggin and G. Breggin, *The War Against Children* (New York: St. Martin's Press, 1994), 196.

20. S. A. Kirk and H. Kutchins, "Deliberate Misdiagnosis in Mental Health Practice," *Social Service Review* 62 (1988): 225–37.

21. As quoted in Wylie, "Diagnosing for Dollars?" 28.

22. M. Scarf, "Keeping Secrets," *New York Times Magazine,* 16 June 1996, 38–41.

23. See, for example, C. Bollas and D. Sundelson, *The New Informants: The Betrayal of Confidentiality in Psychoanalysis and Psychotherapy* (Northvale, N.J.: Jason Aronson, 1995).

INDEX